Frank B. Lewis

Pedes Finium

Or, Fines relating to the county of Surrey, levied in the King's court, from the seventh year of Richard I. to the end of the reign of Henry VII.

Frank B. Lewis

Pedes Finium

Or, Fines relating to the county of Surrey, levied in the King's court, from the seventh year of Richard I. to the end of the reign of Henry VII.

ISBN/EAN: 9783337418366

Printed in Europe, USA, Canada, Australia, Japan

Cover: Foto ©ninafisch / pixelio.de

More available books at **www.hansebooks.com**

PEDES FINIUM;

OR,

FINES RELATING TO THE COUNTY OF SURREY,

LEVIED IN THE KING'S COURT,
FROM THE SEVENTH YEAR OF RICHARD I. TO THE
END OF THE REIGN OF HENRY VII.

EXTRACTED AND EDITED BY
FRANK B. LEWIS, B.A.

SURREY ARCHÆOLOGICAL SOCIETY.
EXTRA VOLUME I.

Guildford:
PRINTED FOR THE SURREY ARCHÆOLOGICAL SOCIETY.
1894.

PREFACE.

The Fines (*Pedes Finium*), which are the subject of this Calendar, form part of a large collection preserved at the Public Record Office. In this collection the fines relating to each county are arranged in a separate series under the name of that county, and the fines which refer to several counties are grouped in two large classes, called 'Divers Counties' and 'Various Counties.' Each fine is numbered at the foot, and the same number appears before the title in the Calendar referring to it, so that if an applicant at the Record Office wishes to see any particular fine, he would refer to it as Surrey Fines, 7 Richard I., No. 1, 9; Henry III., No. 73, etc. The different series date, as a rule, from *temp.* Richard I. (though there are a few earlier) to 1834, when a statute was passed 'For the Abolition of Fines and Recoveries, and the substitution of more simple modes of assurance.'

Probably every member of the Society knows what a fine is, but if perchance there be some who do not, the following brief description may give them some interest in this Calendar, which would otherwise to them be a mere list of names and places.

A fine was so called from the words *Finalis Concordia* with which it begins, and also from its effect in putting a final end to all suits and contentions, was an amicable agreement or composition of the suit (whether fictitious or real) in which it was made.

The fine, which commenced with the words *Hæc est finalis*

Concordia, was the embodiment in a permanent form of the agreement or composition made between the parties with the license of the judges to concord, and was enrolled amongst the Records of the Court in which the suit was commenced: down to the time of Edward I. such enrolment is to be found in the Curia Regis Rolls, and after that date for the most part in the De Banco Rolls. These fines related almost exclusively to free tenements and the incidents arising from or connected with them, such as tenures, services, rents, and grants of freedom, and were the means by which they might be transferred, settled, or limited. Mr. Scargill Bird, in his *Guide to the Documents at the Public Record Office*, says, in the section dealing with Fines and Recoveries: 'They are said to be of equal antiquity with the first rudiments of the law, instances having been produced of them even prior to the Norman invasion, and they no doubt originated in actual suits for recovering the possession of lands or other hereditaments, the possession thus gained being found so sure and effectual that fictitious actions were soon introduced for the sake of obtaining the same security.' The view that what afterwards came to be the process of levying a fine was originally a real action tried before the Court, is supported by the fact that the various stages of the early forms of both are identical, and I have seen cases, *temp.* H. III., where what was apparently a contentious action had been begun and various steps in the action taken, and then the parties have come and prayed for license to concord, which has been given, and a day for the parties to have the chirograph appointed.

The early process of levying a fine was this: A præcipe or writ was issued, and on the fourth day after service the parties appeared in Court and prayed for license to concord, which was granted; the terms of concord were then entered into, sometimes there being an adjournment for this purpose, and a day was given for them to attend and receive the chirograph, when they attended, and each party received

PREFACE. v

a part of this engrossment of the final concord, the third part being enrolled by the Court.

Further information can be obtained by reference to Cruise's *Essay on Fines and Recoveries*, 1794, or for a brief but very succinct account of the fine used as a conveyance, settlement, or transfer, the reader should refer to the article in Mr. Scargill Bird's *Guide to the Public Records*, previously referred to.

In the index of this Calendar I have collected together as far as possible the different variants of the name of a person or place under one heading with cross references, but I would warn those referring to the index that it is almost impossible to do this in every case, and that they must look for possible variants themselves to render their search complete.

The multiplicity of variants in some cases is very perplexing, and would seem to depend in some cases either upon the education or sobriety of the clerk who engrossed the fine, or of the person who instructed him, and in others as to whether the clerk entered on the roll the original English name spelt properly or misspelt, as the case may be, or what he considered to be the French or Latin equivalent of it. For example, see Wandsworth, Windsor, Abinger, and Southwark: amongst the names of places and persons, and amongst the names of persons, 'de molendino,' 'de molendinis,' 'atte mulne,' and 'del Molyn,' or 'atte Strete,' 'de la Strete,' 'del Strete,' and others, etc.

Such entries as 'Robert de Bath fil' Robert de Weston,' p. 28, or 'Thomas atte Doune fil' Richard Puffe,' p. 151, are very interesting topics for discussion, as are the place, trade, and nicknames to be found in this Calendar, and the various theories which have been propounded thereon, but however much one is tempted to do so, this is not the place to enter into a disquisition on such subjects.

The Calendar will be of interest not only to Surrey antiquaries, but also to antiquaries in general, as there are a very large number of fines classified with the county of Surrey which relate to Southwark and the adjacent parishes and manors. In many cases where a party to a fine was a citizen of London, mention is made of the City Guild to which he belonged, and possibly many missing links in genealogy or other debateable points may be traced out and settled.

Some five years ago I wished to obtain some information relative to certain places in Surrey which the county histories of Manning and Bray, Allen, and Walford did not disclose, and to complete my search it became necessary to examine the series of *pedes finium* relating to the county. To my dismay, and probably others have experienced the same feeling, I found that until *temp.* Henry VII., with the exception of Hunter's transcripts, *temp.* Richard I., and John, there was no Calendar, and that I should have to look through about 3,000 Surrey and 7,000 divers counties' fines to see if the information I wished to obtain was to be found amongst them. With a view of making these fines more accessible to myself I compiled this Calendar, and finding it of very great use to myself, I considered that it would be of equal use to Surrey antiquaries and others, and I offered to give it to our County Society provided that it was printed *en bloc*. This offer was accepted, and the result is now put before the members of this society in the hope that by throwing open this, for practical purposes, new source of information as to field names, tenures, services, etc., our local antiquarian research may be generally aided and developed. I must mention that I am greatly indebted to Mr. Mill Stephenson, one of the hon. secretaries of the Society, for the assistance which I have received from him from time to time.

F. B. LEWIS.

11, OLD JEWRY CHAMBERS, E.C.
November 6, 1894.

A CALENDAR
OF THE FEET OF FINES

FOR

SURREY.

7th Rich^d I
1. Mabel de Mumbrai v. the Prior and Convent of Sudwerke in Sudmeresfeld in Banested
2. The Prior of Mereton v. Gilbert Morin in Mordon and Awylton
3. Alexander fil' Henry v. Roger de London in Wallewurd
4. Walter de Windeshores v. Hugh de Polested & Cecilia his wife in Conton
5. Robert fil' Robert v. Richard de Breges in Awell

8th Rich^d I
6. John de Stokewell by Pentecost de Wandeswrd v. Gunnilda de Hesse in Hesse
7. Margaret de Normenwil v. Emma de Normenvile in Titinges Beverink & Mades
8. John Blund of Auton v. William Blund his brother in Auton
9. Julia de Normenwil v. Emma de Normenvil in Titinges Beverink & Mades

10 Rose de Normenvil *v*. Emma de Normenvil in Boverink Totinges & Hame
11 John the Abbot of Waverle by Hugh his Monk *v*. William de Wico in Wickes
12 Reginald de Cornhull *v*. Roger fil' Roger de Sutwerke in Sutwerke
13 Christina fil' Baldwin *v*. Godwin de Certesey in Certesey
14 Robert de Gatton *v*. Eva del Broc in Waibreg
15 Richard Dignus *v*. Thomas fil' Hervey in Sandres
16 Alexander fil' Henry *v*. Edward de Dudelea in Walewrth
17 Godfrey de Tichesey *v*. William fil' Odo de Tichesey in Chelesham and Netlested.

9th $Rich^{d}$ I

18 William de Chiriton *v*. Reginald de Cruce in Mikeleham
19 Pagan fil' Samar *v*. Herbert de Polesdene in Polesdene
20 Martin the Abbot of Certesey and the Convent there *v*. Gilbert fil' Ralph in Certeshey
21 Alan de Wicton *v*. Roger fil' Roger de Sudhiwerke in Wicham & Sudhiwerke
22 Robert fil' Davit *v*. Martin the Abbot of Certesey in Certesey
23 William fil' Robert *v*. Robert de Waleton in Sudmaresfeld (Bansted)
24 Stephen de Bendenges *v*. Simon de Berkes in Wike
25 Gilbert de Pudindene *v*. Odo the Abbot of Battle by Robert le Sauvage in Gamelingedene (near Regate)
26 Mabel de Mumbre *v*. the Prior & Convent of Suthwerk in Benested
27 Christina Smith *v*. Norman Smith in Sudhiwerke
28 Gunilda de Hese *v*. Peter fil' Walter de Badrichesey in Hese
29 Roger fil' Peter *v*. Adam Ruffus in Chelesham
30 Robert de Valeignes & Matilda his wife *v*. William de Pudindene & Lucy his wife in Billesersse
31 William de Hames *v*. Ralph de Penherste in Warlingham

10th Rich^d I

32 Walter de Lingefeld *v.* William de Wonham in Becheswrde
33 Hugh de Beseville *v.* Alexander de Wicford in Aulton
34 Thurbert de Bosco *v.* Richard le Curt in Puteham
35 Philip Mareschall *v.* Wlric fil' Recluse in Edinton
36 Gilbert Kersere *v.* Ralph P... in Kingestun
37 John fil' Ailvard *v.* Richard fil' John in ...
38 Alan de Wicton *v.* Alexander Cecū by Fulk de Ruerhee in Sudhiwerk
38a Herbert de Wandleswrde and Juliana his wife *v.* Henry fil' Robert in Wandleswrde
39 Emma widow of William (de Fenne) *v.* William de Fenne fil' William de Fenne in Fenne
40 Agnes widow of Thomas Malemoillier *v.* Philip de Lehe in Camerwell
41 Juliana Ernhina Emma Alice & Rose by Richard de Coterfaude *v.* Akina widow of Philip Blund and Philip his son in Polested
42 Emma fil' Aldwin *v.* W... Baker & Albrea his wife in Certesey
43 Vitalis fil' Ralph *v.* John de Cruce in Suthton
44 William Pentecost *v.* Geoffrey Warner by Robert de Ruerhee in Reigat
45 Hugh de Beseville *v.* William the Prior of St. Mary Sudhiwerke in Awelton
46 Alexander fil' Ailbric *v.* Alan de Wichton in Sudhiwerk

1st John

1 Walter Tropmell & Avelina his wife *v.* Walter de Hexestede in Kingestun
2 Gocelin fil' Ailward *v.* Robert fil' Gocelin & Estrilda his wife in Bechom
3 Geoffrey the Prior of the Convent of Canterbury by Elias de St. Albans his monk *v.* Editha de Horslee in Horslee

1—2

4 Gilbert de Suthill & Gunilda his wife *v.* Gilbert de la Feld & Matilda his wife in Waleton & Westmoleseie

5 Simon fil' Roger & Richard fil' Hamo by Homund Clerk *v.* Philip de Lega in Camerwell

6 William de Hertmere *v.* Thomas fil' Philip in Hertmere

7 John Cumin *v.* Martin the Abbot of Certesey in Awelton

8 Vitellus fil' Robert *v.* Richard his brother in Banested

9 Peter de Cudinton *v.* William Pentecost in Cherlewude & Cheiham

10 Eva de Broc by Walter de Folebroc *v.* Avice fil' Hugh Bolle by Reginald de Clifton in Waibrige

11 Amabel & Ysabel fil' Ranulph *v.* Suanilda fil' Ranulph in Wikes

12 William Pentecost *v.* Roger Enganet in Batrichesey

13 Hugh de Logos & Margaret his wife *v.* Richard de Dol in Burg Wandleswrth and Remdon

14 Ernald de Mecham *v.* Gilbert de Waleton and John his brother in Mecham

15 Walter de Pirlee *v.* John the Abbot of Hyde by Master Elias in Pirlee & Sandested

16 Walter fil' Hamo *v.* Ralph de Grava in Horslee

17 Eva de Broc by Walter de Folebroc *v.* Adam de Wdeham by Reginald de Clifton in Bifled

18 Robert de Besevill *v.* William Flandr and Matilda de Covel his wife in Awelton

19 Geoffrey (Ben)dinges *v.* Robert de Baseville by Alan de Wicton in Puteham

2nd *John*

20 William le Franceis *v.* Ralph fil' Walter de Cunton in Slifeld

21 Martin the Abbot of Certesey *v.* John Chaper in Clendon

22 William Hansard & his wife Aveline *v.* Walter the Prior of Merton in Kingeswude, Chauvesdone, Tadeswurthe, & Tuleswerthe

3rd John

23 Gilbert fil' Ralph *v.* Robert Mandut in Micheham
24 Philip de Winlesore *v.* William Bastard in Bergh
25 Martin the Abbot of Certesey *v.* Robert fil' Peter in Egham
26 Gilbert de Boveney *v.* Robert Ma(ndut) and Ernald de Mecham in Mecham
27 Beatrice de Sandres *v.* William Maubanc in Sandres
28 Eva de Keisney *v.* Milo fil' Robert & Alice his wife in Dritham
29 Hugh de Loges & Margaret his wife by John Brule *v.* Samson de Mulesey in Geldeford
30 Walter de Hecsted and Matilda his wife *v.* Adam de Wudeham in Halgheford and Biflete
31 Walter de Polesdon *v.* Walter the Prior of Merton by Adam the canon in Fechham and Polesdene
32 Edward fil' Ailwin de Micheham *v.* Odo de Stafald & Juliana his wife & Haenilda her sister in Micheham

4th John

33 Alvina fil' Godwin *v.* Robert de Barevill in Stok
34 Walter fil' Gilbert *v.* Henry fil' Robert in Wenleswrth
35 Robert fil' Reginald de Rinssam *v.* Geoffrey de Middelton in Egeham
36 Robert fil' John by Walter de St. Michael *v.* Peter de Fonte in Cudinton
37 Ralph de Halling *v.* Hugh the Prior of Bermundesey in Waddon
38 Philip Vitdeniers *v.* Hugh the Prior of Bermundesey in Rutherhey
39 Henry Smith *v.* John the Abbot of Waverleg in Ockestate
40 Turebut fil' Tureb(ut) *v.* Osbert fil' Ralph in Effingham
41 Robert Chaplain *v.* Gonilda & Matilda in Geldeford
42 Henry le Engleis & Emma his wife by Henry Bacun *v.* Edward de Budele in Lamhee
43 Theobald fil' Godric *v.* William Akr in Suberton

44 Ranulph de Rokesbir *v.* Walter de Holeherst in Holeherst & Dun
45 Thomas grandson of Adam Cook *v.* Deodatus de Dunes & Agnes his wife in Polesden
46 Elwin fil' John *v.* Roger de Holeg in Holeg
47 Edith fil' Leufric *v.* William Croc & Gunnilda his wife in Horton
48 Alice Magant *v.* Hugh Magant in Cleigat
49 Osbert Hors *v.* Godfrey the Bishop of Wincester by William Testard in Kingestun
50 Theobald de Ferming *v.* Richard de Dol in Badricheshee & Wanlesworth

5*th* John

51 Henry fil' Ailwin *v.* Walter fil' Walter in Waldingham
52 Richard fil' John *v.* Reginald Juvenis in Awelle
53 Geoffrey the Prior of Christchurch, Canterbury, by Elyas his monk *v.* Alan de Wicton by John Clerk in Sudwurk
54 Robert le Crew & Matilda his wife *v.* Richard fil' Ranulf in la Wudecote & Awelton
55 Adam de Cumpewrthe *v.* Henry fil' Ailwin in Waldingham
56 Lecia fil' Walter Vinitor *v.* John le Franceis in Reigate
57 Ralph the Abbot of Westminster *v.* William de Ginnei & Matilda his wife in Badrichesey

6*th* John

58 Ralph Pothel *v.* Walkelin Rabus by John Rabus in Subertone
59 Hamo fil' Gilbert *v.* Norman fil' Hamo & Beatrice his wife in Kingeston
60 Walter fil' Gilbert *v.* Matilda fil' Wlwold in Sudhiwerke
61 Walter de Edelmeton & Juliana his wife *v.* William de la Leie in West Mulesey
62 John the Prior of Newark by William his canon *v.* William Maubanc in Sandes
62a Siward de Ewelle *v.* Reginald Juvenis in Ewelle

6—9 JOHN.

63 Robert prior of the Hospital of Jerusalem by brother Robert de Waie *v.* Thomas de St. Christopher in Horsemad (Suthwark)
64 Robert fil' John *v.* William de Minthurst in Cudinton
65 Brother Robert treasurer of the Hospital House of Jerusalem by Robert de Waie *v.* Cristiana fil' Goding by Ralph Black clerk in Sudwurc
66 Hugh de Dol *v.* Richard de Dol in Loselee and Litlington
67 John de Brius & Margary his wife *v.* Ralph de Cameis whom Hubert de Anesti & Matilda his wife called to warranty in Wissele

8th *John*

68 Alvina widow of Tom by Gilbert her son *v.* William fil' Baldewin in Leddrede
69 John Marescall *v.* Richard fil' William in Awelton
70 Felicia widow of Ernald *v.* Robert Manduit in Mecham
71 Robert Manduit *v.* Walter fil' Gilbert by William Bataille in Mestham
72 John Marescall *v.* Reginald Pinget & Cristiana his wife in Awelton
73 Wulneva widow of Geoffrey *v.* Geoffrey fil' Dunning in Cumbe
74 Hugh de Horsie *v.* Agnes de Heiwude who called to warranty Deodonatus de Dune & Agnes his wife in Heiwude
75 William de Chissedon by Stephen Bonchristien *v.* Germanus de Chissedon in Chissedon (Brian fil' Ralph a.s.c.)
76 Gilbert Blund *v.* Peter Tholy who Robert Blund called to warrant in Kingeston
77 Roger fil' Simon & Alice his wife *v.* Jocelin de Scaudeford in Scaudeford

9th *John*

78 Robert de Lurdune *v.* Walter the Prior of Mereton in Ewelle

79 Robert de Hameledon *v.* William de Brademer in Fecham Ledrede and Hameledon
80 William de Rokesbir *v.* Edgar de la Linde & his wife Gunnilda in Rokesbir
81 Luke de Waleton *v.* William Banastre in Waleton
82 Siward de Ewelle *v.* Reginald Juvenis in Awelle
83 Roger fil' William de Tom *v.* Walter de Holeherst in La Dune
84 Hugh de Windlessores by Roger de Remdon *v.* Michael de Polsted who called to warranty Cecilia de Polsted in Witetrewe and Chidingefald

10th *John*

85 Walter the Prior of Merton *v.* Richard de Bures in Kingeswude
86 William de Sandes & Lucy his wife *v.* Stephen de Turneham & Edelina his wife in Stlifeld

11th *John*

87 Robert le Sauvage *v.* Roger fil' Alan by Stephen Boncristien in Geldeford
88 John the Prior 'de Novo Loco de Andebir' (Newark) by Alexander the canon *v.* Beatrice Maubanc by William de Pappewrth in Sande

14th *John*

89 William fil' Siward *v.* Reginald Juvenis in Ewelle
90 Maisent fil' William Carbonell by Ralph Carbonell *v.* Thomas de Katenham clerk in Katenham
91 Walter the Prior of Merton *v.* Nicholas Malesmeins in Ockel and Holebroc
92 Walter the Prior of Merton *v.* Brian fil' Ralph & Gunnora his wife by Peter de Badelesmere in Meandon
93 Walter the Prior of Merton *v.* Brian fil' Ralph & Gunnora his wife by Peter de Badelesmere in Mandon

15th *John*

94 Letitia widow of William le Bolc by Ralph Chaplain *v.* William le Bolc in Horslee

95 John le Chaloner & Grace his wife *v.* Master Amisius archdeacon of Surrey and master of the New Hospital of St. Thomas the Martyr in Sudwerc, in Sudwerc (S. Archbishop of Canterbury a.s.c.)

96 John le Carpenter & Elena his wife *v.* Master Amisius &c. (see 95) in Sudwerc (S. Archbishop of Canterbury a.s.c.)

97 Ralph de Kameis and Matilda his wife by Philip de Scaudeford *v.* Peter de la Ruebern in la Ruebern

98 Richard fil' Ralph & Cecilia his wife *v.* Master Amisius &c. (see 95) in Sudwerc (Stephen, Archbishop of Canterbury a.s.c.)

99 Walter the prior of Merton *v.* Samson de Mulesey in Muleseye

100 Stephen de Suthwerc clerk *v.* William de Warlingeham in Sutwerc

2nd *Henry III*

1 William Testard *v.* William de Bath in Geldeford

2 Reginald de Kent & his wife Dionisia *v.* Martin le Corder in Suwerc

3 Martin de Covenham & his wife Eva *v.* Gilbert de Abernun & his wife Matilda in Hadlee

4 Alexander de Wikeford & his wife Isabel *v.* Peter de Berg in Berg & Sutton

5 Frechisent widow of William Blenche *v.* Peter de Berges in Awell

6 Roger fil' Albric *v.* Walter de Colle in Colle

7 Alvina de Stokes by William fil' Geri *v.* William, Bishop of London by William de Bukingham in Stokes

3rd *Henry III*

8 William del Geyt *v.* Ralph Manduit in Mecheham

9 Savaric de Stanes *v.* Henry de Middleton in Egeham

10 Robert de Wintersell and his wife Margaret *v.* Roland de Axstede who Herlewin de Traz and William Blund called to warranty in Graweshull and Axstede

11 William de Crauestok *v.* Gilbert de Chabham and his wife Alice in Crauestok
12 Roger Saft *v.* William Sutor in Esse
13 Martin Carpenter and his wife Avice *v.* Robert Blanche in Kinggeston
14 Alice widow of Michael Belet by Walter de Tinbreg *v.* Thomas the Prior of Merton by brother Hugh in Seenes
15 William de Wauton *v.* Aulbrey de Teill in Micheham
16 John fil' Algod and Robert fil' Mathew *v.* Randulf de Burstohe in Horlie (Peter de Berge a.s.c.)
17 Hamo fil' Ralph and William fil' Siward *v.* William de Wicumb and Sailda his wife in Norbinton
18 Walter de Ruda *v.* Geoffrey Heremitam in Hoteressaham
19 Swein Predome and his wife Helewisia and William Sweting and his wife Matilda *v.* William fil' Savaric in Reherth
20 Robert fil' William de Litleton *v.* William Slow of Litleton in Litleton
21 Ailleva fil' Leuric *v.* Richard de Graveneye in Thorp
22 Gilbert de Cruce and his wife Alice *v.* Adam fil' Segar and William Godeman in Suberton
23 Henry Gresley and wife Alice *v.* Alexander de Wicsted in Micheham
24 Gilbert Ruffus *v.* Edelina fil' Osebert de la Dene in Dorkingg
25 Thomas fil' Robert *v.* Jordan fil' Amfred in Ledred
26 Godefrid Chaplain of Kinggeston *v.* Hugh le Stut and his wife Milisant in Kinggestun
27 Harding fil' Semer *v.* Aveline widow of Robert Miller in Kinggestun
28 William the Abbot of Westminster by Stephen de Berkingg *v.* Walter Woderowe in Peyng
29 Adrian fil' Ralph Eswy *v.* Reginald Bretinghull in Pecham
30 Gilbert de Teler *v.* Reginald Clerk and Simon le Wessere in Wikeford

3—5 HENRY III.

31 Robert de Quodeham John Algod and Gunnora de Cudinton v. Pentecost de Wandlesworth in Horle
32 Henry Bataille v. William Aquillun and his wife Johanna in Edinton
33 Alan de Bercherst v. John de Ymbeloge in Bercherst
34 William Long by Elyas fil' Ralph v. Ralph Morin in Thatlefeld
35 John fil' Roger de Heure v. William de Heure in Horle
36 William fil' Edward de Bodel v. Clement de Doure and his wife Isabel in Suwerc
37 Lucy fil' Walter de la Neuland v. Robert master of St. Thomas' Hospital Suwerc in Suwerc
38 William fil' Robert v. Basilia de Ponehurst in Penehurst
39 Hugh de Windlessores v. Hugh de Nevill and his wife Johanna by Roland de Acsted in Horsleg and Okelege
40 Gilbert fil' Roger v. Hugh Kolswein and his wife Beatrix by William de Elmedon in Wodecote
41 Alexander de Wikeford v. Deodatus de Dune and his wife Agnes in Polesdene
42 Roger Harding v. Ordmer Storm in Kingeston

4th Henry III

43 Richard fil' Godwin v. Warin de Chelese in Certesey
44 Richard fil' Godwin v. Ranulf de Stanore in Certesey
45 Richard fil' Godwin v. John le Draper in Certesey
46 Richard fil' Godwin v. Peter de Podeshal in Certesey
47 Thomas fil' Odo de Criol v. John de Criol in Chepstede
48 Margaret Con de Cive widow of Alured le Paumer v. Robert Squattechese in Suthwerc
49 Richard fil' Ralph v. William fil' Hubert in Kamerwell

5th Henry III

50 Reginald de Neubir Clerk v. Robert de Bekeham in Bedinton
51 Geoffrey Goldsmith v. Robert de Bagschate who called to warranty Ralph Hoppeschort in Bagschate

52 Robert de Turri *v.* Reginald de Brittinghurst in Pecham
53 Deodatus de Dune and his wife Agnes *v.* Robert de Puntinton in Coveham
54 Isabel widow of Walter de la Neweland *v.* Geoffrey Godesgrace who called to warranty Ralph fil' Ralph Carbonel in Suwerc
55 Bartholomew Smith and his wife Alice and her sisters Cecilia and Mabel *v.* Reginald Smith in Croherst
56 Richard de Cumbe *v.* Nicholas de Pirile who called to warranty the Abbot of Hide in Sandersted

6th *Henry III*

57 William de Land clerk *v.* Joceus le Pesur and his wife Mary in Retherhey and Bermundesey
58 William de Belce *v.* Godard de Caterham who Gilbert de Pudindon called to warranty in Wudemarethorn
59 Richard de Newedegate *v.* Reginald Juvenis in Ewell
60 Richard de Langhurst and his wife Alice and Thomas de Rumeham and his wife Cecilia *v.* Julian fil' Goda by Gerard fil' Ralph in Slifeld
61 Thomas H...arl *v.* William de Bekeham in Bedinton

7th *Henry III*

62 William fil' Benedict *v.* Henry fil' Henry de Taiden in Micham
63 Philip Vitdeners *v.* John de Tichesey who Agnes de Tichesey called to warranty in Camerwell
64 Ralph Deyrell *v.* Hugh the Prior of Bermundesey in Chelesham

8th *Henry III*

65 Thomas de Banelingham and his wife Mabel *v.* Richard, Bishop of Salesbyr in the Hundred of Godalming
66 Baldewin de Bechum and his wife Johanna by Robert Baillemunt *v.* Matilda prioress of Haliwell by Nicholas the chaplain in Kamerwell
67 Luke de Kingeswod *v.* Luke fil' Robert in Gatton

68 William Pentecost of Wandleswurth *v.* Geoffrey de Parco in Gatton

69a Philip Vitdeners *v.* Matilda prioress of Haliwell by Nicholas the chaplain in Camerwell

69b Hamo de Gatton *v.* Petronilla de Bellevale in Gatton

70 William fil' Benedict *v.* Henry fil' Henry de Taidon in Micham

71 Peter le Poter *v.* Isabel widow of Ralph Lungis in Geldeford

72 William fil' Benedict de London *v.* Philip de D... in Retherhethe

9*th* *Henry III*

73 Philip Vitdeners *v.* Ralph de Wik and his wife Ascelina by Peter le Crisp in Camerwell

10*th* *Henry III*

74 John de Wauton and his wife Alice by Thomas de Grava and William de Kingeston *v.* Thomas the Prior of Tenrugg in Tenrugge

75 John de Wauton and his wife Alice by same *v.* William Earl Warrenne in Herewardesle

76 John de Wauton and his wife Alice by same *v.* John de St. John in Wolknested

77 Hugh the Prior of Bermundesey *v.* John de Tichesey, Reginald de Bretinghurst, Geoffrey le Ridere, William Brun & John Garland in Dilewis & Camerwell

11*th* *Henry III*

78 Hubert de Burg, Earl of Kent and his wife Margaret *v.* Nigell de Hubray in Benested

79 Geoffrey de Saukevill, Richard de Cumbe and Sibilla his wife by Robert de Dene *v.* Petronilla de Belevale and Hamo de Gatton in Gatton

13*th* *Henry III*

80 William Churn *v.* Albred de Strode in Utterwrth

81 William de Colevil *v.* William de Besevile and William de

Besevile who John de Bedinton and his wife Isabel called to warranty in Kersawelton (John Jocelin a.s.c.)

82 Thomas Raven and his wife Sarra *v.* Alban Fisher who the Abbot of Battle called to warranty by Philip de Esford in Sudwerk

83 Richard de Horse *v.* John de Hale in Neudegate

84 Walter fil' John *v.* John de Tichesey who William fil' Reginald called to warranty and John de Tichesey, who Gunnora widow of Reginald Smith called to warranty in Croherst

85 John de Kemesinges and his wife Idonea by Philip de Benchesam *v.* Peter de Bendenges in Benchesham

86 Ralph fil' Robert *v.* William Topplere in Bandon

87 John de Grapelingeham and his wife Acelina and her sister Agnes *v.* William Testard in Cudiford

88 William Tony *v.* William le Greder in Kingeston

89 Ralph de Chetwode *v.* Ralph de Berkinges and his wife Margaret in Berges

90 Gilbert Textor and William de Monasterio *v.* Hugh le Franklein and his wife Alice in Wikford

91 William de Munested *v.* Reginald Giffard in Chedingefeld

92 Mabel widow of Ralph de Halink *v.* Ralph de Halink in Croindon, Waddon, & Bedinton

93 Walter de Uttewrth *v.* Ruald de Sandes in Sandes

94 Ralph fil' John *v.* William Faukes and Alice his wife in Wandleswrth

95 William fil' Ailbric *v.* Walter fil' Britgive in Wolknested (John de Wauton and his wife Alice a.s.c.)

96 Ralph le Mukere *v.* Richard Smith in Kingeston

97 Frichesand' filia William *v.* Gilbert Walensis who William Halpeni called to warranty in Certesey

98 William de Dene *v.* Alwin de Dene & Algar le Fulur and his wife Agnes in Bromlegh

13 HENRY III.

99 William Goldsmith and his wife Roesia *v.* Jordan de Monte in Holecroft
100 Richard de Stafaud *v.* Robert le Bukere in Alfaude
101 Editha de la Stronde *v.* John Ingel and his wife Swonilda in Gingeston
102 David fil' Nicholas *v.* John Newman in Weston
103 William fil' William Carpenter *v.* Robert de la Done in Wandeswrth
104 William Testard by Thomas fil' Simon *v.* John Wode in Geldeford
105 Thomas Pinchun *v.* Gilbert de Oxenecroft in Ledrede
106 Stephen fil' Robert *v.* Hugh le Nappere in Gingeston
107 Henry del Yl *v.* Henry fil' Ralph in Merstham
108 Alice widow of Gerard de Saklesford *v.* John fil' Robert de Essinge in Saklesford
109 Maurice de Ewaken *v.* John de Horton in Horton
110 Maurice de Ewaken *v.* William Croc in Horton
111 Seman fil' Thurston *v.* Lewin Bule in Gingeston
112 John Hardegray *v.* Osbert Peper in Kingeston
113 William de Bakewrth *v.* William Rufin in Cherlwude (Walter de Collye, a.s.c.)
114 John de Bures *v.* John de Scaldeford in Ewell
115 William de Gerston by Richard de Horne *v.* Richard the Prior of Renecester by Alured Tellekin in Blechingeleg
116 William Monke *v.* John de Chereburg who Henry fil' Jordan called to warranty in Ledred
117 Henry fil' Richard *v.* Geoffrey fil' Geoffrey and his mother Agnes and Robert de Tichesey in Kamerwell
118 Almar Knicht *v.* Gilbert fil' Edwin in Kingeston
119 Ivo de Hallink *v.* Ralph de Hallink in Bedinton and Bendon
120 Eylena widow of Henry Cook *v.* William Molde in Sire
121 William Scot and his wife Alice *v.* William de Ditton in Ditton

122 Almar Knicht v. William Greder in Kingeston
123 Pagan Wronge v. Avice de Dorking in Hamsted
124 Adam de la Tey v. John fil' Elias in Wauton
125 William Goldsmith and Roesia his wife v. John Bundy and his wife Margaret in Guldeford
126 Hugh Spring v. Forthwin de Norboton in Gingeston
127 Pagan Wronge v. Richard de Westcote and his wife Avice in Hamstede
128 Richard fil' John v. Richard fil' Gerard in Polsted
129 Walter de Suthwerc and his wife Leuina v. Simon de Chivening in Putinden
130 Walter fil' John v. John de Tichesey who William fil' Roger called to warranty and John de Tichesey who Gunnora widow of Reginald Smith called to warranty in Croherst
131 Bruna de Chedingefeld v. Thomas de Banelingeham, Grant of her Freedom
132 Peter fil' John and wife Lucy v. Robert le Tyg and his wife Matilda & John Baker and his wife Albreda in Gingeston
133 Odo de Prinkeham v. Ailward Crips in Lunnsfeld
134 Walter fil' Warin v. Edward le Paumer and his wife Edith in West Mulesey
135 Geoffrey de Godelegh v. Robert Carter in Chidingefold
136 Robert Baker v. Mathew fil' Geoffrey in Gingeston
137 Alexander de Thorp v. Geoffrey de Starith who Alan fil' Hairun called to warranty in Certesey
138 Reginald fil' Reiner v. Henry le Saltere in Camerwell
139 William Paramurs and his wife Isabel v. Reginald fil' Roger in Suwerc
140 Gilbert de Haywod v. Gunnilda de Polesden in Pollesden
141 Richard fil' Richard v. John Barbarius in Okelinge
142 Mathew de Einton and his wife Juliana by Philip de Benchesham v. John de Tichesey in Crohurst

143 Reginald de Brettingherst *v.* William de Funtenay and his wife Frechesant in Pecham
144 Matilda fil' Edelina *v.* Philip de Henlegee who Robert Fareman and his wife Goda called to warranty in Hanlegee
145 Daniel le Franceis *v.* Gilbert de Holeghe and his wife Margery in Merewe
146 Dionisia fil' William de Wymbeldon *v.* Richard de Wyngth by Robert de Le in Wymbeldon
147 Ralph Morin *v.* Walter de Tatlesfeld in Tatlesfeld
148 Matilda de Kilcham *v.* William de la Rughebern in Horsleg

14th *Henry III*

149 Godefrey Dodekin and his wife Constance and William fil' Robert and Cristiana his wife *v.* John de Chelesham in Chelesham
150 Roger de la Dune and his wife Alice by Robert de Hormede *v.* John Belot who Roger de Shen called to warranty by John Planez in Shene
151 Gregory de la Dune *v.* Robert, Bishop of Salisbury in Ledling
152 William de London *v.* Stephen fil' Thomas Nicolas and Isabella his wife in Rithereye
153 Geoffrey de Frowik *v.* John de Kemesing and his wife Idonea in Benchisam
154 Agnes and Avelina daughters of Mathew de Daunmartin *v.* Katherine, prioress of Rugespere in Newdegate

15th *Henry III*

155 Margery widow of Thomas de St. Martin *v.* William master of St. Thomas' Hospital Suthwerc, in Bedinton and Bandon
156 Thomas de Oldbridge *v.* William fil' Edward de Budele in Budele and Suwerk

16th *Henry III*

157 Hugh de Wendlesores *v.* Hamo de la Wudecote in Horsleg
158 Odo Goldsmith *v.* Geoffrey de Farleg and Helena his wife in Suwerck
159 Thomas Black *v.* Henry Bec & Dionisia his wife in Middleton and Vinecumb
160 Robert de Eggeham *v.* Robert de Sudinton in Sudinton

17th *Henry III*

161 Golda widow of William le Fleming *v.* Humphrey prior of Suwerk, John de Ymewurth, Richard Cokespur, Robert Ruffus & William Duddel in Adinton, Chelesham and Farleg
162 Robert de Watervill *v.* Ralph the Abbot of St. Leofrid by Fulc Chamberlain in Esschere
163 Pentecost de London clerk *v.* Hugh the Prior of Bermundesey who Adam the Chaplain called to warranty in Suwerc
164 Thomas le Neir *v.* Robert de Watervill and Alina his wife in Mikelham
165 Roger de Walecote and Alice his wife by Richard de Walecote *v.* William Mandut who Henry prior of Merton called to warranty in Mecham
166 Roger de London *v.* Robert the Abbot of St. Augustine's Canterbury by brother Robert de Hastinges his monk in Suwerck
167 Henry the Prior of Merton *v.* Alan the Abbot of Certesey by Ralph de Certesey in Sutton

18th *Henry III*

168 William fil' Benedict *v.* Robert de Retherhee and his wife Agnes in Hachesham

19th *Henry III*

169 Geoffrey de Ho and William de la Rude *v.* Thomas de Melewys and his wife Johanna in Wokyng
170 John Crane *v.* William le Taillur and Letitia his wife in Wolkenested

171 Richard le Veil and his wife Goldina *v.* Robert de la Dune in Wendleswurth
172 Henry le Barbur and his wife Helewysa *v.* William de Wakeherst in Thrule
173 Matilda widow of Robert de Basing *v.* Robert de Reingny in Bagshet
174 Mathew Hog *v.* Nicholas Duket in Kingeston
175 Peter Ateruwebern *v.* Roger de Upton in Upton
176 Peter Ateruwebern *v.* Richard Harm in Upton
177 Richard the Prior of Sandon by Gilbert de Sandon chaplain *v.* Roger de Bydon in Brunningesfaud, Wytheresfaud, Ottewurth and Chelewurth
178 Matilda fil' Baldric *v.* Richard the Abbot of Westminster by brother Theobald his monk in Mordon
179 William de Stoke *v.* Peter de Bidun in Twengham
180 Richard Harm *v.* Alan the Abbot of Certesey in Covenham
181 Gilbert Oisel and his wife Richalda *v.* Adam the Prior of Tenrig in Tenrig
182 Thomas the Prior of Newark *v.* Nicolas de Arundell in Sendes (Rualdus de Sandes a.s.c.)
183 William le Parmenter and his wife Edelina and Richard de Tichesey and his wife Viviana *v.* Robert de Molendino in Wolkenested
184 Alice the Abbess of Fontevraud by William the Prior of Leyton *v.* John de Faye in Bromlegh & Ottewurth
185 Richard de Hereford and his wife Felicia *v.* Gerard de Chisenden and his wife Matilda and Alice her sister in Ewell
186 John Oter and Lucy his wife and Mathew de Hurcle and Annora his wife *v.* Robert de Hecstede who Simon de Hecsted, Henry Nutheuseband, Richard Ismanger, Adam Puke, Ralph Sevoghel and Eylerd de Holm called to warranty in Wolkenested
187 William, Bishop of Exeter *v.* John le Chanu and his wife

2—2

Katherine and John le Chanu and wife Katherine who Walter Chaplain called to warranty in Tyting

188 Robert Joye *v.* Ralph de Kameis in Wodeton
189 Ascer de la Dune *v.* William de Watevill in Meandon
190 Gilbert Marescall *v.* Walter de Ottewurth and his wife Ida in Scyre
191 William fil' Ralph *v.* John fil' Wolward in Temes Ditton
192 Agnes widow of Richard Gulafre *v.* Thomas Chamberlain and Thomas Suel in Waleton
193 Richard de Wudecot *v.* Giles de Westwod and Christiana his wife in Waleton
194 Herbert fil' Elias *v.* John de Fay in Danhurst (John de Caburg a.s.c.)
195 Simon fil' Thedruc *v.* William fil' Odo in Dorking
196 Henry de la Ford and his wife Agnes *v.* Ralph de Papeworth in Papeworth
197 Gilbert Kempe *v.* Philip de Henleg in Certesey
198 Beatrice fil' Edgar *v.* Mathew fil' Juliana in Micham
199 William Poleyn *v.* Beatrice fil' Warin Goldsmith in Kyngeston
200 Thomas fil' Richard *v.* Hemeric fil' Hemeric in Suthlameye
201 Alexander de Torp *v.* Ralph de Gardino in Torp
202 Richard de Newdegate *v.* Roger de London who Thomas Testard called to warranty in Newdegate

20th *Henry III*

203 Golda widow of William le Fleming *v.* John de Chelesham who Richard Forester, Lawrence de Straton, Thomas de la Witesand, Drugo de Richescumbe and William Scrift called to warranty in Wolknested
204 John de Lobricth and his wife Felicia *v.* Margaret fil' Cristiana in Katerham Wolkenested Tenrig & La Newlond

21ˢᵗ *Henry III*

205 Brother William Gracien master of the Hospital of St. Mary of Ospreng *v.* Henry de Scrikeston and his wife Beatrice in Merewe

206 Robert de Wyk and his wife Lecia *v.* Laurence de St. Michael, Roger Frilent and Matilda his wife, Vitalis de Burgh and William Frilent in Cudinton

207 Humphrey the Prior of St. Mary Suwerc *v.* William fil' Richard and his wife Tephania in Suwerc

208 John Belemeyns *v.* William de la Mare by Ralph le Engleis, and William de la Mare who Henry fil' William called to warranty in Ested and Newdegate

209 Henry the Prior of Merton by David de Merton clerk *v.* Nicholas de Pyrle and his wife Johanna in Westmordon

210 Richard Ouberkyn by William de Wandleswurth *v.* Paul Blund and Matilda his wife in Suwerk Brugge & Gatton

22ⁿᵈ *Henry III*

211 Felicia the Prioress of Ambresbiry by brother William de Ambresbiry *v.* John de Fay in Bromleg

212 Robert de Haringe *v.* Aldred de Stoke and his wife Alvina in Stok

213 William de St. John *v.* Roger de Clare and his wife Alice in Chepstede

214 Gunnora widow of Mathew fil' Geoffrey *v.* Peter fil' Baldewyn in Kingeston

215 John fil' Ralph *v.* Robert de Reney and the said Robert de Reney who John fil' Robert Godric, Robert fil' Ralph le Naper and his wife Mabel called to warranty in Bageset and Wyndesham

216 Roger de London *v.* Wyschard the Prior of St. Saviour's Bermundesey by brother John de Dunestaple his monk and Geoffrey Pikerin in Rotherhuthe

217 Ralph the Abbot of Battle by John de Iham *v.* Hervey fil'

Fulk and Alice his wife in Suwerk (Ralph de Hibernia a.s.c.)

218 William de Rading and his wife Margery *v*. Robert Feyrchild and his wife Beatrice in Gudeford

219 Master Thomas Aswy *v*. Robert Reeve of Retherhethe and his wife Agnes in Ritherheth

23rd *Henry III*

220 William fil' William de la Rude *v*. William fil' Walter de la Rude and the same person who Richard de Graveney and his wife Editha and Hugh Garget and Dionis his wife called to warranty in Horishill

221 Albreda fil' Aylbright de Horton *v*. John fil' Gilbert de Horton in Horton

222 William de Gyrund *v*. William de Fednes by Hugh Harpur in Kersalton & Cloppeham

223 Walter de Merton clerk *v*. John le Blench of Ewell in Ewell

224 Cristiana widow of Luke de Trye *v*. Simon de Putindene in Lingefeld

225 Reyner de Suthull and his wife Alice, Alexander de Parco and his wife Emma, & Juliana de Pirifrith *v*. Walter de Tangel and his wife Matilda in Werplesden

226 Gilbert de Ewell and his wife Agnes *v*. John le Blench of Ewell in Ewell

227 Roger de Horn *v*. Nicholas de la Nobrith in Wolknested (John de Nobrihte and his wife Felicia a.s.c.)

24th *Henry III*

228 Richard le Pessuner and his wife Alice by Andrew de St. Swythun *v*. Peter fil' John de Suwerk in Suwerk

229 Peter de Pirifright *v*. the Prior of Newark in Pirifright

230 Lucy widow of Richard de la Bere by William de la Bere *v*. William le Duc in Chelesham

25th *Henry III*

231 William de Adburton *v*. Stephen Miller in Crohurst

232 Agnes de Linngefeld and Robert Cook and his wife Mabel *v.* John de Lobright and his wife Felicia, John de Rugge, William Pollard and Edmund atte Neweland in Warlingham, Crohurst and Lingfeld

233 Ralph de Bradel and Basilia his wife *v.* William Baldewin and his wife Mabel in Bradel

234 Hillary fil' Gilbert *v.* Hugh de Windles in Horseleg

235 Simon fil' Mary and his wife Avice by John de Wynton *v.* Henry Inkel in Camerwell

236 Geoffrey the Parson of Tichesey Church *v.* Gilbert Gowbrith and Emma fil' Siward in Tichesey (Hamo de Valoynes a.s.c.)

237 The Abbess of Wherwell by Robert de Sutton *v.* Walter de Ottewurth in Chelewurth

238 John de Berkinges and his wife Alice *v.* William de Stocwell in Betrecheseye

239 Joel de St. German *v.* Thomas de Pollesden and his wife Sarra in Gundeslee

240 Robert de Inegefeld *v.* Agnes de Inegefeld in Crohurst, Lingefeld & Warlingham

241 Thomas Kentwyn and his wife Johanna *v.* William Goldsmith in Tenrigge (Ralph le Cuver a.s.c.)

242 William de Widewell *v.* Gilbert de Basevill in Werplesden

243 William fil' William Picot *v.* the Master of the Hospital of St. Mary Magdalen of Sindon in Chissenden Taleworth (William de Daunmartin a.s.c.)

244 Agnes fil' John de Yenefeld *v.* Hervey fil' Fulc and Godefrey fil' William Cook who Isaac the Jew of Suwerk called to warranty in Suwerk

245 Stephen de Pollingfold *v.* John de la Hale and his wife Editha in Blakehok

246 The Prioress of Haliwell *v.* Henry de Dilewis in Camerwell

247 Ralph de Certesey *v.* Alexander de Thorp in Thorp and Egham

248 John de Lobright and his wife Felicia and Margery Malemeins *v.* Gilbert Malemeyns in Tanerig
249 Hagenilda fil' Roger *v.* Geoffrey Brond in Sutlamehethe
250 Hugh de Clere *v.* Walter de Ottewrth in Ottewrth & Chelewrth
251 Letitia widow of Godefrey Bonejoie *v.* the Prior of Sutwerk in Michham
252 Henry Inkel of Sutwerk *v.* William fil' Richard and his wife Theophania & John de Dunlegh in Sutwerk
253 John fil' Pagan and his wife Emma Augustin le Mercer and his wife Bella, Robert de Lenn and wife Alice by William de Vallibus who William Bolaun called to warranty in Sutwerk
254 Henry Luvel *v.* Richard de Craneford in Craneford
255 Ralph Grasvassal *v.* Nicholas fil' Joceus in Suwerk
256 Robert Herman *v.* Robert le Furber and his wife Anastasia in Geldeford
257 Brother Robert de Sanford master of the Knights Templars in England by brother Hugh de Stokton *v.* Walter de Morton in Adinton
258 Richard de la Horse and his wife Leuina *v.* Andrew de Wigepol and his wife Mabel and Walter de Wigepol in Cherlewod
259 Brother Richard master of the Hospital of the Holy Ghost Sandon *v.* Walter de Ottewurthe in Chelewurth and Ottewurth
260 Robert fil' Augustin *v.* Rodland de Aksted who Isabella de Aksted and Gregory fil' Sampson called to warranty in Aksted
261 Gilbert de Jarpenvill *v.* Richard de Oxehagh and Hugheline his wife in Pinkehurst
262 Margery fil' Ascelina *v.* Ascelina de Wike in Camberwell and Pecham

263 Gunilda de Dorkinges *v.* Thomas de Taynturer and Gilbert Oslang in Dorkinges

264 John de Chayham *v.* The Prior of Suwerk and the Prior of Suwerk who Vitalis de la Dene called to warranty in Bansted

265 Nicholas de Wapfold *v.* Richard de Oxehagh and his wife Hugheline in Abingewrth

266 Brother Robert de Sanford master of the Knights Templars in England *v.* Gilbert Walerand in Merwe

267 Brother Robert de Sanford master of the Knights Templars in England *v.* Roger de Craft by Thurstan fil' Geofrey de Weston in Merwe

268 Michael fil' Michael *v.* Peter fil' John de Suthwerk who William le Wympler called to warranty in Suwerk

269 James Haunsard and his wife Agatha *v.* James le Bel in Fermesham

270 Reginald fil' Walter *v.* Alice widow of Geoffrey le Weyte in Wandleswurth (the heirs of Hamo de Gravelee a.s.c.)

271 Richard de Warwik and his wife Juliana and her sister Johanna *v.* John de Gatwik & John de Gatwik who John de Fulbrok called to warranty in Cherlwod

272 Swan de Weston *v.* Robert de Reygni in Baggesayte

26*th Henry III*

273 The Abbess of Werwell by John de Sutton *v.* John de Parco in Hertindon

274 The Abbess of Werwell by John de Sutton *v.* Richard de Frollebir in Hertindon

275 The Abbot of Battle *v.* Ralph de la Quarere and his wife Agnes in Lymenesfeld

276 Peter de Bedinton by Eudo Moryn *v.* Andrew de Waddon and his wife Avice in Bandon

277 Master Thomas Assewy *v.* Henry Fiscer and his wife Editha in Suthwerk

278 Hymbert prior of Bermundesey *v.* Giles fil' Luke de Trie in Warlingham

279 The Abbess of Wherwell by Robert de Sutton *v.* Jordan de Montibus in Hertinden

27th Henry III

280 Robert prior of Merton by Nicholas de Hegham *v.* Lawrence fil' William in Micham

281 Richard Harm *v.* Hugh de Windesoure in Westhorslegh & Esthorslegh

282 Walter le Bufle and his wife Dionisia by Walter de Lichesfeld *v.* Robert le Brus in Wysselegh

283 John fil' Adrian *v.* William fil' William de Fakeham in Brokham

284 Thomas the Prior of Newark *v.* Henry de Bovill in Saundres

285 Alan the Abbot of Certesey by brother Richard his monk *v.* John de Daggenhal and his wife Agnes in East Cleyndon & West Clendon

286 Master Henry deacon and chaplain of St. Paul's London *v.* Thomas de Dunelm in Geldeford & Stoke

287 Adam de la Thye *v.* John de Berkinkes and his wife Alice in Merstham (Hamo de Shotemere a.s.c.)

28th Henry III

288 Isabel widow of Robert de Wymbeldon by William de Hege *v.* Floerin fil' Robert in Wymbeldon

289 Gilbert fil' William Rauf and his wife Alice *v.* Richard Swyfth and his wife Amabel in Horlee (The abbot of Certesey a.s.c.)

290 Margery fil' Richard de Wyk *v.* Ascelina de Wyke in Camereswell

291 Alice widow of Hamo de la Berwe *v.* Adam Stef in La Berne

292 Alexander treasurer of St. Pauls London *v.* Robert de Talewrth by John de Talewrth in Talewrth

293 John the Prior of Tunebrigg by brother Roger de Thune-

brigg his canon *v.* Bartholomew fil' Bartholomew and his wife Matilda and Hugh fil' Oliver and his wife Mary in Chelesham

294 Thomas Ravon and his wife Sarra *v.* Ralph de Ymewrthe in Ditton

295 Robert the Abbot "de loco sancti Edwardi" by brother Philip his monk *v.* Roger de Clere in Shire

296 John the Prior of Saundelford by Mathew Harand of Herliston *v.* John de Hamme and his wife Matilda in Bromleg

297 Cecilia fil' Ralph Blundel by William Gery *v.* Peter de Bydun in Twangham.

298 Adam le Buteler *v.* William de Camera and his wife Mabel in Taunrigge & Wolknested

299 Laurence fil' William *v.* William Bolle and Agnes his wife in Retherhethe

30*th* Henry III

300 Richard de Hurell and his wife Katherine *v.* William fil' Peter in Wymbeldon

301 William de Wandeleswurth *v.* William de Eytun and his wife Emma in Wymedon

302 William de Ebor reeve of Beverley *v.* Gilbert de Berham and his wife Lucy in Apse

303 John de Abernun *v.* Richard de Stokes and *v.* Richard de Stokes who Adam Dru called to warranty in Fecheham

304 John Adryan *v.* Giles le Neyr in Brocham, Estbechewrth and Mykeleham

305 Robert the Prior of Merton by Robert de Cirencester *v.* William de Suwerk and his wife Theoph (ania) in Suthwerk

31*st* Henry III

306 Symon fil' Richard *v.* Walter de Merton in Mendon, Maldon and Farnl (William de Wattervill and his wife Egidia a.s.c.)

307 Avice widow of James Goldsmith *v.* Laurence fil' William in Retherhethe & Hechesham
308 Brother Robert de Sanford master of the Knights Templars in England by William de Fraxino *v.* Walter de Morton in Adington and Selysdon
309 Warin de Monte Canis by Peter Cardon *v.* Walter the Abbot of St. Wlfmar Bonon in Notfeud
310 Ralph the Abbot of Battle by Richard le Marescall *v.* Geoffrey fil' Jordan in Axstede
311 Master Robert de Bandon *v.* Theobald Cook and his wife Alice in Bandon
312 John fil' Faber *v.* Odo de Crohurst in Crohurst
313 Gyffard the Abbot of Waverle by Richard de Ferkcles *v.* William Braunche and his wife Johanna in Pyperharg
314 Andrew Turbut and his wife Matilda *v.* William Faukes in Wandleswrthe, Totinges & Wymbeldon
315 Geoffrey de Newcastle *v.* Geoffrey le Deveneys and his wife Margery in Hacstede
316 John de Kynardele *v.* Walter de Kynardele and his wife Alice in Kersawelton

32nd *Henry III*

317 Alice fil' Philip Vitdeners & William Bolle and his wife Agnes *v.* Laurence fil' William in Rutherhee
318 Matilda de la Faye by Henry de la Breche *v.* Gyffard the Abbot of Waverle by John de Dunmere in Bromleye
319 Richard de Clare Earl of Gloucester by Richard le Waleys *v.* Ymbert the Prior of Bermundesey by brother Henry de North his monk in Camerwell
320 Roger de St. John *v.* Alice de Daumartin in Wolknested
321 John le Fleming *v.* Robert de Gatton in Gatton and Stanstede
322 Terricus Bunt *v.* William de Clerholt and his wife Alice in Mickelham
323 Robert de Bath fil' Robert de Weston by William de

Glastingebir *v.* Elyas fil' Nicholas de la More in Wymbeldon

324 Peter del Punt *v.* Gilbert fil' William and Rose his wife in Upton
325 Elyas fil' William *v.* Walter de Snodeham in Bromley
326 Geoffrey le Dyn *v.* Thomas the Prior of Newark, Joel de St. Jerman, Henry Pyrun, Robert de Papwrth, Richard de Grava, and Reginald Maubank in Saundes
327 Stephen the Prior of St. Mary Suthwerk *v.* Thomas Gerlonde in Suthwerk
328 Lecia fil' John *v.* Master Adam de Cudinton and *v.* Master Adam de Cudinton who Walter prior of Merton called to warranty in Cudinton
329 John le Morin *v.* Richard Waukelin in Suwerk
330 Henry de Balun, Robert de Waleton and Johanna de London *v.* John de Mickelham in Mikelham
331 Stephen the Prior of St. Mary Suthwerk *v.* Thomas de la Folkelaunde in Adington
332 John Brother *v.* William Bonvadlet in Suwerk
333 William fil' Odo de la Hombreth *v.* Thurstan le Doul in Dorking
334 Stephen the Prior of St. Mary Suwerk by Robert de Stoke *v.* Richard le Cutiller of Suwerk, quit claim of money in arrear
335 Walter de la Sonde *v.* Osbert del Ore and his wife Agnes in Dorking
336 Ralph de Bradele *v.* William fil' Baldewin de Ledred by Philip le Neir in Ledred (Henry le Berker and his wife Sibil a.s.c.)
337 William fil' Ralph *v.* John Burel in Suthwerk
338 Osbert de Cornburg *v.* James Anshard in Effingeham
339 Walter de Brugges *v.* John de Berking and his wife Alice in Wendeswrth and Bruges
340 Henry de la Boxe *v.* Henry de la Forde in Saundis

341 Robert Malemeyns *v.* Adam de Certeshey and his wife Alice in Hadleg
342 Agnes fil' Arnulf *v.* Stephen the Prior of St. Mary Suwerk who John le Estreis called to warranty in Suthwerk
343 Alice fil' Philip and William Bole and Agnes his wife *v.* Saerus fil' Henry in Camerewell and Retherhee
344 Thomas Goldsmith of London Bridge and his wife Cecilia *v.* Master Alan de Stokwell in Suthwerk
345 Alice de la Puyle *v.* Henry Mercator and his wife Gunnora, & Alice widow of Philip le Clerk in Kyngeston
346 Alice de la Puyle *v.* Henry Mercator and his wife Gunnora, & Alice widow of Philip le Clerk in Kingeston
347 Alan the Abbot of Certesey by brother Richard de Certesey *v.* Geoffrey de Bacsete and his brother William in Esse
348 Margery fil' Osbert Clate and her sister Matilda *v.* John fil' Albred in Kingeston
349 Henry de la Lithe *v.* Robert de Hedenescumbe in Bromleg
350 Walter de Hecstede *v.* Robert de Hecstede in Walkested and Lingesfeld
351 Alan abbot of Certesey by brother Richard de Certesey his monk *v.* Robert de Yattelegh in Esse
352 Thomas the Prior of Newark *v.* Matilda de Faye by Ralph de Gattele in Putteham
353 Geoffrey Belami *v.* Herding Lovechild in Dorking
354 Thomas de Ottewirthe *v.* Walter de Otteworth in Bromlegh Ottewirth
355 John fil' Henry de Molendinis *v.* Brother Terricus the Prior of the Hospital of St. John of Jerusalem in England by Brother Robert de Hegham in Suthwerk
356 Ralph de Hybern *v.* William de Say in Suthwerk
357 John Brother *v.* Robert Inkel in Suwerk
358 Lucy widow of Peter de Gardino *v.* Reginald Lutte in Kingeston

32 HENRY III.

359 Symon de Sywelle *v.* William de Arras by William de Pesemere in Est Shenes
360 Imbert the Prior of Bermundesey by brother Henry de Norhamton *v.* John fil' Hervey in Retherhee
361 Matilda fil' William le Clerk and her sister Basilia *v.* Giles de Westcote who Walter le Bachelor called to warranty in Westcote
362 Margery fil' Osbert Clate and her sister Matilda *v.* Richard Clate in Kingestun
363 Imbert the Prior of Bermundesey by brother Henry de Norhamton *v.* Geoffrey fil' Norman and his wife Alice in Wallewrth
364 John Russel and Cecilia his wife *v.* Peter le Templer who Waukelin and his wife Beatrice called to warranty in Kingeston
365 Richard le Saunner *v.* Simon le Clerk of Beremundesey and his wife Margaret in Beremundesey
366 Philip de Fraunkelee *v.* Margery prioress of Keleburn in Middelton
367 Thomas de Warblinton *v.* Alice Damartin in Tanrich, Chepstede, & Effingham
368 John de Bromleg and his wife Matilda *v.* Isaac the Jew of Suwerk in Suwerk (the Prior of Bermundesey a.s.c.)
369 Robert the Prior of Merton by Robert de Cyrencester *v.* Amisius de Wauton in Michham
370 Symon de Sywelle *v.* Elyas de Graphlingesham in Scaudeford
371 Alice fil' Henry *v.* William de Yfelde in Shyre
372 John Baret chaplain *v.* Matilda Baret in Reygate
373 Richard Knotte *v.* William fil' Alexander in Bedington
374 John de Cudinton clerk *v.* John Russel and his wife Cecelia in Kingeston
375 Robert Luvekyn *v.* Ralph de Sulameheth in Sudwerk

376 Peter le Templer *v.* Lucy widow of Peter de Gardino in Kingeston

377 John Russel and his wife Cecelia *v.* William Page in Kingiston

378 Nicholas the Prior of Holy Trinity Canterbury *v.* William de Sayten in Suwerk

378b Peter de Scaudeford *v.* William de Bradmere and his wife Alice in Scaudeford

33rd Henry III

379 Nicholas Malemeins *v.* John de Gatesden and *v.* the said John de Gatesden who Letitia de Gatesden called to warranty in Dorking, Okeleg, Hamsted, & Cumpton

380 William fil' Luth *v.* Johanna widow of William fil' Ralph Karbonell by Thomas de Ardern in Suwerk and Lamiheth

381 Master Thomas Ayswy *v.* William fil' Ralph in Suwerk and Lameye

382 Jordan de Suwerk and his wife Emma *v.* Stephen the Prior of St. Mary Suwerk by Robert de Stock in Suwerk

383 Robert de Temes Ditton *v.* Robert Fisher and his wife Mazeline in Temesditton

384 William de Wendleswrth *v.* Nicholas Prior of Holy Trinity Canterbury in Merstham

385 Agnes de Monte Acuto and Nicholas Malemeins *v.* William le Enfaunt and his wife Alice in Suwerk

386 Ernald Geraudon by Jordan le Chanu *v.* Imbert the Prior of Bermundesey by Brother Richard de Kingeston his Monk, grant of a corrody

387 Brother Robert de Saunford master of the Knights Templars by brother Henry de Safray *v.* Walter de la Grave and his wife Alice in Adinton

34th Henry III

388 Adam Gurdun *v.* William de Cantilupe and his wife Emma in Padesdon

389 Giles the Prior of Saundon *v*. Robert le Butiler and his wife Dulcia in Weston & Waleton
390 Geoffrey de Brayboef *v*. Alexander de la Berne in Cherlewude
391 Imbert prior of Burmundesey *v*. Saerus fil' Henry in Bermundesey and Rotherheye
392 William Prest *r* William le Faunt and his wife Alice in Suthwerk
393 William Smith of Axstede *v*. Walter le Sumeter and his wife Emma in 'villa Pontis Edulfi' (Edenbridge)

35th *Henry III*

394 Peter de Ryvall *v*. Robert de Mikelham in Hoke
395 Stephen Knotte *v*. Stephen de Sutton and his wife Helewyse in Clopham
396 Robert le Pestur and his wife Matilda *v*. Alan the Abbot of Certesey in Certesey and Thorp
397 Johanna de Stangrave *v*. Robert Cook of Blachingeleg and his wife Mabel in Blachingeleg
398 Peter Drui *v*. Adam Drui in Ledrede & Fecham
399 Roger de St. John *v*. John Pypart and his wife Emma and Geoffrey Prest of London and his wife Goldyna in Welkenested
400 John fil' Hamo *v*. John fil' Thomas in Wendleswrth
401 John the Prior of Seleburne *v*. Peter de Ryvall in Sholaund & Putham
402 John the Prior of Seleburne *v*. William de Wintereshull and his wife Beatrice in Sholaund & Puteham
403 Geoffrey fil' Wm. de Ledrede *v*. Ralph de Haling by Ivo de Haling in Croydon
404 Geoffrey de Trie and his wife Idonea *v*. Robert Hardelton in Buddeleg
405 Peter de Ryvall *v*. Valence fil' William de Cesterton in la Sholaunde

406 Thomas de Uttewrth *r.* Walter de Uttewrth in Uttewrth Chelewrth
407 Alice fil' Richard de la Frythe *r.* Ralph de Immewrth in Immewrth
408 Richard Auberkin *r.* John de Berking and his wife Alice in Wendleswrth
409 Henry de Aperdele *r.* William de Aperdele in Ledrede & Mykelham
410 William Michel *v.* John de Berking and his wife Alice in Merstham
411 Andrew Turbut *v.* John de Gravenel in Wendleswirth

37th *Henry III*

412 Elias de Garschirche *r.* Henry Garlaunde and his wife Johanna in Suwerk
413 Richard Auberkin *v.* John de Berekinges and his wife Alice in Wandlesworth
414 Brother Henry master of the Hospital of Reygate *r.* Robert de Watevill in Mikelham
415 Thomas de la Poylle *r.* Richard Testard in Guldeford
416 Peter de Egoblaunch Bishop of Hereford *v.* William de Eyton and his wife Emma in Wymbeldon
417 Adam Gurdun *v.* William de Cantelupe and his wife Eva in Padesdon
418 Sarra de Wodeham *v.* Richerus Maunsel and his wife Cecilia in Hunnewaldeham
419 Johanna widow of William de Honewaldesham *v.* Richerus Mauncell in Honewaldesham
420 William de Swynebroc *v.* Robert le Butiler and his wife Margery in Apse, Waleton, Weston, Moleseye and Tamesditton

38th *Henry III*

421 Nicholas Malemeyns *v.* John de Gatesden in Ockele (Roger de la Hide a.s.c.)

422 Symon de Cheyham *v.* John de Berking and his wife Alice in Cheyham
423 Master John de Cheyham *v.* John de Berking and his wife Alice in Cheyham
424 Nicholas the Prior of Holy Trinity Canterbury by brother John Pykenot his monk *v.* Master William de Ludham in Neuton
425 Gilbert North *v.* Richard Schayl and his wife Inga in Aspe
426 Walter de Merton *v.* Reyner the Prior of Tortington in Farlegh
427 Walter de Kynardesle *v.* John de Colevil and his wife Milicent in Berhes
428 Master Hericus de Witemersse *v.* Reginald de Dorking and his wife Avice in Suthewerk

39th *Henry III*

429 Mathew de Bovill *v.* Cristiana de Ulsefeld in West Clandon
429a John le Minur *v.* John de Bekeham in Kersauton
430 Ralph de Beck and his wife Agnes *v.* William Huskard in Bedington
431 John de Burstowe *v.* Peter de Burstowe in Burstowe
432 Thedric Coleman *v.* William de Sonde in Hemstede
433 Richard de la Barre, William fil' Matilda, Matilda widow of Benedict le Heymonger, Philip le Gresmonger and his wife Beatrice *v.* Elias Maunsell in Geldeford
434 Robert de Spineto *v.* Florius de Wymbeldon in Wymbeldon
435 Master Thomas Ayswy *v.* William fil' William fil' Thomas in Suthewerk
436 Thomas de Weston *v.* John de Weston in Weston
437 Richard de Billingehurst *v.* Gilbert Malemeins in Hascumbe
438 Peter le Chevaler *v.* Henry de Sutherst in Windlesham
439 Alice Wytdeniers and her sister Agnes *v.* John de Tycheseye who Reginald de Rockele and Grecia his wife called to warranty in Kambreswele

440 Adam le Timbermonger *v.* Alan Kockel and Leuina his wife in Suthlamehethe (B. Archbishop of Canterbury and Baldewin de Insula a.s.c.)
441 Adam le Timbermonger *v.* William fil' Luke in Suthewerk
442 John fil' John *v.* Symon le Barbur in Suthewerk
443 Symon de Dunstaple and his wife Beatrice *v.* Peter le Orfeure of Kingeston in Kingeston

40*th* Henry III

89 Thomas de Stokes and his wife Emma *v.* Alan the Abbot of Certeseye in Certeseye
90 Nicholas fil' Hugh and his wife Margery, Gilbert fil' Thomas and his wife Alice *v.* Nicholas Jacob of Geldeford and who Walter de Rugwik called to warranty in Geldeford
91 Thomas fil' Richard de Bandon and his wife Alice *v.* Alured fil' Walter de Wodecote and his wife Cecilia in Bandon
92 Master John de Gloucester cementer *v.* Geoffrey fil' William de Stokewell in Stokewell, Lambeth, Hese and Wyke

41*st* Henry III

93 Dulcia de Meandon *v.* William de Watville who Ascer de la Dune called to warranty in Chyssendon
94 John de Ebbesham *v.* Henry Luvel in Sutton & Kershaulton
95 Pagan fil' Adam and his wife Isabel *v.* Walter le Cordwaner of Suwerk and his wife Beatrice in Suwerk
96 Matilda widow of William Longespey by Henry de Montfort *v.* John fil' Geoffrey in Schaldeford and Eldefolde
97 James Haunshard and his wife Agatha *v.* James le Bel in Fermesham and Pytfaude
98 Richard de Eltham and John de Gatingdon clerk *v.* John de Berking and his wife Alice in Lamethethe
99 Henry Lovel *v.* Richard de la Grave and his wife Alice in Egeham

42nd Henry III

100 William de Kynardele and his wife Alice *v.* William de Berghes in Suttone

101 Quintin de Neuport and his wife Sabinia *v.* Dyonisia prioress of Cestrehunt in Feltham

102 Adam de Basinges and his wife Johanna *v.* Walter de Frowik in Benchesham

103 Robert de Waleton and his wife Beatrice *v.* Thomas de Holeg in Culesdon

104 Fulc, Bishop of London by Robert de Trumpeton *v.* Peter de Pyrefryth in Wockyng

105 William de Meleburne *v.* Robert de Meleburn and his wife Emma Oliver in West Shene

106 John Maunsel treasurer of York and reeve of Beverle *v.* Robert de Meleburn and his wife Emma Oliver in Shene

107 Matilda de Burn by Alexander de Brumle *v.* Symon de Sewell and his wife Isabella in Estshene and Mortelake

108 Hugh le Bigot by Walter de Gernemuth *v.* Alan Basset and his wife Petronilla in Bruges

109 Richard fil' Richard Oysel *v.* Richard Oysel in Newenton extra barram de Suwerk

110 Richard Russel *v.* David le Tynterer and his wife Alice in Mandon

111 John de Wyntereshull *v.* William de Wyntereshull and his wife Beatrice in Bromley, Puteham & Wonerse

112 Thomas de Yford *v.* Aylard de Dorking and his wife Avice in Ewelle & Chepested

113 Ralph the Abbot of Westminster *v.* Richard the Prior of Newark in Horsille

114 Robert de Brywes *v.* Dyonisia widow of Walter de Bufle by John fil' John de Edelmeton in Whysell

43rd Henry III

115 Ralph de Champeneys *v.* John le Lung in Sutwerk

116 Richard the Prior of Newark by brother Adam de Wuburn his canon *v.* Thomas de Hertmere by Phillip de Hertmere his son in Hertmere & Wytleg

117 Richard de Clare Earl of Gloucester and Hertford by Richard de Middelton *v.* Alexander de Rameseye and his wife Matilda in Effingham

118 William de Swynbrok *v.* Hugh de Stok and his wife Agnes in Waleton

119 Gilbert de Dunton *v.* William de Neudegate in——

120 Walter de Areblaster *v.* Warin de Keniton and his wife Cristiana & Thomas le Eluminor and his wife Johanna in Suwerk

121 Richard the Prior of Newark *v.* Geoffrey le Dyne in Saunde

44th *Henry III*

122 Robert de Scothon and his wife Margery *v.* Adam master of the Hospital of St. Thomas de Acre in Colisdon

123 John de Bures *v.* Roger de Stominholl and his wife Isabel in Horle

124 William Cusin and his wife Alice *v.* Henry de Hervy and his wife Aylith in Suthwerk

125 William de Wyndes by William de Forneys *v.* John de Gatesden by Robert de la Hyde in Comton

126 Richard Oysel senior *v.* Richard Oysel junior in Newenton & Suwerk (Alice wife of Geoffrey Norman a.s.c.)

127 Robert de Ludham *v.* Nicholas le Thaylur of Jernemue & his wife Elicia in Suthwerk

128 John fil' William *v.* Robert de Brymarton in Effyngham

129 Richard the Prior of Newark *v.* Walter Wace and his wife Hawyse in Hertmere

130 Gunnilda Maubaunc *v.* Robert Maubaunc in Sende

131 Peter fil' William *v.* William de Strode & Matilda his wife in Cumbe Nevill

132 William de Ebbesham *v.* Nicholas fil' Hugh & his wife

Margaret and Gilbert le Teynturer of Dorking & his wife Alice in Gildeford

133 Heming de Godlaund and his wife Matilda *v.* Osbert le Champeneys in Coveham

134 Joel de la Greston and his wife Philippa *v.* William de Haselwode in la Newlond and Colisdon

135 John le Moyne by Nicholas de Sandon *v.* Richard de Kendal and his wife Cecilia in Suwerk

136 Ingeram de Fenles *v.* Stephen de Sutton in Clopham

137 Ralph abbot of Battle by William de Lewes *v.* John le Blund of Lymenesfeld and his wife Agnes in Lymenesfeld

138 John Knotte of London *v.* Roger Knotte of Kersaulton in Kersaulton

139 Baldewyn de Insula by Adam de Stratton *v.* Alan the Prior of St. Mary Suwerk in Micham

140 Robert le Treur *v.* William de Burdens & his wife Sibil in Geldeford

141 Walter Box of London *v.* Thomas de Godinton & his wife Matilda in Reygate

142 William de Lilleswrth & his wife Alice *v.* William Pykot in Chissendon

143 Peter de Gildeford *v.* John de Welere & his wife Agnes in Gildeford

45th Henry III

144 Henry Walemund *v.* William Schort & his wife Cristiana in Redereye (The Prior of Bermundesey a.s.c.)

145 Johanna abbess of Fontevraud John de Leython *v.* Thomas de Ottewrth, 10 marks

146 Geoffrey le Fraunceys *v.* Walter le Mouner & his wife Elicia in Dilwysse

147 Roger de Mildenhall and his wife Katharine *v.* Henry de Ryselberge and his wife Margery in Mortelak

148 Margery Dygun *v.* Richard Dygun in Benstede

149 Henry de Aspeleg & his wife Matilda *r.* William Gerard in Est Horsseleg
150 Brunning Attewyke *v.* Nicholas Quatremars & his wife Beatrice in Merwe
151 Symon Passelewe *r.* Hugh de Polstede in Cumpton
152 Walter de la Felde & his wife Agatha *r.* John fil' John de Ho, Clement West & his wife Emma, William de la Rude & his wife Beatrice, William de Horyshill & his wife Agatha, Matilda widow of Robert le Turnur in Werplesden
153 John de Nevill by Nicholas de Freton *r.* Peter Goldsmith in Kyngeston
154 William de Mortimer & Master Hugh de Mortimer *v.* John le Moingne in Benchesham
155 Alan abbot of Certesey by Brother John de Waring his monk *r.* Master Andrew le Cunners by William de Vadis in Chabbeham
156 William de Gysilham and his wife Agnes *r.* William fil' Richard the keeper of London Bridge in Pecham
157 Eustace the Prior of Merton by Robert de Hamme *r.* Baldewyn de Insula in Mycham
158 Mathias de Mara, John la Warre, Reginald de Mortinger by William de Mara *v.* Richard the Prior of Newark in Ested
159 John de la Garston *r.* Matilda de la Garston in Blechingleg and Wolkested
160 Brother William master of the hospital of St. Thomas the Martyr ' de Aconia ' by Brother Nicholas de Crawedon *v.* Henry de Lacy in Katerham
161 William le Arblester of Sussex *r.* William le Arblester of la Vacherie in Cranleye
162 Henry Wyppetratel *r.* William de Burdegala & his wife Sibil in Ertedon
163 William de Assesham *r.* Richard le Macone and his wife Emma in Assche

164 Symon the Abbot of Waltham by Thomas de Rankedich *v.* William Hereward & his wife Mabel in Chauledone

165 William le Wyrdrawere & his wife Alice *v.* Pagan le Clerk & his wife Isabel in Suthwerk

166 Nicholas de Wuburn & his wife Matilda *v.* Emma widow of Henry Pyron in Saundres & Horslegh

167 Richard fil' Nigel de Neuton *v.* Isabel de Aldebyr in Micham (Peter fil' William de Aldebyr a.s.c.)

168 John de Wyntereshull *v.* William de Godalming & his wife Johanna in Great Bocham & Wyntershull

47*th* Henry III

169 John the Abbot of Certeseye *v.* John de Wyngham by Robert de Dovere in Horle

170 Eustace the Prior of Merton by Richard de Heyford *v.* Philip le Juvenis of Ewelle in Ewelle (Richard le Constable a.s.c.)

171 Edmund Pippard & his wife Margaret *v.* Eudo de Gudeford in Gudeford

172 Andrew de Dunstanstede & his wife Agnes *v.* John fil' John fil' Geoffrey in Craneley (Peter le Rus a.s.c.)

173 Gilbert Thedric & his wife Mabel *v.* Edmund de Hersetelesheye in Lingefeud

174 Roger de Loges *v.* Geoffrey de Slifeld & Agnes his wife in Effingham

175 William Bolle *v.* Robert Payn in Chellesham

176 Humphrey the Prior of Tanrigge *v.* Thomas de Warblington in Tannerigge

177 Hervey de Hecheham & his wife Isolde *v.* John de Eston & Agnes his wife who William fil' Hugh de Meynyl called to warranty in Dalby de Wauz

178 William de Appilderleye *v.* Mary fil' William Dammartin in Horleye

179 William de Stonehame *v.* Simon de Stonham in Tenregg & Katrehamme

180 Gilbert atte Pyrie *v.* John Haunsard in Effingham & Littille Bokham

181 Margery prioress of Ankerwyk *v.* John de Pappeworth concerning 40s. rent

182 William fil' John de Dorkinge *v.* Ralph atte Herne & his wife Elena in Horleye

183 Henry atte Cherche & his wife Alice, Emeric de Stanstede & his wife Isabel & Roger le Pestur & Cecilia his wife *v.* John de Botteleg in Walkennested

184 Walter de la Poylle *v.* Richard Testard & his wife Felicia in———

185 Jordan de la Stonhall & his wife Agnes *v.* William le Prest & Isabel his wife in Camerwell

48*th Henry III*

186 Gilbert Coleman & Roesia his wife *v.* Richard Spyllebord & his wife Margery in Suthwerk

49*th Henry III*

187 Walter Dragun *v.* Hubert de Haunlegh & his wife Clemencia in Chelesham (John fil' John de Stangrave a.s.c.)

188 William de Chamberleg of Bruges *v.* William de la Sale of Stokes & his wife Lucy in Stokes & Gildeford

189 Roger de St. John by Ranulph de Essex *v.* Odo fil' Walter le Fevere of Tenrigg & his wife Matilda in Wolknestede

190 Alan the Prior of St. Mary Sutwerk *v.* Robert de Beleshale & Lecia his wife in Sutwerk

191 Ralph de Hegstede by John de Merlawe *v.* William the Abbot of Hyde by William de Stanstede in Lyngefelde

192 Gilbert de Ewelle & his wife Agnes by Walter atte Wyke *v.* Robert fil' David de Weston & his wife Matilda in Ewelle

50—52 HENRY III. 43

50*th* Henry III

193 William de Wintereshull & his wife Beatrice by Nicholas Thebaut *v.* John de la Roede who Geoffrey de Braybof called to warranty in Duntesfaud Hassecumbe Bromleg & Tunchamstede

194 John fil' John *v.* John de Suthinton in Heggeham

195 Robert de Ebbegate *v.* Reginald le Fevre in Suwerk

196 Gilbert de Ewelle & his wife Agnes by Walter de Attewyk *v.* John de Yenefeld & his wife Isabel & Elias de la Chaumbre & his wife Johanna by William Dodekin in Ewelle

51*st* Henry III

197 William de Bernewell & his wife Isabel *v.* John fil' Richard Walkelin & his wife Lucy in Suwerk (Brother Arbelard master of the Knights Templars in England a.s.c.)

198 Adam le Treur & Elicia his wife and William fil' Adam and Elicia his wife *v.* Henry fil' Martin in Suthwerk Lamhuth, Arpitle & Longehope

199 Richard Russel *v.* John Gregor & his wife Johanna in Eggeham, Euebrigge & Berttemers

52*nd* Henry III

200 Brother Roger de Ver prior of the Hospital of St. John of Jerusalem in England by John de Dinggeleg *v.* Richard de Bereleye & his wife Margery in Suwerk

201 John fil' Gilbert *v.* William de Bylisersse & his wife Juliana in Lyngefeld

202 Adam le Escot *v.* Saerus fil' Martin by Reginald le Forester in Suthwerk

203 Richard de Derby & his wife Christiana *v.* Alan la Zouche by Henry Martin in Suthwerk

204 John de Ebbegate & his wife Juliana *v.* Nicholas de Kent & his wife Adriana in Neuton

205 John le Mouner & his wife Mabel *v.* Lewin de Sunderesse & his wife Agnes in Suthwerk
206 John de Reygate & Ralph Burouhard *v.* John le Balk in Reygate
207 Ralph de Thorp & his wife Avice *v.* Robert de Bechampton in Cherteseye (Thomas de la Porte & his wife Emma a.s.c.)
208 Geoffrey the Prior of Newark by brother Adam de Wuburn his canon *v.* Henry de Suthhurst in Wyndlesham
209 John de la Fanne *v.* Walter de Snodeham & his wife Emma in le Fanne (William de la Fenne a.s.c)
210 John de Regate *v.* William de Covenham & his wife Alice in Gyldeford
211 Robert fil' Ralph *v.* John fil' Hugh in Wyndlesham
212 William Hervi *v.* Richard Gargat of Merewe & his wife Alice in Merewe
213 Adam le Clive & his wife Elicia *v.* Thomas Lammesse & his wife Alice in Suthwerk & Walewrth.
214 Ralph de Dorsete & Luuina his wife *v.* William fil' Baudric in Bedigton
215 Juliana de Pappewrth *v.* Johanna de Pappewrth in Sende (John de Pappeworth a.s.c.)

53rd *Henry III*

216 William de Wyntereshill *v.* John de Pappewrth & his wife Alice in Bromlegh
217 William le Corniser & Aveline atte Hacche *v.* Matilda prioress of Keleburn in Myddleton
218 Roger de Horne and his wife Matilda *v.* Joel de la Garston and his wife Philippa in Colesdon
219 Gilbert the Prior of Merton *v.* Gilbert de Clare Earl of Gloucester & Hertford in Effingham
220 Gilbert Auberkyn *v.* Isabel widow of Symon de Suwell in Wandleswrth

53—55 HENRY III.

221 Robert de Ebbegate & his wife Juliana *v.* Nicholas de Kent & his wife Adriana in Newton

222 John the Prior of Bermundeseye by Walter de Hallynbir his monk *v.* Adam le Treur & his wife Elicia in Suthwerk (John de Reda & his wife Clemence a.s.c.)

223 Robert fil' Robert le Norreys *v.* Mary la Noresche by Hugh le Noreys in Ronewelle

224 Thomas de Leukenore *v.* Peter de Pylefrith in Chepstede

54th Henry III

225 Roger de Mildenhale & his wife Katharine and Henry de Welwyk & his wife Margery *v.* Christiana Sperlyng in Mortelak

226 William de Mardwyr *v.* Thomas Lammesse & his wife Alice in Neuton

227 John de Warenn Earl of Surrey by Richard de la Vache *v.* William de Gyseleham & his wife Agnes in Suwerk

228 William de Sutton clerk *v.* Walter le Ferur & his wife Margery in Wolknestede

229 Robert de Ebbegate & his wife Juliana *v.* Gilbert le Melkere & his wife Matilda in Neuton

230 John de Welwes & his wife Matilda by Geoffrey Scapereng *v.* Abraham de Osyngehurst & his wife Letitia by Robert de Brynkehurst in Okeleg

231 John de Welwes & his wife Matilda by Geoffrey Scapereng *v.* Abraham de Osyngehurst by Robert de Brynkehurst in Okeleg

55th Henry III

232 Richard le Gras *v.* Nicholas de Basyng & his wife Isabel in Okstede and Lemenesfeld

233 Walter Box *v.* John fil' Adam de Braynford & his wife Agnes in Wendesworth

234 Walter de Rokesle & his wife Lucy *v.* William fil' Baldric de la Wodecote & his wife Agnes in Bandon

235 Robert de Wyveleshole *v.* Thomas atte Hoke of Pudeham & his wife Cristiana in Suthwerk

236 John de Hadestok *v.* Nicholas le Tayllur and his wife Elicia in Suthwerk

237 John le Ferun *v.* Nicholas le Tayllur & his wife Elicia in Suthwerk

238 Editha fil' Hervey *v.* Reginald the Abbot of Battle by William Gyffard in Suthwerk

56*th* Henry III

239 Bartholomew de Heddresham *v.* Peter de Katerham & his wife Alice in Nutfield

240 Margaret de Ynyngefeud by John de Wendleswurth *v.* Robert de Horne in Lyngefeud, Crauhurste and Tanrugge (John fil' John de Stanigrave, a.s.c.)

241 William de Mortimer parson of St. Peter's Church Yweherst *v.* Herbert de Somerbergh in Yweherst

242 Richard le Grant *v.* Reginald de Inworthe & his wife Matilda in Walleton

243 John Marescall of Suwerk *v.* Thomas le Burser & his wife Felicia in Suwerk

244 Master Reginald de Croydon *v.* Ralph de Saunford & his wife Isabel in Burstowe

245 Richard de Derby and his wife Christiana *v.* Peter de Micham and Helewysia his wife in Lambheyth

246 William de Wyntereshull *v.* John de Middelton by John de Rouleboys in Cumpton

247 Robert de Ebbegate & his wife Juliana *r.* Walter le Cordwaner & Dyonisia his wife in Neuton.

248 Richard de Pleyshamel & his wife Johanna *v.* Thomas de Stok & his wife Emma in Certesey

249 Robert de Garscherche *v.* William de Bernewell & his wife Isabel in Suwerk

250 Gilbert de Crawestok & his wife Albreda *v.* John abbot of Certesey by John de Wendlesworth in Chabham

252 Thomas Haunsard & his wife Alice *v.* Walter le Stut & his wife Alice by John de Wendlesworth in Ebbesham

253 Thomas de Tycheseye by William de Kelleshulle *v.* Reginald de Rokesle & his son William by Walter de Bedenested in Chelesham and Tycheseye

254 Hugh fil' Hugh de Wyndesor by Richard de Wyndesor *v.* Ralph de Berners in Westhorslegh, in Schyre, Cranleye, Chydingfald, Sende, Effingham, Wyschele Okham, Okele, Esthorsleg

255 John de Cobham *v.* John de Pettestede & his wife Ada in Bocsted & Manhefeud

256 Ralph de Berners and Cristiana his wife *v.* Hamo de Gatton and his wife Johanna in Westhorsleg

257 Richard de Horton and his wife Johanna *v.* William le Vineter in Suthewerk

258 Reginald de la Hamme *v.* John le Heuere and his wife Johanna in Blechingeleye (John de Stanygrave a.s.c.)

259 Robert de Redinghersth *v.* Eudo de Gyldeford in Gyldeford

260 Henry de Dune and Isabel his wife *v.* William le Ken in Bokham

261 John le Fevre of Certeseye and his wife Margery *v.* John the Abbot of Certesey by Richard de Twangham in Certesey

262 Robert Burnel by Henry de Lenn *v.* Hugh fil' Hugh de Wyndesor by Richard de Wyndesor in Schene (Hamo de Gatton and his wife Johanna, a.s.c.)

263 William Wyleman and his wife Sibil *v.* William atte Muln and his wife Alice in Wolkested (Alice fil' Alice de Welkestede and Amice and Clemence her sisters a.s.c.)

264 Jordan le Barbur by Richard Punchard *v.* John le Rede and his wife Clemence in Suthewerk

265 Mabel fil' John Smith *v.* John le Fevre and his wife Margery in Certesey
266 Philip de Burgate *v.* Richard de Bremingefeld in Dunterfeld
267 Robert de Cokefeld by John Buntyng *v.* Richard de Dereby and his wife Cristiana in Suthewerk
268 John de Souwy and Johanna his wife *v.* James de Wodeham in Honewoldesham
269 Gilbert le Mareschall *v.* Richard Garget and his wife Alice in Merwe
270 Robert Lambyn and his wife Juliana *v.* John de Rameseye and his wife Agnes in Suthewerk
271 Geoffrey the Prior of Newark *v.* Aylwyn de Tywele and his wife Margaret in Gyldeford
272 Robert de Esche clerk *v.* Serlo le Halveloverd of Esche in Esche
273 John the Abbot of Certesey *v.* Symon de Blechynglegh and his wife Emma in Certeseye
274 Vincent le Ferun and his wife Johanna *v.* William Hardel in Suthewerk
275 Roger fil' Peter de Northwode *v.* William fil' William de Northwode in Effingham
276 Geoffrey the Prior of Newark *v.* John de Henle in Essinge
277 William fil' Peter *v.* Peter de Chabeham and his wife Matilda in Chabeham
278 Reginald de Domere *v.* William de Dommer and his wife Margaret in Fernham
279 John de Newenham *v.* William le Pestur & his wife Matilda in Effingeham
280 John de Dommere *v.* William de Dommere & his wife Margaret in Fernham
282 Matilda de Certesey *v.* Walter Auverey & his wife Edith in Ockele, Ewakne and Wudeton

1ˢᵗ *Edward I*

1 Hugh de Oyldebof *v.* Symon Bernard and his wife Roysia in Polstede
2 William Davy *v.* Jordan le Barbur and his wife Alice in Suthwerk
3 Gilbert the Prior of Merton by William de Mildenhall *v.* Adam le Treur and his wife Elicia in Suthwerk
4 Peter Cosin *v.* Richard de Derby and his wife Cristiana in Lameth
5 William de Storteford *v.* Geoffrey le Bakere and his wife Beatrice in Suwerk
6 William de Breuse by Robert Rose *v.* Nicholas le Tayllur and his wife Elicia in Suthwerk

2ⁿᵈ *Edward I*

7 John de Boclaunde and his wife Johanna *v.* Thomas de Terling in Suthwerk
8 Robert Pykeman, fishmonger of London *v.* Robert de Ebbegate and his wife Juliana in Neuton, Walewurth and Suthwerk
9 John de Flore *v.* Ralph Maunsel and his wife Alice in Wolkenstede & Tanrugge and *v.* Roger fil' Ralph Maunsel and his wife Isabel in Wolknestede
10 John de Flore *v.* Ralph Maunsel in Wolknested & Tanrugg.
11 Geoffrey Turgis and his wife Matilda *v.* John Sauntere and his wife Agnes in Certeseye
12 Richard le Graunt v. Hugh de Stokes and his wife Agnes in Waleton
13 Master Odo de Westminster *v.* Peter de Montfort and his wife Matilda in Reygate
14 John fil' William *v.* William le Paumer of Radesole in Puteham
15 Peter Cusyn *v.* William de Tothill and his wife Felicia in Lamhythe

3rd Edward I

16 Hugh de Oyldebof *v*. William le Hare and his wife Johanna in Polstede

17 Master Reginald le Sauser *v*. Edmund de Wrotting and his wife Margery in Gyldeford

18 Geoffrey de Walehale *v*. Robert de Beverlay and his wife Cecilia in Puryford

3rd Edward I and 55th Henry III

19 Roger de Covert *v*. John Haunsard and Gundreda his wife in Chelvedon (James Haunsard a.s.c.)

20 James Haunsard *v*. Gundreda Haunsard by Herbert de Candevere in Kateram

4th Edward I

21 William Trug and his wife Olivia *v*. Roger le Tayllur and his wife Agnes in Lamhuthe

22 John fil' John de Ryppeleye *v*. Reginald de Chelsham and his wife Alice in Saundrestede

23 Robert de Campania *v*. Robert de Crevquor in Tatlesfeld

24 Ernald de Suthwerk Clerk and his wife Johanna *v*. William de Bernewell and his wife Isabel in Suthwerk

25 Edmund de Wrottyng and his wife Margery *v*. Thomas de Pyuelesdon and his wife Elena in Mycham.

26 Adam de Blechingeleye *v*. Ralph de St. Laudo and his wife Beatrice in Blechingel

27 Peter de Wyntreshull parson of Neweton Church *v*. John fil' Richard le Lymbernere and Johanna his wife in Neuweton

28a Bartholomew the Abbot of Certeseye by brother Thomas de Ocham *v*. Geoffrey de Walehale and his wife Matilda in Certeseye.

29 Peter de Cramplingesham and his wife Margery *v*. Richard Stacy of Longeditton and his wife Matilda in Kingeston and Longe Ditton

5th *Edward I*

28 Roger fil' Walter *v.* Henry de Watdone in Merstham (Robert Polbre and his wife Margery a.s.c.)

30 Matilda widow of Roger de Horne *v.* Stephen de Graveshende and his wife Amy by Geoffrey Gyan in Effingham

31 William de la Leye *v.* Thomas de Merewe and his wife Alice in Effingham

32 John fil' Juliana and his wife Alice *v.* Stephen de Graveshende and his wife Amy by Geoffrey Gyan in Kersauton and Bedinton

33 Bartholomew the Abbot of Certeseye by brother Thomas de Ocham his monk *v.* Thomas Haunsard and his wife Alice in Coveham

34 John de Warenn Earl of Surrey by Robert de Chamberleyn *v.* Hugh de Laval and his wife Matilda in Kenyngton extra London

6th *Edward I*

35 William de Buritton *v.* Nicholas the Prior of Tenrugge in Chepstede

36 Hugh Prowet *v.* William Wenche and his wife Johanna in Guldeford

37 Geoffrey Norman by John de Gretton *v.* Robert de Mortimer and his wife Jacosa by William de Deveneys in Suthwerk

38 Brother Joseph prior of the Hospital of St. John of Jerusalem in England *v.* Richard de Schorne of Littelington and his wife Matilda in Kingeston

39 John de Dudham and his wife Matilda *v.* Ralph de Dunton and his wife Johanna in Chelesham.

40 Robert le Croys *v.* Adam de Chelesham and his wife Lora by Adam de Scheyntone in Chelesham & Maldon

41 Henry le Marschal of Guldeford *v.* Richard le Dyke and Nichola his wife in Guldeford

42 Gilbert prior of Merton by Richard de Merton *v.* Henry Brunyng and his wife Gunnilda in Kyngeston

43 William Baudri and his wife Mabel *v.* Agnes prioress of Bromhale by William de Ford in Wyndlesham (John Baudri a.s.c.)

7*th* Edward I

44a Robert fil' John de Stangrave junior by Philip de Podyndenn *v.* Luke de Hecstede in Crowehurste & Lyngefeld

44b William Aumesas and his wife Johanna *v.* Bartholomew the Abbot of Certeseye in Kersanton

45 Robert de Beregh and his wife Matilda *v.* John de Yenefeld and his wife Isabel in Banested, Mikelham, Ebbesham, Ewell and Codynton

46 William le Suur of Waleton and his wife Amabel *v.* Peter le Knyt and his wife Beatrice in Micham

47 Richard le Peyntur of Certeseye *r.* Roger de la Stret and his wife Beatrice in Certeseye

48 Margaret fil' Robert de Fremeswrth *r.* John de Thorp and his wife Alice in Bocham

49 Henry de la Felde and his wife Johanna *v.* Henry de la Sonde in Dorkyng

50 Thomas de la Fenne *v.* Laurence de Yatele and his wife Isabel in Godalming and Fenne

51 John Heythorn and Helewisia his wife *r.* Geoffrey the Prior of Newark in Sende

52 John de Thorp *r.* William de Forde and his wife Beatrice in Certeseye

53 Walter le Parker and his wife Paulina *r.* John de Warenn Earl of Surrey by Ralph le Messager in Reygate

54 William Hervy of Guldeford *r.* Henry de la Doune and his wife Alditha in Stok juxta Guldeford

55 Master Peter de Abyndon master of the 'domus scolarius' of Merton *r.* Walter de Portesmuth in Cudynton

56 Richard de la Watere and his wife Avice, John le Parmenter and his wife Alice & Clementina de Shyrefeld *v.* William atte Melne of Wolkestede in Wolkestede

57 Frechesenta fil' Hamo de Brecia, Hugh fil' Letitia and John fil' Isabel by Peter de Mallyng *v*. Peter the Prior of Beremundeseye in Retherheth

58 Mabel Abbess of Wherewell by Master Walter de Tychefeld *v*. Thomas de Ottewrthe in Chelewurth and Ottewrth

59 Walter de Codeston *v*. Robert Attefrith and his wife Alice in Tenrygge (Thomas fil' William de Warblington a.s.c.)

60 John de Puthurst *v*. John de Wykeford and his wife Margaret in Chetyngfaud

61 Henry le Mareschal *v*. Walter Purbyk and his wife Dulcia in Guldeford

62 Frechesenta widow of Thomas de Codeham by Peter de Mallyng *v*. Peter the Prior of Beremundeseye in Retherheth

63 Imbert de Monte Regali by Henry de Guldeford *v*. Walter le Parker of Guldeford in Guldeford

64 Walter Herman and his wife Margaret *v*. Laurence de la Sale and his wife Isabel in Gyldeford

65 Edward Lovekyn and his wife Matilda *v*. Hugh del Molyn and his wife Alice in Kyngeston

66 Robert Deumars *v*. Robert de Merton and his wife Avice in Kyngeston

67 Richard le Gros and his wife Margery *v*. Thomas le Gros in Kyngeston

68 Robert Bishop of Bath and Wells by John de Berewyk *v*. Ralph de Berners and his wife Cristiana in Shene

69 Laurence de Suwelle *v*. Edmund de Totenhale and his wife Margery in Wendlesworth

70 Geoffrey the Prior of Newark *v*. Peter de la Wode and Alice his wife in Sendes

8th *Edward I*

71 William Aumbesas and his wife Johanna *v*. Ralph de Hegthon and his wife Roesya in Bechinton

72 Peter Cosyn citizen of London *v*. Alexander de Tothull and his wife Emma in Lamheth

73 John le Orfevere of Kyngeston *v.* Hugh atte Melne and his wife Alicia in Kyngeston
74 Robert le Mareschal *v.* Laurence de Yatelegh and his wife Isabella in Guldeford & Wokynghe
75 Walter Herman *v.* Laurence de Yateleghe and his wife Isabella in Guldeford
76 Robert Bishop of Bath and Wells by Richard de Middelton *v.* Laurence de St. Michel by Robert de Batesford in Retherheth and Wolwyg
77 John fil' John Adryan of London and his wife Cecilia *v.* Reginald de Immeworth and his wife Matilda in Farnecumbe
78 William de Northwode and his wife Agnes *v.* Roger Chapre in Ocham
79 Simon de Bosco *v.* John fil' Simon de Bosco in Cumpton & Farncumbe
80 Henry de Somerbyr *v.* Nicholas Malemeyns in Wodeton

9*th* *Edward I*

81 William de la Rithe and his wife Cecilia *v.* Alan atte Oke in Clendon Abbatis
82 Ernald de Tangel *v.* William Brokere and his wife Edith in Bromleye
83 William de Wendlesworth *v.* John de Braynford and his wife Agnes in Wendlesworth
84 Henry de Bonynges by John de Wyndlesor *v.* Robert de la Nedre in Marsham
85 Roger de Berking *v.* Henry de la Venele and his wife Isabella in Suwerk
86 William Aumbesas and his wife Johanna *v.* John de Yenefeld and his wife Isabella & Richard Regaud and his wife Matilda in Sutton
87 Geoffrey de Gedding and Walter his son by John de Wyndesor *v.* William de la Legh and his wife Margaret in Bromlegh

88 John de Hadestok *v.* Philip de Brummore and his wife Johanna in Suthwerk
89 Thomas de la Strode and his wife Agnes *v.* Henry Picot and his wife Alice in Wandlesworth
90 Thomas Box and Christiana his wife *v.* Stephen de Slapton and his wife Alice in Wendlesworth

10*th* *Edward I*

91 Alan le Surugien of London *v.* John May and his wife Chelsa in Camerwelle
92 John de la Sale *v.* Richard de Goderinton and his wife Beatrice iu Kyngeston
93 Robert de Ludham *v.* Thomas fil' Robert de Pappeworth by Warin de Lund in Sende
94 Baldewyn le Buscher of London *v.* William le Bromere and his wife Lecia in Kyngeston
95 Robert Deumars *v.* John de Horton in Horton & Ebesham
96 Richard the Bishop of London by John fil' Alan *v.* Henry de Andham in Stoke and Guldeford
97 John de Padebrok and his wife Cassandra *v.* Geoffrey Rydere and his wife Cristiana in Tycheseye
98 Thomas Box and Cristiana his wife *v.* Geoffrey le Poer and his wife Alice in Wendlesworthe
99 Henry Pyrot *v.* Thomas de Tychesye in Camerwelle
100 Hugh de Hengham *v.* Robert de Munpelers and Roesia his wife in Eweykene
101 Master Geoffrey de Haspale *v.* Symon de Pudingden in Lingfeud Crowehurst, Axstede & Lemnefeud
102 William Norman *v.* Nicholas fil' Richard de Kertling and his wife Alice, Richard Lythfot and his wife Isabel, & Sarra fil' Thomas le Fevere in Suwerk
103 John le Mouner and his wife Emma *v.* Thomas the Prior of Christchurch Canterbury by William de Grenehulle in Waleworth
104 William Aumbesas and his wife Johanna by Hugh de

Cresauton *v.* Thomas Vyel and his wife Cecilia in Kersalton

105 Thomas Box and Cristiana his wife *v.* William de Perham and his wife Johanna in Wendlesworth

106 John de St. John and his wife Margaret *v.* Walter Dragun in Nobrychte

107 William Norman *v.* Peter the Prior of Bermundeseye by Richard Marchall in Suwerk

11th *Edward I*

1 Master Odo de Westminster *v.* Richard de Lodebur and his wife Isabel in Mycham

2 Walter le Blunt *v.* Richard de la Penne and his wife Elicia in Suthwerk

3 Robert de Preston and his wife Margaret *v.* Richard de la Penne and his wife Elicia in Suthwerk

4 John Adrian and his wife Cecilia by John Hadinham *v.* Gilbert de Mikeleham and his wife Alice in Mikeleham

5 John de Brewes and his wife Eva and their daughter Beatrice and Robert fil' William Burnel by Geoffrey de Staundon *v.* Robert Bishop of Bath & Wells by Robert de Boclinton in Wyssele

6 Robert de Hengham *v.* William fil' Robert Gerveys in Est Bechesworth

12th *Edward I*

7 Roger de Northwode *v.* Robert le Ken of Glastonia and his wife Isabel in Suthwerk

8 Henry le Mareschal *v.* Ralph de Stofold and his wife Beatrice, Robert le Foghel and his wife Matilda in Bromlegh

9 Robert de Drat and his wife Alice *v.* John de Baerne and his wife Felicia in Retherhethe

10 Henry de la Croiz and his wife Agnes *v.* William Trug in Suthlamhuth

11 Walter de Chabeham and his wife Sibil v. William fil'
   Peter de Chabeham and his wife Alice in Chabeham
12 Ralph le Fissere and his wife Alice v. William le Barbur
   and his wife Dionisia in Kyngeston
13 Richard Russel and his wife Matilda v. Gilbert de Gravemere in Esere-Wateville
14 William Trug citizen of London v. Robert de la Hide and
   his wife Alditha in Suthlamheth
15 Henry de Dereby v. Richard de Dereby and his wife
   Christiana in Suthwerk
16 Johanna widow of Adam de Crokford v. Lucy fil' Adam de
   Crokford in Certesey
17 Edmund de Ottewrthe v. Laurence de Ottewrthe in Bromleghe
18 Richard the Bishop of London v. Robert le Parker and
   Elicia his wife in Stok
19 John de Boveleye v. Peter de Watevile and his wife Agnes
   in Ledrede
20 William Ambesas and his wife Johanna v. Elyas de la
   Chaumbre of Opping and his wife Johanna in Sutton,
   Horle & Elesdon

13th *Edward I*

21 Master Odo de Westminster v. Richard de Ledebury and
   his wife Isabel in Micheham
22 William de Lychpol and his wife Johanna v. Robert de la
   Sale and his wife Alice in Chelesham
23 Idonea de Hadestok v. Hamo de Campo clerk in Retherhythe
24 Ralph de Hengham v. Gilbert de Bocland and his wife
   Cristiana in Estbechesworth
25 Thomas de Welaund v. Richard de Holebrok in Sutwerk
26 Roger Sharp v. John de la More painter and his wife Ida
   in Blechinglegh

27 Walter Gerlaunde of Kingeston *v.* Thomas de Waltham and his wife Isabel in Kyngeston
28 John de la Mare *v.* Richard de Ledebury and his wife Isabel in Micham
29 Richard Elys *v.* Laurence de Ingeston and his wife Matilda in Micham
30 John le Tymbermongere of Kingeston and his wife Julia *v.* James le Orfevere and his wife Beatrice in Kyngeston
31 Robert de Clopton and his wife Alice *v.* Adam de Waleton and Leneva his wife in Cersauton

14th *Edward I*

32 Thomas de Tycheseye *v.* John fil' John de Crawhurst in Crawhurst
33 Ralph de Hengham *v.* Richard le Warnyr and his wife Alice in Dorkinge
34 Ralph de Ditton and his wife Johanna *v.* Robert de Waleton and his wife Isabel in Sandrestede & Sellesdone
35 John den Ensinge clerk *v.* William le Rus and his wife Agnes in Lymenesfeud
36 Symon de Micham *v.* Richard de Bandon in Bandon, Bedinton, Wodecote and Micham
37 John fil' Reginald de Badeham *v.* John de Lincoln and his wife Katherine in Suthwerk
38 William de Wykyngeston *v.* Walter de Rokeslee and his wife Lucy in Bedinton

15th *Edward I*

39 John Iwun of Gyldeford *v.* William Wyring and his wife Alice in Hertingdon
40 John le Jevenis *v.* Gilbert le Wlf and his wife Margery in Suthwerk
41 Thomas Box *v.* Walter West and his wife Isabel in Wendlesworth
42 John de Badeham *v.* Robert le Preston and his wife Margaret in Suthwerk

43 Robert de Basinges Citizen of London and his wife Margery *v.* William fil' Reginald de Rokeslee in Kamerewell
44 John de Ely *v.* William Trug and his wife Olivia in Suthlamhuth
45 Ralph de Hengham *v.* William Aguilun in Estbechesworth
46 Roger Sket of Westone *v.* William de la Hegge and his wife Elena in Westone
47 & 48 The King *v.* Brother Robert the Abbot of St. John's Church Colcestre in Ledrede
49 Hawysia widow of John le Savage *v.* William de Brewes in Gumshelf

16th *Edward I*

50 Peter de Kulsham *v.* Godefrey le Leper and his wife Margery in Coveham
51 Master Beumunde de Visia *v.* Ralph de Dytton and his wife Johanna in Bandon
52 John le Tymbermongere of Kingeston and his wife Juliana *v.* Nicholas de Hadresham and his wife Emma in Kyngeston
53 Walter Attenovene of Pekham *v.* Richard le Carpenter of Suthwerk and his wife Emma in Suthwerk
54 Henry Gerard of Gildeforde *v.* Thomas de Leukenore and his wife Lucy in Taleworth (Erneburga fil' Ralph de Bray a.s.c.)
55 Pavya de St. Fide *v.* Gilbert de St. Fide of Sendes in Sendes
56 John de Badeham *v.* Geoffrey Sauvage and his wife Aveline in Suthwerk

17th *Edward I*

57 Richard de Litlemondene and his wife Agnes *v.* Bartholomew Tassel and his wife Margery in Suthwerk
58 Symon le Kyng *v.* John Oky and his wife Elena in Suthwerk

59 William de Marisco *v.* Richard Dikes and his wife Isabel in Mitcham (Richard le Fraunkelyn and his wife Sabina a.s.c.)

18*th Edward I*

60 Henry Gerard of Guldeford *v.* Thomas de Leukenore and his wife Lucy in Suth Taleworth
61 William de Oksted and Godefrey de la Hethe *v.* John de Westwode and Leticia his wife in Caterham
62 Gilbert de Appeltrefeld *v.* John de Berewyk in Tylemundesdon and Lynglegh (John fil' Roger de St. John a.s.c.)
63 Michael de Wynton *v.* Nicholas de Wynton and his wife Matilda in Esshere-Watevill.
64 James fil' James de Wodeham *v.* Robert atte Otlond and his wife Sibil in Weybrigg
65 Robert de Boclynton and his wife Alice *v.* Richard de Boclynton in West Clendon (John fil' Mathew de Bovile and his sister Petronilla a.s.c.)
66 Cecilia de More *v.* John de Breynford and his wife Alice in Suthwerk
67 Philip Burnel *v.* Isabel widow of Thomas de Heygham in Retherhethe & Camberwell
68 Robert Bishop of Bath & Wells *v.* Thomas fil' Thomas de Heygham in Retherheth
69 John fil' Nicholas de Guldeford *v.* Richard de la Grave in Sende

19*th Edward I*

70 Walter le Bachelor junior *v.* Agnes widow of Walter le Bachelor senior in Westcote
71 Walter le Collye *v.* John de Wyntereshull and his wife Johanna in Farenham
72 John de Cobeham *v.* Ladereyna de Valoynes by Peter de la Done in Werplesdon
73 Henry de la Hathe *v.* Adam Ace of Brokham and his wife Hilditha in Neudegate

74 Richard fil' Gilbert de Waltham and Thomas his brother v. Gilbert de Waltham of Wandlesworth in Wandlesworth

75 Laurence atte Hethe v. John de Burstowe and his wife Alice in Chelesham

76 Philip Burnel by Robert fil' William v. John de Northwode by Richard de Norton in Retherheth

77 William Bernard of London v. Geoffrey le Clerk of Weyminster and his wife Amflisia in Bandon

78 Ralph de Cheyny v. Henry de Wyntersell in Schaldeford

20th *Edward I*

1 Roger de Wetham v. Johanna atte Spottenes in Chyssyndon and Taleworth

2 William Paynel v. Mathew de Foleburn and his wife Cristiana in Suthwerk

3 Adam Wytlock and his wife Hilditha v. Adam le Rus and his wife Letitia in Ewelle

4 Ralph le Barbur of Suthwerk v. William le Fevre of Suthwerk and his wife Petronilla in Waleton

5 Aunger de Rypon v. John fil' John de Bokelaund in Suthwerk and Lamehyth

6 Thomas Pope v. Roger de Hamme and his wife Gunnora in Kyngeston

7 William de Marisco v. Richard le Frankeleyn and his wife Sabina in Micham

8 Eustace de Hacche v. John de Brokes and his wife Cristiana in Ledred

9 Walter Deys v. Robert atte Byrchette and his wife Edith in Gomeshulne

10 Nicholas fil' Nicholas atte Brugge and his wife Beatrice v. Richard le Fevre de Sythwode in Sythwode and Coresbrokes

11 William de Marisco v. John le Cornmangere and his wife Edith in Kersalton

12 John le Conners and his wife Johanna *v.* John le Mouner and his wife Emma in Lameheth

13 John de Shakeleford and his brothers Hugh and Richard *v.* Juliana de Shakeleford in Godelmynge

14 Robert le Cros of Warlyngham and his wife Agatha by Ralph de Kirkeby *v.* Ralph de Dunton and his wife Agatha in Chelesham

21*ˢᵗ Edward I*

15 Thomas Reyner and his wife Isabel *v.* John Reyner and his wife Johanna in Esthorslegh

16 Nicholas fil' John de Ledrede and his brother John by John atte Hale their guardian *v.* John de Ledrede in Ledrede

17 Beatrice widow of William de Wyntreshull by William Springaunt *v.* Adam le Despenser in Burgham & Toresworth

18 Guy Ferre junior *v.* John de Wauton senior in Bukelonde

19 Martin de Ambresbury and his wife Rosamund *v.* Pinus de Florence Merchant and his wife Alice in Lamheth and Leshurst

22*ⁿᵈ Edward I*

20 Henry fil' Adam atte Forde of Baggeshete and his wife Alice *v.* Nicholas Gerveys and his wife Agnes in Ryppeleye

21 John de Horne *v.* Thomas de Tycheseye in Chelesham

22 Robert de Rattescroft and his wife Alice *v.* John le Mareschal Bywesten de Gyldeford and his wife Agnes in Ertyndon

23 Master Peter de Newcastle *v.* Robert de la Lese and his wife Matilda in Bedynton

24 Henry Gerard of Gyldeford *v.* Ingeram de Blechingelegh and his wife Agnes in Ewell and Longeditton

25 Alan fil' Walter Hereman of Guldeford *v.* Richard fil'

Thomas le Tannere and his wife Emma in Bromlegh and Schaldeford

26 Thomas de la Strode and his wife Agnes *v.* Peter de Brygeford and his wife Lucy in Cherteseye

27 Lambert Clays of Ipre and his wife Margaret *v.* John de Otteford and his wife Juliana & Nicholas de Gloucester and his wife Matilda in Bermondeseye

28 Henry Gerard of Gyldeford *v.* John le Lumbard and his wife Lucy in Ewell

29 William de Weston and his wife Alice *v.* Henry de Somerbur and William fil' Nicholas le Mouner of Weston in Seende and West Clendon

30 Alan le Chaundeler and his wife Johanna *v.* Thomas atte Watere of Wymbeldon and his wife Alice in Miccham

31 Thomas Pope of Kyngeston *v.* William de Maldon and his wife Alice in Kyngeston

32 John de Lovetot senior by Peter Child *v.* John de Wauton senior in Wauton

33 John de Berewyk *v.* John de Wauton senior in Becchesworth

34 Thomas le Romayn and his wife Juliana *v.* Humfrey de Dunsterre in Stockewell, la Hethe, Lamehuthe & Batericheseye

35 Thomas Box and his wife Cristiana *v.* Elias de Edelmeton and his wife Nicholaa in Wandlesworth

23rd *Edward I*

36 Thomas de Skernynges and Roger fil' Vincent de Skernynges *v.* John Lumbard of Mutina and his wife Lucy in Maldon, Chissingdon, Ditton, Thaleworth & Kyngeston.

37 Richard de la Goldhord and Isabel fil' Alice *v.* Thomas atte Watere and his wife Alice in Wymbeldon (Gilbert de Dorking and his wife Agnes, Richard Child and his wife Letice, Adam le Chaundeler and his wife Johanna a.s.c.)

38 John de Balesham *v.* Master Clement de Wyk in Cherlewode
39 John de Ditton clerk *v.* Richard le Eremite and his wife Alice in Tamesditton
40 Robert de Hastyngg *v.* Richard de Derby in Suthewerk
41 Adam Scot of Westminster *v.* Gilbert de Dorkyng and his wife Agnes in Wymbeldon
42 Thomas le Romayn and his wife Juliana *r.* John le Conners and his wife Johanna in Lamheth
43 John de Walyngford and his wife Alice *r.* Richard de Sherton and his wife Alice in Ingefeld and Egeham
44 Walter de Wengham *r.* Thomas de Jarpenvill in Abingworth (Geoffrey fil' Warin and his wife Johanna a.s.c.)
45 John le Mareschal of London *r.* Henry le Estrishe and his wife Margery in Newenton juxta Suthwerk
46 Edmund le Chaumberleyn and his wife Lucy *r.* John de Colecester and his wife Johanna in Suthwerk

24*th* *Edward I*

47 John fil' William de Pirle *r.* Simon le Ruge and his wife Dionisia and her sister Isabel in Whatedon Colesdon Chabiedon Merstham
48 Isabel de Gulderegg *r.* John de Colecestere and his wife Johanna in Suthwerk
49 William de Frollebur and his wife Johanna *v.* Thomas fil' William de Frollebur in Puteham, Werplesdon & Cumpton
50 Thomas Yon of Suthwerk and his wife Agnes *r.* John de Colcestre and his wife Johanna in Sutwerk
51 Robert le Rede *v.* Ralph Belebarbe and his wife Dionisia in Cherteseye
52 John de Metyngham *v.* Adam Seman and his wife Avice in Neuton
53 Elias Aygnel and his wife Edith *v.* Gilbert fil' Robert de la Grave and his wife Cristiana in Suthwerk

54 Thomas de Wykeford *v.* Margery widow of John de Wykeford in Werplesdon
55 Robert de Middelton *v.* Simon le Lung and his wife Agnes in Neweton
56 John le Peystur of Suthwerk and his wife Margery *v.* Arnald de Suthwerk and his wife Avice in Suthwerk
57 Robert de la Holilande *v.* Thomas de Horncumbe and his wife Cristiana in Notfeld
58 Godwyn de Polesden *v.* Simon de Harleford and his wife Margaret in Boukham
59 Thomas de Sende and his wife Alice *v.* Richard de Ludham and Roger de Ludham in Sende (Walter Prior of Newark juxta Guildford a.s.c.)
60 John de Gatewyk *v.* William Aiquillun of Dorking and his wife Emma in Mersham

25*th Edward I*

61 Cristiana de Marisco *v.* John de Boveneye in Ledrede & Pachenesham
62 John fil' John de Northrugge and his sister Agnes *v.* John de Northrugge and his wife Beatrice in Cherteseye
63 Peter de Huntingfeld and his wife Ismania *v.* John fil' Henry de Cherteseye in Cherteseye
64 Adam de Bray *v.* John de Holeburne and his wife Mabel in Suthwerk
65 Peter de Huntingfeld and his wife Ismania *v.* Thomas de la Strode and his wife Agnes in Certeseye
66 Robert de Middleton by Hugh de Scrouby *v.* John de Parys and his wife Alice in Suthwerk and Lamhethe
67 Robert de Middleton by Hugh de Scrouby *v.* Maurice de Adyngton of Lambeth and his wife Editha in Lamhethe
68 Thomas de Bekensfeld and his wife Johanna *v.* John fil' Hugh atte Thorn of Mordon and his wife Matilda in Kersaulton and Bedinton

69 Peter de Tauresio and his wife Isabel *v.* Robert le Eyr and his wife Felicia in Schaldeford juxta Guldeford

70 Peter de Tauresio and his wife Isabel *v.* Richard de Apsele and his wife Emma in Schaldeford juxta Guldeford

71 Henry atte Blakefenne *v.* Roger le Colyer of Cranstok and his wife Alice in Cranstok

72 Walter Curteys *v.* John Priur and his wife Lecia in Ertindon

73 Peter le Child *v.* Idonia widow of Hugh le Barbur in Cambrewelle

74 Richard de Horton clerk *v.* Richard Primerole of Kyngeston and his wife Cecilia in Ebsham

26th *Edward I*

75 Peter del Ewe *v.* William del Ewe and his wife Matilda in Sende

76 Walter de Westok and his wife Avice *v.* Hugh Dunning and his wife Johanna in Kyngeston

77 Eustace de Malevill *v.* Gilbert de Etton and his wife Alice in Tycheseye

78 Peter parson of Wodemersthorne and Henry atte Hulle *v.* Adam de Chyvenyngg in Wodemersthorn

79 Henry Gerard of Guldeford *v.* Thomas le Wulmangare of Kyngeston and his wife Agnes in Taleworth

80 Walter atte Gate *v.* Richard atte Gate and his wife Johanna in Chierteseye

81 Robert de Chelberton and his wife Beatrice *v.* Thomas de Merstham, Clerk, in Merstham

82 Robert de Burghton & his wife Sarra *v.* John de Immeworth in Egeham

83 John de Matham & his wife Isabel *v.* Thomas de Jarpenville in Waleton

84 Robert le Bekere *v* Thomas de Jarpenville in Waleton (Geoffrey fil' Warin & his wife Johanna a.s.c.)

85 John fil' Walter de Holehurst *v.* Walter de Holehurst in Brumlegh and Shyre

86 Walter atte Hulle *v.* Walter de Canefold and his wife Margery in Uhurst

87 William Hughe of Mayford *v.* Roger fil' William de Cranstok & his wife Isabel in Mayford

88 Hugh de Tychewell chaplain *v.* Robert Pyrun of Neuton & his wife Alice in Neuton juxta Lameheth

27*th Edward I*

89 Richard the Bishop of London *v.* Adam de Tayllur of Biddyk & his wife Johanna in Croydon

90 Henry de Myddelton & his wife Matilda *v.* John de Maurdyn in Egeham & Thorp

91 Thomas de Chirefold *v.* Robert de Gatton in Chypstede & Merstham

92 Thomas fil' Gilbert de Waltham of Wandlesworth by Robert de la Brok *v.* Gilbert de Waltham by Richard de Tetteburi in Wandlesworth

93 Christiana Isabel & Roesia fil' Gilbert de Waltham of Wandlesworth by Robert de la Brok *v.* Gilbert de Waltham by Richard de Tetteburi in Wandlesworth

94 William de la Strode by Ralph le Whelere *v.* John de Heo and his wife Elena in Kyngeston

95 Ralph fil' William de Finchingfeld and his wife Margaret *v.* Roger fil' William de Crawestok and his wife Isabel in Crawestok

96 Roger de Redenhale and his wife Amicia by Ralph de Berleston *v.* Thomas de Abecroft and his wife Beatrice in Farnham

30*th Edward I*

97 Reginald de Thunderle of London and his wife Margery *v.* Martin de Aumbresbir and his wife Rosamund in Lomhethe

98 Robert de Middelton *v.* Richard de Felton and his wife Sibil in Suthwerk

99 Adam le Chaundeler by John de la Bataille *v.* Richard de

Chikewell and his wife Agnes by John de Mawardyn in Wymbeldon

100 Guy Ferre junior by Thomas de Verlay *v.* Guy Ferre senior by John le Peyntur in Bokelonde (John de Wauton a.s.c.)

31st *Edward I*

101 Roger de la Garston and his wife Sarra by John le Botiller *v.* Reginald de la Garston and Roger de Abboteston in Blachinglegh and Wolknested

102 Martin Schench and his wife Clarice *v.* John fil' John le Sauvage and his wife Lucy in Okstede

103 Walter de Medburn by Ralph de Waldon *v.* John de Fyenles by James de Muscote in Kersaulton

104 Robert Yon of London by Fremund de Assherygg *v.* Robert atte Lese of Muleseye and his wife Matilda in Muleseye

32nd *Edward I*

105 Richard de Sumerbury by Clement Buck *v.* Godefrey atte Church and his wife Dionisia in Cudyngton

106 Gilbert de Horslegh and his wife Margery by John Mauser *v.* Bartholomew de Haueldersh in Merwe West Horslegh & Est Horslegh

107 Richard de Wulurenehampton *v.* Ralph de Hengham in Ockele

108 William de Brokhale and his wife Johanna *v.* Simon de Beauchamp and his wife Petronilla in Effingham

31st and 33rd *Edward I*

109 John de Uvedale by William de Uvedale *v.* Gilbert de Ecton and his wife Alice by Eustace de Malevill and John de Westwyk and his wife Margery in Tycheseye

110 John de Uvedale by William de Uvedale *v.* Gilbert de Ecton and his wife Alice by Eustace de Malevill and John de Westwyk and his wife Margery in Camerwell (John de Horne son and heir of Roger de Horne a.s.c.)

33rd *Edward I*

111 William Paynel and his wife Margaret *v.* William le Armeror and his wife Emma in Suthwerk
112 John de Grendon *v.* John de Brokes in Estherslegh
113 Thomas Duraunt of Wyndelesham *v.* Robert le Peyntur of Certeseye and his wife Johanna in Wyndelesham
114 William de Melksope *v.* Lora widow of Adam de Chelesham in Maldon
115 Alice de la Hacche *v.* Stephen Abbot in Suwerke
116 Thomas fil' Thomas de la Strod *v.* Thomas de la Strode and his wife Agnes in Certeseye
117 William de Lutegareshale clerk *v.* Hugh de Dygneneton and his wife Cecilia in Suthwerk
118 Richard le Rous *v.* Philip Savery of Westbury and his wife Agatha in Bandon
119 Nicholas de Okham clerk *v.* Henry de Stockwell and his wife Agnes in Suthlamheth
120 Reginald de Thunderle and his wife Margery *v.* Roger fil' Thomas de Piwelesdon and his wife Emeline in Lamheth
121 Richard fil' John atte Legh and his wife Isabel & John fil' Richard fil' John atte Legh *v.* John fil' John de Poneshurst and his wife Alice in Ledrede

34th *Edward I*

122 Robert de Ashurst and his wife Alice *v.* Robert de Godelegh and his wife Alice in Wytle
123 Peter fil' Richard le Fevre and Matilda in la Hurn *v.* Ralph fil' Robert le Tannere of Kingeston and his wife Agnes in Kingeston
124 Henry Huse and his wife Isabel *v.* Robert de Rydingers and his wife Matilda in Hascumbe and Bromlegh
125 William de Melksope *v.* William de Henle and his wife Isabel in Chelesham and Tycheseye
126 Roger Wodeloc *v.* William de Horwode and his wife Cristiana in Haywode juxta Covenham

127 Milo de Stapletone and his wife Johanna *v.* Stephen de Saham and his wife Matilda in Suthwerk
128 Peter de Grenewych and his wife Letice *v.* John Aleyn de Suthwerk and his wife Margery in Bermundeseye
129 Walter de Gloucester and his wife Hawise *v.* Giles de Henxton and his wife Margery in Certeseye, Egeham and la Lynde
130 Henry de Sumerbury and his wife Margaret *v.* John atte Vyne and his wife Sarra in Cranle
131 Felicia fil' John de Medersh *v.* Stephen de Tothull in Shyre
132 Hugh de Wythham of Certeseye and his wife Margery *v.* Robert le Rede and his wife Mabel in Certeseye
133 Henry Husee by Peter Toly *v.* William de Henle and his wife Isabel in Bromleye and Hascumbe
134 Ralph de Cammeys and his wife Margaret by William Thebaud *v.* Mary widow of William de Brewosa by William de Bosco in Effingham and Little Bokham (Peter de Brewosa and William de Brewosa lord of Brembre a.s.c.)
135 William de Mees clerk by Peter de Goddalmynge *v.* Master Roger de Radenhale and his wife Amicia in Farnham
136 Henry Gerard of Guldeford clerk *v.* John Gerard of Guldeforde in Guldeforde, Ertyndon, Merewe & Stoke juxta Guldeford
137 Johanna de Aulburn by William de Wytewell *v.* Agatha de Aulburn by Peter Toly in Werplesdon (John le Hewere and his wife Agnes a.s.c.)
138 John Turpyn and his wife Cecilia *v.* Walter fil' Robert Randolf of Farnham and his wife Emma in Farnham
139 Ralph de Heuere and his wife Hawyse *v.* Rolland Huscarl in Bedynton
140 John de Abernun and his wife Constance *v.* Henry de Stocwell and his wife Agnes in Suthlambeth
141 Alice de Aulburn by William de Wythewell *v.* Agatha de Aulburn by Peter Toly in Werplesdon

142 John de Berewyk *v.* John de Henle in Kyngeston
143 John de Burstowe and his wife Alice *v.* Gilbert de Wolkenestede chaplain in Burstowe
144 William atte Hale *v.* John atte Longebregge and his wife Alice in Abbyngworth
145 Reginald de Chelesham and his wife Dionisia *v.* John de Moneketon by John Sauser in Chelesham

35th *Edward I*

146 Thomas Romeyn and his wife Juliana *v.* William Aumbesas and his wife Johanna in Clopham
147 John de Northwode *v.* William de Northwode in Effingham
148 Stephen de Chanente and his wife Cecilia *v.* Henry le Sygher of Gildeford clerk in Gildeford
149 John le Glovere de Ebor of London *v.* John de Longo Champo in Camberwell
150 Henry de Say and his wife Johanna *v.* John Gerard of Guldeford and his wife Johanna in South Taleworth & Ewell
151 Walter Poydras of Dynesle *v.* Nicholas le Fort of Kersaulton and his wife Agnes in Kersaulton
152 John de Ebor of London le Glovere *v.* Roger de St. Giles and his wife Emma in Suthwerk
153 Thomas Romeyn and his wife Juliana *v.* William le Clerk of Clopham and his wife Johanna in Clopham
154 Richard Bundy of Guldeford and his wife Margaret *v.* Roger de Stretton in Guldeford and Ertinden
155 John de Malton and his wife Isabel *v.* Peter de Grenewych and his wife Letitia in Bermundeseye
156 Roland fil' Robert Roland *v.* Margaret widow of John de Wykford in Werplesden

35th *Edward I & 1st Edward II*

1 John fil' John de la Chaumbre of Kersalton *v.* John de la Chaumbre of Kersalton in Kersalton
2 Milo de Stapleton *v.* John de Ebor of London in Suthwerk

3 Thomas Faukes and his wife Gunnilda *v.* John de Ponesherst and his wife Alice in Ledred
4 William fil' Walter de Butteford *v.* Thomas le Tailliour of Werplesdon and wife Agatha in Werplesdon
5 Stephen de Frollebery and his wife Alice *v.* Robert fil' Richard de Westebrok in Farnham (Johanna widow of William de Frolleburgh a.s.c.)
11 Henry Huse and his wife Isabel *v.* Henry Sturmy in Hascumbe

1st *Edward II*

6 Stephen Otte and his wife Alice and Stephen fil' Stephen Otte of Nuttefeld *v.* William de Waure and his wife Cristiana in Nutefeld
7 Henry de Say *v.* Thomas de Polton and his wife Isabel in Guldeford
8 Nicholas atte Parkgate of Burghstowe *v.* William de Waure and his wife Cristiana in Notefeld
9 Richard de Langeford clerk *v.* Geoffrey de Heyford and his wife Emma in Heyford and Wandlesworth
10 Thomas de la Pyle of Eshing and his wife Alice *v.* Edmund de Thurstan of Bensted in Hertmere & Eshyng
12 William le Frutyer and his wife Alice *v.* Thomas de Mikkesham and his wife Isabel in Kyngeston
13 John de Gaysham *v.* William de Waure and his wife Cristiana in Notfeld
14 John de Hamme and his wife Alina *v.* Thomas Saunterre of Certeseye in Hamme and Stanore
15 Thomas Faukes and his wife Gunnilda *v.* John de Punshurst and his wife Alice in Leddrede
16 Thomas atte Wyke and his wife Isabel *v.* John Otte of Blechingelegh and his wife Alice in Blachingeleye
17 John atte Asshe of Godalminge and his wife Isabel *v.* William le Frenshe of Chuddingfold in Godalmyngge

2nd Edward II

18 John de Apperdele *v.* Nicholas de Apperdele and his wife Alice in Leddrede
19 Peter Toly *v.* Richard le Hen of Ludlingg and his wife Juliana in Godalmyngg
20 John de Geysham *v.* William de Waure and his wife Cristiana in Nutfeld
21a Hugh le Despenser *v.* John de Vautort in Westshene Combe and Baggeshete
21b Stephen de Preston *v.* Sarra widow of William de Rokesle in Retherhethe & Bermundeseye
22 William fil' William Glade of Bromlegh *v.* Margery widow of William Glade in Bromlegh
23 John Fisher of Kyngeston clerk and his wife Alice and John their son *v.* Adam le Rede of Kyngeston and his wife Edith in Kyngeston
24 John Lumbard *v.* Constance widow of John Baldewyne in Suthwerk
25 Roger fil' Walter le Gateward *v.* Walter le Gateward of Ticheseye in Ticheseye
26 Henry de Gildeford *v.* William de Paynel and his wife Margaret in Compton and Bromleyghe
27 Bartholomew de Shire and his wife Alice *v.* Peter de la Knolle in Shire
28 John Maunsel parson of Creyndon Church and Alice fil' Robert Payn of Bandon *v.* William Aumbesas and his wife Johanna in Bedynton
29 John Elis and his wife Elena *v.* Ralph le Fisshere atte Mede and his wife Emma in Bermundeseye
30 Thomas Godefray of Polstede *v.* John Godefray of Polstede in Polstede
31 Richard de Swyneford and his wife Agnes *v.* Henry Mokway and his wife Johanna in Kyngeston

32 Henry de Somerbur and his wife Margaret *v.* Walter le Machun and his wife Agnes in Neudegate
33 Thomas Romeyn and his wife Juliana *v.* Lora widow of Adam Crosse of Chelesham in Maldene and Berardesfeld
34 Richard atte Grove and his wife Beatrice *v.* John de Wachesham and Adam atte Grove in Croweherst
35 Gilbert Thurbern of Twyford *v.* Bartholomew atte Lythe of Weston and his wife Cecilia in Farnham
36 Martin Polle and his wife Emma *v.* William Sebright and his wife Eufemia in Suthwerk
37 Hugh le Despenser *v.* John de Vautort in West Shene Coumbe and Baggeshete
38 William le Frenshe and his wife Johanna *v.* William de Euyton and his wife Juliana in Chuddingfeld
39 Thomas Romeyn and his wife Juliana *v.* Pinus Bernardini and his wife Alice in Wyk juxta North Lambuth
40 Cecilia fil' John Pynchon *v.* Thomas de Ledrede and his wife Mabel in Ledrede
41 Thomas de Parnycote clerk *v.* Richard atte Goldhorde and his wife Alice in Batricheseye and Legham
42 William Fraunceys *v.* John Prodomme and his wife Johanna in Wyssly Puryford and Waleton
43 John de Lucy Carpenter *v.* William de Chesthunte and his wife Margery in Croydon

3rd *Edward II*

44 John de Chabeham and his wife Margery *v.* Thomas de Swafham in Est Bechesworth
45 Reginald de Chelesham and his wife Dionisia *v.* John de Ifeld in Chelesham
46 Alan de Suffolk of Kingestone and his wife Johanna *v.* Richard Darnel of Wakeringg in Kingeston
47 William Petit of Cranle and his wife Emma *v.* Bartholomew de Grauetye and his wife Matilda in Suthwerk

48 William de Ockeleye and his wife Matilda *v*. Nicholas de Weston in Ockeleye
49 Richard de Langeford and his wife Johanna *v*. Thomas Ande and his wife Edith in Suthewerk
50 Thomas Ande and his wife Edith *v*. Auda Coleman in Suthwerk (cf. 125)
51 John de Hadyngden *v*. Master John atte Halle clerk in Lyngefeld
52 Thomas le Heore of Berners and his wife Isabel *v*. William de Barton and his wife Johanna in Berners
53 William Inge and his wife Margaret *v*. Ralph de Heure and his wife Hawise in Bedynton
54 Robert de Asshyndon and his wife Cecilia *v*. Thomas de Ledrede and his wife Mabel in Ledrede
55a Gerard Dorgoyl of London merchant *v*. William Norman in Suthwerk
55b Edward Sherewynd of Certeseye and his wife Elena *v*. John atte Hulle of Certeseye and his wife Sarra in Certeseye
56 Ralph atte Strete of Wendovere *v*. Richard David and his wife Alice in Kyngestone
57 Robert de Scoteslye *v*. William de Chussebury & his wife Dionisia in Wytlye Godalmynge Hasulmere and Fernhurst
58 Master Philip de Barton clerk *v*. Mathew de Tournenfuy seler of London & his wife Dionisia in Bermundeseye
59 Philip fil' Thomas de Solderne & his wife Isolde *v*. Adam le Coupere & his wife Isabel in Suthewerk
60 William fil' William atte Uvere of Benstede & his wife Emma *v*. William atte Churche of Fermesham in Fermesham
61 Henry de Guldeford *v*. Geoffrey de Pernestede and his wife Isabel in Wyttle

4th *Edward II*

62 William atte Horseheye & his wife Alice *v.* Robert atte Churche in Neudegate

63 Henry de Thurston *v.* Master William de Tunstalle in Certeseye

64 Richard del Goldhord & his wife Alice *v.* John le Chapman of Croyndon & his wife Letice in Wymbeldon

65 John atte Stoket & his wife Matilda *v.* Robert fil' Gregory de Langenhurst & his wife Alice in Oksted and Lymefeld

66 Richard fil' Richard Sweyn *v.* Richard Sweyn in Guldeford

67 John de Barbour de Bifeld de London & his wife Hawyse *v.* John de Reygate of London & his wife Cristina in Dylewish in Camberwell

68 Margaret fil' Simon de Bernewell *v.* Simon de Bernewell & his wife Agatha in Suthewerk

69 Daniel de Preston clerk *v.* Richard Ermeners & Cristina his wife in West Grenewyche

70 Reginald de Chelesham & his wife Dionisia *v.* John de Ifeld in Chelesham Crouhurst and Bandon

71 John Payn & Simon his son *v.* John de Ponishurst & his wife Alice in Ledrede.

72 Robert Joun of London *v.* Richard de Hoo tannur of Kingesston & his wife Agnes in West Moleseye

73 John de Netoelfeld *v.* Thomas le Belde of Dorkingg & his wife Gunnilda in Middelton

74 & 75 Henry de Chinthurst & his wife Cristina *v.* John de Ponishurst & his wife Alice in Ledrede

76 John Lucas of London *v.* Richard de Chygewell & his wife Agnes in Suthwerk

77 Cristina fil' Norman de Karingeham *v.* Felicia widow of Norman de Karingeham in Bromlegh

78 Richard atte Legh *v.* John Payn & his wife Lucy in Ebesham

79 Nicholas fil' Robert de Heure *v*. Mabel widow of Robert de Heure in Bletchyngeleye & Notfeld
80 William Bouch & his wife Agnes *v*. William atte Wode & his wife Juliana in Bedinton

5*th* *Edward II*

81 Roger Elys of Cranstock *v*. William Elys of Cranstock in Purefright & Mayford
82 Walter Gras *v*. William Aumbesas & his wife Johanna in Sutton Horlee & Colusdon
83 Robert Lovekyn of Kyngeston & his wife Emma *v*. Roger de Stretton in Kyngeston
84 Adam le Chaundeler & Edward his son *v*. Edith de Westminster in Wymbeldon
85 John de Gaysham & his wife Matilda & their son John *v*. William de Waure & his wife Christiana in Notfeld
86 Thomas fil' William de Northwode *v*. William de Northwode in Effingeham
87 Ingelran Berenger *v*. Perceval Simion & his wife Elizabeth in Suthwerk
88 Martin Gerveys & his wife Johanna *v*. Nicholas Letice in Merstham
89 Richard Wolmar *v*. Johanna fil' John le Ken in Suthwerk (Simon de Bernewelle a.s.c.)

6*th* *Edward II*

90 Adam atte Rodgate & his wife Matilda *v*. John Payn de Chudyngfold in Chudyngfold
91 Ralph fil' Peter de Chakedon *v*. Emma widow of Peter de Chakedon in Burgham
92 Adam de Gulden & his wife Catherine *v*. David de Brounyerd & his wife Margery in Guldeford
93 John de Botteleye *v*. Richard de Wyford and his wife Alice in Certeseye
94 John Dabernun *v*. Edmund le Taillour de Alegate & his

wife Johanna & William de St. Edmund & his wife Johanna in Lambehith.

95 Henry de Horkesle *v.* William de Monte Acuto & his wife Fyna in Bermundeseye

96 Bogo de Wauton & his wife Margery by Durand de Widmerpol *v.* Roger de Brisle in Suthwerk Walton & Leye juxta Becheworth

97 Richard Seward de Godelmyng *v.* Walter de Cokfeld Mareschal & his wife Cecilia in Shaldeford (Richard de Heyfull & his wife Margaret a.s.c.)

98 John de Losenerssh *v.* Thomas de Covereworthe & his wife Alice in Iwehurst

99 Roger de Brisle by Durand de Widmerpol *v.* Bogo de Wauton in Suthwerk, Walton & Leye Juxta Becheworth

100 Richard fil' William Jermeyn de Iwode & his wife Agnes *v.* John le Brid of Fermesham & his wife Alice in Fermesham

101 William le Baker of Ledderedd & his wife Alice *v.* John de Wolveston & his wife Johanna in Ledderedd

102 Walter de Pappeworth & his wife Alice *v.* Robert Richard of Dodington in Sende

103 Walter de Bobyngeworthe poleter & his wife Isolde *v.* John Freshfish barber & his wife Johanna in Suthwerk

104 William Odyerne & his wife Juliana *v.* William de Danhurst in Bromlegh & Aldfold

105 Henry de Lutgereshale *v.* Roger Welusworth & his wife Clarice in Okstede

106 John le Noreys of London *v.* Seman Clement of Ipswich & his wife Alice in Ewekene & Dorkyng

107 Roger de Wellesworth & his wife Clarice *v.* Henry de Lutgareshale in Okstede

108 John Tygre *v.* John de Padbroke in Tycheseye

109 Peter le Parker & his wife Cassandra by William de Northwyk *v.* Peter le Taillur of Shire & his wife Eustachia in Shire.

6*th* & 7*th Edward II*

114 John de la Mare & his wife Alianor *v.* Nicholas de Chelmereford & his wife Katharine in Suthwerk and afterwards 7 Edward II between Philip de Orreby & his wife Florence daughter and heir of John & Alianor and the same

7*thEdward II*

110 Stephen de Cuslyngehurst *v.* Robert de Arundell in Okele

111 Henry de Thorp & his wife Emma *v.* Robert de Certeseye in Certeseye

112 Walter Snoute of Tanrugge *v.* Henry Stiker & his wife Florence in Tanrugge

113 Salomon le Marler de Horle & his wife Johanna *v.* Robert le Marler of Horle in Horle

115 Henry de la Knolle & his wife Kassandra *v.* Bartholomew de Shire in Shire

116 Richard de Dunle *v.* William de Depyng & his wife Ismania & Richard de Dunnom in Rutherheth & Hacchesham

117 Geoffrey de Brandon of London *v.* John de Suthwyk & his wife Mary in Micham

118 Alice de Preston & Robert fil' Philip de Colevill *v.* Robert le Vavassur in Caterham

119 William de Harewedon parson of Waleton Church *v.* Richard Freytmauntel in Baggeshute & Wyndelesham

120 Thomas atte Grene de Bermundeseye *v.* Richard le Longe de Wormele & his wife Emma in Hacchesham

121 William de Russham & his wife Petronilla *v.* William Gilles of Egeham & his wife Alice in Egeham

122 Richard le Hunte of Alrebrok & his wife Emma *v.*

Thomas fil' John de Sandon in Thames Ditton & Alrebrok

123 Walter le Benere of London & his wife Johanna *v.* Richard de Waleden & his wife Alice in Suthwerk

124 John de Wyk & his wife Alice *v.* Gilbert de Wythewell in Werplesdon & Westwode

8*th* *Edward II*

125 Thomas Ande & his wife Edith *v.* Thomas Coleman in Suthwerk

126 William de Hallingbury *v.* John Pukelyn & his wife Matilda in Caterham and Bletchinggeleghe

127 Robert Waldecart de Luda by William de Norwich *v.* John de Byfeld of London barbur & his wife Hawyse in Dylewysh and Camerwell

128 Robert atte Holilonde *v.* Matilda widow of Robert atte Holilonde in Horlee and Cherlewode

129 William Inge *v.* Fulc de Archiaco in Wodemeresthorne, Chepstede, Mestham & Ewelle (Cecilia widow of John de Bello Campo and John de Bello Campo a.s.c.)

130 John fil' Thomas Wermere *v.* Walter le Hunt of Maufeld & his wife Agnes in Croyndon

131 Thomas Horlok & his wife Alice *v.* Robert Noel in Est Horslegh

132 William Tukke & his wife Margery by Thomas de Stanes *v.* Stephen le Clerk of Walyngford & his wife Emma in Certeseye

133 William de Alreford *v.* Gilbert le Webbe of Dorkinge & his wife Gunnilda in Westbechesworth

134 Oliver de Burdegala *v.* Adam Romyn & his wife Cecilia in Dunttesfold and Bromleghe

135 William de Alreford *v.* Robert le Webbe of Dorking & his wife Matilda in Westbechesworth

136 John Wytheued & his wife Beatrice *v.* Thomas de Haytfeld in North Lambhethe

137 Robert Yon of London *v.* Robert atte Leese & his wife Matilda in West Moleseye

138 John atte Watere & his wife Johanna *v.* Robert atte Watere in Asshe & Werplesdone

139 Roger de Taverner of Kyngeston & his wife Agatha *v.* Edmund de Alegate in Kyngeston

9*th* *Edward II*

140 John de Loxelegh & his wife Alice *v.* Robert le Taillour atte Wyle in Bromlegh

141 Geoffrey Purte of London *v.* Adam atte Rose pottere & his wife Cecilia in Suthwerk

142 Thomas fil' Geoffrey de Heyford and his brothers Adam & Stephen *v.* Geoffrey de Heyford in Wandlesworth

143 Edmund de Hersheteslegh *v.* John fil' Edmund de Hersheteslegh in Lynggefeld

144 William de Basyngestok & his wife Matilda *v.* David Laurence of Kyngeston & his wife Agnes in Kyngeston

145 Richard le Clerk of Suthwerk & his wife Johanna *v.* Richard de Paris of London & his wife Matilda in Suthwerk

146 John fil' Walter de Rontele *v.* Walter de Rontele in Wockyng

147 John Vanne *v.* Gerard Dorgoyle in Lamhuth

148 Roland de Wycford & his wife Alice *v.* Hugh de Bynteworth & Richard de Aubervyle in Werplesdone

149 John fil' James le Beel of Fermesham *v.* Richard fil' William Germeyn of Iwode & his wife Agnes in Fermesham

150 Adam de Bandon *v.* John Moyse & his wife Johanna in Bedynton

151 Symon de Deyere of Wendlesworth & his wife Matilda *v.* Robert Melksop & his wife Cecilia in Wendlesworth

152 Henry le Brun *v.* Hamo le Brun in Lemnesfeld and Croweherst

153 Roger Coldmawe & his wife Matilda *v.* John de Ponshurst & his wife Alice in Leddrede

154 Robert Aufray *v.* Thomas fil' Thomas de Rokenham le Fevre & his wife Annora in Ockele

155 Geoffrey le Scrop *v.* Geoffrey de Brandon in Micham

156. Richard le Parys of London & his wife Matilda *v.* Richard le Clerk & his wife Johanna in Suthwerk

157 John de Hampton & his wife Juliana *v.* Richard le Lokyere of Kyngeston & his wife Matilda in Kingeston

158 Richard de Farnbergh & his wife Matilda & their daughter Johanna *v.* Richard de Foleham & his wife Johanna in Suthwerk

159 Stephen Otte & Stephen his son *v.* William de Wauere & his wife Cristiana in Nutefeld (John de Gaysham a.s.c.)

160 Geoffrey de Heyford & his wife Emma *v.* Thomas Ande of Suthwerk & his wife Edith in Suthwerk

161 Hawyse de Hautot *v.* Johanna widow of William de Lichepole in Apse, Waleton, Weston, Tamyseditton, Taleworth, West Moleseye & Longeditton (Ralph Hervey of Finchingfeld & his wife Margaret & Thomas atte Felde & his wife Isabel a.s.c.)

162 Walter Mounde & his wife Johanna *v.* Adam de Garboldesham & his wife Cristiana in Bedynton

163 Stephen Aleyn & Henry le Feure of Suthwerk *v.* William de Stanford & his wife Johanna in Suthwerk

164 Lora widow of William Peyforer *v.* Stephen de Chelesfeld & his wife Johanna in Suthwerk

165 Robert de Waleton & his wife Juliana by William Chatkulne *v.* John de Waleton in Banstede & Chepstede.

166 Richard de Gatewyk *v.* John Lucas of Launcyng in Chepstede & Merstham (Katharine de Gatewyk & her sisters Elizabeth & Margery a.s.c.)

167 Richard Horn of London fishmonger *v.* Walter le Costretbyndere & his wife Agnes in Retherhethe

168 Andrew Horn & his wife Isabel *v.* Robert de Ely & his wife Alice in Suthwerk

169 Richard Horn of London fishmonger *v.* Geoffrey Maundevile & his wife Alice in Retherhethe

170 William le Latymer *v.* John de Frendesbury in Holebrouk

171 Adam de Garboldesham & his wife Cristiana *v.* John de Chesewyk in Bedynton & Creshaulton

10*th* *Edward II*

172 John de Wolneston *v.* John de Poneshurst & his wife Alice in Ledrede

173 Walter atte Rude senior *v.* Walter fil' Walter atte Rude junior & his wife Anastachia in Chabeham, Horesulle & Pureford (William de Carleton & his wife Alice and John atte Twychene & his wife Alice a.s.c.)

174 William de Whythewell & his wife Alesia by John de Wyke *v.* Reginald de Claygate & his wife Juliana in Werplusdon

175 Richard atte Hulle *v.* Thomas atte Hacche & his wife Matilda in Croyndon

176 Roger de Stretton & his wife Matilda by William de Coleshull *v.* William fil' Walter de Geddyng in Reygate & Horle

177 Walter Waldeshef & his wife Johanna by William de Bentele *v.* Roger de Seyntgyle lymbernare & his wife Emma in Suthwerk

178 William atte Horseye & his wife Alice *v.* Henry de Summerbury in Neudegate

179 Richard de Wyk & his wife Johanna *v.* Master Peter of Newcastle under Lyme surgeon in Wyk

180 Robert de Northrugge & his wife Margery *v.* Robert le Rede & his wife Mabel in Certeseye

181 Hawyse de Hautot *v.* Gilbert North of Apse in Apse, Waleton & Molesye

182 Robert de Keleseye *v.* Ralph de Ditton & his wife Johanna in Sanderstede
183 Richard de Chevynton *v.* Richard atte Bure & his wife Alice in Nutfeld
184 Johanna fil' William atte Lye of Mayford junior *v.* Philip atte Felde of Sande & his wife Grecia in Mayford
185 Richard de Berners *v.* Cristiana widow of Ralph de Berners in Westhorsley, Effingeham, Sende & Wysshelaye
186 Henry de Guldeford citizen of London & his wife Cristiana *v.* Robert fil' Walter Curteis of Guldeford in Aldham
187 John de Chedwode senior *v.* Robert de Twyford in Preston (Walter de St. Andrew & his wife Johanna a.s.c)
188 Laurence de Rustyngton *v.* Thomas le Barber & his wife Beatrice in Suthwerk & Bermundeseye
189 Richard le Brewere of Stanes *v.* John le Neweman of Inggefeld & his wife Matilda in Eggeham
190 Richerus de Resham & John de Resham *v.* John le Coupere of London and his wife Eufemia in Suthwerk
191 Robert de Certeseye & William fil' John le Wayte of Hoo *v.* Richard de la Sale of Thorp in Thorp, Egeham & Certeseye (Johanna fil' Ralph de Thorp & John her son a.s.c.)
192 Walter de Codestone *v.* William Geffrey & his wife Cecilia in Lyngefeld
193 Guy fil' Simon de Goldeburgh *v.* William fil' Roger de Eton & his wife Agnes in Egeham & Ingefeld
194 Robert de Bretinghirst & his wife Johanna *v.* John Lambyn in Pekham
195 Robert de Buchurst *v.* Peter le Cotiler and his wife Emma in Godalmyng
196 Walter atte Bregge of North lamhethe & his wife Margery and William his son & his wife Margery junior *v.*

Henry Canyn of Breynford & his wife Lucy in North Lamhethe (Edmound fil' Thomas de Lamhuthe a.s.c.)

197 Roger fil' Adam de Aperderle *v.* William Ewelle of Ledrede & his wife Alice in Ledrede

198 William de Rikethorn & his wife Elena *v.* Henry le Taillour of Suthewerk & his wife Cecilia in Suthewerk

199 Robert de Kellesey *v.* Henry Moukoy & his wife Isabel in Sandrestede

200 John le Ros of Lymmefeld *v.* Thomas de Ocstede in Ocstede

201 William Abbot *v.* Simon le Taillour of Farnham and his wife Johanna in Farnham

202 Adam le Chaundeler & his wife Johanna *v.* Richard le Clerk of Suthwerk in Wendlesworth

203 John atte More *v.* Anselm le Fourbur & his wife Margery in Suthewerk

11*th* *Edward II*

204 Richard de Rouebern *v.* Ralph de Rouebern in Esthorsleye

205 Adam Prodhomme & his wife Emma *v.* Gilbert Postel & his wife Margery in Kyngeston

206 Walter le Poleter & his wife Isolde *v.* Margery widow of Nicholas le Verrer of Suthwerk in Suthwerk

207 William atte Chert *v.* Roger le Belde & his wife Alice in Dorkyng

208 Richard fil' William Agyloun of Dorkyngg & his wife Dionisia *v.* Richard le Muleward of Dorkyngg in Dorkyngg & West Bechesworthe

209 Robert atte Sonde of Dorkyngg & his wife Alice *v.* Richard le Muleward of Dorkyngg in Dorkyngg

210 William de Waleton *v.* Elisea widow of Walter le Kyng in Waleton & Kersaulton

211 John de Merehurst & his wife Agnes *v.* Gilbert Broun forester & his wife Agnes in Werplesdon

212 John de Jarkevill *v.* Robert de Morlane and his wife Mabel in Est Hampton
213 John Froil Cirger of London *v.* William Rykyld of Kingeston & his wife Haverilda in Kyngeston
214 Margaret fil' John atte Nasshe & her sister Johanna *v.* John atte Nasshe of Potenham in Potenham
215 Roger Dammory & his wife Elizabeth by John de Chelmersford *v.* Walter de Gloucester in Suthwerk
216 Paulina de Heghham *v.* Ralph fil' Ralph de Ditton & his wife Johanna & Margaret fil' John de Ralegh in Werplesdone
217 Roger Dammory & his wife Elizabeth by John de Chelmersford *v.* Walter de Beauchamp & his wife Hawyse in Suthwerk
218 John Maheu de Chepyngnorton clerk *v.* Henry Kanyn & his wife Lucy in Northlambehuth
219 Thomas de Elingham & Richard de Bernham *v.* John de Uvedale & his wife Isabel by Robert de Benyngworth in Tycheseye Bendestede Crowehurst Camerwelle & Pecham
220 Nicholas de la Beche & his wife Johanna by Nicholas de Stapelston *v.* William de Echyngham in Suthwerk
221 & 222 Henry de Lutegarshale clerk *v.* John de Hamme & his wife Alina in Okstede
223 Walter de Froggewelle & his wife Isabel *v.* Adam le Sakkere of London & his wife Edith in Stokwell
224 Roger Husebond of London *v.* John de Rytlyng & his wife Cristiana in Hachesham
225 William Farman senr. & his wife Constance *v.* John fil' Ralph de Asshe in Asshe
226 Thomas de Colyngham of London *v.* Robert le Tannere & his wife Margaret in Kyngeston
227 Robert de Meldon *v.* Eustace Crullyng & his wife Agnes in Blechingleye

228 William de Blakelond & his wife Margery *v.* John Wymund of Lyngefeld in Lingefeld
229 Ranulph de Lightebirches & his wife Alice *v.* Henry de Horkesle in Suthwerk
230 John Bouk & his wife Matilda *v.* John Walkelyn of Kyngeston & his wife Isabel in Kyngeston
231 Richard Gylekyn of Farenham *v.* Ingelran de Farenham in Farenham
232 Roger Sauvage armurer & his wife Isabel *v.* Adam atte Rose potter & his wife Cecilia in Suthewerk
233 Philip de Orreby & his wife Florence by John atte Cherche *v.* Hillary Roce & his wife Margery in Micham
234 Hillary Roce & his wife Margery *v.* Phillip de Orreby & his wife Florence who Alianor widow of John de la Mare by Walter Ryvel called to warranty in Micham
235 Henry May de Batricheseye *v.* John Nichole of Batricheseye & his wife Scolastica in Batricheseye
236 William de Bekennesfeld *v.* William Aumbesas Kt. & his wife Johanna in Kersalton & la Wodecote
237 Andrew le Conestable of Guldeford *v.* Walter le Conestable of Guldeford in Guldeford, Merwe, Sende, Stoke & Ertedon
238 John de Arderne & his wife Agnes *v.* John de Tighele & his wife Avice in Busseleye
239 William de Rameshulle & Roger fil' Agnes atte Crouche *v.* Agnes atte Crouche de Leddrede in Leddrede
240 Richard le Hunte & his wife Emma & their daughter Isabel *v.* John fil' Edward Lovekyn of Kyngeston and his wife Cecilia in Kyngeston
241 John fil' William le Mareschal *v.* William le Mareschal de Flexwere in Asshe
242 John Cole & his wife Rosamund *v.* William atte Hacche & his wife Matilda in Bromlegh juxta Guldeford

243 Humfrey de Bohun Earl of Hereford & Essex *v.* Walter de Langeton Bishop of Coventry & Lychfeld in Waleton

244 John de Merkyngfeld clerk *v.* Roger de Munketon in Neweton Waleworth Suthwerk & Hachham

245 Thomas Ande of Suthwerk *v.* John Deyvill of Suthwerk in Suthwerk

246 John de Hurle *v.* John de Wy. & his wife Sibil in Camerwell

247 The Abbot of Certesey by William de Wikkewane *v.* William Andrew of Certesey & his wife Mabel in Certeseye

248 John Dunnyng & his wife Margaret *v.* John Walkelyn of Kyngeston & his wife Isabel in Kyngeston juxta Thames

249 William de Spersholte of London *v.* William Cosyn of London & his wife Beatrice in Effyngham

250 Scodland de la More & his wife Cristina *v.* Amicia widow of Nicholas le Eyr of Bromham in Bedyntone & Mychham

251 John le Latymer *v.* John Horn & his wife Jeremia in Estshene Mortelake & Wymeldon

252 John de Henley *v.* John de Norton in Northlambhithe

253 Thomas de Baggeworth *v.* Thomas de Leycester in Croyndon

13th *Edward II*

1 Robert de Kelleseye *v.* William de Henle & his wife Isabel in Warlingham & Chelesham

2 Walter de Verney & his wife Margery *v.* Ralph le Carpenter of Certeseye in Suthwerk

3 Hugh le Hettere of Croydon *v.* William Morris & his wife Cristina in Croydon

4 Roger Sauvage of London armurer & his wife Isabel *v.* John de Rokelond & his wife Margery in Suthwerk

5 Ralph Postel of Kyngeston *v*. Thomas le Spicer of Lewes & his wife Matilda in Kyngeston on Thames

6 William de Tangelegh and his wife Agnes *v*. Gilbert de Wythewell in Werplesdon (Thomas de Danehurst, Robert de Danehurst and Thomas de Tangeleye a.s.c.)

7 Robert Lovekyn & his wife Emma *v*. Gilbert de Saleby & his wife Matilda in Kyngeston

8 Adam fil' John le Tannere of Kyngeston *v*. Lucy widow of John le Tannere of Kyngeston in Kyngeston

9 Master John Walewayn *v*. Walter fil' Walter of Gloucester in Certeseye

10 John le Ellerker junior *v*. Walter de Geddyng & his wife Margaret in Est Pollesden Mikelham & Feccham

11 William Olyver *v*. Thomas Olyver in Saunderstede

14th *Edward II*

12 John de Mockyngg & his wife Idonia *v*. Elias le Barber & his wife Juliana in Suthwerk

13 Hugh le Despenser junior *v*. Thomas Corbet & his wife Johanna in Taleworth (Agnes widow of Ingelran de Horton a.s.c.)

14 Hugh Draghsper of Wyndesore *v*. Richard de Burewe of Croydone & his wife Matilda in Croyndone

15 Robert le Fissher of Kyngestone *v*. Gilbert de Saleby & his wife Matilda in Kyngeston

16 John le Ellerker junior *v*. Walter de Geddyng in Est Pollesden Mikelham Dorkyng & Lederede

17 Thomas le Heywood of Wolkstede & his wife Katharine *v*. James de Hadersham in Wolkstede

18 Master John Walwayn by Nicholas de Eton *v*. Walter de Geddyng in Leghe & Effingeham

19 John Dunnyng and his wife Margery *v*. Thomas le Ferour & his wife Alice in Kyngeston

20 Lawrence de Rustinton *v*. Gilbert atte More of Effyngham and his wife Isabel by John de Wyk in Effingham

21 Master John Walewayn *v.* Walter de Geddyng & his wife Margaret in Effingham
22 Thomas le Heyward & his wife Katharine *v.* John de Bodekesham & his wife Rose in Wolknestede
23 John Turney of Kyngeston & his wife Matilda *v.* Stephen le Suur of Kyngeston juxta Tamisiam in Kyngeston super Tamisiam
24 Richard la Veille *v.* John de Haudlo & his wife Matilda in Hachesham
25 John de Hastynges *v.* Nicholas Bachelor in Dorkyngg & Bokham
26 Peter Poulche of Kyngeston & his wife Beatrice *v.* Stephen le Suur of Kyngeston in Kyngeston on Thames
27 William de Herle *v.* Philip de Orreby & his wife Florence in Miccheham (Walter fil' Arnold de Wykford a.s.c.)
28 John de Brudeford *v.* Edward de St. John & his wife Eva in Cumpton juxta Guldeford
29 William Bonet & his wife Matilda *v.* Peter atte Velde of Great Bokham in Great Bokham
30 John de Latymer & his wife Johanna and Edmund fil' John le Latymer *v.* Lambert de Thrikyngham in Crawestok
31 Elias le Caller of London & his wife Matilda *v.* Henry de Hatton & his wife Anabel in Newenton "Beate Marie."
32 John Beswill *v.* Robert de Lincolle & his wife Alice in Suthwerk
33 John Morice of Orsete *v.* John Dunnyng & wife Margery in Kingeston on Thames
34 Robert Sauser of Gildeford *v.* John fil' John Nichole of Gildeford and his wife Johanna in Gildeford and Stok juxta Gildeford
35 Robert Fraunceys & his wife Agnes *v.* John Richard in Camerwell

36 John de St. John of Lageham & his wife Margery by
Robert Pultebem *v.* John de Ifeld in Lageham &
Meryden

15*th* *Edward II*

37 Ralph Smerehele & his wife Gunnilda *v.* Richard Wylegyng & his wife Johanna in Ledrede

38 Thomas Godard & his wife Isabel *v.* Richard Wodebat in Godalmyng

39 Thomas Godard & his wife Isabel *v.* Richard Wodebat in Godalmyng

40 Richard Hurelond *v.* Adam Gerlaund & his wife Alice in Bromlegh

41a William Dyry of Esshemeresworth *v.* Robert Frere of Stokes juxta Guldeford & his wife Johanna in Sende

41b John le Attorne & his wife Agnes *v.* John Roger & his wife Johanna & Thomas Wygayn & his wife Alice in Kersaulton & Bedynton

42 John de Horne & his wife Alice *v.* John de Badesulle in Horne

43 Andrew Godard and his wife Cristiana *v.* Simon Horn of Stretford atte Bowe and his wife Matilda in Suthewerk.

44 William de Tanrugge & Godefrey de Tanrugge *v.* John de la Stoket in Crowhurst

16*th* *Edward II*

45 William de Tanrugge *v.* Godefrey de Tanrugge in Tanrugge, Wolkstede, Okstede, Crowhurst, Lynggefeld and Waldyngham

17*th* *Edward II*

46 Nicholas de Thorp Costentyn (cf. No. 68 Nicholas Costentyn) chaplain and Simon his brother *v.* Thomas Grick of London in Micham

47 Hugh le Despenser junior by Richard Hillary *v.* John de Crumbewell and his wife Idonia in Schaldeford

48 John de Houghton *v.* John de Burghton and his wife Johanna in Certeseye aud Egeham
49 Geoffrey le Lacer citizen of London *v.* Johanna fil' Walter de Asshesham, Robert le Mileward of Halresshet, Richard fil' Walter Andrew and Gilbert Hachewulf in Asshe
50 Simon Turgys of London *v.* John atte Walle of Camberwelle and his wife Cristina in Pekham
51 John fil' James de Hadresham *v.* John fil' William de la More of Lyngefeld in Lyngefeld
52 Richard de Berkynge of Wendlesworth by William de Brecles *v.* Robert Fabian of Wendlesworth and his wife Johanna in Wendlesworth
53 Gilbert de Balesham of London cealer *v.* John Nichol of Batricheseye and his wife Scolastica in Batricheseye
54 Robert de Syndlesham and his wife Agnes by Nicholas del Marreys *v.* John atte Greene and his wife Johanna in Padyndene
55 Walter Oliver of London *v.* Richard de Coggeshale and his wife Johanna in Suthwerk
56 Michael de Houghton and his wife Johanna *v.* William Aumbesas and his wife Elizota and William Cross and his wife Agnes in Bedynton
57 John le Rede of Alemaigne and his wife Alice *v.* William de la Quenhethe trumpour and his wife Avice in Suthwerk
58 John le Wermore and his wife Emma *v.* Walter le Smyth in Croyndon
59 Hugh le Despenser Earl of Wynton *v.* John Bishop of Bath and Wells in Pirifright
60 John de Ifeld *v.* John le Spenser and his wife Isabel in Chelesham
61 Adam Prodhomme of Kyngeston bucher and his wife Emma *v.* John de Longebrigge and his wife Avice in Kyngeston

62 Walter Thorberne of Kyngeston and his wife Juliana and their son Walter *v.* Thomas le Ferrour of Kyngeston and his wife Alice in Kyngeston super Tamisiam

63 William fil' William le Cornmangere and his wife Edith *v.* Richard de Hameldon and his wife Alice in Ledrede

64 Henry fil' Henry Hawys *v.* William Hawys of Thorncombe in Bromligh

18*th* *Edward II*

65 John fil' John le Norreys of London *v.* Seman Clement and his wife Alice in Dorkynge

66 John Scot *v.* Thomas Corbet and his wife Johanna in Carshalton

67 Hugh de Wytham *v.* William Andrew of Certeseye and his wife Mabel in Certeseye

68 Nicholas Costentyn *v.* Thomas le Rees and his wife Matilda in Croyndon

69 John fil' Robert le Marler *v.* Robert le Marler of Horle in Horle

70 Charles de Segesford of Cullesdon clerk *v.* Thomas Vyel chaplain in Caterham

71 William Stilewell *v.* Richard Merk of Farnham and his wife Alice in Farnham

72 Simon le Sire of Litleton and his wife Juliana *v.* Agnes Goylyn of Eppewell in Strode and Egeham

73 Andrew Horn of London *v.* Robert le Bisshopeston and his wife Johanna in Suthwerk

74 William de Bray and his son Nicholas *v.* John Payn of Kyngeston and his wife Johanna in Kyngeston

75 William fil' William de London *v.* William de London senior in Cherlewood and Horle

76 Simon fil' William le Clerk of Croyndon and John his brother *v.* William Morys and his wife Cristina in Croyndon

77 Johanna widow of William Aumbesas of Kersalton *v.*

William de Bekenesfeld and his wife Cristina *v.* Richard fil' John de Kymberle of Cantebrigg in Kersalton Bedyngton and Cloppeham

78 Robert atte Fenne and his brother Walter *v.* Thomas atte Fenne in Godalmyng

79 Ralph de Brokshote and his wife Johanna *v.* William Olyver in Piryford

80 The Abbot of Certeseye *v.* Charles de Canductu parson of Colesdon Church in Colesdon (John fil' John de Horne and Roger fil' John de Horne a.s.c.)

81 William Ingelard *v.* John de Tyle and his wife Avice in Cherteseye Walleton and Chabeham

82 Gilbert de Burefeld *v.* John le Em of Compton in Farncombe and Cateshulle (Walter Roger a.s.c.)

83 John le Em of Compton and his wife Elizabeth by John de Wyke *v.* Gilbert de Burghfeld in Ertyndon and Lytleton

84 Alan Herman of Guldeford and his wife Margaret *v.* Henry de Guldeford and his wife Cristiana in Aldham

85 Simon de Parys and his wife Agatha *v.* Richard le Clerk of Suthwerk and his wife Johanna in Suthwerk and Neuwyngton juxta Suthwerk

86 Thomas Brian of Suthwerk and his wife Alice by Giles de Gatton *v.* Simon de Parys and his wife Agatha in Suthwerk

87 Thomas Bryan of Suthwerk and his wife Alice by Giles de Gatton *v.* Richard de Langeford clerk and his wife Johanna in Suthwerk

88 Thomas Brian and his wife Alice by Richard de Bolingbrok *v.* William de Sarum and his wife Amicia in Suthwerk

89 Agnes de Papeworth *v.* Ralph de Hoo, Alexander de Sarterie ismonger and his wife Alice, Alianor fil' Ralph de Hoo and her sister Johanna in Sande

90 Walter Roce *v.* Richard fil' Geoffrey de Heyford in Heyford and Wandelesworth
92 Henry fil' Simon de Stanhamme *v.* Simon de Stanhamme Senr. in Lymmesfeld and Okested
93 Walter fil' Robert de Wodeham *v.* Robert de Wodeham and his wife Sibil in Weybrigge juxta Byflet
94 John Paul of Kyngeston juxta Tamisian *v.* Richard Machun and his wife Cristina in Kyngeston juxta Tamisian
95 William de St. Michael of Codyngton *v.* Adam Pykeman of London fishmonger and his wife Matilda in Suthwerk
96 Adam de Wouburn taillur *v.* John de Burton and his wife Johanna in Certeseye

19*th Edward II*

91 Robert Myles clerk *v.* Hugh Madefrey and his wife Juliana in Suthwerk
97 William de Wanting and his wife Agatha *v.* Richard Purse and his wife Agnes in Burgham
98 Gilbert le Glovere of Ledrede *v.* William Ewelle of Ledrede and his wife Alice in Ledrede
99 John de Pokenord and his wife Juliana by William de Siddene *v.* Thomas fil' Philip de Hascumbe in Godalmyngge
100 Thomas atte Chirchegate of Dorkyngge *v.* John le Clerk of Reygate and his wife Dionisia in Reygate
101 Andrew Payn and his son Robert *v.* Petronilla la Kynges in Suthwerk
102 William fil' John de West Pirle and his wife Juliana *v.* Emma widow of William Petit of Cranle in Suthwerk
103 Robert Oliver *v.* John Child and his wife Agnes in Merstham
104 Richard de Biterle *v.* William le Barbour of Hynton and his wife Cecilia in North Lamhethe

105 Richerus de Resham *v.* John fil' John Vanne in Suthwerk
106 Henry Monkoye and his son Thomas *v.* Giles de Gatton and his wife Alice in Suthewerk
107 Simon le Bedel and his wife Felicia *v.* John de la Bere and his wife Johanna in Cherlewode and Neudegate (John de Gotwich and his wife Agnes, Thomas le Man and his wife Matilda, Robert atte Bernette and his wife Juliana, John Ventre and his wife Elena, John de Godwich junr. and his wife Alice a.s.c.)
108 Alan de Hekestede and his wife Eva *v.* Walter Potyn and his wife Margaret in Lyngefeld and Lemefeld
109 Richard Payn and his wife Johanna *v.* John Payn of Kyngeston and his wife Johanna in Kyngeston
110 Thomas de Hamme and Matilda fil' Adam Page by Philip Payn her guardian *v.* Robert de Hamme Parson of Kayrwent church in Hamme
112 William de Monte Acuto by William de Merston *v.* Thomas Chaumterel and his wife Alesia in Wandlesworth
113 Andrew le Eyr of Guldeford *v.* Robert le Eyr of Guldeford and his wife Felicia in Guldeford, Godalmyng, Bromlegh and Stoke juxta Guldeford.

20*th* *Edward II*

111 William de Weston *v.* William Bocher of West Clendon and his wife Matilda in Est Clendon
114 John Scot of Guldeford *v.* Roger le Taillour of Kyngeston and his wife Matilda in Kyngeston
115 Andrew Horn of London *v.* Simon de (Stowe) and his wife Alice in Suthwerk
116 John de West Pirle *v.* Robert de Bourstalle parson of Sanderstede Church in Sanderstede, Watyndon, Colesdon, Chalvedon, Merstham and Waddone
117 John de Brugford *v.* John Prodhomme and his wife Johanna in Waleton super Tamisiam

118 Roger de London of Reygate and his wife Alianor *v.* Thomas fil' Walter de Collee in Reygate and Cherlewode

119 John de Ifeld by William de Langele *v.* William fil' William de Porkele, John Roland and his wife Juliana, & Thomas de Cleye and his wife Lora in Chelesham

1st Edward III

1 Thomas de St. Michael *v.* John Botayle and his wife Margery in Ewelle

2 Thomas de Weston & his wife Matilda *v.* John Cole & his wife Rosamund in Bromlegh

3 Thomas Brian of Suthwerk *v.* Thomas Spereman of Suthwerk & his wife Wimarca in Suthwerk

4 Isabel fil' James de Wodeham *v.* James de Wodeham in Weybrugg & Certeseye

5 Simon de Stanstede *v.* Ralph le But in Mayford

6 Roger Frenshe *v.* Simon le Butiller in Tanrigge & Welknestede

7 Walter le Ladde & his wife Agnes *v.* William fil' Walter le Ladde in Purefrith

2nd Edward III

8 John de Dudeswell & his wife Letice *v.* Richard de Bokelynton chaplain in Sende

9 Walter le Benere & his wife Johanna *v.* Henry Wymond of London in Suthwerk

3rd Edward III

10 Stephen Lytewyne *v.* John Lytewyne & his wife Agnes in Certesie

11 Alan de Warwyk & his wife Emma *v.* Roger fil' Ralph Saleman & his wife Alice in Burstowe

12 Robert le Pyp *v.* Walter fil' Robert de Snodeham in Bromlegh

13 Bartholomew Gatyn of Guldeford & Alice fil' Walter atte

Chirche v. Peter de Totenham of Guldeford in Guldeford, Shaldeford, Bromlegh, Irtyngdon & Stok juxta Guldeford

14 John fil' Ralph de Storich & his wife Alice v. Thomas de Slappeleghe & his wife Alice in Certeseye

15 Peter de la Spineye & his wife Margaret by Thomas Prat v. Thomas de Puttenhuthe in Wymbeldon

16 William de Tanrugge v. John de Crowhurst & his wife Agnes in Tanrugg

17 Richard atte Grene of Ellisworth vicar of Shaldeford church v. Francis de Wyntreshull & his wife Juliana in Bromlegh & Godalmyng

18 William de Wyggepyrye v. William de Covelyndenne & his wife Juliana in Horle & Cherlewode

19 Gilbert de Wythewell & his wife Cecilia v. Peter vicar of Wambergh Church in Westwode & Rykford

20 Peter atte Burnebrig of Thorp v. Robert de London & his wife Matilda in Thorp

21 John de Warrenne Earl of Surrey by John de Assheby v. Francis Bachemus & his wife Johanna in Wauton (Philip de Drokeneford a.s.c.)

22 Adam de Kyngeston v. John Fot of Oxford & his wife Margery in Suthwerk

23 Nicholas Fraunceys & his wife Florence by John Profale v. Alan le Fraunceys of Wrydelyngton & John Seman of Berton in Micham & Mordon

24 William de la Solere of Est Grensted v. Peter de St. John of Wolkenestede

25 William de Thorbern v. Thomas le Ferour & his wife Alice in Kyngeston

26 John Gold and his son John v. Richard le Whyte & his wife Hawyse in Certeseye

27 Adam de St. Albans v. Gocelyn Osbern & his wife Margery in Kersalton & Bedynton

28 John de Hayton v. John Botaile & his wife Margery in Ewell & Codynton
29 John Germin chivaler & his wife Alice v. Robert Power of Wyham & his wife Lucy in Suthewerk juxta London
42 Roger fil' Ralph Saleman v. Roger fil' Roger atte Loge of Burstowe in Burstowe

4th Edward III

30 Thomas de Lodelowe & his wife Katharine v. Adam Poignaunt in Miccham & Toting Graveneye
31 William atte Bregge v. Walter atte Bregge of Lambeheth & his wife Rose in Wandlesworth
32 John de Mockyngg of London fisshmonger & his wife Nichola v. John de Beseville in Suthewerk
33 Robert Storm of London v. John Scot of Kersalton & his wife Cecilia in Bedynton & Kersalton
34 Richard atte Rigge v. John de Sothenye & his wife Agnes in Bromlegh
35 Reginald fil' Robert de Wodeham v. Hugh de Shrimpelersh & his wife Margaret in Certeseye
36 William Milcent & his wife Beatrice & their daughter Alice v. Thomas Richard & his wife Johanna in Werplesdon
37 Stephen de Frollebury & his wife Margaret v. Robert de Dool in Werplesdon, Compton & Farnham
38 Robert le Shephard of Strode v. Henry de Thorp & his wife Isabel in Egeham
39 Anthony Citronen & Nicholas de Salvo of London cytesein v. John de Felton chivaler & his wife Sibil in Suthewerk
40 John de Dunstaple parson of Wittelegh Church v. William Buristrete of Wordi Mortimer in Farnham
41 John de Ifeld & his wife Margery by William Papellioun v. Johanna widow of John de Gatewyk in Chelesham & Tycheseye
60 Robert Storm of London v. Johanna widow of John de Upton in Kersalton and Bedyngton

43 William de Walberton chaplain *r.* Nicholas Bachelir & his wife Johanna in Westhorsligh Okham & Sende
44 Letice fil' John de Wodesham *r.* Letice de Langenacre in Shyre, Dorkyngg, Newdegate & Shaldeford (Margery fil' John de Wodesham a.s.c.)
45 John atte Nalerette junior & his wife Johanna *r.* Letice de Langenacre in Shyre, Dorkyngg, Newdegate & Shaldeford (Margery fil' John de Wodesham a.s.c.)
46 John de Warenne Earl of Surrey *r.* John de Malton chaplain in Wauton
47 John Plomer of Kyngeston & his wife Johanna *r.* John Payn & his wife Johanna in Kyngeston
48 Nicholas fil' William le Cornemonger of Leddrede *r.* Robert de Eylenehaghe & his wife Johanna in Mickelham
49 John Latymer *r.* Peter fil' John de St. John of Lageham in Nobright & Welknested
50 Robert de Stangrave chivaler & his wife Johanna *r.* Hugh de Audele & his wife Margaret in Blecchyngleye
51 Roger the Prior of Newark (Novo loco juxta Guldeford) *r.* John Prodhomme & his wife Johanna in Coveham
52 Thomas le Webbe of Bedenescumbe *r.* Richard Champyon of Bednescumbe in Farncumbe
53 William fil' Thomas Alfroun *r.* John le Clerk & his wife Alina in Thames ditton
54 John Dunnyng of Kyngeston *r.* Thomas Ferrour of Kyngeston & his wife Alice in Kyngeston
55 Nicholas de Haytfeld & his wife Matilda *r.* John de Wodesham & his wife Matilda in Shyre, Dorkyngg, Newdegate and Shaldeford (Margery fil' John de Wodesham a.s.c.)
56 William fil' Richard atte Fen *v.* Walter le Potager & his wife Agnes in Suthwerk
57 Simon Rote of London pelter *v.* John de Chelmeresford

clerk in Bedyngton, Bandon, Wodecote, Waleton, Waddon & Michham

58 Thomas de Betoigne & his wife Johanna *v.* Nicholas de Besseford clerk in Camerwell, Pekham, & Hachesham

59 John de Croydon of London fishmonger *v.* John atte Doune of 'Waltham Sancte Crucis' & his wife Alice in Croydon

5*th* *Edward III*

61 Ralph de Hoo & his wife Juliana *v.* Henry Baynard in Wokkyngg & Bromlygh

62 Thomas fil' Philip de Depyng of Merstham *v.* Robert de Depyng & his wife Margaret in Wandelesworth

63 John fil' Richard le Smyth junr. *v.* Richard le Smyth of Okstede in Okstede

64 Nicholas Keete of Wandlesworth & his wife Emma *v.* Robert le Warde vicar of Wandlesworth Church in Heyford and Wandlesworth

65 Peter de Roughberne *v.* William de Braybrok & his wife Margery in Effyngham, Esthorslegh & Sende

66 John de Foxton *v.* Thomas de Waltham & his wife Isabel in Stretham

67 Andrew le Conestable & his wife Mirabel by Richard Frye *v.* Baldewin de Wansted in Stok juxta Guldeford (Walter le Conestable a.s.c.)

68 John Pentecost *v.* John de Ardern & his wife Agnes in Chabham

69 John atte Hoo & his wife Alice *v.* William fil' Hugh Uppelegh in Bromlegh

70 John de Warrenne Earl of Surrey *v.* John de Malton chaplain in Wauton

71 Stephen Chelesfeld *v.* William Gerberd & his wife Margery in Suthwerk

80 Richard de Hamme & his wife Matilda *v.* William Brigham

& his wife Alice and Roger le Rakyere & his wife
Haginilda in Kyngeston

82 Walter Conestable de Guldeford & his wife Juliana *r.*
Thomas Conestable parson of the Church of St. Mary
Guldeford in Guldeford, Merewe, Sende, Irtyndon &
Stok juxta Guldeford

83 Nicholas de Northwode *r.* Edmund fil' John de Badeshill
& his wife Anna in Gatton

84 Roger fil' Ralph Saleman *r.* Edmund fil' John de Badeshill
& his wife Anna in Gatton

5th and 6th *Edward III*

79 William de Castleacre & his wife Alice *r.* William le
Pedelere parson of Streatham Church in Lamehith
(Thomas de Shenholton a.s.c.)

81 William le Pedelere parson of Stretham Church *r.*
William de Castleacre in Lamehith (William de Henholte a.s.c.)

85 Thomas Huscarl *r.* Master William de —— in Badynton

6th *Edward III*

72 Thomas de Merston de Depyng *r.* Robert de Depyng & his
wife Margaret in Est Shene

73 Richard de Morton & Robert de Remenham *r.* Thomas de
Remenham in Cumpton (Richard son & heir of Johanna
fil' Henry Mabaunk of Remenham a.s.c.)

74 William Roce of Totingbek *r.* Richard de Patmere & his
wife Clemence in Batricheseye

75 William fil' Richard atte Fenne *r.* John de Wyncester of
Suthwerk & his wife Johanna in Suthwerk

76 Roger fil' Ralph Saleman & his wife Alice *r.* Richard
parson of Burstowe Church in Burstowe & Horlee

77 Ralph fil' Roger de London & his wife Katharine *r.*
Alianor widow of Roger de London and her son Roger in
Collee

78 Roger fil' Roger de London & his wife Alice *r.* Alianor

widow of Roger de London in Reygate, Bechesworth & Horlee

86 William de Jarpunvyll *r.* Roger de Jarpunwyll & his wife Lora in Abingeworth & Dorkyngg (Henry de la Marlere & his wife Margaret & William Fraunkelyn of Guldesburgh & his wife Margery a.s.c.)

87 John de Tidilmynton clerk *r.* Bartholomew de Malvern of London & his wife Alesia in Ashtede

88 John Plummer & his wife Johanna by William de Morton *r.* John le Bruys & his wife Alice in Kyngeston

89 Richard vicar of Ebesham Church *r.* Nicholas de Tunstalle & his wife Johanna in Bettegrave

90 William Roce of Totynggebek *r.* William le Pedeler parson of Stretham Church & Roger de Syleby chaplain in Suthwerk, Stretham & Totynggebek

92 Robert atte Hulle of Okele *r.* William Stoute & his wife Helewise in Nudegate

91 William de Herle & his wife Margaret *r.* Nicholas Fraunceys & his wife Florence in Micheham & Mordon

92a Henry fil' Geoffrey atte Doune *r.* Richard Longys of Guldeford & his wife Cecilia in Ertendon

93 Richard atte Stone *r.* William le Hounere & his wife Alice in Shaldeford

94 Henry fil' William Henry & his wife Isabel *r.* Walter de Codyngwych & his wife Johanna in Mayford

95 Thomas Gerveys *r.* Martin Gerveys & his wife Johanna in Merstham

96 Roger fil' Roger de London *r.* John de Madham in Immeworth

103 Henry de Thorp & his wife Isabel *r.* John de Sodynton & Bartholomew de Walingford in Certeseye

104 Stephen Bures *r.* Alan Bures & his wife Juliana in Suthwerk

105 Nicholas de Bibury chaplain *v.* Thomas de St. Michael of Codynton in Codynton

106 John de Wy & his wife Sibil *r.* John de Hurle in Lambhethe & Camerwell

108 Richard fil' Henry de Somerbury & his wife Johanna by John le Bel her Guardian *r.* Henry de Somerbury in Shire

109 Thomas Coleman *r.* Adam Coleman in Suthwerk & Pekham

7th *Edward III*

97 Ralph le Baker & his wife Amphusia *r.* John de Sellesdon & his wife Amicia in Croydon

98 Edmund de Reynham of London & his wife Isolde by Thomas de Totchewyk her Guardian *r.* Geoffrey de Hugendene in Kersaulton

99 Henry atte Knolle & his wife Matilda *r.* Henry Baynard & Walter le Taillour of Uhurst in Bromlegh

90 Robert de Westbrok & his wife Bona *r.* Walter atte Garston in Godalmynge (Richard le Frenshe of Chuddyngfold a.s.c.)

101 John Wythorn of Dounton chaplain *r.* Richard Doppelane of Salesbiry turnour & his wife Katharine in Suthwerk

102 Walter de Okkelyghe & his wife Agatha *r.* Richard parson of Abbyngeworth Church in Gomshelne & Est Shaldeford

107 John fil' Peter Baret of Eton & his wife Agnes by William de Northwyk *r.* Richard atte Novene of Ledrede in Ledrede (Gilbert le Hore of Ledred, Mabel widow of Thomas atte Novene, William de Ewelle & Thomas Pynchon a.s.c.)

110 Richard de Farneberwe of London coffrer *r.* Thomas de Dunlee of Camerwell & his wife Matilda in Camerwell

111 Robert le Grouere & his wife Alice *r.* Adam atte Hille in Chertiseye & Waleton
112 Robert de Medersh *r.* John de Medersh in Wonersh
113 Nicholas fil' Henry de Bergh *r.* William de Croft & his wife Johanna in Croyndon
114 Robert Swote & his wife Agnes *r.* Robert Storm in Suthwerk
115 Thomas Shaplee & his wife Alice & John le Foghel of Cherteseye in Cherteseye

8*th* *Edward III*

116 Robert atte Gote of Wynthorp *r.* John de Temeford & his wife Alice in Bermundeseye
3 Robert de T—— *r.* William Man & his wife Letice in Polyngfold (Robert de Polyngfold a.s.c.)
72 John de Molyns *r.* John fil' Robert de Domelton of Wandlesworth in Wandlesworth

9*th* *Edward III*

70 John de Covert & his wife Margaret *r.* John Cafhous parson of Esshynton in Chalvedone
71 William de Weston and his wife Margery *r.* Richard de Boclynton parson of West Clendon Church and William de Sydeneye in West Clendon & Sende

9*th* and 10*th* *Edward III*

4 William de Weston *r.* Richard de Boclynton Parson of West Clendon Church & William de Sydenye in Aldebury & Shire (Robert fil' William atte Walter of Ware a.s.c.)

10*th* *Edward III*

54 John le Beel of Fermesham *r.* Robert de Pernecote in Fermesham & Elstede

11*th* *Edward III*

2 William atte Fenn *r.* Peter de Alemaiyne & his wife Margaret in Wimbeldon & Mortelak
8 Stephen, Bishop of London *r.* William Vygerous parson of

Fulham Church & William Mogge parson of Wyleye Church in Benchesham (Thomas de Gravesende a.s.c.)

10 Richard Munnyng *r*. John Deneys fisshere & his wife Emma & William Deugard & his wife Agnes in Seende (John fil' John de Mickelham a.s.c.)

12 Edmund de Covyntre *r*. Peter de Thorne & his wife Alice in Blecchyngligh

13 John atte Hulle & his wife Agnes *r*. William atte Wode & his wife Juliana in Kersalton

15 John de Heghfeld & his wife Cecilia *r*. John Brocas in Bromlegh, Ertyndon & Chidyngfold

19 William de Upton chaundeler & his wife Johanna *r*. Robert de Bruge of London pelter & his wife Juliana in Suthwerk

24 Master John de Ayleston clerk *r*. Isabel de Castelacre in Leshurst

51 Thomas Aude of Suthwerk *r*. Nicholas Kete & his wife Emma in Suthwerk

52 Peter Pyrye of Kyngeston *r*. Thomas le Ferour of Kyngeston & his wife Alice in Kyngeston

60 Master John de Ayleston *r*. William de Castelacre & his wife Alice in Leshurst

61 John fil' Edmund de Berners & his wife Elizabeth *r*. Thomas fil' Richard de Berners in West Horslegh

65 John de Gaynesford & his wife Margery *r*. Nicholas le Hert & his wife Matilda in Wolknestede & Horne

67 Isabel widow of Henry Husee & Henry Husee chivaler *r*. William de Henle chivaler in Wytle, Chuddyngefold, Bromle & Guldeford

11th and 12th *Edward III*

16 John de Croydon citizen & fishmonger of London *r*. John atte Doune of Waltham & his wife Alice in Croydon

12th Edward III

1. Maurice Turgys & his wife Katharine *v*. Henry Whissh & his wife Katharine in Lambhuth
11. John Dewy & his wife Margery *v*. John de Mickelham in Mickelham
18. William Gomme junr. *v*. William Gomme senr. in Guldeford & Stok juxta Guldeford
37. Simon de Mussendene & his wife Margery *v*. John de Brokas & his wife Margaret in Guldeford, Stok, Sende, Ertyndon & Clendon Regis
38. John fil' Robert Box of London & his wife Margaret *v*. John de Foxton clerk & his wife Juliana in Wanlesworth
47. Maurice Turgis citizen and draper of London & his wife Katharine *v*. Stephen Vanne citizen & barber of London & his wife in West Grenewyk
48. John de Recchynge *v*. John de Sterteforde & his wife Alice in Croydon
49. Richard Maunsel *v*. William fil' Geoffrey le Helere of Ledred & his wife Alice in Croydon
53. Richard Mounyng & John Colston *v*. Roger de Bolton & his wife Agnes in Sende
54. Alice widow of Richard de Graveneye *v*. Miles de Wodeham chaplain in Thorp & Egeham (Richard fil' Richard de Graveneye a.s.c.)
56. Nicholas Hosebonde of London & Alice Hosebonde *v*. Laurence Sely & his wife Agnes in Retherheth
57. John de Gaynesford & his wife Margery *v*. Robert de Stangrave & his wife Johanna in Crouhurst Lynggefeld Lemenesfeld & Okstede
58. William de Herle *v*. Nicholas Fraunceis of Wrydelyngton & his wife Florence in Miccham & Morden
63. John de Bures senr. *v*. Alan de Bures & his wife Juliana in Suthwerk

66 John de Bures senr. *v.* William atte Doune & his wife Margery in Estbechesworth
68 William atte Fen *v.* John Trappe of London pelter & his wife Agnes in Wymbeldon Shene & Mortlake

12*th* & 13*th* *Edward III*

35 Miles de Stapelton & his wife Isabel by John de Northland her guardian *v.* Nicholas de Stapelton chivaler in Suthwerk
39 John Aleyn of Slyfeld *v.* John Lytholf of Merewe in Stok juxta Guldeford

13*th* *Edward III*

7 William de Herle *v.* Nicholas Fraunceys & his wife Florence in Suthwerk
14 John de Okstede & his wife Isabel *v.* Juliana widow of Peter Purye in Kyngeston
17 Maurice Turgis citizen & draper of London & his wife Katharine by Geoffrey Baudewyn *v.* Laurence Sely citizen & skinner of London & his wife Agnes in Hachesham
23 Jordan de Coushete & his wife Agnes *v.* John de Wythewell in Purefright & Chabeham
25 William de Grenstede & his wife Johanna *v.* John Pope in Okham, Seende, Westhorslegh & Dorkyng
29 Edmund de Wyke of London taillour & his wife Johanna *v.* John Yago & his wife Agnes in Suthwerk
30 John le Parker of Guldeford *v.* Walter le Parker of Guldeford & his wife Agnes by William Gomme in Guldeford
31 Thomas fil' Thomas de Roukeslee & his wife Johanna *v.* John de la Mandeleyne in Worplesdon
32 Geoffrey Horn of London fisshemonger *v.* William de Maddeleye & his wife Matilda in Suthwerk, Bermundeseye & Retherhethe
33 William de Maddelee of Bermundeseye & his wife Matilda *v.* Stephen Van of London & his wife Margaret in Bermundeseye

34 William de Longhurst & his wife Edith *v.* John de Longhurst in Ockelegh & Abyngeworthe

36 Henry fil' Henry de Hatton & his brother Stephen *v.* Thomas Reyner of Suthwerk & his wife Cristina in Suthwerk

40 William de Cheyham citizen of London & his wife Agnes *v.* Walter le Gras chivaler in West Cheyham.

41 John de Horton *v.* Walter le Hore & his wife Alice in Ewell

42 Stephen de Frollebury & his wife Katharine *v.* John de Resham & William Clerk of Shakelford in Puttham, Werplesdon, Cumpton, Ibenerth & Waneburgh

43 Reginald le Forester & his wife Matilda *v.* John le Forester in Beddyngton, Bandon & Waleton

44 Maurice Turgis citizen & draper of London & his wife Katharine by Geoffrey Baudewyn *v.* William Maddele & his wife Matilda in Hachesham

13th & 14th *Edward III*

59 Robert de la Blakefanne *v.* Henry de la Blakefanne in Wokkyng & Mayford

14th *Edward III*

5 William de Baggeshete of Ryppele & his wife Johanna *v.* Symon atte Beche & his wife Emma in Ryppele

6 Robert de Uttokeshather *v.* Ralph le Taillour of Cherteseye junior & his wife Johanna in Cherteseye

20 William atte Gate & his wife Johanna *v.* Thomas de Bovyndon & his wife Alice in Worplesdon

21 Henry Whissh & his wife Katharine *v.* Robert de Staunford & his wife Isabel in Suthwerk

22 Richard atte Wylle *v.* William Wreyford in Compton juxta Guldeford

26 John fil' William de Piriton *v.* Alianor widow of Guy Ferre Knight in Waldyngeham, Tanrugge, Wolkestede, Crouhurst & Lyngefelde

27 Henry de Kyngeston & his wife Agnes *v.* Richard de Swyneford & his wife Agnes in Kyngeston (John fil' Richard de Swyneford of Kyngeston & William Osebern of Stanes a.s.c.)

28 John Poleyn & his wife Alice *v.* Richard le Smyth of Purefright in Purefright

45 William Box *v.* Edmund de Reyngham & his wife Isolda in Karsalton

46 John de Ridyngersh & his wife Margery *v.* Hugh de Colewyk parson of Cranlegh church in Bromleygh, Chelesham & Ticheseye

50 Roger Saleman *v.* William de Waure & his wife Cristiana in Nutfeld

62 William atte Lee carpenter *v.* Walter de Canterbury perler & his wife Margery in Suthwerk

64 Thomas de Lincoln *v.* Richard Andrew shereman & his wife Matilda in Wandelesworth & Batricheseye

69 Roger Saleman *v.* Thomas de Charlewode & his wife Juliana in Cherlwode & Horlee

72(a) Thomas (Er)mener *v.* Peter de Totenham & his wife Emma in Guldeford

14th & 15th *Edward III*

1 Thomas de Pynkhurst & his wife Letice *v.* Walter Pynkhurst in Shire, Shaldeford, Dorkyngg, Neudegate & Houwyke

2 William Glade & his wife Alice *v.* Henry le Bocher in Bromlegh

3 Edmund de Coventre & his wife Margaret by John de Hull *v.* Geoffrey de Hadresham & his wife Alice & their son John in Blecchynlegh

4 John le Parker of Kenyngton *v.* Robert le Taillour of Horeshull & his wife Johanna in Cherteseye

15th *Edward III*

5 Robert Burgeys of Ledrede & his brother John by John

de Ofham *v.* William Marewe & his wife Isabel in Ledrede & Stoke Daberoun

6 Henry Wyssh & his wife Katharine by Henry Wykwan *v.* John de Ryngwode & his wife Juetta in Suthwerk

7 John Moy Flemmyng of London Cyteseyn *v.* John de Sarum of London glover & his wife Cecilia in Southwerk

8 Richard de Rothyng citizen & vintner of London *v.* William Gilbert & his wife Margaret in Wauton, Bechesworth & Leygh

15*th* & 16*th* *Edward III*

17 Richard de Rothyng citizen & vintner of London *v.* William Gerberd & his wife Margery in Wauton, Bechesworth & Legh

20 John Potom of Cranlegh *v.* Henry le Lokiere of Cranlegh & his wife Matilda in Shire

21 Elias de Farnecroft of Banstede *v.* Adam de Farnecroft of Banstede & his wife Cecilia in Kyngeston

16*th* *Edward III*

9 Walter le Gras chivaler *v.* Nicholas de Chynham in Croyndon & Cranham

10 William de Briklesworth & his son John *v.* Robert Swote & his wife Agnes in Suthwerk

11 Thomas de Lincoln by Henry Wykwan *v.* Walter Shakespye & his wife Emma in Wandlesworth

12 John de Croydon of London fishmonger *v.* John de Bures & his wife Johanna in Suthwerk

13 John Bouet & his wife Alice *v.* Henry de Brugeford in Walton, Coveham & Wyssle

14 Adam de Radelee & his wife Matilda *v.* Philip de Aylistone & his wife Katherine in Lamhethe

15 Thomas de Weston senior *v.* Thomas de Weston junior & his wife Johanna in Sende, Merwe & West Clendon

16 Thomas Stote of London fyshmongere *v.* Thomas Malet of Ixnyngge & his wife Agnes in Suthwerk

18 John le Hende & his wife Johanna *v*. Thomas de Moundele & his wife Johanna in Farnham

19 Nicholas Kete & his wife Emma *v*. John de Langgeton vicar of Wandlesworth Church in Heyford & Wandelesworth

16*th* & 17*th* *Edward III*

25 Henry Whissh & his wife Katharine by Henry Wykwan *v*. John Lyon & his wife Alice in Suthwerk

17*th* *Edward III*

22 Isabella de Muskham & John de Hoo chaplain by William de Neubrigg *v*. Ralph Aunger & his wife Isabel in Bletchyngleye

23 John de Fremelesworth & his wife Johanna *v*. William de Wythewell & his wife Alesia in Asshe

24 Adam de Wodeham *v*. John atte Hoke of Cherlewood & his wife Isabel in Certeseye & Horesulle

26 John de Gaynesford & his wife Margery *v*. William de Colverdene & his wife Johanna in Crouhurst

27 William atte Barre & his wife Johanna *v*. John de Radesole & his wife Margaret in Stoke juxta Guldeford

28 Simon de Stonle & his wife Isabel *v*. John Horncastel & his wife Johanna in Kyngeston

29 William de Stanesfeld *v*. Alice widow of John de Walyngford in Egeham & Thorp (John de Walyngford a.s.c.)

30 Peter de Beroudon *v*. William de Dounton & his wife Alice in Ledrede

31 Roger de Suthcote *v*. Robert le Taillour in Horeshulle

32 William de Brewosa & his wife Isabel by Richard Pruet *v*. Robert Gervays & his wife Johanna in Bromlegh

33 Sarra widow of James le Palmere *v*. James le Palmere in Wandlesworth & Batricheseye

34 William de Felyhurst & his wife Alice *v*. William le Scolmaystre chaplain in Est Shaldeford

35 Thomas de Hokkele and his wife Isabel *v*. Amiel de

17—18 EDWARD III.

Sabrichesworth Melleward & his wife Johanna and Roger Berlyng & his wife Matilda in West Dilwysh

36 John de Wythewell & his wife Constance by Richard Pruet *v.* William le Hokere & his wife Johanna in Worplesdon

37 Andrew Braunche chivaler *v.* Henry de Stoghton & his son Thomas & Margaret his wife in Piperhargh

38 Henry atte Knolle & Richard Arnold & his wife Matilda in Shire

39 John de Gaynesford & his wife Margery by John atte Hull *v.* William le Venour & his wife Agnes in Crouhurst

40 Alan de Warewyk & his wife Emma by John atte Hull *v.* John de Shiple & his wife Mabel in Burstowe

41 Adam Lucas of London cyteyn *v.* Walter Turk of London cyteyn & his wife Idonia in Suthwerk & Neweton

42 William de Nytymbre & his wife Margery *v.* Ralph de Hangelton chaplain & Robert le Monek of Rugwyk in Wodeton

43 John de Stonore by William de Poynton *v.* John de Aulton in Camerwell & Pekham

43a Thomas de la Vyne of Certeseye senior & his wife Hawyse & Thomas fil' Thomas de la Vyne & his wife Elena *v.* Robert de Storith vicar of Certeseye Church in Certeseye

44 Thomas de Burgh of London & his wife Cecilia *v.* John Anio of Rippele & his wife Dionisia in Sende

18*th Edward III*

45 Thomas Broun citizen of London & his wife Margaret by Henry Wykwan *v.* Gilbert de Elkinton of London flecchere & his wife Isabel in Hachesham & Camerwell

46 John de Gaynesford & his wife Margery *v.* William atte Bissh & John atte Tunbregg in Crouhurst

47 Walter Frysel & Richard fil' Alan Longy *v.* Peter Maubaunk of Sende and his wife Alice in Bromlegh

48 Gilbert de Ledred & his wife Johanna by Thomas de

Sleford *v.* Richard fil' Henry de Somerbury in Wodeton, Codynton & Ewelle

49 Richard fil' Alan Longy *v.* John atte Lane & his wife Johanna, William Godesfeld & his wife Felicia, Alice Walsheman & Margaret Walsheman in Guldeford & Bromlegh

50 Adam Leuote of London *v.* John Smart of London muneter & his wife Alice in Longeditton and Taleworth

51 John de Wauerchyn *v.* Simon atte Beche of Okham & his wife Emma in Okham

52 Richard de Somerbury *v.* Thomas de Dagworth & his wife Alianor in Somerbury, Codynton, Ewell, Shire & Wodeton

53 Nicholas le Taillour of Certeseye & his wife Agnes *v.* Thomas Slaplegh & his wife Alice in Certesey

54 John Makenheved of London *v.* Robert de Depyng & his wife Margaret in Wandelesworth

55 Robert de Howell & his wife Ela by Gilbert de Berdefeld *v.* William de Cheyham citizen of London & his wife Agnes in West Cheyham

56 Roger parson of Okstede Church & Peter de Escote *v.* Robert de Stangrave chivaler & his wife Johanna in Okstede

57 Thomas de Slaplegh & his wife Alice *v.* Thomas atte Halle of Chabeham & Nicholas le Taillour of Certeseye and his wife Agnes in Certeseye

57a Peter Semere of Guldeford & his wife Tiphania and their daughter Johanna *v.* Henry Gomme of Guldeford & his wife Johanna in Guldeford

58 Nicholas Pynnok clerk *v.* Robert atte More of Suthwerk in Suthwerk and Neuton juxta Suthwerk

17th & 19th *Edward III*

62 Richard Trut & his wife Katharine *v.* Robert Patrik of

Guldeford & his wife Isabel *v*. John de Radesole of Farnham junior & his wife Margaret in Wockyng

63 Henry de Stoghton & his wife Johanna by Henry de Loxlee *v*. Peter atte Wode of Clandon chaplain in Stoghton

18*th* & 19*th* Edward III

59 John de Stangrave chivaler & his wife Johanna by William Neubrigg *v*. Giles atte Ware & his wife Margery in Blecchynggelegh & Katerham

19*th* Edward III

60 John Abbot of Certeseye *v*. Edmound Canoun of Brambelegh & his wife Johanna in Certeseye & Thorp

61 Thomas de Uvedale chivaler & Margaret fil' John de Isdle of Gatecombe by Henry Wykwane *v*. John atte Stokette junior & Richard de Elbrugg in Tycheseye, Chelesham, Lyngfeld & Crouhurst

64 Adam le Tannere of Est Grenestede *v*. Henry Whyssh' & his wife Katharine in Suthwerk

65 Bartholomew de Burghersh chivaler senior *v*. John de Badeselle & his wife Alianor in Ockele, Middelton & Dorkynge

66 Isabel Parnyng by Thomas de Sandeford *v*. Adam de Radelee & his wife Matilda in Lamhethe

67 Richard Pruet & his wife Johanna *v*. Roger Purbyk & his wife Margaret in Guldeford

68 Adam Maunsel of Croydon *v*. William de Hoghelere of Leddred & his wife Alice in Croydon

69 Thomas de Lincoln *v*. Stephen Hauberger of Bodynton & his wife Margery in Wymbelton & Wandelesworth

70 John de Yellyng clerk *v*. William atte Fen of London tableter & his wife Margaret in Suthwerk

71 William de Naples by Thomas de Sleford *v*. Geoffrey West of Worton & his wife Juliana in Kyngeston

72 Adam le Tannere of Estgrensted *v*. John atte Spytele of

Luyton & his wife Alice in Tanregge, Horne & Wolknestede

73 Peter le Beroudon *v.* Thomas fil' John atte Grove of Ledred & his wife Felicia in Ledred

75 John fil' Peter de Purle *v.* Peter atte Wode & Nicholas de Chynham in Sanderstede, Coulesdon, Wodemersthorn, Kersalton, Bedyngton, Micheham, Lyngefeld, Beghenham, Adyngton & Farleye

76 John fil' Peter de Purle & his wife Alice *v.* Peter atte Wode & Nicholas de Chynham in Croyndon, Bedyngton, Burstowe & Horne

78 Henry Whissh & his wife Katharine by Henry Wikwan & Thomas fil' Robert de Michelham & Amisius de Leuesham taillour & his wife Agnes in Suthwerk & Pekham

18th & 20th *Edward III*

79 William Marlyn of Potenham & his wife Matilda *v.* William le Leche in Potenham & Godalmynge

19th & 20th *Edward III*

80 John Lyon & Henry Whissh & his wife Katharine in Southwerk

82 Peter Wodbat & John le Leche *v.* William le Leche & his wife Alice in Potenham & Godalmynge

20th *Edward III*

74 Nicholas fil' John de Chetwode & his wife Alice *v.* John de Chetwode chivaler & his wife Lucy in Preston juxta Benstede

77 Robert de Ledrede *v.* William atte Denne of Horsham & his wife Johanna in Ledrede & Stoke Daberon

81 John de Thorp & his wife Alice *v.* Ralph atte Tyele & his wife Johanna in Egham

83 Henry Gomme *v.* John fil' Reginald de Wyckele in Guldeford

84 William de St. Omer by Thomas de Tochewyk *v.* William

de Grenstede & his wife Johanna in Westhorslegh & Okham

85 Thomas Broun & his wife Margaret v. Henry de Bekewell in Pekham & Camerwell

86 William Chaynel & his wife Alice v. John atte Estmulle & his daughter Juliana & her sisters Johanna & Matilda by Richard Pruet v. John de Wodeford vicar of Wonerhs Church in Shaldeford

87 John de Bodekesham & his daughter Alice v. Richard Cabous & his wife Juliana in Blecchyngleghe

21* *Edward III*

1 William Goldmore & his wife Isabel v. Geoffrey de Upton & his wife Isabel in Wockyng

2 Richard de Wylughby Knight senior & his wife Elizabeth v. Walter de Kenele & his wife Isabel in Bedyngton

3 Geoffrey de Twywell chaplain v. Richard de Felde & John le Mareschal of Changeton in Duntesfold, Bromlegh & Godalmyng

4 Guy de Briane junior v. the Abbot of Certeseye in Bretesgrave

5 Henry de Buxton & his wife Emma v. Edward Toly & his wife Agnes in Kyngeston

6 Reginald le Forester of Bandon v. William Mareys of Micham & his wife Alice in Micham

7 John Elys & his wife Johanna v. Peter le Lavender of Berselegh & his wife Agnes in Leddrede

8 John Pyard of Clone v. Nicholas de Tunstalle & his wife Johanna in Chissendon, Maldon, Kyngeston, Longeditton, Tamisditton, Hoke & Talleworth

9 Henry de Strete citizen & vintner of London v. William de Herle Knight in Miccham & Mordon

10 Richard de Birton v. William atte Burgate & his wife Johanna & William de Pakenham & his wife Lucy in Legh

11 William de Roderham *v.* John de Horne & his wife Alice in Horne

12 Henry del Strete citizen & vintner of London *v.* William Mareys & his wife Alice in Miccham

13 Thomas de Udelicote & Adam de Aldefeld of Henlee chapeleyn *v.* Richard atte Hulle & John de Petresfeld & his wife Alice in Piryford, Sidwode, Wodeham & Horeswell

32 William de Aldestede *v.* Peter Richebele & his wife Isabel in Merstham

33 Richard de Wylughby Knight senior & his wife Elizabeth *v.* Thomas fil' Robert Stout in Kersalton

22nd *Edward III*

14 Richard de Hardebrigg *v.* John Hughelot & his wife Matilda in Waleton

15 John Alfray of Estgrenstede & his wife Agnes *v.* William atte Stret of Bourstowe & his wife Alice & Michael le Vaps & his wife Agnes in Wolknestede

16 Thomas atte Quarrere *v.* Robert le Tollere of Wayflete & his wife Rose in Kyngeston

17 Richard de Potenhale citizen of London and his wife Rose by Henry Wykwan *v.* John de Ebesham & his wife Matilda & Philip le Spenser of Wynbelton & his wife Elizabeth in Wandlesworthe

18 William de Braybrok & his wife Margery *v.* William de Fyndon parson of Est Horslegh Church in West Horslegh

19 John fil' William de Burstowe & his wife Margery by Michael Huet *v.* William Warde of Preston & his wife Juliana in Preston, Banstede & Ewell

21st & 22nd *Edward III*

20 Richard atte Welle *v.* Johanna daughter and one of the heirs of Peter de Heysulle in Chuddynfold

31 William de Carreu & Nicholas de Carreu by Henry Wyke-

wan *v.* William le Smythe of Waddon and his wife Johanna in Bedyngton

37 Richard de Basyngstok goldsmith junior & his wife Patronilla *v.* Nicholas le Blake citizen & vintner of London & his wife Alice in Suthwerk

22nd *Edward III*

21 William de Wyrcestre citizen of London *v.* John Fogel of Suthwerk & his wife Agnes in Suthwerk

22 Richard Earl of Arundel *v.* Roger de London & his wife Alice in Reygate Estbechesworth Horlee & Neudegate

23 Richard de Birton & his wife Johanna by William de Medewell *v.* Adam de Derleton clerk in Legh

24 Henry Maunsel clerk *v.* John fil' Thomas Olyver & his wife Katharine in Croydon & Sanderstede

25 Thomas de Bury *v.* John de Salisbury taillour & his wife Margaret in Aldebrok

26 Oliver Brokas & his wife Margaret *v.* Ralph Hervy of Fynchyngfeld & his wife Margaret in Apse, Waleton, Temseditton & Molseye

27 Hugh de Dalynton & Roger de Farndon & his wife Matilda *v.* John Boys & his wife Johanna in Kyngeston

28 Adam de Podyndenne & his wife Johanna *v.* John fil' John de Rugge junior & John fil' Adam de la Toche in Lyngefeld, Crouhurst & Okstede

29 Richard atte Stret *v.* John atte Stret in Burstowe

30 Ralph de Birton *v.* Robert le Spenser & his wife Alice in Legh

34 Edmund Mabaunk *v.* Peter Mabaunk & his wife Alice in West Clandon

35 Peter atte Wode & his wife Margery by Henry Wikwan *v.* Ferand Manion & his wife Margery in Bedyngton, Kersalton & Wodemersthorne

36 Reginald le Forester of Bandon & his wife Matilda by

Henry Wykwan *v.* Ferand Manion & his wife Margery in Bedyngton & Kersalton

47 Thomas Godard of Micham *v.* Richard Martyn & his wife Mabel in Micham

21st & 23rd *Edward III*

42 Richard de Wylughby senior Knight & his wife Elizabeth *v.* William de Hertforde & his wife Amicia in Bedyngton

22nd & 23rd *Edward III*

38 John fil' John Adrian of Brokham & his wife Margaret *v.* Henry de Frouwyk & William de Fynchyngfelde in Brokham

44 John de Stoghton & his wife Juliana by William de Neubrigg *v.* William fil' William atte Lane of Sutton & his wife Agnes in Stok juxta Guldeford

23rd *Edward III*

39 Margery de Chaumpayn, John de Marlebergh chaplain & William Mortemer *v.* Thomas Mortemer & his wife Johanna in Caterham & Warlyngham

40 Guy de Bryene Knight by Nicholas de Carreu *v.* John de Bures chivaler in Kersalton

41 John Randolph and his wife Elizabeth *v.* Henry de Tytyngge in Farnham & Compton juxta Waverle

43 John de Wyndesore parson of Clyve Church, Edmund de Acres parson of Merstham, Walter de Merstham parson of Lemenesfeld *v.* Nicholas le Frensshe in Tanrugge Wolkestede & Crouhurst

45 Simon fil' Walter atte Churche & Thomas de Michenhale by William de Neubrigg *v.* John de Stoghton & his wife Matilda in Godalmyng, Bromlegh & Catteshull

46 Richard de Notyngham of London mercer *v.* Walter Boys & his wife Katharine in Bernes Esthampton Rokehampton & Puttenhyth

48 Reginald Forester & his wife Matilda & their son William

by Henry Wykwan *v.* Thomas Gylemyn chaplain & Robert Corbet in Bandon

24*th* *Edward III*

49 John Madefray *v.* William Cosyn in Effyngham
50 John Danyel *v.* William Colles & his wife Matilda in Blecchynglegh & Caterham
51 Roger Daber *v.* Robert Aspey & his wife Isolde in Caterham & Blechynglegh
52 The Master of the Hospital of St. Thomas the Martyr of Suthwerk *v.* John Asshebourne & his wife Elizabeth in Suthwerk
53 Henry del Strete of London *v.* Henry le Scrop Knight in Miccham
54 Otto de Grandisson & Theobald de Mounteny by Richard de Norwich *v.* Elias Godard & his wife Alice in Camerwell & Pecham
55 Thomas de Shelveleye *v.* Elias Godard & his wife Alice in Ticheseye & Crouhurst
56 John Adam of Luk citizen of London & his wife Katharine *v.* John Pynselegle of Gene citizen of London & his wife Katharine in Hacchesham
57 John de Burton parson of Market Overton Church *v.* Thomas de Sumpton of London chaundeler & his wife Margaret in Bermundeseye
58 William de Tudenham citizen & mercer of London *v.* Edmund de Coventre & his wife Margery in Blecchyngleye
59 Thomas de Uvedale & his wife Margaret by Richard de Ellebrugg *v.* Elias Goddard & his wife Alice in Ticheseye
60 John Roce of London fisshemonger *v.* Henry Flemyng & his wife Alice & her sister Margaret in Suthwerk
61 John Suwell of Wandelesworth & his wife Emma by Robert Fyneford *v.* Robert le Hyrde & William Curdhope in Wandelesworth

62 John de Wyndesore clerk *v.* John de Asshebourn & his wife Elizabeth in Suthwerk
63 Nicholas atte Welle *v.* John fil' Roger de Kent & his wife Isabel in Waldyngham & Chelesham

22nd & 24th *Edward III*

64 John fil' Nicholas atte Welle *v.* Robert de Sellyng in Chelesham

24th *Edward III*

65 Robert Fyneford *v.* John de Chestre & his wife Agnes in Wandlesworth
66 John de Wyndesore clerk *v.* John le Porter of Berkyngge & his wife Alice in Suthwerk

25th *Edward III*

67 William Cosyn & his wife Johanna *v.* John Madefray in Effyngham
68 John Mounkoy citizen & fishmonger of London & his wife Alice *v.* William Rolf of Kyngeston & his wife Agnes, Peter Vale & his wife Johanna & Richard Hardyng of Kyngeston & his wife Agnes in Kyngeston & Surbeton
69 John de Baddeby clerk *v.* John de Vautort & his wife Johanna in West Shene
70 John Chene of Tortyngton *v.* John de Shirbourn & his wife Katharine in Merewe
71 Simon Plomere *v.* John Fisshere & his wife Alice in Suthwerk & Pekham
72 Richard Freland of Ockham *v.* Richard atte Churchegate & his wife Beatrice in Ocham & Coveham
73 Richard de Lyftwych & his wife Isabel *v.* John Goythur chaplain & Robert Corbet in Bedyngton & Micham
74 William Menne clerk *v.* John Fisshere of Aillesford & his wife Alice in Suthwerk & Camerwell
75 John de Tamworth *v.* John de Salford of Wakerle & his wife Alice in Miccham, Bedynton, Bandon & Waleton
76 Richard Doxhey & his wife Alice *v.* Roger Bernard & his

wife Katharine & William atte Twychene in Horesulle Chabeham & Pyreford

24th & 26th Edward III

82 William de Notton & John de Fourneux *r.* Thomas le Latimer of Carleton in Lyndrik chivaler in Wodeton

26th Edward III

77 Walter de Grendon & William Moryn *r.* Gilbert de Beauchamp & his wife Juliana in Kyngeston

78 John Fencote & Alan le Hattere of London & his wife Amicia in Carsalton

79 Adam de Podydene *r.* William Neubrugge & Roger Daber in Lyngefeld Crouhurst & Okstede

80 William de Lambhith clerk *v.* Thomas de Durele clerk in Suthwerk & Bermondeseye

80 (a) Robert de Denton chaplain *r.* John de Yakesley & his wife Alice in Suthewerk

81 John de Worldham *r.* Robert de Chusendale in Chudyngefold

83 John de Worstede of London & John Fauconer chaplain *v.* Henry de Bekewell & his wife Agnes in Camerwell

84 Salamon Faunt citizen & fellemongere of London *r.* John Dyueyn & his wife Matilda in Niewyngton

85 Gilberte le Hunte of Longe Ditton *v.* Adam Spicer & his wife Johanna in Temseditton

86 Robert de la Puylle and his wife Margaret by William Neubrigg *v.* Cristina widow of Fremond Inge and William Watford and his wife Mariota in Newedegate and Charlewode

87 William de Hatfeld chaundeler *r.* Thomas le Whyte and his wife Margery in Suthwerk and Newenton

88 Robert de Eldynge and his wife Nicholaa *v.* Thomas Basket and his wife Isabel in Croydon

89 Robert Swote citizen and fishmonger of London and his wife Agnes and William fil' William Swote and his wife

Katharine *v.* Roger de Boresworth chaplain in Suthwerk

90 John de Stodeye and Robert de Ramseye *v.* Herlewin de Houweton citizen and vintner of London and his wife Amicia in Southwerk

27*th* *Edward III*

91 Walter de Fryland clerk *v.* Thomas Orgar and his wife Alice in Suthwerk

92 William Gras and his wife Cristiana *v.* William de Notton and his wife Isabel in Suthwerk

93 Peter Noreys of Fecham *v.* John de Asshebrok and his wife Alice in Fecham

94 Richard Markwyk *v.* John de Asshebrok and his wife Alice in Ledrede

94a Ralph de Halstede citizen and woolmonger London and his wife Cristina *v.* Thomas de Mortymer Knight and his wife Isabel in Lenehurst

94b Thomas de Mortuo Mary chivaler *v.* John de Wythewell and his wife Matilda in Caterham and Werlingham

95 Nicholas Pynnok clerk *v.* William de Spridlyngton and Thomas de Hockele in Suthwerk and Neuton juxta Suthwerk

96 Robert de Eldyngge citizen and vintner of London and his wife Nicholaa *v.* Reginald Tayllour and his wife Isabel in Croydon and Adynton

97 William Holbech of London draper *v.* Henry de Bokewell and his wife Agnes in Camerwell

98 William de Clynton Earl of Huntyngdon *v.* Roger de Notyngham and his wife Matilda in Hamme

99 John Halyday of Weybrigge *v.* John Derlyng and his wife Alice in Waleton super Tamisiam

100 John de Blonham of Suthwerk and his wife Cristina by John de Ofham *v.* Henry de Ebor of London smyth and his wife Alice in Suthwerk

101 Elias de Braghynge of Southwerk and Laurence de Merkyngfeld of Newynton *v.* Nicholas atte Fen of Ingworth and his wife Margaret and Robert Hereward of Eylesham and his wife Agnes in Southwerk

102a John Pollowe *v.* Reginald de Wodham in Waybruge

102b Nicholas atte Helde of Farnham and his wife Johanna by John Crukerne *v.* John atte Chaumbre and his wife Johanna in Farnham

103 William de Careu Portioner in Bedyngton Church and Nicholas de Careu *v.* Roger Pylgrym and his wife Agnes in Bedyngton

104 Robert atte Doune of Wandlesworthe *v.* William Jacob of Guldeford Soutere and his wife Alice in Wandlesworthe

105 Simon Plomer of Southwerk *v.* John Fisshere of Aldeford and his wife Alice in Southwerk

26th & 28th *Edward III*

106 Robert atte Doune of Wandlesworthe *v.* Robert de Stratford citizen and shoemaker of London and his wife Dionis in Suthwerk

28th *Edward III*

107 John atte Water and his wife Edith *v.* Thomas Walle and his wife Emma in Padyngden and Ockele

108 Nicholas atte Helde and his wife Johanna *v.* John atte Chaumbre and his wife Johanna in Farnham

109 Henry Lechford and Thomas le Freynssh *v.* Robert de Howell and his wife Ela in West Cheyham

110 Nicholas atte Hatche *v.* John de Melkesope and his wife Margery in Nutfeld

2 John Maltesone *v.* Richard Redhond and his wife Alice in Bromlegh

25th & 29th *Edward III*

6 Nicholas de Lageham and his wife Margaret *v.* Roger fil' John de St. John of Lageham chivaler in Lageham, Mereden and Wolknestede and afterward between

Nicholas de Lageham and Peter de St. John next of kin and heir of Roger de St. John

28th & 29th *Edward III*

10 Walter Wodelond of Guldeford *v.* Thomas Osebarn of Wassyngham and his wife Margaret in Guldeford, Stoke juxta Guldeford, Ertyngdon, Merwe and Wokkynge

29th *Edward III*

1 John de Rokwyk *v.* Walter Pernersh and his wife Johanna and Simon atte Nore and his wife Juliana and Simon Mabonk and his wife Alice in Shire

3 John Rose and his wife Cristina *v.* John atte Dene of Aldebury in Ertyngdon

4 Simon Ropere of Croydon *v.* Thomas Birchedenne and his wife Cecilia in Croydon

5 Adam Geffray of Horsham and his wife Letice *v.* William le Rideler of Horsham in Ruggewyk, Cranlee, Shaldeford and Dorkyngg

7 John de Saghiere de la Capele and his wife Johanna by Walter de Warnham *v.* Adam Pynkehurst and his wife Johanna and Adam Geffray of Horsham and his wife Letice in Dorkyngg and Becchesworth

8 Nicholas de Slyfeld *v.* Robert Wynepol of London and his wife Alice in Great Bokham

9 William atte Smyth and his wife Matilda *v.* John de Okhurst of Wysbergh in Bromlee

11 Thomas Babbe of Kyngeston and his wife Agnes by William de Neubrigge *v.* William Fitzmichel and his wife Johanna in Suthwerk.

30th *Edward III*

12 John de Hampton parson of All Saints' Church 'ad Fenum' London *v.* John Dyveyn clerk and his wife Matilda in Newenton

13 John de Rothyng of London mercer *v.* John de Suwell of Wandelesworth and his wife Emma in Wandelesworth

14 Richard fil' Roger atte Lane and his wife Margery by Robert de Nethersole *v.* John Page of Kyngeston super Tamisiam and his wife Alice in Wandelesworth

15 Bartholomew Frestelyng citizen of London *r.* Roger de Wyth and his wife Agnes in Batrichsaye

16 John de Rothyng and his wife Emma by William de Neubrugge *r.* Walter Elys of Hendon and his wife Alice in Wandelesworth

17 Henry de Stoughton and his wife Johanna by William de Neubrigg *r.* William Dunmowe chaplain in Guldeford, Sende and Stoke juxta Guldeford

18 Thomas Dolsely and his wife Johanna *r.* Henry de Bekwell and his wife Agnes in Camerwell

18a William Danel of Bromblegh *v.* Walter fil' Adam de Bursebrigg and his wife Alice in Godalmyng

19 Richard Burgeys of London and his wife Johanna *r.* Gilbert Burgeys of Ledred and his wife Johanna in Cudyngton and Ewell

20 Thomas Keynes clerk and William de Bugbrigge clerk *v.* Elias Asselyn and his wife Margery in Wandlesworth

21 Richard fil' Richard de Bursebrigg *r.* William Wysdom and his wife Juliana in Godalmyng.

31*st* *Edward III*

22 Thomas Fissh of Suthwerk hosyere and his wife Alice *v.* Ralph Grynford citizen and goldsmith of London and his wife Matilda in Suthwerk

23 Henry Lechford *v.* Laurence Herfray and his wife Matilda in Cherlewode

31*st* *and* 32*nd* *Edward III*

24 John de Gaynesford *r.* John Sogehamme and his wife Margery in Crowhurst and Lyngefeld.

32*nd* *Edward III*

25 John de Briklesworth of London *r.* Reginald de Langeton

of Wandelesworth and his wife Florence in Wandelesworth

26 Philip de Hamme and his wife Agnes by John de Rouleye *v.* John atte Lythe and Richard de Heghfeld in Hamme

27 John de Dighton and his wife Hawise by her guardian Thomas de Stapelho *v.* Alan le Botiller of Cherteseye and his wife Juliana in Coveham, Horle, Okham and Walton

28 Richard Webbe and his wife Matilda by William de Neubrigg *v.* Robert Nowel and his wife Alice in Bromlegh

29 Henry atte Stonhouse of Guldeford *v.* William atte Barre of Guldeford in Guldeford and Stoke juxta Guldeford

30 Hamelin fil' Sampson de Matham *v.* Sampson de Matham in Muleseye

31 Richard Sankhurst and his brother William *v.* Elias Burgoyne of Brokham and his wife Juliana in Brokham

32 Walter le Hakkere of Iwehurst *v.* William de Wyntryngham and his wife Johanna in Gomshulne

33 Richard de Boxhale *v.* William Sergeant and his wife Matilda in Shire

34 John atte Bere *v.* John Scamaile and his wife Sibil in Dorkynge

35 John Ismongere *v.* Robert Brabasun and his wife Masera in Blecchyngelegh

33rd *Edward III*

36 John de Okebourne and his wife Margery *v.* John Wenbrigge and his wife Johanna in Kyngeston super Tamisiam

37 Henry Bocher of Bromle *v.* John Godard and his wife Alice in Kyngeston super Tamisiam

32nd *and* 33rd *Edward III*

38 Roger de Haghe *v.* Robert de Loxeleye and his wife Margaret in Suthwerk and Retherhythe

39 Margaret Burdeyn and John her son *v.* John de Canefeld chaplain in Suthwerk

33rd Edward III

40 John de Wysebech junior *v.* Simon de Dryfeld and his wife Isabel in Kyngeston super Tamisiam

41 The King *v.* William fil' John de Molyns Knight and his wife Margery in Henle juxta Guldeford

42 Johanna de Burton *v.* Richard de Podenhale and his wife Margaret in Wandlesworth and Bachericheseye

43 John de Bryghtlamton and his wife Johanna *v.* William le Chernere parson of Worplesden Church and Richard Pole chaplain in Puryfryght

44 John atte Bere and his wife Johanna *v.* Peter Pirie and his wife Alice in Newdegate

45 Richard de Asshurst *v.* Gilbert de Ledred and his wife Johanna in Wodeton and Ockelegh

46 William Calke chaplain *v.* John de Molond and his wife Agnes in Reygate

47 Richard le Webbe of Cranlegh *v.* John Lygard of Clendon and his wife Disoria in Shire

48 Gilbert de Leddrede *v.* John Boltford and his wife Margaret in Leddrede and Asshestede

49 Robert Garkyn and his wife Johanna *v.* Philip de Upton and Richard de Lyntesford chaplain in Wandesworth

50 Nicholas le Pulter *v.* John le Taillour of Eghtham and his wife Alice in Lymnesfeld and Lygnefeld

32nd & 34th Edward III

62 John de Bourstalle citizen and vintner of London *v.* Salaman Faunt citizen and felmongere of London and his wife Matilda in Newenton Lambhuth and Southwerk

33rd and 34th Edward III

51 Nicholas de Slefeld *v.* John Boltford and his wife Margaret in Leddrede and Asshestede

34th Edward III

52 William atte Brugg clerk *v.* Walter Norman and his wife Johanna in Northlamhuth

53 Richard Dane *v.* Thomas de Lincoln citizen and goldsmith of London and his wife Johanna in Lyngefeld

54 Stephen Child and his wife Isabel *v.* William Trigge of Batricheseye and his wife Emma in Batricheseye

55 William Cherde and his wife Isabel *v.* Walter Norman and his wife Johanna in Northlambeheth

56 William de Crokford *v.* Thomas de Welles and his wife Odierna in Wodham

57 William de Burton citizen and goldsmith of London *v.* John fil' John de Leycestr in Cherteseye and Egeham

58 Robert Rundel of Kyngestone and his wife Juliana *v.* Thomas le Carpenter of Kyngeston senior and his wife Johanna in Kyngestone

59 Thomas de Ronthhale and his wife Margery *v.* William de Langeley of Rikmeresworth and his wife Alice in Feecham Stoke Dabernoun and Pachenesham

60 Ralph le Hert of Kersaulton *v.* John Withewell and his wife Matilda in Kersaulton

61 Thomas atte Hurst and his wife Alice *v.* Walter Prou of Papeworth and his wife Agatha in Bourgham

63 John atte Roughebern chaplain and John atte Hall of Est Clandon *v.* Richard atte Pleystowe and his wife Alice in Esthorslegh

64 Philip de Herlawe citizen and armourer of London and his wife Agnes *v.* William atte Castelle hauberger & citizen of London and his wife Isabel in Suthwerk juxta London

65 John fil' Robert Folvyll and Margery widow of William atte Feen *v.* Simon le Plomer and John Typet in Suthwerk

66 John Colneye of Kyngeston *v.* Thomas Carpenter of Kyngeston senior and his wife Johanna in Kyngeston super Tamisian

67 Philip Rauns *v.* Richard atte Hegge and his wife Johanna in Worplesdon

68 John Gargat of Bedynton *v.* Richard Kyng of Croydon and his wife Hawise in Croydon

69 Walter de Twyneham *v.* Simon de Clopton of Walden and his wife Isabel in Kyngeston super Thamisiam

71 William Brown baker of Suthwerk and his wife Johanna *v.* John Broun and his wife Sarra in Lambhith and Camerwell

72 Ralph le Pope of Wyndlesham *v.* Walter atte Pole of Chabeham and his wife Johanna in Wyndelesham

35*th Edward III*

70 Thomas atte Fynersh and his wife Alice *v.* Walter atte Hoo of London skynnere and his wife Alice in Horlee

73 William de St. Omer *v.* Richard Dent and his wife Agnes in Okham and Sende

74 John de Wolhampton and his wife Johanna *v.* Thomas Johan vicar of Wolkenestede Church in Wolkenestede Tanerigge and Blechynglye

75 Walter Nappere of Suthwerk *v.* William Cras of Suthwerk and his wife Cristina in Suthwerk

76 John de Watford and his wife Margaret by Thomas de Bledelawe *v.* Henry Colas of Guldeford taverner and his wife Johanna in Stoke juxta Guldeford

77 William de Debenham sergeant of the Lord King *v.* Thomas Russham of Egham junior and his wife Hawise in Certeseye

36*th Edward III*

78 Richard Earl of Arundel by Walter de Warnham *v.* Walter atte Howe and his wife Alice in Reygate

79 Richard atte Dene and his wife Cristina *v.* John Broun and his wife Sarra in Northlambhith

80 William Tirwhit clerk *v.* Robert Ruch— and his wife Margery in Suthwerk

81 Thomas Cook clerk Thomas Jekes clerk Robert de Chaddesle clerk and Adam de Hadresham by Walter de

Warnham *v.* Henry Mot of Waldon and his wife Alice in Kersalton and Micham

82 John Muryweder and his wife Alice by William de Warnham *r.* Walter Hackere and his wife Agatha in Shaldeford, Gomshelne, Wodeton, Dorkyngg and Bromlegh

83 Bernard Brokas clerk *r.* Walter de Hamme and his wife Agnes in Bromlyghe

84 Nicholas de Carreu and Johanna widow of Andrew de Bekenesfeld *r.* Henry Mot and his wife Alice in Bedyngton and Wodecote

85 Walter le Smyth of Kyngeston *r.* John de Lychefeld and his wife Alice & John Joye and his wife Juliana in Kyngeston

86 Robert Garkyn and his wife Johanna by Richard Heryng *r.* John Sely in Wandesworth

87 Richard le Dyghere and his wife Alice *r.* Henry le Muleward and his wife Alice in Kyngeston super Tamisiam

88 Adam Sleddale clerk *v.* Thomas Shordych and his wife Amicia in Wymbeldon

89 Adam atte Wode *r.* William Godsub and his wife Isabel in Batricheseye

90 John de Mokkyng citizen and vintner of London and his wife Alice by Richard de Fifhid *r.* William de Kyngeston citizen and fishmonger of London and his wife Alianor in Southwerk

91 Richard atte Wyle *r.* John Cokogh and his wife Juliana in Bromlegh

92 John atte Greuette *r.* Richard Doxeye and his wife Sabina in Horeshull, Chabeham, Waleton, Cherteseye & Pureford

93 William Ivory citizen & butcher of London *r.* John de Caversham of Hertford & his wife Johanna in Suthewerk

37th *Edward III*

94 Richard de Chesham citizen of London & John Forster chaplain *v*. Richard de Lambhithe & his wife Agnes in Suthewerk

95 Robert de Denton chaplain & Thomas Brown *v*. John de Tichefeld of Suthwerk & his wife Matilda in Suthwerk

96 Adam Cosyn *v*. John Morvile & his wife Felicia in Shire

97 Nicholas de Carreu *v*. Elizabeth widow of Richard de Wylughby Knight in Bedyngton

98 Peter Semere *v*. John Semere of Guldeford & his wife Isabel in Guldeford, Stoke juxta Guldeford & Worplesdon

99 Simon atte Churche of Slyfeld *v*. John Semere & his wife Isabel in Bromlegh, Slyfeld, Stoke juxta Guldeford & Werplesdon

100 Edward Prince of Aquitaine & Wales & his wife Johanna *v*. Eustace Dabrichcourt & his wife Elizabeth in Wokkynge, Sutton & Baggeshote

101 John Fot *v*. Robert de Appelby & his wife Alice in Michham

102 William de Neudegate & Henry Leccheford *v*. John Reynald of Cranle & his wife Mabel in Cherlwode

103 Master John Goseden, Thomas fil' John Hochard William Berard and Richard Pruet of Guldeford by Walter de Warnham *v*. John Hochard & his wife Alice in Shaldeford, Bromlegh & Clandon

104 Thomas Mounteney, Robert Burle & John Corpsty citizens and mercers of London *v*. Nicholas atte Cruch of London & his wife Agnes in Suthwerk

105 William Goldemor of Wokkynge *v*. John de Lotegereshale & his wife Matilda in Wokkynge & Sende

106 William de Northbury & his wife Johanna *v*. Thomas Serle & his wife Agnes in Suthwerk

107 Nicholas Wavendon chaplain *v*. Andrew Pykeman & his wife Johanna in Lambheth & Suthwerk

108 Mathew Redmane *v.* William Filiol & his wife Mary in Neobright

109 Thomas Balle of Kyngeston *v.* John Burgeys of Kyngeston & his wife Margery in Kyngeston

110 Thomas Parker and his wife Emma *v.* William le Duc & John Fynch in Batricheseye

38th *Edward III*

111 Robert Base and his son William & daughter Agnes by Robert Norwych their guardian *v.* John de Levedale & his wife Johanna in Chelesham

112 Richard Totehale & his wife Agnes by John Rous *v.* Nicholas Thurbarn & his wife Beatrice in Horsull

113 William Reson of Bandon *v.* Nicholas Fissher & his wife Johanna in Bandon

114 William de Hamptede citizen & pepperer of London *v.* John Boydon bocher citizen of London & his wife Alice in Southwerk

115 William Harkestede & his wife Agnes *v.* William atte Sydney & his wife Katharine in Bromlegh & Cranleye

116 Richard Earl of Arundell & Surrey by Walter de Warnham *v.* John de Levedale & his wife Johanna in Gatton

117 Peter atte Wode *v.* John Mershton & his wife Scolastica in Wodemeresthorn

118 William de Sleford clerk *v.* John Goderyk in Suthwerk

119 John de Bursebrugg & his wife Rose *v.* Walter de Hamme & his wife Agnes in Somerbury

120 Walter Selot chaplain *v.* Thomas Lumbard & his wife Matilda in Guldeford, Shaldeford, Ertyngdon & Stoke juxta Guldeford

121 Michael de Ponynges chivaler *v.* John Tournour of Suthewerk bocher & his wife Johanna in Suthwerk

37th and 39th *Edward III*

2 Richard Chanri of Oksted *v*. Roger Edlon of Kyngeston on Thames & his wife Emma in Oksted

38th and 39th *Edward III*

3 John de (Ge)ttelee *v*. Henry le Webbe atte Stretende of Borden & his wife Felicia in Godalmyngg

10a Thomas le Heyr *v*. Robert Nowell & his wife Matilda in Shire

39th *Edward III*

1 Thomasina widow of John de Dageworth chivaler *v*. Roger Fynch & his wife Alice in Wandlesworth & Batriseye

4 Robert Raven & his wife Johanna *v*. John Mowbray of the Island of Axiholm chivaler & his wife Elizabeth in Suthwerk

5 John de Kenyngton *v*. Richard de Gadynton & his wife Alice in Cherteseye

6 John Clerk polter & citizen of London *v*. John Pope chaundeler & citizen of London & his wife Johanna in Cudyngton & Ewelle

7 Ralph Thurbarn *v*. William Reynold sherman & his wife Johanna and Henry Broun & his wife Isabella in Kyngeston & Longditton

11 John le Hore of Croydon, Brice le Tanner of Croydon *v*. William de Burghersh & his wife Alice in Bristowe, Nuttefeld, Croydon, Horne & Caterham

40th *Edward III*

8 Henry Colas taverner & his wife Johanna & their son Walter by Walter de Warnham *v*. Robert Hollewey of Worplesdon & his wife Margaret in Guldeford

9 William de Neudegate *v*. Richard Talbot & his wife Alice in Neulond & Hocklegh

10 John Greneholde & his wife Isabella *v*. William (Cul)ham of London & his wife Agnes in Kyngeston on Thames

12 Robert de Bonebroke *v*. Richard le Taillour of Cherteseye

& his wife Margaret & John Child & his wife Matilda in Shakelford

13 Robert de Denton chaplain *v.* John de Yakeslee & his wife Alice in Suthwerk

14 Walter atte Grene citizen of London *v.* John Clerk pulter & citizen of London & his wife Alice in Cudyngton & Ewelle

15 Robert de Loxle & his wife Margaret by John Hemery *v.* William Seward & his wife Sibil in Polstede & Compton

16 Richard Earl of Arundel & Surrey by Walter de Warnham *v.* Walter Scamaille & his wife Dionis in Brokham

17 William de Sandford junior *v.* William de Weston & his wife Johanna in Suthwerk

18 William de Cottesdon & his wife Johanna & Isabella daughter of William *v.* Richard fil' Richard le Cartere in Sende

19 John de Chaddesle & his wife Cristina *v.* Henry atte Gate of Merton in Suthwerk

40th and 41st *Edward III*

23 Robert atte Lote & his wife Alice by John Hemery *v.* Richard Peshauwe of Dorkyng & his wife Agnes in Hedleghe

41st *Edward III*

20 Richard de Thoron clerk *v.* William de Wyghton & his wife Katharine iu Suthwerk

21 John de Clynton by Simon de Lichefeld *v.* Richard Ponte & his wife Johanna in Suthwerk

22 John Duk of Cherteseye *v.* Henry Alfat & his wife Johanna in Certeseye

24 Henry atte Helde of Blecchynglegh *v.* Andrew Bagod of Blecchynglegh & his wife Alice in Blecchynglegh

41st and 42nd *Edward III*

27 Nicholas de Slyfelde *v.* Nicholas atte Houke & his wife Hawise *v.* Walter Rykoun & his wife Alice in Bokham

42nd *Edward III*

25 William de Guldeford *v.* Master Robert Danhurst & his wife Agnes in Ertyngdon & Guldeford

26 John de Cherteseye *v.* Richard Cadyngton of Brokesbourn & his wife Alice in Cherteseye

28 John de Mockyng & his wife Alice & Martin fil' William le Clerc of Felbrygg *v.* Roger de Shirbrok of Plumstede & his wife Margaret in Suthwerk

29 John de Colney senior *v.* John Wynchestre & his wife Emma in Walton on Thames

30 John de Asshburnham & his wife Johanna *v.* Laurence Benstede & his wife Agnes in Lyngfeld

31 William Topy *v.* Thomas Conners & his wife Elena in Great Bokham

32 Roger atte Wode carpenter, Roger Chaunce of Reygate, Robert atte Wodehacche Adam le Tanner of Horlie *v.* Stephen Wasthuse of London girdeler & his wife Margaret in Horlee

33 Katharine fil' Robert de Danhurst *v.* Robert de Danhurst in Certesey Thorp & Egham

34 John le Parkere & his wife Alice *v.* Reginald de Lokedon & his wife Alice in Ewell

35 Katharine fil' Robert de Danhurst *v.* Thomas de Russham & his wife Hawise in Egham & Certesey

36 Bernard Brocas clerk *v.* John Chapman vicar of Godalmynge & Geoffrey Edyth chaplain in Piperharwe

37 John Boyle *v.* James de Inyngfeld & his wife Dionisia in Lyngefeld

38 William de Neudegate *v.* John de Garton & his wife Margaret in Newelond and Ockelegh

39 Richard Dane of Lyngefeld *v.* Richard Willam & his wife Agnes in Lyngefeld

40 John Boyle *v.* William Wodye of Grenstede & his wife Dionisia in Lyngefeld

46 Robert Brokhull of Suthwerk *v.* John Thoursway citizen & fisshmonger of London & his wife Agnes in Suthwerk

43rd *Edward III*

41 Thomas Cartere *v.* Robert Bures in Effyngham

42 Ralph atte Watre *v.* William Bedel of Fynchamstede & his wife Avice in Chabeham & Cherteseye

43 Robert de Wetherdeleye clerk & Walter de Multon clerk *v.* Roger atte Strete citizen and mercer of London & his wife Johanna in Wandelesworth

44 John de Wadelehurst & Stephen de Wadelehurst *v.* Adam de Wadelehurst & his wife Agnes in Themese ditton & Long ditton

44a Walter Smyth of Kyngeston on Thames & his son John *v.* John Wysbech junior of Kyngeston on Thames & his wife Alice

45 Walter Whithors *v.* John de Weston citizen & baker of London & his wife Idonia in Benchesham

47 Richard Hurt *v.* John Toly of Chydynggefold & his wife Alice in Chydynggefold

48 Robert Rus citizen of London & his wife Katharine *v.* John Quyntyn of Shorne in Suthwerk

49 John Colneye senior *v.* William Melbourn & his wife Margaret in Haverychesham & Walton on Thames

50 John fil' Thomas Coumbe of Reygate *v.* William Waleys & his wife Agnes in Reygate

51 William Mose & John Okwod & his wife Alice in Cranleye

52 John de Pottenhethe of Kyngeston & his wife Margaret *v.* John Wysebeche & his wife Alice in Kyngeston on Thames

53 John Cok of Godalmyng clerk, John Melersh *v.* Robert Bonebrok & his wife Isabel in Poteham, Compton, Farnham, Chudyngefolde & Godalmyng

54 John de Hermesthorp clerk & John de Ravenser clerk *v.* Adam Forester & his wife Alice in Egham

55 Richard de Wydden *v.* John Vyncent & his wife Alice in Bedyngton & Cassalton
56 Nicholas Exton & John Rous *v.* Robert Lytle & his wife Johanna in Camberwell
56a Ralph Thurbarn *v.* John atte Church & his wife Emma in Kyngeston & Longditton
57 Richard Gonayre of Egeham *v.* Henry Page of Warefeld & his wife Agnes in Egeham
67 Roger parson of Sutton Church & Henry atte Gate *v.* John de Tamworth in Bedynton, Bandon, Waleton & Micham

43rd and 44th *Edward III*

66 William de Walleworth citizen & alderman of London, Master Richard de Warmyngton junior, Ralph de Horlete chaplain *v.* William de Culham citizen of London & his wife Agnes in Kyngeston on Thames
68 John Farman chaplain *v.* Walter Chapman vicar of Dorkyng Church *v.* Robert Sebarn & his wife Margaret & William Baldewyne & his wife Alice in Dorkyng
73 John de York of Croydon *v.* Nicholas Mymmys & his wife Emma in Croydon

44th *Edward III*

58 William Neuport citizen & fishmonger of London *v.* Walter Norman & his wife Agnes in Lambheth
59 James Andreu by Richard Wylden *v.* Ralph Double & his wife Alice in Suthewerk
60 John de Whitewell & Thomas Pernel chaplain *v.* Robert de Fynefford of Wandelesworth & his wife Alice in La Doune
61 John atte Hale & William Knappere *v.* Adam Ermyte & his wife Agnes in Horne
62 William Weggewode of Saundrestede *v.* Adam Lyndon in Saundrestede
63 Ralph Gundewyne & his wife Agnes *v.* Henry Brokwode & his wife Matilda in Horisull

64 Peter atte Wode & his wife Laurence by William Olmestede *v.* John atte Wode clerk & Edmund Guonshale clerk in Bedyngton, Kershalton & Wodemeresthorne

65 Ralph Lorchon & his wife Juliana *v.* Nicholas Thurbarn & his wife Beatrice in Horishull

69 Thomas Basset *v.* Laurence de Bedenstede & his wife Agnes in Chelsham

70 Richard de Wydden *v.* Henry de Wydden & his wife Agnes in Bedyngton & Carsaulton

71 William de Walleworth citizen & alderman of London & his wife Margaret by Hugh de Westwyk *v.* John de Weston citizen & bread-seller of London & his wife Idonia in Suthewerk

72 William de Walleworth citizen & alderman of London & his wife Margaret by Hugh de Westwyk *v.* John de Foxton citizen & apothecary of London and his wife Johanna in Suthwerk

74 William Wortyngge of Bansted *v.* William Culham citizen of London & his wife Agnes in Banstede

75 William de Walleworth citizen & alderman of London & his wife Margaret *v.* John Folevill & his wife Mary in Hacchesham & Peccham

76 John Page & Adam atte Water *v.* Thomas de Wylforde of London fishmonger & his wife Cristina in Suthwerk & Bermondeseye

79 Adam Pynkhurst *v.* John Puttuk & his wife Margaret & Emerus Puttuk & his wife Isabella in Bromlegh

80 Roger Lumbard *v.* Matilda fil' Alan Herman of Gyldeford in Gyldeford, Shaldeford, Bromle & Stoke juxta Gyldeford

45th *Edward III*

77 John de Uvedale *v.* Thomas Beuchamp chivaler & his wife Johanna in Suthwerk

78 John de Hadresham *v.* Thomas de Stopundon & his wife Elizabeth in Lyngefeld & Crouhurst

81 Thomas de Middleton *v*. Richard de Lakenham & his wife Cristina in Miccham
82 Gilbert de Despenser chivaler *v*. Richard Jolyf & his wife Beatrice in Feccham
83 William atte Lee & his wife Isabella *v*. Nicholas de Reynham & his wife Alesia in Clopham
84 Walter atte Broke & his wife Agnes *v*. Robert le Kyng of Guldeford carpenter & his wife Matilda in Guldeford
85 John Legg *v*. Roger Goghemere & his wife Alice in Merwe
86 Roger Tonebrugge & John Ismongre *v*. Henry atte Pyrie & his wife Agnes in Crouhurst & Lyngfeld
87 William Walsshe *v*. Stephen Edolfi & his wife Beatrice in Chorlwode
89 William atte Bisshe & his sister Agnes *v*. John Capenore & his wife Isabella in Horne
93 Richard atte Leye of Adynton *v*. Richard atte Stulpe citizen of London & his wife Isabella in Horne

46th Edward III

90 Willlam Fitz-Johan *v*. Robert Danhurst & his wife Agnes in Hamme
91 John Chesere of Chedyngfold *v*. John Martyn of Tydd St Giles in Cambridgeshire & his wife Emma in Clopton
91a William atte Cornere of Kyngeston *v*. Nicholas (Bla)were of Kyngeston & his wife Matilda in Kyngeston on Thames
92 Nicholas Carreu William Tank, William Hoghton, John Olyver junr. John Mokkyng senior, John Mokkyng junior & Nicholas Mokkyng by William Hoghton *v*. Reginald Haywode of New Sarum & his wife Agnes in Suthwerk
94 John Burdon chaplain & Thomas de Pathorn *v*. William Braynt citizen of London & his wife Alice in Kyngeston on Thames
95 John Lorchun & John atte Bradeford of Chabeham *v*. John atte Watere of Chabeham & his wife Johanna & their daughter Matilda in Chabeham

96 John atte Mere *v.* Robert atte Shagh & his wife Agnes & William atte Lynde & his wife Beatrice in Horlee & Cherlwode

97 Robert Solace *v.* Richard atte Vyne of Suthwerk & his wife Johanna in Suthwerk

98 Walter de Freland clerk *v.* Henry Wylewes clerk in Ockam, Coveham & Sende

99 William Cressewyk & Nicholas Potyn *v.* John de Hampton of London skynnere & Alianor one of the daughters & heirs of John Stoket in Okestede & Tatlesfeld

100 Walter Mareschal & his wife Alice by William Chivaler *v.* John Aldenham & his wife Alice in Suthwerk

101 Henry fil' Mark Husee Knight & his wife Margaret *v.* Richard Ardern citizen & skinner of London & his wife Alice in Bermondeseye

102 John Hethere of Lyngefeld & his wife Agnes *v.* Richard atte Pende & his wife Johanna in Lyngefeld

104 John Fayrehere of Southwerk & his wife Margaret *v.* John Wardedu & Thomas Pathorn in Southwerk

105 John Person & John Sherman of Camerwell & his wife Cristina in Bromlegh & Catteshulle

106 Robert Taverner of Kyngeston on Thames & his wife Idonia *v.* William Culham citizen & merchant of London & his wife Agnes in Kyngeston on Thames

107 Richard Bonvalet *v.* Thomas Leuesone & his wife Agnes in Cherteseye

46*th* and 47*th* *Edward III*

109 William Halden Roger Digge, Thomas Garwynton of Welle, William Horne, Nicholas Heryng & John Wacche *v.* Roger Shipbroke & his wife Margaret in Southwerk

47*th* *Edward III*

103 Peter atte Merssh & his wife Alice *v.* Peter de Culcham & his wife Agnes in Coveham

108 William Bénefait & his wife Constance v. Laurence atte Hoke & his wife Isabella in Merstham
110 John de Hadresham & his wife Emma v. Richard Karbonel & his wife Johanna in Crauhurst & Lynggefeld
111 Richard Earl of Arundel & Surrey by John Hemery v. Thomas de la Ryvere & his wife Isabel in West Bechesworth
112 Henry Vanner citizen & vintner of London by John Hemery v. Nicholas Reynham citizen & fishmonger of London & his wife Alesia in Totyng
117 William Holeweye v. Stephen atte Harryes & his wife Alice in Farncumbe
118 William de Walworth citizen of London, William de Halden, John Whitewell, John Bays & Richard de Wermyngton clerk v. John Wenge of Kyngeston upon Thames in Kyngeston upon Thames
119 Thomas Askern & his wife Cristiana v. Peter atte Wode of Worpulston & his wife Patronilla in Farnham
46th and 48th *Edward III*
122 William de Harewell & John Lysurs v. William Gibbes of Lyngefeld & his wife Riĉa & John Clerk of Crowehurst & his wife Isabel in Welkestede & Tanrugge
124 William Leccheford v. William Coupere & his wife Juliana in Horle
47th and 48th *Edward III*
120 John Middelton, John Wentebrigg, John Ive clerk, Peter Wysebech clerk v. Robert Little citizen of London & his wife Johanna in Camberwell
48th *Edward III*
113 Robert Symond chaplain, Philip Tylare chaplain, John Hunteleye v. Thomas Cosynton & his wife Alice in Kyngeston on Thames
114 William Spenser, John Walet senior & William Hauker v.

William Beaufoy & his wife Agnes in Catteshull & Ertyngdon

115 Robert Broun *v.* Roger Libbesofte & his wife Johanna in Weston & Alrebrok

116 John atte Barre of Reygate *v.* William atte Helde of Okstede & his wife Agnes in Reygate

121 Nicholas de Carreu *v.* Henry Mot & his wife Alice in Kershalton Bedyngton & Clopham

123 Gilbert Flemyng chaplain & John Tumby *v.* John Rusthall of Speldherst & his wife Agnes in Wolkestede, Tanrugge, Lyngefeld & Horne

125 Ralph Knight clerk *v.* William atte Lee & his wife Isabel in Clopham

48*th* and 49*th* *Edward III*

126 John Legg *v.* Walter atte Fan of Gildeford & his wife Margaret in Gildeford

130 Richard Diridenne & his wife Emma *v.* Robert Deumars & his wife Johanna in Ebesham

49*th* *Edward III*

127 John Chontere *v.* John Carpenter of Assh & his wife Matilda in Assh

128 Richard atte Broke parson of Stapelhurst Church *v.* Henry Husee fil' Mark Husee & his wife Margaret in Bermondeseye

129 Thomas de Lye *v.* John Ledet & his wife Margaret in Walton on Thames

133 William Alvyne & William Arnold *v.* Robert Lyndwyk citizen of London & his wife Alice in Horlee

48*th* & 50*th* *Edward III*

136 Robert Northrug of Kyngeston bakere & his wife Alice *v.* John Burgeys of Kyngeston on Thames & his wife Margery in Kyngeston on Thames

49*th* & 50*th* *Edward III*

134 Richard Moushirst of Okstede *v.* Richard Carbonel of Okestede & his wife Johanna in Okestede

50th *Edward III*

131 Simon de Mordon stokfisshmongere citizen of London & his wife Alice *v.* Benedict Hardele smith & citizen of London & his wife Margery in Camerwell & Lambeheth

132 John Salyng & his wife Margaret *v.* Richard atte Churche, Thomas de Barnett & Henry Yevele in Gildeford, Stoke, Sende, Crawestoke & Clandon

135 William Denyas *v.* John Wysbech of Kyngeston & his wife Alice in Kyngeston

137 John Skinner of Oksted & Richard Dase *v.* Simon Durant & his wife Margaret in Ocstede

138 John Hyrner of Croydon *v.* John Westbury & his wife Alice in Croydon

139 Roger Lumbard *v.* Robert Kempton & his wife Margaret in Bromle & Stoke juxta Guldeford

141 James Gylot parson of Burstowe Church *v.* Andrew Pykeman & his wife Johanna in Lambythemersh & Suthwerk

51st *Edward III*

140 Robert Notebourne *v.* Robert Kempton & his wife Margaret in Bromlegh, Guldeford, Worplesdon, Merewe & Stoke juxta Guldeford

142 Robert Notebourne *v.* Robert Kempton & his wife Margaret in Bromlegh, Guldeford, Worplesden, Merewe & Stoke juxta Guldeford

143 William Randolph & his wife Katharine *v.* John Aleyn Clerk & Robert Gaydon Clerk in Leddrede & Feccham

144 William de Wyntryngham *v.* Cristofer de Shokkeburgh & his wife Agnes in Suthwerke (St. Olave's)

47th *Edward III* & 1st *Richard II*

15 Thomas fil' Roger de Clifford & his wife Elizabeth *v.* Roger de Clifford chivaler in Shaldeford

1st *Richard II*

1 William Bys of London stokfisshmonger *v.* Godefrey atte

Bury of Hermondesworth & his wife Alice in Bedyngton, Croydon and Creshauton

2 John Pollard of Sandrestede *v.* John Bruggeman of Croydon & his wife Alice in Croydon

3 Nicholas Pego *v.* Eustace Rothyng of Neuton & his wife Cristina in Newton

4 Thomas de Middelton clerk & Robert de Wyclyff clerk *v.* James de Strete in Rasebery, Micham & Mordon

5 Richard Rothyng citizen & stokfisshmongere of London *v.* William Herry of Porkeleye in Porkeleye, Caterham, Warlyngham & Chelsham

6 Henry Michelgrove *v.* John atte Pende & his wife Agnes in Kershalton

7 William atte Nayssh *v.* Richard Tayllour of Wallyngton & his wife Johanna in Wallyngton

8 Nicholas de Carreu *v.* Robert Alexaundre & his wife Margaret & Roger Berwell and his wife Katharine in Wodemeresthorn

9 Frebern Petresfeld chapman *v.* John Fuller of Great Bookham & his wife Johanna in Chabham

10 John Bonet & Robert Broune clerk by John Blast *v.* William Robyn citizen & shoemaker of London & his wife Alice in Walton, Coveham & Wisshele

1st & 2nd *Richard II*

12 John de Hadresham & his wife Emma *v.* Edmund Herneys & his wife Elizabeth in Crowehurst, Lyngefeld, Malet, & Lemefeld

2nd *Richard II*

11 John Aubyn junior *v.* John Hystede & his wife Hilda in Reygate

3 John Mayster clerk, Gilbert Acton & Richard Horpol *v.* Robert Alisaundre of Kersalton & his wife Margaret, Roger Birwell & his wife Katharine & John Kiriell & his wife Alianor in Kersalton & Badyngton

14 Nicholas de Carreu *v.* John Kyryell & his wife Alianor in Wodemeresthorn

16 John de Thorp junior *v.* John Welde of Thorp & his wife Margaret in Thorp and Egeham

17 John Welburn citizen & goldsmith of London & his wife Cecilia *v.* William de Braynte & his wife Alice in Kyngeston on Thames

18 William Asketyn *v.* John Ufford of Kyngeston & his wife Isabel in Croydon

19 William Pelham & his wife Johanna *v.* Thomas Balsham & his wife Matilda in Lambheth

20 Richard atte Mere of Chelsham *v.* John Sigmond & his wife Agnes in Croydon

21 John Cheyne chivaler, John Roulond clerk, William Burcote clerk, Thomas Charleton, William Wodelef & John Wodelef *v.* Henry Marchall of Southwerk & his wife Agnes, John Waryn citizen and butcher of London & his wife Margaret in Southwerk

2nd & 3rd *Richard II*

24 Roger de Freton clerk *v.* John Kentyngg of Dorkyngg & his wife Isabel in Dorkyngg

26 John Chaumberleyn of Coveham *v.* Michael atte Grove & his wife Sibil in Coveham

22 John Hore & Walter atte Grene *v.* John Donyle & his wife Alice in Croydon

23 Roger Gate *v.* John Mote junior & his wife Cecilia in Farnham

25 Robert Leeper vicar of the Church of St. Laurence London by Henry Jolipace chaplain *v.* John Dony & his wife Katharine in Suthwerk

27 Richard Rook, Thomas Aston, John Kymbell & Reginald atte Wode by Henry Oundel *v.* William Hunte junior & his wife Margery in Wendelesworth

28 John Gatyn citizen & fishmonger of London & his wife

Rose *v.* Peter Shep citizen of London coffrer & his wife Katharine in Bermondesey

29 Thomas Crowe of the parish of Lyngefeld *v.* William fil' Giles Benet & his wife Isabel in Lyngefeld

30 William Fitz Johan & his wife Agnes by Thomas Walbroun *v.* Robert Danhurst & his wife Agnes in Chertesay & Egeham

31 John Bys citizen & stokfishmonger of London & his wife Matilda *v.* Peter Shep coffrer citizen of London and his wife Katharine in Bermondesey

32 John Fressh citizen & mercer of London *v.* Robert Rus brasier & citizen of London & his wife Katharine in Suthwerk

33 Robert West, Thomas Thorne, & John Semere *v.* John Thorne & his wife Margaret in Guldeford

4th Richard II

34 Katharine atte Rouberne & Ralph Agmundesham & his wife Isabel *v.* John atte Rouberne clerk in Esthorsle, Effyngham & Litel Bookham

35 John Kirketon, William Goddisson & John Southwell clerk *v.* John Hokele & his wife Mary & Mathew Langriche & his wife Margaret in Southewerk

36 William de Wykeham Bishop of Winchester *v.* William Baret of Farnham & his wife Johanna in Farnham

37 Thomas Lumbard *v.* Robert Trapes of Guldeford & his wife Alice in Guldeford

38 Alexander Bykenore of Kent & his wife Agnes by William Gysburn *v.* James Taillour & his wife Agnes in Kyngeston on Thames

5th Richard II

39 William Smyth fil' Laurence Smyth of Raygate *v.* Richard Cook & his wife Alianor in Raygate

40 Edmund Fitz-Johan *v.* William Fitz-Johan & his wife Agnes in Hamme

41 William Ancroft citizen of London & William Hirnyng of
London *v.* John Boydon citizen & butcher of London &
his wife Alice in Suthwerk

42 Adam Lucas of Brewe *v.* Reginald Kentebury & his wife
Alice in Walton & Banstede

43 Robert de Plesyngton chivaler *v.* John de Nevill of Raby
chivaler in Rasebery, Micham & Moredon

44 Philip Broune *v.* Richard Skynnere of Reygate & his wife
Johanna in Reygate

45 William de Walberton chaplain *v.* Nicholas de Bachelir &
his wife Johanna in Westcote

45a Stephen atte Merssh & his wife Margery *v.* William
Cressewyk of London & his wife Alice in Camberwell

6th *Richard II*

46 Geoffrey Michel, John Bray, William Hore, Edmund Heryng,
John Sergeant, Thomas Bocok, Thomas Sewale & William
Gosselyn of Arnyngton by Richard Waltham *v.* Thomas
de Legh of Shellegh & his wife Anna in Walton on
Thames

47 John Kentecoumbe *v.* William Maybank senior & his wife
Agnes in Seende

48 Roger Slak & his wife Agnes *v.* Robert Pountfreyt citizen
of London & his wife Juliana in Kyngeston on Thames

49 William Spycer *v.* Thomas Lanewell & his wife Isabella in
Kyngeston on Thames

50 John Worsted & his wife Agnes *v.* Robert Litle & his wife
Johanna in Bredynghurst

7th *Richard II*

51 John Redyng citizen of London & his wife Cecilia by
William Wakefeld *v.* Thomas Rolf of Northlambehethe
& his wife Emma in Northlambehethe

52 Nicholas de Carreu senior *v.* John Fairher citizen &
goldsmith of London in Suthwerk

53 John de Burton clerk, Richard Holm clerk, Geoffrey Martyn

& John de Bretton *v.* John Melbourne senior & his wife Isabella in Eshere Watervyle & Sandon

54 William Ancroft citizen of London, John Burwell of London stokfisshmonger & William Hernyng of London *v.* John fil' Richard Horn citizen & fishmonger of London & his wife Alice in Suthwerke

55 Walter Grene & his wife Johanna by Nicholas Peny *v.* Thomas Kent & his wife Alice in Croydon

56 Roger Cheldewell *v.* John Bourer & his wife Johanna in Kyngeston on Thames

57 Robert Clay & his wife Margaret *v.* John Bourere & his wife Johanna in Kyngeston on Thames

58 William Horscroft citizen & skinner of London *v.* John le Man of Wandelesworth & his wife Alice in Wandelesworth

59 Thomas Thurbarn & his wife Johanna *v.* William Rydere of Merstham & his wife Alice & John Taillour of Ebesham & his wife Johanna in Guldeford

60 Alexander Bykenore & his wife Agnes *v.* Ralph fil' James Taillour & his wife Philippa in Kyngeston

8*th* *Richard II*

61 John Chamberleyn clerk & Thomas Broun *v.* John Dony citizen & mercer of London & his wife Katharine in Suthwerk

62 Margaret widow of Ralph de Norton chivaler *v.* William Weston and his wife Johanna in Clandon

33 John Cok clerk & Peter atte Wode of Godalmyng *v.* John Arnald of Heydon & his wife Cristiana in Godalmyng

64 William Fitz Johan *v.* John Grenestrete of Chidyngfold & his wife Alice in Cherteseye

65 John Kent of Suthwerk shoemaker *v.* William Furneux of Leuesham Kent & his wife Amy in Suthwerk

66 William de Wykeham Bishop of Winchester, Nicholas de Wykeham clerk, John de Bukyngham clerk, John de

8—9 RICHARD II. 151

Campeden clerk, John de Wykeham clerk, John de Ketene clerk *v.* William Merston of Sele juxta Farnham & his wife Margaret in Farnham

67 John Lytewyn *v.* Thomas atte Doune fil' Richard Puffe in Chertesey

68 Robert de Dyneley & his wife Margaret *v.* John de Swanton & his wife Margaret in Estshene

69 John Stepere & John Donmowe *v.* William Maldon & his wife Alice in Est Bechesworth

70 William Fitz Johan *v.* Robert del Sauserye of Cherteseye & his wife Matilda in Cherteseye

71 Ralph Basset of Drayton chivaler, John de Olneye & Walter de Althorp *v.* John Hughes of Romford & his wife Margery in Suthwerk

72 John Beket of Fernebergh & his wife Matilda *v.* William Pykeslegh lately parson of Fernebergh Church in Suthwerk

73 William Ermyn clerk, Thomas Breaux Knight, Robert Chisenhale, Richard Bedewynd & William Brantyngham *v.* William Weston & his wife Johanna in Catteshull

74 Thomas le Man *v.* William Bottlegh & his wife Johanna in Horne, Wokenysted & Tanrugg

75 William Weston & his wife Johanna *v.* William Brantyngham in Ertyngdon

9th *Richard II*

76 John Smert of London bocher & his wife Matilda *v.* John Bonet of London fleccher & his wife Agnes & John Vylers of London & his wife Agnes in Lambheth

77 William Horscroft citizen & skinner of London, Robert Markle citizen & skinner of London & his wife Beatrice in Wandlesworth

78 William Rikill *v.* Thomas Elriche & his wife Alice in Padyngdon & Abyngeworth

79 John Kene of Merton *v.* Thomas Baker of Ledrede & his wife Margery in Totyng

80 John Marlere parson of Garboldesham Church Norfolk, John Doreward of Rewenhale, John Beneroche chaplain, John Chabbok of Felstede, Richard Clerk of West Merseye, William Fitzpiers of Halstede Essex, John Inthenaldres of Halstede & Nicholas Brayham of Great Leighes by Richard Waltham *v.* Adam Peche & his wife Mary in Newenton & St. George's Parish (Newenton)

81 Robert Vynt *v.* Peter Gonayre & his wife Margaret in Guldeford

82 Henry Boghay clerk & John Boghay & Henry his brother *v.* William Clerk & his wife Agnes in Bermondeseye

2nd & 10th *Richard II*

85 John Carbonel, William Stamyndenne & Thomas Bureham *v.* John Somervylle & his wife Katherine in Wandesworth, Southwerk & Kyngeston on Thames

10th *Richard II*

83 John de Campeden clerk *v.* Alice widow of Thomas Fysche hosyer of Suthwerk in Suthwerk

84 Robert March and his wife Agnes by Thomas Thwayt *v.* Robert Adam & his wife Elizabeth in Duntesfolde, Chudyngfold & Kerdesforde

86 William de Wykeham Bishop of Winchester, Nicholas de Wykeham clerk, John de Wykeham clerk, John de Campeden clerk, Robert Cherlton, & William Ryngeburn *v.* John Griffits & his wife Grace in Ewelle, Ebbesham, Codynton, Horton, Shaldeford, West Cheyham, Tallworth, Long ditton and Brittegrene

87 John Brenchelee of Suthwerk *v.* Roger Mark bladsmyth & citizen of London & his wife Cristina in Suthwerk

88 John Clerk pulter, Robert West pulter, & Robert Betaigne goldsmith *v.* William Cappe of London pulter & his wife Elizabeth in Suthwerk

89 John Sutton of Kyngeston & his wife Johanna *v.* Richard Ardern and his wife Isabella in Kyngeston

90 Henry atte Wode citizen of London *v.* Richard Notyngham & his wife Isabella in Barnes, Rokehampton & Puttenhethe

91 John Hadrisham senior *v.* John Mot & his wife Juliana in Crouherst

92 William Robkyn & his wife Alice by Walter Mason *v.* John Webbe & his wife Johanna in Burstowe

93 William Fitz Johan & his wife Agnes *v.* Robert Loxele junior and his wife Agnes in Charteseye

94 John Sutton of Kyngeston on Thames & his wife Johanna *v.* John Welburn citizen & goldsmith of London & his wife Cecilia in Kyngeston on Thames

95 Walter atte Grene of Croydon *v.* John Hampton & his wife Sibil in Croydon

96 John Gatyn of London fisshemongere *v.* Walter Wodeland of Guldeforde & his wife Johanna in Guldeford & Stoke

97 Henry Donne of Coveham, Thomas Freke citizen & wodemonger of London & John Punshurst citizen & wodemonger of London by William de Faseby *v.* John Banell & his wife Cristiana in Batricheseye

98 Robert Loxle senior & John Weston *v.* Robert Loxle junior & his wife Agnes in Ertyngdon & Guldeford

99 Walter Knolles *v.* Henry Whyssh & his wife Johanna in Bromlegh

100 William Trofford clerk & William Ardern *v.* Richard Ardern & his wife Isabella in Ewell

101 John Brymmesgrene chaplain & John Chipstede citizen of London *v.* Thomas Jolyf & his wife Agnes in Feccham

102 Elias Fedecok & his wife Alice *v.* William Brutteby & his wife Beatrice in Kyngeston on Thames

10th & 11th *Richard II*

104 Richard Wyddene *v.* Nicholas Yepeswych & his wife

Beatrice & John Vyncent in Carselton, Benyngton & Walyngton

11th *Richard II*

103 John Stok & John Chipstede *v.* Thomas Jolyf & his wife Agnes in Leddrede

105 William Eynesham, John Eynesham & John Cros *v.* John Hampton & his wife Sybil in Benchesham

106 Robert Hardyng *v.* William Symme & his wife Agnes in Kyngeston on Thames

107 Henry Yevele mason & his wife Katherine, William Hochepount chaplain, John Clifford mason, & Martin Seman clerk, *v.* John Kerle & his wife Margaret in Suthwerk

108 Henry Yevele mason & his wife Katherine, William Hochepount chaplain, John Clifford mason, & Martin Seman clerk *v.* John fil' John fil' William Rous in Suthwerk

109 John Lorkyn clerk *v.* Richard Polynge & his wife Matilda daughter & next heir of Richard Wrotham lately citizen & apothecary of London in Suthwerk

110 Thomas Wynter, & Richard Woghere *v.* John Hampton & his wife Sibil in Croydon

111 Robert Dyneley, & his wife Margaret *v.* William Hunte of Potenhethe & his wife Margery in Est Shene

112 William Chipstede citizen & fishmonger of London, John Claydon, John Palmer, William Bridbrok *v.* Ralph Double & his wife Alice in Suthwerk, West Grenewych & Lambhethe

113 Robert Vynt *v.* John Person & his wife Alice in Bromlegh

114 John Gerveys *v.* Nicholas Slifeld & his wife Johanna in Sende

12th *Richard II*

1 John Innocent clerk & John Benteley *v.* John atte Castell & his wife Agatha in Waweton, Bechesworth & Leghe

2 Richard Erneld *v.* William Bys citizen & stokfishmonger of London & his wife Atianora in Kersalton & Bedyngton

3 John Conde *v.* Henry Martyn & his wife Lucy in Stoke juxta Guldeford
4 Peter atte Wode & his wife Petronilla *v.* Henry Martyn & his wife Lucy in Stoke juxta Guldeford
5 William Fitz Johan *v.* Robert Northrigge of Coveham & his wife Johanna in Cherteseye
6 William Makenade, John Appelton & Thomas atte Hay *v.* John Balham & his wife Juliana in Wyttele & Hasulmere

13*th* Richard II

7 Henry Payn & his wife Agnes *v.* Henry Elyot & his wife Agnes in Bromlegh
8 John Colman, John Underdych, Robert Popy, John Puddyng & William Sprygy *v.* William Sporier of Kyngeston & his wife Agnes in Kyngeston on Thames
9 Nicholas Horsele of Guldeford bowyer & his wife Agnes by William Wymeldon *v.* Richard atte Hone of the parish of Wokkyng and his wife Agnes in Worplesdon
10 Thomas Wely *v.* Henry Whisshe & his wife Johanna in Suthwerk
11 Nicholas Bysshop *v.* John Walter of Okstede & his wife Alice in Okstede
12 Henry Halstede *v.* Walter Shepherd of Okstede & his wife Isabella in Okstede

13*th* Richard II

15 John Longereg junior & Richard Benek *v.* John Chytyngelegh & his wife Margaret in Lyngefeld and Croweherst
15a John Whelere of Elstede *v.* William Dyne & his wife Cecilia in Guldeford & Ertyngdon

13*th* & 14*th* Richard II

13 Richard Cartere of Badshute *v.* Simon le Thecchere of Hethlegh & his wife Johanna in Badshute
14 John Wantele *v.* Richard Crikebade & his wife Alice in Wonersh, Aldebury and Bromlegh

14th Richard II

16 John Marlere parson of Garboldesham Church, Norfolk, John Doreward of Rowenhale, William Broke of Stistede senior, John Beneroche chaplain, Richard Parlebien chaplain, John Inthenaldres, William Fitz Piers of Halstede Essex, John Chabbok of Felstede, Nicholas Brayham of Great Leighes & John Jour of Stistede *v.* John Broke of Stistede in Essex, & his wife Margaret in Newenton & Suthwerk

17 Simon Barton chaplain, John Thurston & Thomas Aston by Henry Oundel *v.* John Norton in Batricheseye, Wandelesworth & Rydon

18 Thomas de Coumbe, John de Yardburgh of the County of Lincoln and Elias Brown citizen and butcher of London *v.* Thomas Wyght citizen and grocer of London & his wife Cecilia in the Parish of St. Mary Magdalene juxta Southwerk

19 Robert Chonneson *v.* Johanna fil' Thomas Aleyn in Godalmyng

20 Master Arnald Brokas and Salamon Oxeneye *v.* John Adam of Guldeford ferour and his wife Johanna in Guldeford

21 John fil' William Hadresham *v.* Geoffrey Bristowe citizen of London fuller and his wife Agnes in Lyngefeld & Croweherst

22 John Woderone *v.* John Porter & his wife Agnes in Ledride

23 Giles Taillour, Thomas Rolf & John White *v.* Hugh Netelfold & his wife Johanna in Dorkyng

24 Robert Frye citizen of London *v.* Henry Brown citizen of London & his wife Isabella in Long Ditton & Kyngeston

25 Walter Colgrym *v.* Roger Wethewelle & his wife Letice in Whatedone, Colesdone, Caterham and Warlyngham

27 Gilbert Piryman & his wife Matilda *v.* William Averay of London & his wife Cecilia in Suthwerk

28 Master Nicholas de Wykeham clerk & Master John Campeden clerk *v.* Roger de Fridelee in Mikelham
29 Master Nicholas de Wykeham clerk & Master John Campeden clerk *v.* Peter Chapman & his wife Matilda in Waleton-on-Thames
30 Laurence Tayllour of Kyngeston on Thames *v.* John London of Kyngeston on Thames & his wife Johanna in Kyngeston on Thames
31 Master Nicholas de Wykeham clerk & Master John Campeden clerk *v.* John le Freke of Feccham in Mykelham
25 William Salman *v.* Henry Brette of Hampton & his wife Johanna & William Dyke of Cherteseye & his wife Amicia in Cherteseye

15*th* Richard II

32 Master Nicholas de Wykeham clerk & Master John Campeden clerk *v.* John Apperdele fil' John Apperdele of Ledrede in Mykelham
33 Robert Savage senior, Baldewyn Berford chivaler, Druo Barentyn & Thomas Vynent *v.* John Paas of Eton & his wife Johanna in Wandelesworth
34 John Weston & his wife Milicent *v.* William Weston & his wife Johanna in Papeworth
35 Richard atte Port *v.* Robert Wegge & his wife Matilda in Dorkyng
36 John Woderone, Thomas Gaytford & William Mirfeld *v.* John de Heton & his wife Elizabeth in Le Legh

15*th* & 16*th* Richard II

37 Philip Sotenham & his wife Juliana *v.* Robert Colyn of Ryppele & his wife Alice in Ryppele
38 John Gylys clerk, John Aleyn clerk, William Cokerell clerk & John Walford *v.* Robert Bromersshe & his wife Emma in Worplesdon

16*th* Richard II

39 Robert Pobelowe parson of Westbourne, John Bonet,

Walter Lange & Thomas Pacchyng *v.* Henry Jop of Guldeford & his wife Johanna in Guldeford

40 Walter Humfray *v.* John Howel mason & his wife Agnes in Lyngefeld

41 William Ingram & his wife Johanna *v.* Johanna Renehawe junior & his wife Annora in Est Clendon

42 John Pygas of Rippele bocher *v.* William Wysebeche of London barbour & his wife Matilda in Rippele

43 Peter Hatter *v.* Walter Lambard of Chalk & his wife Agnes in Croydon

44 William Redeston of Suthwerk *v.* Thomas Serle citizen & malemakere of London & his wife Agnes in Suthwerk

72 Walter Chudham, John Richer clerk, John Aleyn & Thomas Remys *v.* William Bys citizen & stokfisshemonger of London & his wife Alianora in Bandon

17*th* *Richard II*

45 William Leddrede & his wife Juliana *v.* Thomas Bakere & his wife Idonia in Leddrede

46 Robert Clay of Kyngeston on Thames *v.* Simon Prodom of Kyngeston on Thames & his wife Johanna in Kyngeston on Thames

47 Thomas Yokflote archdeacon of Berkshire, John Cosyn of London, John Thorne, William Wymeldene & John Astone parson of Est Horsle Church by William Wymeldene *v.* John Shordiche & his wife Alice in Kyngeston on Thames

48 William Vale citizen & fishmonger of London & his wife Margery *v.* Thomas Wymund citizen & fishmonger of London & his wife Agnes in Suthwerk

49 John Bursebrygg *v.* Geoffrey atte Dene & his wife Alice in Farncombe & Godalmyngg

50 John Gybbe & his wife Johanna *v.* John Telgherst junior & his wife Agnes in Tanregge & Tyngefeld

51 William Savage, Thomas Colrede & Thomas Joop by John

Hilton v. William Wymeldon & his wife Margery in Mikelham & Leddrede

52 John Waryng v. John Colyns & his wife Alice in Camberwelle & Lambhythe

17th and 18th Richard II

53 Thomas Brocas & his wife Elizabeth v. William Sheperde carpenter & his wife Margaret in Godalmyng, Werplesden and Compton juxta Guldeforde

18th Richard II

54 John Underhelde & John Wehbe v. William Profyt and his wife Alice in Lyngefeld

55 Master Arnald Brocas clerk v. William Shepherd carpenter and his wife Margaret in Litelton juxta Guldeford

56 Nicholas Carreu v. Thomas atte Mote & his wife Johanna in Croydon

57 Thomas Serle citizen & malemaker London v. Thomas Botiller of Southewerke & his wife Alice in Southewerk

58 Nicholas Carreu v. Godfrey atte Pyrye & his wife Alice in Bedyngton & Croydon

59 Richard Virley & his wife Alice v. John Selverton & his wife Johanna in Hoorne, Burstowe, Nutfeld, Blecchynglegh, Wolkenested, Lyngfeld & Croweherst

60 John Selverton & his wife Johanna v. Richard Virley & his wife Alice in Hoorne, Burstowe, Nutfield, Blecchynglegh, Wolkenested, Lyngefeld & Croweherst

61 William Do & his wife Matilda by John Halle v. Thomas atte Mote & his wife Johanna in Croydon, Sellesdon, Sanderstede & Adyngton

62 Richard Morannt of Wolknestede & his wife Agnes by Walter Hoke v. John Roghheye & his wife Johanna in Wolknestede

63 John Waddysle citizen & goldsmith of London & Thomas Prentys citizen & fleccher London v. John Langeston of

the county of Buckingham & his wife Elizabeth in Leshurst

64 Henry Fleynsford & his wife Agnes *r.* Geoffrey Bircham & his wife Juliana in Reygate

19th *Richard II*

65 Thomas Chapman *r.* Reginald Kentebury & his wife Alice in Wauton on the Hull

66 John Stanton & John Spycer *r.* John Olyver & his wife Johanna in Suthwerk & Retherhithe

67 William Powe of London & Edmund Dene *r.* Thomas Colney & his wife Alice in Doune in Coveham

68 William Gascoigne, Nicholas Gascoigne, William Hornby & Thomas Hornby *r.* James Dyneley & his wife Elena in Est Shene & Westhall

69 Richard Shepherde of Nutfelde *r.* John Halpeny of Hertford & his wife Petronilla in Leghe & Horlee

17th *& 20th Richard II*

70 John Hull *r.* William atte Welle & his wife Johanna in Wannesworth

20th *Richard II*

71 Walter atte Hoke & Thomas atte Helde *r.* Andrew Bagot & his wife Alice in Blecchynglegh

73 John Fremantel & Gilbert Cowper *r.* Walter atte Hethe & his wife Rose in Wyndlesham

74 John Wyntershull *r.* John Holyngburn & his wife Alice in Aldebury, Shire & Gomeshulne

75 John Walworth & Henry Janecok coupere *r.* Geoffrey Janecok & his wife Margaret in Newenton

76 Nicholas Upton & his wife Johanna *r.* John atte Doune & his wife Margery in Hedlegh and Wauton

77 Thomas Prophet clerk *r.* John Solas & his wife Johanna in Suthwerk & Newenton

78 John Brokere clerk *r.* Roger Cheldewell & his wife Alice in Kyngeston on Thames & Tameseditton

20—22 RICHARD II. 161

79 John Champ & his wife Johanna *r.* Roger Walden clerk &
   John Preston in Gildeford, Worplesden, Stokes, Shaldeford, Ertyngdon, Merwe & Tydyng
   20th & 21st *Richard II*

83 Henry Rosefeld & his wife Alianor *r.* Richard Caym & his
   wife Sarah in North Lambehith
   21st *Richard II*

82 John Hunt of Slagheham by Richard Wakehurst *v.* John
   Pratyn & his wife Agnes in Burstowe

84 Thomas Barbour of Reygate *v.* Hugh Merdene of
   Merstham & his wife Alice in Reygate

85 John Balton vicar of Kyngeston on Thames Church &
   Alexander Bykenore *v.* John Sutton of Kyngeston on
   Thames & his wife Johanna in Kyngeston on Thames &
   Longeditton

86 Richard Dulle & his wife Agnes *v.* Henry Cobbe & his wife
   Isabella in Batricheseye

87 James de Billyngford, Thomas Grace junior, & William fil'
   Richard Grace *r.* John Northwod & his wife Juliana &
   John Lodere & his wife Johanna in Suthwerk &
   Newenton

88 Robert Deny Kt. & his wife Anna *r.* Thomas Deny & John
   Smert citizen & butcher of London & his wife Matilda
   in Lambhithe

89 Ralph Reed citizen of London & his wife Petronilla *r.* John
   Calan citizen of London & his wife Isabella in Suthwerk

80 Robert Prior of Merton *r.* Robert Alot & his wife Agnes in
   Bedynton

81 John Barat *r.* John Trumpyngton & his wife Alice in
   Bermundeseye
   21st & 22nd *Richard II*

90 John Inggram *r.* Peter Wyke & his wife Agnes, John Mede
   of Blecchyngleye & his wife Margaret & William Langle
   & his wife Emma in Fecham & Great Bocham

91 William Sydeneye by Robert Bussebrigge *v.* Ralph Agmondesham & his wife Isabella in Bromlegh

22nd *Richard II*

92 Stephen Wyke lately parson of Coveham Church *v.* Thomas atte Penne in Purbryght

93 Robert Carpenter chaplain *v.* Richard Stacy & his wife Agnes in Kyngeston on Thames

94 John Gravesende & his wife Isabella *v.* Walter Pembroke & his wife Margery in Long Dytton, Thamyse Dytton & Kyngeston on Thames

95 Richard Nevile of Suthwerk *v.* Thomas Spencer citizen of London & his wife Johanna in Suthwerk

96 John Solas of Suthwerk *v.* Robert Brown & his wife Anna in Suthwerk

97 William Weston & his wife Idonia *v.* Richard Virley citizen of London & his wife Alice in Suthwerk

98 Richard Marchant of Okested & William atte Hirst of Okested *v.* John Marchant of Crouherst & his wife Margaret, William Marchant of Crouherst & his wife Katherine & John atte Halle of Crouherst & his wife Johanna in Crouherst

99 William Coventre, William Venour, Thomas Beaupeny & John Stapelford *v.* Ralph Whythors chivaler & his wife Elizabeth in Benchesham

100 Johanna Muriele by Robert Bussebrygge *v.* Richard Whenelare & his wife Margaret in Farnham

101 Richard Crokhere *v.* John Stakeford & his wife Isabella in Walton on Thames & Waybrug

1st *Henry IV*

1 William Loveney & his wife Margaret *v.* Richard Snell & his wife Emma in Kyngeston

1b William Loveney & his wife Margaret *v.* John Ammory & his wife Juliana in Kyngeston

1c Richard 'that was the parisshe prest' of Wynelesham &

Walter atte Hethe v. Gilbert Couper & his wife Isabella in Wynelesham

1ˢᵗ & 2ⁿᵈ Henry IV

8 John Burgh & Thomas Prentys of London fleccher v. Thomas Hanlegh of Cressalton senior & his wife Johanna in Cressalton & Bedyngton

2ⁿᵈ Henry IV

1d Richard Gatyn v. Edmund Stapelford & his wife in Duntesfold & Chidyngfold

2 Thomas Sippenham v. John Flemyng of Croydon in Surrey bocher & his wife Juliana in Croydon

3 Thomas Aylesham tylemaker v. Thomas Short of Dylwysh in the parish of Camerwell & his wife Alice in Camerwelle

4 Edmund Bolton citizen & stokfysshemonger of London & his wife Margaret v. Richard Virse of Suthwerk & his wife Agnes in Suthwerk

5 John Bronnyng v. Thomas de la Hay & his wife Johanna in Leygh juxta Derhurst

6 Ralph Cobham of Kent esquire, Roger Genowe clerk, John Brook & Thomas Joop v. John Bierden & his wife Elizabeth in Croweherst, Lemnysfeld, Lyngefeld & Ocstede

7 Henry Halstede v. William atte Melle & his wife Agnes in Lyngefeld

9 John Scarlet & John Roke by John Norton v. Adam Bocher of Croydon & his wife Mary in Croydon

10 Richard atte Denye of Wendesham & William Robelot of Chabeham v. Robert atte Denye of Horseld & his wife Matilda in Chabeham

11 John atte Holylonde v. Thomas Mesyngleghe & his wife Margaret in Notfelde

12 William Brampton citizen & stokfisshmonger of London, William Skeene, William Sekyngton stokfisshmongere & citizen of London & John Bryan junior v. John Seymour of London & his wife Johanna in Southwerk

13 Thomas Flete of Suthwerk & his wife Alice *v.* Peter Huet & his wife Agnes in Suthwerk
14 Robert Brayton clerk, Thomas Karlill clerk *v.* John Bromehale & his wife Alice in Suthwerk & Bermondesey

1ˢᵗ & 3ʳᵈ *Henry IV*

15 John Bremmesgrave clerk, John Hadresham, John Asshurst & Thomas Haytone *v.* Richard Pernersshe & his wife Matilda in Cherlewode

3ʳᵈ *Henry IV*

16 John Wyntershull *v.* William Standen & his wife Agnes & Hugh Upfold & his wife Johanna in Bromlegh
17 John atte Lee & John Willersey clerk *v.* Thomas Stoghton & his wife Johanna in West Shaldeforde
18 Richard Porter of Nuttefeld *v.* Thomas atte Stone of Bedyngton & his wife Johanna in Nuttefeld
19 William atte Howe of Guldeford *v.* John Pylton & his wife Margaret in Guldeford
20 Robert Gildesburgh of London brasyere *v.* John Frenssh in Worplesdon

4ᵗʰ *Henry IV*

21 Thomas Prentys citizen and fleccher of London, Robert Dokesworth, John Bynham, Henry Botolf, John Dunnyng, John Asplion & John Broghton *v.* John Norton & his wife Johanna daughter and heir of Hugh Quecche in Wodemeresthorne, Bedyngton & Kershalton
22 Robert Ede clerk, Henry Hyde clerk, Robert Gamelyn clerk & Otto Haunsard by William Wymeldon *v.* Henry Swyft citizen of London and John Swyft citizen of London and his wife Johanna in Leddred, Feccham, Hedlegh and Waweton
23 William atte Lote and his wife Margaret by William Wymeldon *v.* John Ekton citizen of London and his wife Alice in Leddred, Mikelham and Feccham
24 Robert Sharsulle & Richard Yngeram *v.* John Pylton & his

wife Margaret in Guldeford, Shaldeford & Stoke juxta Guldeford

25 Thomas Wheoly of Bentele in the County of Southampton senior *v.* Henry Wysh & his wife Johanna in Southewerk

26 Laurence Trussebut, John de Shuldham, John Carvile, Thomas Derham, William Narburgh, Thomas Styward of Swafham Market, Robert Petirburgh clerk, John Walden, Thomas Priour, Nicholas Morys, John Burgoyne, William Aleyn and John Hore *v.* Thomas Morys of the county of Cambridge & his wife Lucy in Suthwerk

27 John Walden, Thomas Priour, Nicholas Morys, John Burgoyne, William Aleyn, John Hore & Robert Petirburgh *v.* Thomas Morys of the county of Cambridge & his wife Lucy in Croydon, Benyngton, Southcote, Coumbe & Benchesham

28 Thomas Stoghton *v.* John Pilketon & his wife Margaret in Stoke juxta Gildeford

105 Robert Fitz Robert, William Sevenok & Thomas Prat *v.* Robert Savage of Wandesworthe senior & his wife Johanna in Wandesworthe

5*th* Henry IV

29 Richard Squery *v.* Adam Boucher & his wife Mary in Croydon

30 Thomas Warden *v.* Thomas Multon & his wife Agnes in Kyngeston on Thames

31 William de Wykham Bishop of Wynchester *v.* Robert Weston & his wife Elizabeth & Nicholas Wolbergh & his wife Margaret in Esshere Episcopi and Esshere Waterville

32 Robert Standon of Pekham *v.* John Parker citizen & barber of London & his wife Alice in Pekham

33 Richard Lentewardyn & Richard Teweisle *v.* John Norton & his wife Johanna in Ocham, Coveham, Sende, Horsle & Wockyng

34 Adam Storin of Croydon in the county of Surrey *v.* William Doo & his wife Matilda in Croydon

35 Thomas Clerk vicar of Horsham Church *v.* Walter Wrig & his wife Johanna in Reygate & Gatton

6th *Henry IV*

36 Thomas Chipsted & John Bishopton *v.* William Fouler & his wife Alice in Suthwerk

37 Thomas Shropshire *v.* John Hunte of Lyngefeld & his wife Dionisia in Wolknestede

38 Roger Tuttebury *v.* Thomas Currour of Croydon & his wife Mary in Croydon

39 John Willersey clerk & Robert Sauser clerk *v.* Robert atte Mille & his wife Alice in Guldeford

40 Henry Hothom clerk *v.* John Woppefold & his wife Matilda in Dorkyng

41 Robert atte Sonde & his wife Matilda by John Chiryngworth *v.* John Spicer & his wife Matilda in Dorkyng

42 John Ters of Croydon & Richard Cobbe of Croydon *v.* Robert Lancock of Croydon esquire & his wife Ismania in Croydon

43 John Brymmesgrave clerk John atte Mille & John Holyngborne *v.* William atte Welle & his wife Johanna in the Hundred of Emelbrigge & in Imworth, Aldebrok & Cleygate

44 John Combe senior & John Combe junior & his wife Johanna *v.* John Braunthwayt & his wife Alice in Clopham

45 John Loxsley & John Bowebrok of the parish of Dountesfold by John Bray *v.* John Wheler alias John Abbot of Dountesfold & his wife Edith in Dountesfold

46 Adam Buk hatter, John Swofeham hatter & Henry Bylney *v.* William Causton citizen & hatter of London & his wife Alianor in Suthwerk

47 Stephen atte Lee *v.* John atte Halle & his wife Johanna in Okstede

48 Nicholas Bisshop & John Ters of Croydon *v.* John Wynter of Croydon & his wife Agnes in Croydon
49 John Gaynesford *v.* John atte Halle & his wife Johanna in Croweherst, Tanrugge, Lyngefeld & Okstede
50 John Burgh, Thomas Remys, Thomas Holmes & Robert Kene of Croydon carpenter *v.* Robert Alayn & his wife Juliana in Croydon

7th & 8th Henry IV

51 John atte Coumbe of Croydon junior & his wife Margery by Robert Valaunce *v.* John Rede & his wife Isabella in Croydon

8th Henry IV

52 John Weston of Okham *v.* John Tuerslee & his wife Alice in Sende, Okham, Coveham and Esthorsle
53 Nicholas Fitz John & his wife Johanna *v.* Peter Wylcombe & his wife Agnes in Hamme
54 Richard Moushurst & John Macche of Tanregge *v.* John Turnour of Ocstede & his wife Alice in Ocstede
55 John Burgh, Stephen Speleman & John Garland of London carpenter *v.* Walter atte Grene of Croydon & his wife Johanna in Croydon

8th & 9th Henry IV

56 Matilda Huet *v.* John Huet & his wife Margaret in Blecchynglye
60 Ralph Wymeldon & Richard Ware *v.* William Longe & his wife Beatrice in Ledrede

9th Henry IV

57 Thomas Ingram *v.* John Pilton & his wife Margaret in Sende & Wokkynge
58 John Frelond citizen & vintner of London *v.* John Teweresle & his wife Alice in Suthwerk
59 William Duke citizen of London, Richard Merlawe citizen of London & Thomas Sweyne of Chertseye *v.* John Stapenhull & his wife Johanna in Chertseye

60 Ralph Codyngton *v.* William North of Ewell in Chyssyngdon, Kyngeston on Thames & Longditton
62 Edmund Lodlowe *v.* William Brokham & his wife Johanna in Est Bechesworthe
63 Robert Coventre citizen and grocer of London & his wife Emma *v.* Richard Cace of Kersalton & his wife Agnes in Kersalton

9th and 10th *Henry IV*

64 Richard Mousherst, Thomas Best, John Regge, John Bele & John Barton *v.* John Tebald & his wife Agnes in Wolksted & Blecchynglegh

10th *Henry IV*

65 Robert William of Suthwerk *v.* William de Mounpelers & his wife Margery in Suthwerk
66 Thomas atte Wyle de la Wode of the parish of Croydon *v.* Thomas Wynter of Croydon & his wife Agnes in Croydon
67 Richard Norton, John Martyn, John Denne clerk & William Weston *v.* Richard Berners in Westhorsle
68 William Bergh clerk, William Weston citizen & breadseller of London, Henry Hogham chaplain, John Matthewe chaplain & Thomas Ive citizen & breadseller of London *v.* Robert Denny Kt. & his wife Anna in Camerwell and Southlambehethe
69 Gilbert Hamme, Henry Payn, William Pedeweyn & John Waleys *v.* Robert atte Heelde & his wife Johanna in Shaldeford & Godalmyng
70 Henry Fleynesford *v.* William Coumbe & his wife Alice in Reygate
71 Master John Cateryk clerk, William Walton, John Willershey parson of the church of St. Mary Guldeford & Geoffrey Colet *v.* John Clipsham & his wife Alice in Guldeford, Shaldeford, Merwe, Stoke, Eshyng, Lyttylton, Haselmere & Imbham

72 Thomas More *r.* John Heter & his wife Nicholaa in Lyngefeld

73 Gilbert Asshurst citizen & wodmonger of London *r.* John Langlee & his wife Margaret in Kyngeston on Thames

74 William Crophill chaplain *r.* John Norton of London & his wife Margery in Kynggeston on Thames

75 William Asshurst junior *v.* Stephen Hervy & his wife Agnes in Est Bechesworthe

76 Walter atte Rude, Richard Rotour & Walter atte Denye *r.* John atte Rude & his wife Cristiana in Bagshete

20th *Richard II* & 11th *Henry IV*

82 Richard Foldhay, James Chuddelegh Kt, Elias Beere, John Frankcheyney & William atte Burgh *r.* William Wallyng & his wife Isabella in Estbury & Compton juxta Guldeford

10th & 11th *Henry IV*

80 William Bright of Blacchynglegh & his wife Johanna *r.* Richard Heldere & his wife Alice in Blecchynglegh

11th *Henry IV*

76a Peter Brikelisworth, John Clement and William Besouth clerk *r.* Simon Dockyng of Camerwell & his wife Johanna in Camerwell

77 John Richard of Croydon *r.* Richard Scory of Croydon & his wife Johanna in Croydon

78 Thomas Pryntys, Robert Dokesworth & William Feveresham *r.* John Kyriell senior & his wife Cristiana & John Kyriell junior in Waleton & Bedyngton

79 Robert Chesterford & Alan Walsyngham *r.* John Chesterford citizen & leathersellere of London & his wife Johanna daughter and heir of John Park in Southwerk

80 Richard Foulmere *r.* John Bokenham & his wife Alice in Kyngeston on Thames

83 Thomas Lemman of Wodecote Surrey *r.* John Shorman

alias John Corfe of Bedyngton & his wife Agnes in Bedyngton

84 John Bremysgrove clerk, John Cornwaleys & Thomas Hayton *r*. Thomas Remys esquire in Bandon

85 Richard Somer of Croydon *r*. William Doo & his wife Matilda in Croydon, Adyngton, Sellesdon & Saunderstede

86 William Cole of Cherteseye *v*. John Lecche & his wife Alice in Cherteseye

12*th* Henry IV

87 William Bures, Alan Seint Just & John Kyng clerk *r*. John Shapewyk clerk in Southwerk

88 William Lee & Thomas Moraunt *v*. Robert Childewale & his wife Alice in Cherteseye

89 John Colyer & his wife Alice *r*. William Prentys & his wife Margaret in Pyrbright

90 Thomas Saundre & Simon Longehurst *r*. Richard Asshurst & his wife Johanna in Newedegate, Capell and Dorkyng

91 John Holcombe clerk, Richard Wokkynge & John Grovere *v*. John Cok of Guldeford & his wife Agnes in Guldeford, Stoke juxta Guldeford & Ertyngdon

92 Richard Wokkyng *r*. Ralph Eyton & his wife Tiphania in Ertyngdon juxta Guldeford

93 Thomas Squyry, Bartholomew Squyry, Richard Mounford & John Meyne *v*. William Heyward of Totyng Graveney & his wife Johanna in Adyngton

94 John Wyntreshull & Richard Eton *v*. Ralph Eton of Ardern & his wife Tiphania in Purbright

12*th* & 13*th* Henry IV

95 John Alfray of Est Grenstede senior & his son John *v*. William Asshele & his wife Johanna in Chepstede

13*th* Henry IV

96 Thomas Knolles, William Symond & John Credy junior *v*. Robert Denny chivaler & his wife Anna in Lambhythe

96a Richard Moraunt bocher *v.* Walter Naward & his wife Margery in Wolkstede

97 William Flete citizen and fishmonger of London, John Moordon citizen and fishmonger of London & Thomas Hoo chaplain *v.* Thomas Welton citizen and pulter of London & his wife Johanna in Southlambhethe

98 John Lonestede, John atte Lye junior, William Basset & Thomas Lygon *v.* William Wysham & his wife Margaret in Burstowe Horne & Wolkestede

99 Thomas Brydlyngton citizen & tailor of London, Thomas Sutton citizen & tailor of London, John Colbroke citizen & tailor of London *v.* Thomas Morestede & his wife Juliana & John Combe & his wife Juliana in Clopham

100 John Chylterne clerk *v.* Nicholas Ryngewode of London & his wife Emma in Kyngeston on Thames

13*th* & 14*th* Henry IV

101 William Longe of Warlyngham Surrey & his wife Agnes *v.* Roger atte Park of Farleghe Surrey & his wife Juliana in Warlyngham

14*th* Henry IV

102 William Horn tayllour *v.* William Nicolet & his wife Johanna & Henry Broke & his wife Alice in Adyngton

103 William Knight felmongere & Robert Wityngham taillour *v.* Robert Blake citizen & haberdasher of London & his wife Constance *v.* John Pilton & his wife Margaret in Effyngham

104 Thomas Alwyne & his wife Juliana *v.* John Cok & his wife Agnes in Shaldeford

14*th* Henry IV & 1*st* Henry V

1 John Lovestede, John atte Lye junior, William Basset & Thomas Lygon *v.* John Wysham & his wife Katharine in Burstowe, Horne & Wolkestede

1st Henry V

2 Walter Blundell *v.* Richard Pertrych & his wife Margery in Tanrugg

3 John Combe junior *v.* John Combe senior & his wife Margery & John Rede of Hakeney & his wife Isabella in Croydon

4 William Wytte of Pekham *v.* William Penne citizen & tailor of London & his wife Isabella in Camerwell

8 Walter Cotton, Hugh Cary & Edmund Rede *v.* John Warberton or Warbulton & his wife Isabella in Miccheham

9 John Weston *v.* Richard Pirye & his wife Alice in Sende

10 Philip Palmer & Thomas Palmer *v.* Peter Lyveryng of Leuesham Kent & his wife Johanna in Suthwark

11 John Umfray junior *v.* John Croweherst & his wife Dionisia in Lyngefeld

10th Henry IV & 2nd Henry V

12 Henry Hyde clerk, Richard atte Sonde, Thomas Asshurst of Westcote & William Wymelden *v.* John Dolfyn & his wife Agnes in Reygate & Horle

12th Henry IV & 2nd Henry V

6 Nicholas Randolf *v.* William Wymelden & wife Margery in Lederedd & Ffeccham

7 Henry Hyde clerk, Richard atte Sonde, Thomas Asshurst of Westcote & William Wymeldon *v.* William Lanere & his wife Matilda in Reygate & Horle

14th Henry IV & 2nd Henry V

14 Henry Shelford clerk Thomas West & William West of Gildeford *v.* William Andrewe of London & his wife Alice in Gildeford

2nd Henry V

5 Richard Pavy esquire *v.* Robert Gildesburgh & his wife Alice in Piribright

13 John Longeregge *v.* John Holderness & his wife Agnes in Croydon

2nd & 3rd *Henry V*

18 Roger Chaunce, John Barton & John atte Leghe *v*. John Hill & his wife Edith in Newedegate

3rd *Henry V*

15 John atte Wode & his wife Isabella *v*. Adam Boweland of Croydon & his wife Margery in Totyng Graveneye

19 Thomas Stoghton & Ralph Wymeldon *v*. John Hergreve & his wife Juliana in Effyngham

16 John Peres junior *v*. John Ferthyng & his wife Mary in Addescompe

17 William atte Welle and William Gybbons *v*. William Melbourne & his wife Agnes & their son Richard in Shaldeford and Ewell

20 Thomas Calle clerk, William Bakepuz esquire, Richard Osbarn citizen of London *v*. Thomas Boteler of London draper & his wife Alice in Suthwerk

4th *Henry V*

21 John Deraunt *v*. Geoffrey Dale & his wife Johanna in Tycheseye

22 John Payn of Cheyham, Nicholas Wydene & Richard Shirefeld *v*. Ingelrann Priour & his wife Matilda in Sutton

3rd & 5th *Henry V*

24 Walter Vytele citizen & armorer of London & John Chesilden clerk *v*. Robert Wotton & his wife Johanna in Suthewerk

4th & 5th *Henry V*

23 John Gaynesford *v*. William Lytelgrome & Thomas Byfeld in Lyngefeld

5th *Henry V*

25 John Sayer, John Peny chaplain & Edmund Benge *v*. Robert Chichele & his wife Elizabeth in Garston

5th & 6th *Henry V*

26 John Sandeford, Robert Tatersale, John Sandewych vicar

of Camerwell church & Robert Valance *v.* Henry Milward & his wife Isabella in Camerwell

6*th* Henry V

27 John Martyn, John Andrew, William Scarbrugh & John Kympton *v.* John Bacon of London vynter & his wife Katherine in Stokwell

28 Henry Haweles & his wife Margaret *v.* William Seynt John, John Mulle, John Eryth & his wife Agnes, Robert Durbarn & his wife Anna & William Goldemore & his wife Agnes in Longeditton

29 William Cheyne, John Gaynesford & Stephen parson of the church of Wauton on the Hill *v.* Alice widow of Richard Virley, Elizabeth widow of Edward Herveys & John Sylverton & his wife Johanna in Coumbe Nevyle

30 Richard Bures, William Prentys & William Tymmell citizens & mercers of London *v.* Thomas Colman of Southwerk & his wife Anne in Southwerk

31 Henry Pakkere *v.* William Tyngewyke & his wife Agnes in Gyldeford & Shaldeford

32 Richard Coweper, John Wylkyn & John Dane *v.* Richard Woddesdon & his wife Isabella in Okestede

7*th* Henry V

33 William Sedenye *v.* Walter Herman & his wife Alice, and William Rombem & his wife Isabella in Bromlegh & Shaldeford

34 Richard Wakeherst, Walter Urry, William Asshurst & Roger Chaunce *v.* Henry atte Stone & his wife Isabella & Thomas Bornere & his wife Johanna in Notefeld

35 Robert Hodersale *v.* Robert Childewall & his wife Alice in Dunstall

36 Robert Clerk of Codyngton *v.* John Scot of Codyngton & his wife Agnes in Ebbesham

6*th* & 8*th* Henry V

40 Ralph Wymeldon & Thomas Asshurst *v.* Richard Snowe of Bedynton in Dorkyng

37 John Lacy, Richard Forder and Richard Danyell *v.* John Knyght & his wife Johanna in Wandlesworth
38 John Tyndale citizen and fishmonger of London and John Pressen *v.* John Benteley of Wauton & his wife Johanna in Waweton, Bechesworth, & Legh
39 John Underheld *v.* Richard fil' Stephen atte Lee of Wolkenested & his wife Cristiana in Lyngefeld

8th & 9th *Henry V*

41 John Hegger of Creshalton *v.* Thomas Hanley of Creshalton & his wife Johanna in Creshalton
42 William Wygyndenne, John Gaynesford, Thomas Sessyngham & John Rote *v.* William Kyng of Maydestone & his wife Johanna in Horne
43 William atte Grene of Walyngton *v.* Thomas Hanlee of Cresalton & his wife Johanna in Cresalton & Benyngton
49 John Folke clerk & William atte Wode *v.* Thomas Eylone & his wife Elizabeth in Blecchynglegh & Tatelysfeld

9th *Henry V*

44 John Corf & Thomas Mitford *v.* Henry Spencer of Carselton & his wife Johanna in Wandesworth.
45 John Byngle *v.* Nicholas Bisshop & Richard Batyn & his wife Johanna in Croydon
46 John Beel & his wife Suzanna *v.* John Craan of New Alresford & his wife Johanna in Fermesham
47 Robert atte Sonde *v.* John Godeson & his wife Matilda in Dorkyng & Estbechisworth
48 Robert Dodche & his wife Margaret *v.* John Stevynton & his wife Agnes in Lyngefelde
50 Richard Sherefeld & his wife Elizabeth *v.* John fil' Reginald Cobeham esquire in Burstowe & Hoorne
51 Henry Merston clerk, Roger Crome, Nicholas Baynard clerk, William Pynwell, Peter Stukle clerk, John Kirkeby of Haddam, Richard atte Watre of Ware,

Robert Quynaton, William Rokesburgh, John Yonge of Hoddesdon, John Brond chaplain & and John Pykworth *r.* John Skenefeld Gumshelne

10th Henry V

52 John Goolde & his wife Johanna & John atte Welle & his wife Matilda *r.* Alan Luggeford & his wife Alice in Tanrugge, Lyngefelde & Wolkestede

1st Henry VI

1 Robert Holand, John Pyrye *r.* John Holym & his wife Margaret in Batrichesey

2 Nicholas James, John Burgh of Waleton, John Cokayn, William Cambrugg, John Perveys, John Welles, William Symmes William Botiller & John atte Welle of Watford *r.* James Brampton in Suthwerk

3 John Clipsham esquire, John Malton, Adam Levelord & William Stokes *v.* Thomas Pycard & his wife Agnes in Suthwerk.

4 John Bacoun citizen & woolmonger of London, Richard Osbarn citizen of London, Richard Claidich citizen of London, William Thorp chaplain *r.* William Alfrede of Bermondeseye & his wife Agnes in the parish of St. Mary Magdalene in Bermondesey.

5 William Otteworth, John Weriton & his wife Katherine in Merwe

2nd Henry VI

6 John Heynes of Chertesey *r.* John Credy senior & his wife Agnes in Chertesey

7 Henry Martyn citizen & stokfisshmongere of London, William Ellefor clerk, William Sharp citizen & stokfisshmongere of London, Richard Claidich clerk & Ralph Brounyng of Great Yarmouth *r.* Nicholas Ryngwode citizen & bladsmyth of London & his wife Emma who was the widow of Richard atte Revere in Kyngeston on Thames

3rd *Henry VI*
8   William Inkpenne & his wife Petronilla *r.* Thomas Burgeys & his wife Johanna in Farnham
9   Philip Ammotson, John Bolney, Ralph Cowefold & Richard Shirfeld *r.* John Langrygge of Waltham Crosse & his wife Blanche in Micheham & Bedyngton
10 William Alfrede & Stephen Caunterbury *r.* William Symson citizen & skinner of London & his wife Johanna in Suthwerk
11 Stephen Balhorn *r.* John Sewale & his wife Cristina in Dorkynge
12 William Wymeldon *v.* William Redeforde & his wife Johanna in Mikelham & Westbechesworthe
13 Robert Fayreford & his wife Juliana *v.* John Jakeman and his wife Cecilia in Suthwerk

4th *Henry VI*
14 John Wyntereshill, Edmund Rede, Philip Amotesham, Ralph Wymeldon Thomas Grene & Richard Pawelyn *r.* Richard Axsmyth & his wife Anna in Westhorsleghe
15 Arthur Ormesby & Almaric Matany *v.* John Corve & his wife Alice in Suthwerk
16 William Hanewell, Robert Holand & John Pyrye *r.* Richard Freman & his wife Agnes & John Iter & his wife Agnes in Baterycheseye
17 John Horspole clerk, Robert Fitz-Robert of London, John Lemman of London & John Leycestre *v.* Thomas Henley of Crassalton & his wife Johanna in Crassalton & Walyngton
18 Thomas Macche of Lempnesfeld & John Syngere of Okstede *v.* John Macche of Okstede & his wife Agnes in Okstede.

5th *Henry VI*
19 John Asshwell, Robert Wydyngton & Salamon Oxeneye *v.* Roger Aleyn & his wife Katherine in Newenton

20 William Sydeney senior *r.* Robert Danhurst & his wife Margaret in Ertyngdon
21 Stephen Bryt *r.* William Ogger of Wyndesore in Berkshire chaundeler & his wife Johanna in Reygate
22 Hugh Glene *v.* Henry fil' William Herle & his wife Alice in Cherteseye
23 Thomas Heryng, William Smyth & Bartholomew Fuller *v.* Roger Brentfeld & his wife Alice, Reginald Dyer & his wife Agnes, Richard Chaundeler clerk, Simon Prentont citizen & wexchaundeler of London, & John Bracey citizen & talogh chaundeler of London in Croydon
24 Roger Bolton *r.* William Tyngewyke & his wife Agnes in Gildeford Stoke juxta Gildeford & Bromle
25 Thomas Godewyne of London esquire & his wife Johanna *r.* Thomas Caperon & his wife Margaret in Suthwerk
26 John Weston, John Corve, Thomas Stoughton, Thomas Eliot, John Pycas & John Nantes *r.* John Freke in Cranle & Shyre
28 Robert Bouth clerk, Thomas Stoghton *r.* William Tyngewyke & his wife Agnes in Guldeford, Stoke juxta Guldeford, Ertyngdon, Merwe & Shaldeford

6th Henry VI

27 Nicholas Wotton citizen & alderman of London, John Fray & John Symond *v.* Robert Wotton & his wife Elizabeth in the parish of St. Olave in Suthwerk
29 Godefrey Selde of Chelsham in Surrey *r.* Richard Brode of Hese in Kent & his wife Johanna in Chelsham
30 William Tolymond of London *r.* John Thomas of Lincoln & his wife Johanna in Lambehythemershe

6th & 7th Henry VI

31 Philip Amondesham, Ralph Wymeldon & Thomas Grofham *r.* John Gerard & his wife Matilda in Okkeleghe & Wotton

7th *Henry VI*

32 Thomas Rolf, William Daventre, Robert Aubrey & Thomas Cok *v.* Robert Mokkyng in the parish of St. Olave Southwerk

33 John Gylle & his wife Margery *v.* Thomas Colman of Suthwerk & his wife Anna in Suthwerk

34 Alan Luggeford, John Umfrey & Andrew Fleccher *v.* Richard Weller & his wife Cristiana in Wolkestede, Lyngefeld and Tanrugge

35 William Daventre, Robert Aubrey & Thomas Coke *v.* Robert Mokkyng in the parishes of St. Mary Magdalene & St. Olave in Southwerk

36 Robert Caxton of Stenyng in Sussex & Bartholomew Huller of Croydon v. William Shobyngdon of Croydon & his wife Alice in Croydon

8th *Henry VI*

37 Robert de Ponynges, William Fynderne, William Sideneye, John Bolne & John Halle *v.* William Halle & John Aston in Lagham Merden, Brustowe & Heggecourte

38 Thomas Caxton of Tenterden in Kent, Bartholomew Fuller & William Pulpit *v.* John Cokke of Croydon cordewaner & his wife Dionisia in Croydon

39 John Burgh and his wife Katherine *v.* William Walworth of London & his wife Margaret in Suthwerk

40 John Corff, William Estfeld citizen & mercer of London, John Carpenter junior & Richard Claydiche *v.* John Burgh & his wife Katherine in Wodemeresthorn

41 Robert Mildenhale of London junior *v.* Thomas Clay & his wife Johanna in Kyngeston

42 John Thorp & William Skirne *v.* Thomas Neweam & his wife Matilda in Chertesey

43 Peter Savereye & his wife Juliana *v.* Walter Grene & his wife Alesia & Thomas Motte & his wife Margaret in Suthwerk

44 William Ekton & his wife Matilda *v.* Thomas Godewyn & his wife Johanna in Southwerk

45 Johanna Russell of Chertesey *v.* John Reffawe & his wife Margaret in Pyryford

46 Johanna widow of Nicholas Bekwell *v.* John Carter of Frankyngham & his wife Agnes & John Smyth of London & his wife Johanna in Pekham & Camerwell

9th *Henry VI*

47 John Cook *v.* Robert Brounyng of Croydon & his wife Agnes in Croydon

48 Thomas Catteslond & his wife Johanna *v.* Geoffrey Mugge & his wife Johanna in Guldeford & Stoke juxta Guldeford

49 Robert Cawode, Robert Otteley John Fray, Thomas Broket, William Askewe & Thomas Hereford *v.* Nicholas Libard & his wife Isabella widow of Thomas Byssh late of Suthwerk in Suthwerk

50 William Ferrour of London brewer, Nicholas Newetymbyr gentilman, Robert Smith of London brewer, John Reyner of London brewer & William Porland of London clerk *v.* John Stacy citizen & glover of London & his wife Johanna in Chertesey

10th *Henry VI*

51 Thomas Lucas & his wife Margaret *v.* William Dogge & his wife Johanna in Lambehithe & Streteham

10th and 11th *Henry VI*

55 John Bracy of London chaundeler, Peter Aumener & John Horell of London dyer *v.* John Neudegate esquire in Horle, Legh & West Chayham

59 Thomas Laton *v.* John William & wife Johanna in Wandesworth

11th *Henry VI*

52 Henry Brampton & Thomas Morton *v.* Robert Morton & his wife Agnes in Blecchynglegh

53 John Iwardeby & his wife Katherine *v.* Nicholas Banastre in Guldeforde & Stoke juxta Guldeford
54 John Corve, Thomas Haydok & Ralph Wymeldon *v.* John Feriby esquire & his wife Johanna in Westhorslegh
56 Thomas Morstede esquire *v.* Roger Camoys K^t in Wotton
57 Adam Levelord, Thomas Haydok, Nicholas Preest & Thomas Cowper *v.* Thomas Caperon & his wife Margaret in the parish of St. Mary Newenton
58 John Potyer of Wokkyng *v.* Robert Tendale esquire & his wife Alice in Kembryssheford

12th *Henry VI*

60 Reginald Cobham Kt., Richard Wakehurst & John Gaynesford *v.* Robert Dodche & his wife Margaret in Lyngefeld
61 Henry Purchase citizen & grocer of London, Thomas Cowper of Suthwerk *v.* John Cross citizen and wexchaundeler of London & his wife Alice in Kersaulton
62 Augustin Haukyns & his wife Agnes *v.* Alianor Covert wedowe & Thomas Covert in Chalvedon
63 John Onderheld of Lynghefeld senior & John Onderheld junior *v.* John Woghere & his wife Margery in Lynghefeld

13th *Henry VI*

64 John Janyn & Hugh Assheby *v.* John Skelton & his wife Katherine in Gildeford & Stoke juxta Gildeforde
65 John Janyn & Hugh Assheby *v.* Walter Stirkland esquire & his wife Elizabeth in Gildeforde & Stoke juxta Guldeford
66 William Kyng of Suthwerk, William Brook clerk, Adam Levelord, William Kirketon & Thomas Cowper *v.* Robert Faireford & his wife Juliana in the parish of St. George Suthwerk
67 Stephen Lylborn & his wife Johanna *v.* William Grovere clerk & William Hayward in Farnam
68 John Gouderyche esquire & his wife Margery *v.* Thomas Caperon of Suthwerk & his wife Margaret in Suthwerk

69 Robert Symond of Byflete *v.* John Preston of Gyldeford & his wife Johanna in Puryforde, Biflete & Coveham

70 Thomas Waram, Thomas Heryng & Thomas Chambre of Croydon *r.* Hugh Spark of Croydon & his wife Margaret in Croydon

71 William Ludlowe *v.* John Aubrey & his wife Johanna daughter of Robert Russell in Pyryford

72 Thomas Arblaster & John Harpur *v.* Humfrey Earl of Stafford & his wife Anna in Blecchynglee

14*th* Henry VI

73 John Gaynesford senior, Richard Derman & William Derman *r.* John Stokwod & his wife Agnes in Lyngefeld

73a John Gaynesford senior, John Kyme clerk, Nicholas Sibile & Richard Derman *r.* John Dierden & his wife Elizabeth in Lyngefeld, Crowehurst, Oxstede & Lemensfeld

74 John Feryby esquire *r.* Richard Grene of Goryng & his wife Alice in Pirford

75 John atte Crouche of Penge & his wife Elena *r.* William Plegge of Bekynham & his wife Agnes in Penge

76 Robert Wyntereshull, Thomas Slyfeld & Thomas Elyot *r.* Thomas Waller & his wife Johanna in Guldeford & Stoke

77 Thomas Elyot, Thomas Bryght & Peter Northbrigge *r.* John Arle & wife Agnes in Guldeford, Stoke juxta Guldeford, Shaldeford & Ertyngdon

78 William Hervy, John Spenden *r.* John Newerk & his wife Katharine in Egham

15*th* Henry VI

79 Thomas Browne esquire & Alianor Arundell *r.* John Burdens esquire & his wife Johanna widow of Thomas Arundell Kt. in West Bechesworth

80 John Gaynesford, Nicholas Sibile, John Kyme clerk & Alan Luggesford *r.* Richard Hayward & his wife Margaret in Crouherst, Oxstede & Lemmenesfeld

81 William Chauntrell, Robert Caundyssh, John Hedy,

Richard Coronere clerk, John Foche clerk, William Clerk clerk, Thomas Groveherst & John Norton *v.* Robert Ponyngges K*t* in Suthwerk

82 John Aleyn citizen & vintner of London, John Hampton & William Abraham *v.* John Grymesby citizen & fishmonger of London & his wife Margaret in Wandelesworth

16*th* *Henry VI*

83 John Ripon *v.* William Brynke & his wife Margaret & John Rand in Hamme juxta Kyngeston

84 Master Nicholas Ryxton clerk Thomas Beaumond salter & Thomas Hale fishmonger *v.* Stephen Hayne carpenter & his wife Johanna in Wymbeldon

85 John Gaynesford, Nicholas Sibyle, Richard Jay & Alan Luggesford *v.* John atte Halle & his wife Johanna in Crouherst, Tanrugge & Oxstede

9*th* & 17*th* *Henry VI*

93 Thomas Joop & Adam Storme *v.* Adam Pykeman & his wife Emma in Croydon

17*th* *Henry VI*

86 John Savage citizen & vintner of London, Richard Browene citizen & chandler of London & Thomas Maldon chaplain *v.* John Deys citizen & mercer of London & his wife Elizabeth widow of John Perneys son & heir of John Perneys citizen & alderman of London & John Maldon citizen & grocer of London in Bencham

87 Richard Wether & his wife Lucy *v.* John Smyth of London brewer & his wife Johanna in Camerwell

88 John Stopyndon clerk, William Skerne & Richard Drax *v.* John Beverley & wife Johanna in Talworth

89 John Reynold master of the school of St. Paul's London *v.* William Cosyn & his wife Elizabeth in Batrycheseye

90 Adam Levelord & William Kirketon *v.* Nicholas Hough & his wife Katherine in the parish of St. Margaret Suthwerk

91 Stephen Mugge *v.* Hugh Asshebury & his wife Johanna in Guldeford

92 John Wynter, John Fountaynes & Matthew Foucher *v.* Henry Lynster & his wife Margaret in Lambehithe, Camberwell & Streteham

94 Thomas Osbarn of Petteworth *v.* Thomas Somur & his wife Johanna in the parish of Chydyngfold

95 Abam Levelord *v.* Thomas Capron of Suthwerk & his wife Margaret in Newenton and in the parish of St. George Suthwerk

18*th* *Henry VI*

96 John Crosse, Richard Saxilby chaplain, Nicholas Silverton *v.* John Borley & his wife Matilda in Batersey

97 Roger Fenys Knight & James Fenys esquire *v.* John Bitterley esquire & his wife Juliana in Wandesworth & Batersey

98 William Thwaytes & his wife Margaret *v.* Richard Hyldere & his wife Johanna daughter of John le Mose late of the parish of Charlewode in Charlewode & Newedegate

99 John Brokholes clerk *v.* John Leycestre of Creshalton & his wife Alice in Creshalton, Sutton & Moorden

100 Richard attè Yerd senior *v.* John Macche & his wife Agnes in Oxstede

19*th* *Henry VI*

101 Robert Cawode, Thomas Kyrkeby clerk, Thomas Wharff, John Thorley esquire, Simon Waynflete clerk, William Saundyr & Richard Forde *v.* John Denewey of Suthwerk & his wife Agnes in the parish of St. George Suthwerk

102 John Stopyndon clerk & John Kyryell *v.* Margaret Kyryell, John Frolbury & his wife Johanna in

Sanderstede, Croydon, Waddon, Colysdon, Whatyndon, Chalvysdon & Mestham

103 John Bate clerk *v.* John Salisbury & his wife Alice in Farnham

104 Roger Bukyngham *v.* Richard Hunte of Shene & his wife Alice in Kayowe

18th & 19th *Henry VI*

105 William Kyrketon, Adam Levelord & William Brook clerk *v.* Thomas Caperon & his wife Margaret in Bermondesey

19th *Henry VI*

106 Thomas Sexteyn *v.* William Richard of Reygate & his wife Johanna in Reygate

107 John Janyn & his wife Elizabeth *v.* Robert Tendale & his wife Alice in Worplesdon

108 Thomas Warreham, Richard Dawene esquire, Ralph Leigh esquire, William Thwaytes, John Sutton & William Clow scrivener of London *v.* Lawrence Hay citizen & girdler of London & his wife Juliana in Croydon & Benchesham

16th & 20th *Henry VI*

115 William Lee of Aston & John Bykerton clerk *v.* Henry Pevensey & his wife Johanna in Padyngdon & Abyngeworth

19th & 20th *Henry VI*

110 James de Legh esquire & his wife Alice *v.* John James & his wife Agnes & John Byrkehede clerk in Northlambehythe

20th *Henry VI*

109 Nicholas Wyfolde, Robert Horne, John Bartlot, John Langwich, John Deys & Thomas Heryng *v.* John Kyghle & his wife Isabella in Benchesham & Croydon

111 James Janyn & his wife Elizabeth *v.* John Puttok Junior & his wife Anabel in Croydon

112 John Bracy & John Bedford *v.* John Blaunche of London grocer & his wife Alice in Suthwerk
113 Thomas Galley, William Thyrsk gentilyman & Thomas Hert *v.* Philip Fysschwyk & his wife Agnes in Cherteseye, Thorpe, Egham & Coveham
114 William Fitz-Water, Ralph de Legh, William Clun, Thomas Heryng senior & Thomas Warham *v.* John Kyghle & his wife Isabella in Croydon & Adyscomp
116 Thomas Heryng senior, William Gaynesford & Robert Dodge *v.* John Puttok Junior & his wife Anabel in Croydon
117 Peter Stucle clerk, William Laken, Henry Sever clerk, Edmund Plofyld, Thomas Heryng, George Boys & John Borneford *v.* Arthur Ormesby & his wife Mercy in Wodmersthorn & Merstham
118 Thomas Ledredd *v.* John Parker & his wife Margaret in Okle
119 Simon Leviger & John Baker *v.* Thomas Goodman & his wife Elizabeth in Southwerk

21*st* *Henry VI*

1 Margaret Bate of London widow of John Gedner breadseller citizen & alderman of London, Simon Bate citizen & fishmonger of London & John Ludford citizen & dyer of London *v.* Alan Brymmesgrove citizen & gurdeler of London & his wife Alice daughter & heir of Thomas Henley & his wife Johanna lately of Cressalton in Cressalton Walyngton, Bedyngton & Ewell
2 John Stanley esquire *v.* Robert Botreux & his wife Johanna in Wandesworth
3 Henry Pakkere *v.* Richard Wodeward & his wife Johanna in Mayford
4 Walter Moylle *v.* John Davesoun & his wife Margaret in Clopham

21—22 HENRY VI. 187

5 John Merston esquire, & his wife Rose *v.* Thomas Warden & his wife Agnes in Britgrave

22nd *Henry VI*

6 Mathew Foucher & Thomas Lavyngton *v.* John Boteler of Staunton Drewe in Somerset esquire & his wife Isabella in Suthwerk

7 Henry Goode of Dorkyng, John Shirefeld of Merton, William Shirley & Henry Carpenter of Dorkyng *v.* Thomas Berton & his wife Alice in Dorkyng

8 Roger Cok & John Hatheway of Estgrenewiche *v.* Richard Sampson of Lesnes & his wife Margaret in Retherhithe

22nd *Henry VI*

9 Adam Lovelord & Thomas Couper *v.* John Parker & his wife Margaret in the parish of St. George Southwerk

10 John Taylord of Godalmyng, Henry Lederede clerk, John Payne & Thomas Elyot *v.* Walter atte Kythe & his wife Juliana & John Ottour & his wife Isabella in Haselmere

11 Henry Hale *v.* Walter Pollebroke & his wife Alice in Reygate

12 Lawrence Pygot, Alan Johnson, John Sturgeon, Robert Langford, Robert Byllyngey *v.* Archangelus de Pettys & his wife Margaret in Bermondesey

13 Thomas Gryfwold & Thomas Brown of Rothyng *v.* John Parker & his wife Margaret in Southwerk

14 William Gaynesford, Richard Colkok senior & William Moraunt *v.* Thomas Cheteman & his wife Alice, George Boys & his wife Katherine, John Cantelon & his wife Deonisia & Henry Rolf & his wife Johanna in Wolkested

15 Thomas Eliot, Nicholas Consell, William Thwaytes, John Fitz John, Peter Norbrigge & John Mundy *v.* Richard Wodeward & his wife Johanna in Guldeford & Stoke juxta Guldeford

20th & 24th *Henry VI*

17 William Saundre, Thomas Saundre senior, William Gray & Richard Forde *v.* Thomas White of Cherlewode senior, & his wife Alice in Cherlewode

23rd & 24th *Henry VI*

16 Thomas Lad & Thomas Gosse & his wife Isabella in Bokelond

24th *Henry VI.*

18 Nicholas Ayssheton, John Yerd esquire, William Venour, John Blewet John Wydeslade & Robert Clay *v.* Robert Godeston & his wife Johanna & Thomas Fraunsoys & his wife Agnes in Godiston, Walkenstede, Tanregge, Blecchynglegh & Caterham

19 Richard Gylmyn & Thomas Gylman *v.* John Milys senior & his wife Alice in Burstowe

20 Robert Charteseye *v.* John Lawrence of Colbroke & his wife Elizabeth in Horshill, Chabeham & Puryford

25th *Henry VI*

21 John Wotten & John Malton *v.* William Suthcote & his wife Katherine & Richard Langham in Retherhithe

22 John Kemsale *v.* Richard Longe & his wife Agnes in Chelsham

23 John Fastolf, John Malton & John Gargrave *v.* William Southcote & his wife Katherine & Richard Langham in Suthwerk

26th *Henry VI*

24. Thomas Lemman *v.* Richard Poynt of Bedyngton & his wife Alice in Bedyngton

25 William Rous, William Redeston, Robert Groute, William Thwaytes, William Clon & Thomas Warham *v.* Robert Rodelond & his wife Elena in the parish of Croydon

26 John Merston esquire, Mathew Philip citizen & goldsmith of London, William Burton & Simon Burton *v.*

John Moushill citizen & browederer of London & his wife Margaret in West Cheyham & Codyngton

27th *Henry VI*

27 John Crakall *v.* John Seman & his wife Edith in Ferryng
28 William Walesby clerk, William Fallan, Robert Kyrkham clerk, Geoffrey Goodlok esquire & William Godyng of Suthwerk *v.* Henry Wroughton & his wife Margaret in Northlambethe
29 Nicholas Consell, Henry Pakker, Thomas Mugge & Henry Fraunceys *v.* William Brygge & his wife Agnes in Guldeford

28th *Henry VI*

30 William Wedowysson & John Wedowysson & his wife Isabella in Mikelham
31 Walter Moille, William Moille & Roger Moille *v.* John Skarburgh & his wife Anna in Croydon
32 Stephen Balhorne & John Grene of Neudegate *v.* William Myre citizen & talghchaundeler of London & his wife Letice in Neudegate, Cherlewode, Okle, Lederede & Capell
33 Richard Forde & his wife Marcia, William Saundre & his wife Johanna & John Colard *v.* Thomas Sayer esquire & his wife Agnes in Westbergh, Banstede, Ewell & Sandon

29th *Henry VI*

34 Henry Fraunceys, Nicholas Counseyll & Henry Pakker *v.* Benedict Brocas & his wife Cecilia in Guldeford
35 Philip Leweston, John Stanley esquire & William Skerne *v.* Richard Marshall esquire & his wife Alice in West Shene
36 John Chancy junior esquire & his wife Johanna *v.* Nicholas Sylverton & his wife Johanna in Batrichesay & in Wandesworth
37 John Stopyndon clerk, John Brokholes clerk, Henry Gairstaing & John Gerveys *v.* Robert William fil' John William in St. Mary Magdalene Suthwerk

38 John Alvyn v. John Pycher of Horsham & his wife Margaret in Horle
39 Thomas Warham, William Thwaytes & William Clon v. Hugh Kyngeston & his wife Johanna v. Thomas Wesenham esquire in Croydon, Adescompe & le Wode
40 William Wode & Richard Estney v. Thomas Mortymer & his wife Elena in Micham

31st Henry VI

41 John Elmebrugge & William Burton chaplain v. Thomas Eylone & his wife Elizabeth in Blecchyngley
42 William Skerne v. Philip Leweston & his wife Margaret in Wymbildon, Maldon & Wandesworth

32nd Henry VI

43 John Gaynesford esquire, John Kympynden & Philip Amondesham v. Ralph Amondesham & his wife Milicent in Apese, Rypley, Wokkyng & West Horsley
44 John Bruton & Elias Ingulf v. William Ode & his wife Agnes in Pekham
45 John Penycot esquire & his wife Johanna v. Thomas Wyntershull senior esquire & his wife Johanna in Chakedon & Worplesdon
46 William Holt citizen and mercer of London, John Pontrell esquire, Humfrey Hayford citizen & goldsmith of London & William Skerne gentilman v. Thomas Grene esquire & his wife Matilda in Karsalton
47 The Master & Chaplains of the College of St. Peter of Lyngfeld v. Ralph Earl of Westmerland & his wife Margaret & Thomas Cobham Kt. in Hexstede, Bylysshersh, Lyngefeld, Suthwerk & Lymynesfeld
48 Nicholas Sybyle & Richard Derman v. Ralph Earl of Westmerland & his wife Margaret & Thomas Cobham Kt. in Lyngfeld
49 John Stone of London taillour & his wife Margaret, John Prynce, Thomas More & William Lynde v. John Chancy

junior esquire & his wife Johanna in Batersey & Wandesworth

50 Richard Colcock senior & John Skynner *v.* Richard Merston esquire & his wife Margaret in Kyngeston on Thames & Talworthe

51 Thomas Cook of London draper *v.* Thomas Chaloner & his wife Margaret in Watviles, Chelsham, Adyngton & Farleygh

33rd & 34th *Henry VI*

55 William Gaynesford, John Clerk, & Ralph Agmondesham *v.* Thomas Chaloner of Cokefeld in Essex & his wife Margaret in Lambhith & Camerwell

34th *Henry VI*

52 Thomas Eliot *v.* Arnald Brocas esquire & his wife Margaret in Shaldeford

53 Robert Whyte, Thomas Palshudde, Henry Pakkere, William Dernwynd John Sturmyn & Roger Bolton *v.* John Edyngton of Guldeford barbour & his wife Alice in Guldeford, Stoke juxta Guldeford & Shaldeford

54 Thomas Warham, William Thwaytes, William Clon, & William Warham *v.* William Kyng of Suthwerk & his wife Kersandria in Suthwerk

56 William Aclond *v.* John Stone late of Bedyngton & his wife Alice in Walyngton Cressalton & Sutton

57 John Belde of London dyer, Thomas Chambre, William Pulpyt & John Bartlot *v.* Thomas Leget of London goldsmyth & his wife Johanna in Croydon

58 Arnald Brocas & his wife Margaret *v.* William Brocas esquire & Thomas Dauberichecourt in Guldeford & Ertyngdon

35th *Henry VI*

59 Robert Wode *v.* Henry Appulton & his wife Florence in Camerwell & Bredyngherst

60 Reginald, Bishop of Coventry & Lichfield, John, Bishop

of Hereford, John Barre Kt., William Catesby Kt.
Thomas Mille esquire & Henry Honsom esquire *r.* John
Chancy & his wife Johanna in Batrichesey & Wandeles-
worth

61 Thomas Wesenham, John Skynner & Roger Wullowe *r.*
James Janyn & his wife Dionisia & Thomas Warham
of Croydon in Walyngton & Cressalton

62 John Grene of West Shene & William Sonde *r.* John
Benet of Wodemancote & his wife Johanna in
Newedegate

64 Robert Burstowe & Richard Jay *r.* John Maryotte & his
wife Alice in Horley

63 Robert Whyte *r.* John Weston esquire & his wife Johanna
in Farnham & Puttenham

65 Thomas Bulchild *r.* Richard Lambert & his wife Margaret
in the parish of St. Mary Guldeford

66 Richard Pykeman & his wife Johanna *r.* John Wastell &
his wife Agnes in Croydon

37th Henry VI

67 Richard Flemmyng Nicholas Marchall iremonger, &
Thomas Fermory *v.* Thomas Leget citizen & goldsmith
of London & his wife Johanna, John Parker & William
Walton in Croydon

68 William Gaynesford, William Moraunt & John Bedell *r.*
John Maynard & his wife Agnes, Richard Luggesford &
his wife Matilda & Richard Cook & his wife Sibil in
Tanregge, Okstede, Wolkestede & Croweherst

69 John Tudham & John Weller of Wolkestede *v.* John
Maynard & his wife Agnes, Richard Luggersford & his
wife Matilda & Richard Cook and his wife Sibil in
Horle, Cherlewode, Bokelond & Reygate

70 Thomas Warham, William Clon & Thomas Elyot *r.*
Richard Lynder & his wife Isabella & William Baven &
his wife Margaret in Croydon

71 Emma Bodely widow, John Skynner, John Molton, Henry Balford & William Povy *v.* Richard Culpeper esquire & his wife Sibil in the parish of St. Margaret Suthwerk

72 Henry Rukbare clerk *v.* Robert Lovell & his wife Johanna in West Chayham

1st *Edward IV*

2 John Underhill *v.* Thomas Aleyn & his wife Cristina in Wolkestede

3 Richard Byndewyn gentilman, & Edward Stone gentilman, *v.* William Stone & his wife Isabella & Henry Riseberger & his wife Agnes in Kyngeston on Thames

4 Philip Squery & John Squery *v.* John Chattok & his wife Johanna in Hamme Shyrley & Croydon

2nd *Edward IV*

5 John Elmebrygge & his wife Isabella *v.* Thomas Hexstall & his wife Anna in Suthwerk

3rd *Edward IV*

6 William Kele clerk *v.* John Wode senior esquire & his wife Elizabeth in Mulsey

4th *Edward IV*

7 William Burstowe & Robert Burstowe *v.* Robert Boweman of London draper & his wife Isabella one of the daughters & heirs of Thomas Englond in Horlee

8 Thomas Wattys citizen & breadseller of London, William Syward otherwise Peryn of Northampton mercer, John Gybbon chaplain & Richard Bray citizen & fuller of London *v.* William Skryeven of Wandelsworth & his wife Agnes in Wandelesworth

9 John Snell, Thomas Snell, Reginald Shirley, William Redeknapp & Robert Snell *v.* John Rumney & his wife Johanna in Croydon

5th *Edward IV*

10 Reginald Shirley & William Rawelyn *v.* John Chattok & his wife Johanna in Croydon

6th *Edward IV*

11 Thomas Danyell citizen & dyer of London, Humfrey Starky gentilman, Robert Vaus gentilman, Thomas Lewes citizen & vintner of London & Henry Benet *v.* John Lyende of Westhorslegh & his wife Elizabeth in Shaldeford and Bromle

12 William Stede William Rotheley & Peter Morison *v.* John Reynold & his wife Margaret in Totyng Graveney

13 Richard Illyngworth Kt. Chief Baron of the Kyngs Exchequer, John Denham esquire, Hugh Fenne, William Essex & Henry Merland *v.* Richard Forde & his wife Mercia, William Saundre & his wife Johanna & John Collard in Westburgh, Bansted, Ewell & Sandon.

14 John Scot Kt. James Goldwell clerk Thomas Goldwell Thomas Wynbussh & John Goldwell *v.* John Sellyng esquire & his wife Margaret in Bencham

8th *Edward IV*

15 Richard Aubrey *v.* Alexander Fayreford & his wife Agnes in Strode

16 Nicholas Bray & John Skynner *v.* William Bray & his wife Johanna in Nutfeld

9th *Edward IV*

17 John Goryng & Thomas Covert *v.* William Clement & his wife Johanna widow of John Fitz John in Guldeford & Shaldeford

18 Richard Illyngworth Kt. Nicholas Gaynesford Peter Baxster clerk, Henry Merland & Robert Bardsey *v.* William Wower & his wife Johanna in Coveham & Walton on Thames

19 Edmund Shaa, John Assheton Kt., Henry Balknap esquire, John Norbury esquire, Nicholas Gaynesford esquire,

Geoffrey Dowenys, Henry Merland & John Shaa *v.* Thomas Slyfeld & his wife Anna in Pollesdon, Great Bokeham, Dorkyng, Chertesey, Lethered & Stoke-dabernon

11th *Edward IV*

20 William, Bishop of Winchester, David Husbond clerk, William Gyfford clerk, John Neel clerk, Ralph Legh esquire, Thomas Pounde esquire & William Danvers *v.* Laurence Dowens & his wife Margery in Suthwerk

21 John Nutfeld *v.* William Walter & his wife Johanna *v.* Thomas Motte & his wife Agnes in Lemmesfeld

12th *Edward IV*

22 Thomas Stonor esquire, Humfrey Forster, Thomas Hampden esquire Thomas Ramsey esquire & William Weston clerk *v.* John Arundell Kt. & his wife Katharine in Ravenesbury

23 Ralph Wolseley *v.* Stephen Cole & his wife Agnes one of the sisters of John Martyn son & heir of Henry Martyn lately of Retherhithe & John Gary & his wife Cristina the other sister of John Martin in Retherhithe

24 Robert Hughlot *v.* John Grace & his wife Johanna in Wyndlesham & Bagshote

13th *Edward IV*

1 William Welbek citizen and haberdasher of London John Welbek gentilman, Richard Welbek gentleman & Robert Billesdon alderman citizen & haberdasher of London *v.* Nicholas Gaynesford esquire & his wife Margaret in Wymbeldon, Potenhith, Est Shene, Westhall, Hampton & Mortlake

2 William Essex gentilman & John Shelley citizen & mercer of London *v.* Thomas Bassett esquire & his wife Amy in Clandon, Burgham, Terrisworthe, Worplesdon, Chidynge-folde & Bramley

3 Laurence, Bishop of Durham, Thomas Bryan Chief Justice "de Banco" of the Lord King, Guy Fairfax & Richard Pygot sergeants at law of the Lord King, Hugh Damlet clerk, Thomas Portyngton clerk, Gervase Clyston esquire, Robert Forster & Robert Marler *v.* Roger Philipot & his wife Johanna in Batersey

4 Thomas Shouve *v.* John Mersher & his wife Alice in Horle

5 William Welbek citizen & haberdasher of London & Richard Welbek gentleman *v.* John Aunger citizen & vintner of London late of London vyntener & his wife Alice in Wymbeldon

16th *Edward IV*

6 Nicholas Gaynesford esquire, John Forster esquire, William Cornu esquire, Edward Gower esquire, Richard Skynner, Richard Tynkylden & John Slowe citizen & stokfysshemonger of London *v.* John Walshe & his wife Alice & Simon Arnold & his wife Agnes in the parish of St. Olave's Southwerk

7 John Apsle, Richard Apsle, Edmund Crofter clerk & Henry Belknapp *v.* William Uvedale & his wife Anna & Elizabeth Sydney in Godelmyng, Compton, Wonersshe, Shaldeford, Chedyngfold & Seynt Nicholas in Gylford

16th & 17th *Edward IV*

8 Walter Forde, Edmund Denny & Valentine Dunne *v.* William Merston esquire & his wife Anna in Britgrave

17th *Edward IV*

9 William Michell, Thomas Ryngston, Robert Hoge & John Mawetson *v.* Thomas Michell & his wife Elizabeth in Bedyngton

18th *Edward IV*

10 Robert Bardesey *v.* Robert Broke & his wife Margery, Arnald Danse & his wife Agnes & William Gryffyn & his wife Matilda in Walton, Coveham & Wysshele

11 John Saundir & his wife Margaret *v.* Richard Edward of

Colbroke in Buckinghamshire chapman & his wife
Elizabeth in Egham

12 John Holgrave, John Skynner & Ralph Tykkyll *v.* Thomas
Aylove & his wife Agnes in Nutfield, Blecchynglegh &
Horley

19*th* *Edward IV*

13 John Perkyns & his wife Agnes *v.* William Wyghtryng &
his wife Johanna in the parish of St. Mary Guldeford

14 William Collowe sergeant at Lawe, Thomas Trennayle
sergeant at law, Hugh Stepulton gentilman, William
Donnyngton gentilman, Nicholas Lathell Gentilman,
Thomas Burgh gentilman, & Robert Rede Gentilman
v. William Lettres & his wife Agnes in Suthwerk

15 Edmund Dantre, John Threle esquire, Henry Samford
gentilman, John Westbroke gentilman & Arnald Champyon *v.* John atte Hyll & his wife Alice in Dunsfold &
Hascombe

19*th* & 20*th* *Edward IV*

16 John Fenys Kt, Thomas Bourghchier Kt, Thomas Fenys
esquire, John Devenyssh, Thomas Oxbrygge, John Randolf, John Hardy & John Codyngton *v.* Thomas Burgh
of Walyngton in Surrey gentleman & his wife Alice in
Walyngton

20*th* *Edward IV*

17 John Exwold senior & his wife Margaret *v.* William Scotte
& his wife Agnes in Worplesdon

18 John Couper & William Couper *v.* John Kirkeman & his
wife Johanna in Nutfeld

19 John Graunt *v.* Thomas Eylove & his wife Agnes in
Blecchynglegh

21*st* *Edward IV*

20 The King *v.* Thomas Stanley of Stanley Kt. & his wife
Margaret Countess of Richemund in Bagshote

21 Robert Bradsha goldsmith, Richard Chawry salter, Thomas

Wode goldsmith & Richard Chambre *v.* James Piers & his wife Johanna in Croydon & Adescombe

22 Roger Philpot & Richard Cobham *v.* Nicholas Silverton & his wife Johanna in Kentisshestrete

23 Thomas Bowre citizen & baker of London *v.* John Byrte citizen & fuller of London *v.* Thomas Gwynne & his wife Juliana widow of John Rykkell in Wandelesworth

24 Richard Scopeham & his wife Katherine, Edward Wydevyle Kt, Thomas Bourghchier Kt, Thomas Pynde, Richard Kelet & Valentine Doune *v.* Robert Thornton & his wife Amy & Thomas Shirwode & his wife Margaret in Newenton & Waleworth

22nd Edward IV

25 Thomas Wheler of Stoke & John Wheler *v.* William Vernon & his wife Johanna in Guldeford, Shalford & Stoke juxta Guldeford

1st Edward V (inserted as 1st Edward IV in the last bundle)

1 John Thetcher, John Burton, Thomas Billyngton & Richard Bengeman *v.* Richard Stevenson & his wife Margaret, William Warboys & Thomas Bate in Suthwerk

1st Richard III

4 Reginald Sondes esquire *v.* William Gage esquire & his wife Alice, Thomas Hoo esquire, Richard Leukenore esquire senior, William Hapton clerk & John Byssh in Lyngefeld

1 Humfrey Conyngesby, Robert Worthyngton & John Agmondesham *v.* Ranulph Billyngton & his wife Johanna in Bermondesey

2 Roger Johnson *v.* John Edward & his wife Alice in Croydon

3 Richard Skymer *v.* William Swayneslond & his wife Alice in Chipstede

5 John Holnherst, Oliver Knyght, Thomas Palmer, Richard Martyn & William Webbe *v.* Richard Morden & his wife Alice in Sutton

6 John Benet *v.* John Bank of Est Horsley & his wife Margery in Lethered

7 William Capell esquire, Roger Philpot gentleman, John Broun gentleman *v.* William Vernon of London grocer & his wife Johanna in Suthwerk

1ˢᵗ *Henry VII*

5 Henry Saunder *v.* John Kirkeman & his wife Johanna in North Talworth, South Talworth & Long Ditton

2ⁿᵈ *Henry VII*

13 John Dynham Kt Lord Dynham *v.* John Grave & his wife Anna in Lambheth

15 John Bevyll notary & Richard Fenrother chaplain *v.* Edward Waker & his wife Margery in Waybrigge

2 William Capell Kt, John Gardener & Ranulph Bank *v.* Clement Naylyngherst & his wife Elizabeth in Croydon

3ʳᵈ *Henry VII*

18 Richard Tyngylden, William Bukke & William Milbourne *v.* Richard Forde & his wife Agnes in Suthwerk

5 Thomas Wilkynson clerk *v.* William Slefeld Kt. & his wife Alianor in Wymbaldon

38 Robert Rede sergeant at law, Richard Higham, Robert Weston, Stephen Jenyn & Thomas Vocatour *v.* Edward Hexstall & his wife Elizabeth in Croydon & Streteham

4ᵗʰ *Henry VII*

10 Thomas Bourghchier Kt, Christofer Warde Kt, Nicholas Lathell a Baron of the King's Exchequer, John Fitzherbert, William Barowe, John Westbroke, Richard Elyot, William Wode, John Polstede & Henry Norbrigge *v.* William Wyghtryng & his wife Johanna in Wurplesdon & Sende

25 Nicholas Nynes & Maurice Taillour *v.* John Hert & his wife Isabella, Thomas Denton & his wife Margaret, Robert Boughton & his wife Margaret, & John Barnard & his wife Alice in Barnes

24 Richard Chawery, Thomas Twisaday, Richard Adyff, Robert Haukyns & Reginald Pegge v. John Wodesdon & his wife Dionis in Wolstede

5 Richard Steven & his wife Johanna v. Thomas Compton & his wife Margaret in Blechynglegh

5th *Henry VII*

25 John Legh & Edmund Deny v. John Yong & his wife Alice in Padynden & Abingeworth

39 Henry Somer citizen & haberdassher of London v. Richard Puttok & his wife Margaret in Croydon

37 John Mathewe citizen & alderman of London, John Hawe, Cristofer Hawe mercer & Henry Wodecok scrivener v. Edward Hexstall gentleman & his wife Elizabeth in Croydon

3 Edward Willoughby & John Skylle v. William, Marquis of Berkele in Reygate, Dorkyng, Guldeford & Suthwerk

20 John Legh & Edmund Denny v. John Yonge & his wife Alice in Guldeford

5 Owen Rydlay & Roger Rydlay v. William Vernon & his wife Johanna in Chertesay

6th *Henry VII*

7 Henry Colet Kt., Robert Turburvyle esquire, John Parker, John Bigge, Gilbert Girpen & Robert Parys & his wife Alice v. John Abell & his wife Elizabeth in Chirchsey

18 John Otwey v. William Bisshop & his wife Alice in Ferneborowe & Aldebury

22 John Legh esquire, John Banaster clerk, William Fissher gentleman, Ralph Tykhill gentleman, Richard Haweles gentleman, Richard Merland gentleman, Richard Illyngworth gentleman, Richard Skynner gentleman, Edmund Denny gentleman, John Skynner gentleman & John Rodford v. John Down of Effyngham Surrey gentleman & his wife Johanna in Effyngham & Legh

20 Thomas Bowre citizen and baker of London, William

Maryner citizen & salter of London & Henry Somer citizen and haberdasher of London *v.* Thomas Gwynne & his wife Juliana widow of John Rikhill senior of Wandelesworth & Richard Rikhill son of John Rikhill in Wandlesworth

14 Ralph Tikhill, Richard Illyngworth, Thomas Elyngbrigge, John Legh of Stokwell, John Legh of Adyngton & Richard Merland *v.* John Marchall gentleman & his wife Elizabeth widow of Richard Iwe late of London gentleman & Thomas Iwe gentleman in Sandirstede, Waddon, Colesdon, Whatyngdon & Mestham

8*th* Henry VII

2 Reginald Bray Kt., John Elryngton gentleman, Richard Stone & Henry Barnes late of Horndon on the Hill in Essex son & heir of Richard Bernes & his wife Anna in Sydewode, Busshelegh, Pyreford & Horshull

18 Henry Heyward *v.* John Castell & his wife Johanna in Wokkyng

25 William Batyson tailor, Richard Barley skinner & Henry Clough tailor & citizens of London *v.* Alianor Martyn widow of John Martyn late citizen and mercer of London in Bedyngton

32 John Wylde, Richard Skynner & Thomas Burgeys *v.* Cecilia Wyther widow one daughter & heir of William Elmet late citizen & dyer of London & Richard Aubrey citizen & haberdasher of London & his wife Elizabeth the other daughter & heir of the said William Elmet in Newenton

36 William Curteys, Bartholomew Reed, John Shaa, Cristofer Elyot & Elyot & Henry Wodecok *v.* Henry Vavasour & his wife Alice in Suthewerk

19 Thomas Morton esquire, John Morton, Henry Edyall clerk, Thomas Madys clerk, Robert Turbervyle esquire & Clement Clerk *v.* Richard Pole esquire & his wife Eliza-

beth one daughter & heir of John Goldwell & Henry
Wadlose & his wife Emma another daughter & heir of
the said John Goldwell in Benchamp & Croydon

6 Ralph Tykhull gentleman, Frank Marycie & his wife Isoda
in Oxsted

15 Thomas Grace & his wife Johanna *v.* William Lyon & his
wife Margeret & Johanna Grove widow in Sutton &
Micham

17 Richard Eliot & John Neuton *v.* Laurence Normanton &
his wife Mary in Wandelesworth

9*th* *Henry VII*

28 William Goldsmyth clerk *v.* Henry Stoughton senior in
Stoughton & Stoke juxta Guldeford

45 John Legh, Ralph Legh & Edmund Denney *v.* Thomas
Baker & his wife Johanna *v.* John Bolle junior & his wife
Margaret in Lambehith

33 Ralph Legh & Edmund Denney *v.* John Neudegate senior
& his wife Isabella in Westlond, Ewehurst, Okeley,
Wotton & Abingeworth

46 Michael Skynner, John Scote & John Skynner *v.* Cristofer
Middelton & his wife Margaret in Colde Abbey

8 Edward Bouchier esquire, Robert Tywell, Henry Tykkell,
Thomas Schurley, Richard Cooke, Robert Dawse & John
Potter senior *v.* Richard Potter & his wife Johanna in
Croydon

22 Anna Seyntleger, Gregory Skipwith, John Westbroke,
Thomas Clyfforde & Richard Hungerford *v.* Richard
Marten & his wife Elizabeth in Shaldeford

25 Thomas Thwaytis Kt *v.* Roger Leukenore esquire son of
Roger Leukenore Kt & his wife Anna in Barnes, Put-
teneth & Mortlake

18 Reginald Bray Kt, David Phylyp, John Shawe, Bartholomew
Rede & John Argentyne clerk *v.* Thomas Allerton & his

wife Johanna widow of Thomas Warner in Waybrugge & Walton

13 Henry Wodecok, Thomas Butsyde, Edmund Tasburgh & Henry Walter *v.* Thomas Baker & his wife Johanna in Lambeheth

10*th* *Henry VII*

22 John Legh esquire, Edmund Denny, Ralph Legh, Thomas Barbon & Nicholas Elyot *v.* Cristofer Burford & his wife Agnes in Asshested

24 Lawrence Aylmere & Thomas Aylmere *v.* Thomas Fenys Kt, Lord Dacre son & heir of John Fenys Kt. & his wife Anna in Walyngton & Bedyngton

31 William Bishop of Lichfield & Coventry, William Hody Kt, Hugh Oldam clerk, Richard Emson, William Cooke, Humfrey Conyngesby & Nicholas Compton *v.* James Seynt-Leger in Shire, Vachery & Aldfold

29 The same *v.* William Boleyn Kt in Shire, Vachery & Aldfold

27 The same *v.* Thomas Ormond Lord Ormond, William Boleyn Kt. & his wife Margaret & James Seynt Leger esquire, & his wife Anna in Shire, Vachery & Aldfold

11*th* *Henry VII*

16 John Comporth of Adyngton & John Atwode of Croydon *v.* William Wody & his wife Elizabeth in Croydon

20 Thomas Benet *v.* William Lylly & his wife Elizabeth in Water Lambhith

2 Robert Haukyns & Richard Spencer *v.* George Gaynesford esquire & his wife Isabel in Hourne

8 John Brystowe senior *v.* Robert Cornwaleys & his wife Elizabeth in Horley

15 Thomas Giles *v.* William Byknell in Worplesden

6 Henry Norbrugge *v.* Henry atte Lee & his wife Margaret in Guldeford

25 Lawrence Aylmer, John Alymer, Thomas Aylmer, & John

Chaunterell *v.* Henry Hunte & his wife Margaret & William Horseham & his wife Mercy in Bedyngton & Cressalton

12*th Henry VII*

4 Thomas Elmebrigge, John Legh, Richard Carewe, Robert Gaynesford, John Gaynesford, Edward Ferrers, Henry Burton & Henry Saunder *v.* John Newdegate senior & his wife Isabel in Nutfeld

2 William, Bishop of Lincoln, Reginald Bray Kt, William Hody Kt, Hugh Oldam clerk, Humfrey Conyngesby sergeant at law, Richard Emson, & William Coope *v.* James Audeley of Audeley Kt, & his wife Johanna in Craineley & Shire

7 John Archer clerk, John Pasmer & John Worsop *v.* Adam Grene & his wife Agnes in Nudegate, Capell, Occle & Charlewode

13*th Henry VII*

29 John Wylde, John Skynner, William Burgeys *v.* Robert Hunte & his wife Isabel in Cullesdon, Caterham & Watyngdon

19 John Danhurst & his wife Johanna *v.* John Montgomery & his wife Cristina in Chertesey, Walton on Thames & Chabeham

3 Robert Haukyns *v.* William Wode in Totyng Graveney

9 Andrew Tudham *v.* Thomas Kyng & his wife Agnes in Horne

27 George Nevill of Burgavenny Kt, Lodewic Clifford, Walter Roberth, Walter Culpepyr, John Gaynesford of Crowhyrst, John Rober, William Assheburneham, Hugh Pemberton, Reginald Pympe, Robert Nayler & William Brent *v.* Richard Culpepyr & his wife Margaret & Nicholas Culpepyr & his wife Elizabeth in Ockeley, Bysshecourt, Roweley, Ockeley, Abymoure, Dorkyng,

Hoorne, Byrstowe, Goddestone, Charlewode, Craweley & Ifelde

21 Bartholomew Rede citizen & goldsmith of London, John Shaa Kt, Henry Wodcok & Christofer Elyot *v.* John Arnold & his wife Johanna daughter of Elizabeth daughter of John Wodham & one of the next heirs of John Wodham in Waybrigge & Biflete

34 William Mede & his wife Edith *v.* John Scotte & his wife Agnes in Micham

14th Henry VII

4 Roger Thorney & John Pykeryng *v.* John Colyns mercer in Suthwerk

44 William, Bishop of Lincoln, Reginald Bray Kt, William Hody Kt, John Shaa Kt, Hugh Oldam clerk, Humfrey Conyngesby sergeant at law, Richard Emson, William Coope & Nicholas Compton *v.* Richard Bysbrygge & his wife Katherine in Cranley

47 John Legh esquire, Ralph Legh & Edmund Denny *v.* George Gaynesford in Godstone & Wolkestede

15 Roger Grove citizen & grocer of London, William Spynk & William Carkeke *v.* Richard Constabull & his wife Johanna in Suthewerk

32 John Agmondesham *v.* John Rympyngden in Leddrede & Fetcham

39 Ralph Legh, Edmund Denny & Richard Clerk *v.* John Myllys & his wife Margaret in Wolkensted & Tanrygge

43 John Agmondesham, John Legh of Stokwell esquire, Richard Merlond & John Caryll *v.* Thomas Ryall in Pachenesham

12 Amy Merston *v.* Henry Frowyk & his wife Margaret & Anthony Forde in Bryttesgrave

34 Gilbert Stoughton & Henry Norbrugge *v.* John Haccher & his wife Katherine in Est Horseley, Effingham, Okham and Byflete

33 Ralph Merton & his wife Juliana v. Thomas Carter & his wife Rose in Effyngham, Est Horslegh, Little Bokham, Chertesey and Wokkyng

27 William, Bishop of Lincoln, Reginald Bray Kt, William Hody Kt., Hugh Oldham clerk, Humfrey Conyngesby sergeant at law, Richard Emson, William Cope & Oliver Sandys v. Thomas Huchecok son & heir of Richard Huchecok & his wife Alice in Alfold

18 William Danvers a Justice of the Common Bench & Thomas Danvers gentleman v. William Fynall & his wife Johanna in Saint Margaret's Suthewerk

13 John Hurste & his wife Elizabeth v. John Scrace citizen & vintner of London late of London vyntner & his wife Margery in Suthwerk & Newenton

14th & 15th *Henry VII*

19 Henry Heyward v. Thomas Colney in Walton on Thames

15th *Henry VII*

22 Mathew Brown Kt, Richard Marlond, Henry Burton, Robert Wodford gentleman & Thomas Horncastell clerk v. Thomas Wode & his wife Johanna in Est Chenam, West Chenam and Codyngton

23 Robert Bilby, John Brown, Henry Waleram & John Rynge v. William Pygot & his wife Alianor in Kyngeston on Thames

54 John Stone & John Gardener v. John Benyk & his wife Agnes in Croydon

20 Philip Hardys v. John Baker & his wife Agnes in Tattysfeld, Tytsay, Codeham and Westram

35 John Agmondesham, Thomas Champeneys & Cristofer Hawe v. John Rympynden & Thomas Rympynden his brother in Leddrede and Fetcham

13 Gilbert Stoughton & Thomas Purnoche v. Johanna Westbroke in Loseley, Imham, Godalmyng and Compton

23 Lawrence Aylmer v. Leonell son & heir of John Donton

- in Totyng Graveney, Totyng Beke, Moredon, Mecham & Walyngton
4 John Reed, Bartholomew Reed, Hugh Peyntwyn clerk & Richard Laken *v.* Humfrey Riggeley & his wife Alice in Walton on Thames
27 Brian Palmes, Walter Ruddeston, Guy Palmes, Edmund Burton, Edward Greene, John Ryplyngham clerk *v.* John Hurst & his wife Elizabeth in Suthwerk & Newyngton

15th & 16th *Henry VII*

30 John Shaa Kt., Thomas Frowyk sergeant at law, Edmund Dudley, John Mondy & William Capell *v.* Robert Woneham & his wife Margaret in Wolkestede, Godstone & Tanrugge
56 William Shert *v.* John Wrethier & his wife Alice in Shalford, Hascombe, Dunfold & Brande

16th *Henry VII*

77 John Wylde senior, Richard Masham & Humfrey Wylde *v.* John at Hyll & his wife Margaret daughter & heir of Cristina Pode in Camberwell & Lambehithe
8 Henry Knyght *v.* Mathew Mylshe & his wife Alianor in Croydon
9 Edward Alye, William Stratford clerk, John Alye & John Longherst & his wife Alice *v.* John Wyllot & his wife Agnes in Abyngeworth
12 Philip Hardys *v.* Thomas Kempsall & his wife Sibil in Tytsey & Westram
14 Thomas Kempsall *v.* Philip Hardys & his wife Alice in Tatesfeld & Codam
13 John Legh of Abyngeworth & John Auncell *v.* Robert Godman & his wife Johanna in Capell & Mylton

17th *Henry VII*

20 Richard Illyngworth & his wife Anna *v.* Richard Trewe & his wife Agnes in Mycham

33 Thomas Vicars *v.* Thomas Doyle & his wife Alice in Guldeford

7 Walter Champyan *v.* John Wryther & his wife Alice in Guldeford

8 John a Lee & Humfrey a Lee *v.* Nicholas Daly & his wife Johanna in Okley

18*th* *Henry VII*

49 John Legh Kt, Ralph Legh, Edmund Denny, Anthony Forde, Thomas Barbon & Richard Clerk *v.* Nicholas Daye & his wife Margaret in Bokeham

38 Thomas Kneesworth citizen & fishmonger of London, Edmund Denny gentleman & John Smith citizen & fishmonger of London *v.* Thomas Fulbourne & his wife Katharine in Suthwerk

21 Henry Ive & William Blundell *v.* Stephen Hylle gentleman & his wife Elizabeth widow of Humfrey Barton in Croydon & Adescompe

16 John Grigge clerk, Richard Marlond, Thomas Purwoche & Henry Wykes *v.* Richard Hert & William Andrewe & his wife Alice daughter & heir of Robert Constable gentleman in Maldon

27 Richard Aubrey, Eustace Knyll, Hugh Lechard & James ap Meryk *v.* William Bonde & his wife Johanna in Strode & Egham

38 John Kyngesmyll sergeant at law, Edmund Dudley, Richard Hungerford & John Otewell *v.* Thomas Fenys of Dacre Kt & his wife Anna in Wandelesworth, Batersey, Totyng & Putney

5 Thomas Marowe & William Smart *v.* William Irelond & his wife Johanna in Clapham

16*th* & 19*th* *Henry VII* (*this is in the last bundle*)

31 John Legh esquire, Ralph Legh & Edmund Denney *v.* James Homwode & his wife Oliva in Merstham & Gatton

18th & 19th *Henry VII*

40 John Skynner John Scott senior *v.* Thomas Tylle & his wife Alice in Lambhith

19th *Henry VII*

14 John Mongar & William Hamond *v.* Henry Norbrigge & his wife Alice in Bramley, West Shalford, Donnysfold & Guldeford

11 Richard Carpenter *v.* William Fygge & his wife Alice in Fernecombe

10 William Penycod & John Payto *v.* Anna Basset widow of Richard Basset in Chydyngfold

33 Edmund Hyll, Edward Hyll, Richard Martyn & John Redforde *v.* William Wynchester in Ditton on Thames & Emworth

24 John Legh Kt & Edmund Denny *v.* John Doune, son & heir of Thomas Doune & his wife Samithia, & his wife Margery Cade in Effyngham & Legh

20th *Henry VII*

3 Henry Norbrugge *v.* Thomas Westbroke & his wife Alice in Guldeford

5 William Warre & his wife Agnes *v.* Thomas Squyrry & his wife Juliana in Croydon and Addescombe

31 Reginald Pegge, William Buttrye & George Turton clerk *v.* Thomas Barnewell & his wife Margaret in Bernes, Mortlake, Rokehampton, Putneth & Wymbelton

33 Henry Wyatt esquire, Richard Wyatt, William Buttry, Reginald Pegge & George Turton clerk *v.* Thomas Lucas & his wife Isabel in Barnes

36 Henry Wyatt, esquire, John Scott, John Skynner *v.* John Sande & his wife Cristina in Walworth

17 William Irelond, William Yong, Bartholomew Spardour clerk and John Mydenale *v.* Amy Debenham widow daughter & one heir of William Edward late citizen & alderman of London in Clapham

21ˢᵗ *Henry VII*

62 George Monouxe & his wife Amy *v.* Peter Skarisbrig & his wife Cecilia in St. Olave Suthwerk

31 Robert Fenrother, Henry Worley, Nicholas Worley, Robert Hardyng, Thomas Caterall & William Kebyll *v.* William Stoure & his wife Elizabeth in Longe Ditton, Temmys ditton & Kyngeston on Thames

23 John Legh Kt & Edmund Denny *v.* Richard Govell & his wife Margaret in Reygate

4 John Legh Kt, Richard Sutton, Ralph Legh, John Sutton, George Sutton & John Legh clerk *v.* Roger Legh & his wife Agnes in Wodmersthorn, Chepstid, Purbright, Cold Abbey, Nutfeld, Pekham & Kynworsley in Horley

11 Nicholas Hughson & Thomas Hyldersham *v.* Thomas Calcot in Pachenesham, Letherhed & Feccham

16 John Gaynesford esquire & his wife Anna *v.* Richard Underhyll & his wife Elizabeth in Lyngefeld & Croweherst

21ˢᵗ & 22ⁿᵈ *Henry VII*

7 Giles Daubeney Kt, Charles Somerset Kt, David Owen Kt, Thomas West Kt, Edmund Dudley esquire, Jasper Owen gentleman, William Greyvyle & John Neudigate *v.* John Gage esquire & his wife Philippa in Wolkestede

22ⁿᵈ *Henry VII*

33 John Reed *v.* John Scotte gentleman & his wife Anna in Suthwerk

11 John Couper, John Fenner, Thomas Polsted, John Skynner junior & Nicholas Merden *v.* Thomas Fulbourne & his wife Katharine & Anna Fulbourne in Lynkefelde, Reygate & Gatton

29 John Richardson senior, William Marston, Henry Saunder, John Grofham, Richard Godman, Edward Hogeson & Richard Tayllour *v.* John Hatton & his wife

Johanna, Richard Wenright & his wife Clemence, John Vese & his wife Margaret & Anna Mersher in Nutfeld

4 William Sharp, John Degon & Robert Stanford *v.* John Gaynesford of Croweherst esquire & his wife Anna in Lyngfeld & Crowherst

22 George Emeryson, Richard Wyatt clerk & Henry Wyatt esquire *v.* Richard Hole & his wife Margaret in Waleworth & Horsmongerlond in Neweton

23rd *Henry VII*

45 John Scott, Mathew Broun, Henry Wyatt, John Skynner senior & John Skyner junior *v.* Edward Burton & his wife Isabel in Kennersley, Carshalton, Sutton, Mordon & Walyngton

13 Robert Fenrother, Henry Warley & William Kebyll *v.* Lambert Drax & his wife Cecilia in Kyngeston on Thames and Longditton

15 John Scott, John Lewes, John Skynner gentleman & John Scragge citizen of London *v.* Thomas Wode & his wife Johanna in Bermondesey

49 John Cokkys senior, John Bysshop, John Chowne, Thomas Burnell & John Cokkys junior *v.* Benedict Foscue & his wife Matilda in St. Olave's (Suthwerk)

32 Richard Broke, Anthony Fitzherbert, Thomas Polstede & Richard Marble *v.* John Pecche Kt & his wife Elizabeth in Bermondesey

8 Nicholas Hughson & Thomas Hildersham *v.* Thomas Cotton in Pachenesham, Letherhed & Feccham

1 Thomas Best, John Best, John Ravelyn & Richard Derby *v.* William Kebyll & his wife Elizabeth in Wandelesworth

14 John Legh Kt, Ralph Legh & Edmund Deny *v.* Richard Lee late of London gentleman in Est Cheham & Codyngton

24th *Henry VII*

59 John Legh Kt, Ralph Legh & Edmund Denny *v.* Stephen Rommyng & his wife Anna & Thomas Playter & his wife Juliana in Asshestede

24 William Batell senior, William Brayborne, John Mylle, Thomas Brayborne & John Brayborne *v.* Thomas Wryght & his wife Elizabeth in Farneham

DIVERS COUNTIES.

10th *Richard I*

61 Stephen de Turnham & his wife Edelina *v.* the Abbot of Westminster in Patricheseie

UNKNOWN COUNTIES.

13th *Henry III*

50 William de Colevile *v.* William de Besevile & William de Colevile *v.* William de Beseville who Johanna widow of Hugh de Besevile called to warranty and William de Colevile *v.* William de Besevile who John de Bedington & his wife Johanna called to warranty in Kersawelton

41st & 42nd *Henry III*

133 Fulc the Bishop of London by Robert de Trumpeton *v.* Peter de Pyrefryth in Wokyng

52nd *Henry III*

155 Adam de Stratton *v.* John fil' Saerus in Retherheth

54th *Henry III*

158 Adam de Stratton *v.* John fil' Saerus in Retherheth

DIVERS COUNTIES.

7th *Henry III*

25 John, prior of Holy Trinity Canterbury by William le Curteis *v.* Hugh de Nevill & his wife Johanna in Walewurth & Neweton

13th Henry III

69 William de Nortoft & his wife Matilda, Ralph de Ralegh & his wife Mabel & Godelot sister of Matilda & Mabel *v.* John de Lascy the Constable of Chester in Condington

14th Henry III

72 John fil' Geoffrey *v.* Roger de Dantesy & his wife Matilda by the Prior extra Bissopesgate in Ditton

15th & 16th Henry III

89 Margery widow of Odo de Daumartin *v.* John de Wauton & his wife Alice by William de Kingeston and the said Margery *v.* Roger de Clare & his wife Alice in Chipsted Effingeham & Mikelham

21st & 22nd Henry III

137 Ralph de Freschenevil *v.* William, Earl Warenne in Dorking

24th Henry III

156 Roger de Bavet & his wife Sarra by Sampson de Balesford *v.* John de Sey in Hachesham

160 Roger de Bavent & his wife Sarra *v.* Peter de Codington who called to warranty Walter de Merton in Farlegh

25th Henry III

170 Ralph de Cameys' *v.* John le Haud in Wudeton

26th Henry III

179 Master Thomas Ayswy *v.* William de Wylehal in Clopham

28th and 29th Henry III

199 John fil' Geoffrey *v.* Roger de Shyre & his wife Matilda in Shyre

32nd Henry III

228 Saerus fil' Henry *v.* William fil' William in Retherhe & Hagesham

33rd Henry III

239 William de Wintreshull & his wife Beatrice *v.* Phillippa de Nevill in Bromleg, Puttenham and Uners

37th *Henry III*

292 Eustace de Tycheseye *v.* John de Tycheseye in Chelsham, Codeham & Wycham

37th and 38th *Henry III*

297 Emma Belet *v.* John de Valetort & his wife Alice in Westshenes

39th *Henry III*

311 Richard de Mares & John & Henry his Brothers *v.* William de Mares in Tetlesfeld

42nd *Henry III*

338 William de Brademere *v.* John de Ynglesham in Kyngeston & Ditton

344 Katharine de Ely by Henry le Enveyse *v.* Edward de Westminster in Suthwerk

43rd and 44th *Henry III*

372 The King *v.* Peter de Sabaudin in Wytteleye

52nd *Henry III*

427 Walter de Merton *v.* Philip Basset & his wife Ela Countess of Warwick by Henry de Meleburn in Leddrede.

52nd and 53rd *Henry III*

447 Adam de Stratton *v.* John fil' Saerus in Retherheth

54th *Henry III*

462 Adam de Stratton *v.* John fil' Saerus in Retherheth

465 Johanna widow of Umfrey de Bohun by Adam Russel *v.* Umfrey de Bohun Earl of Hereford & Essex in Waleton

471 William la Zuche *v.* William de Wylburham & his wife Emma in Shenes

55th *Henry III*

482 Master Peter de Abyndon keeper of the Scholars House of Merton *v.* Walter de Merton in Meldon, Farleg & Leddrede

55th and 56th *Henry III*

491 Richard de Breous & his wife Alice *v.* William de Breous by Nicholas de Dytton in Brumleg

56th Henry III

500 Ela widow of Philip Basset by Milo le Messager *v*. Roger de Bygod Earl of Norfolk & Marshal of England & his wife Alina by John de Livermore in Wockyng and Sutton

VARIOUS COUNTIES.

30th Henry III

62 Roger de Clere by William fil' Symon *v*. John de Gatesden by Richard de Gatesden in Shyre & Crayle.

39th Henry III

123 Walter de Merthon *v*. Cecilia de Gravenel in Chissyndon and Mendon

DIVERS COUNTIES.

1st and 2nd Edward I

11 Adam, Prior of St. Mary Suthwerk by Brother Hugh de — his canon *v*. John fil' William Haunsard and James fil' William Haunsard in North Adeworth and Little Bocham.

12 John, the Dean and the chapter of St Paul's London *v*. Richard le Frauncseys & his wife Pagana in Bernes

2nd Edward I

18 The King *v*. John de Burgh in Bansted

6th Edward I

70 Richard de Knolle *v*. Alan de Haweman & his wife Amicia in Bagshete, Wyndesham & Chabeham

7th Edward I

82 Henry de Boun *v*. Humfrey de Boun Earl of Hereford & Essex in Waleton

9th Edward I

104 Nicholas Kyriel *v*. Roger de Northwode in Crawham

10th Edward I

121 Nicholas de Cryel fil' Nicholas de Cryel *v*. Agnes fil' Robert de la Lese of Eyneford in Crawham

122 William de Kirkeby & his wife Cristiana by Robert de Babbegrave *v.* Agnes fil Robert de la Lese of Eyneford in Crouham

124 William de Kirkeby & wife Cristiana by Robert de Babbegrave *v.* Agnes fil Robert de la Lese of Eyneford in Crouham

14*th* *Edward I*

163 John fil' Peter de Montefort *v.* Peter de Montefort in Assested

15*th* *Edward I*

179 Robert de Litlebury *v.* William de Hoo in Kyngeston

16*th* *Edward I*

189 Reginald de Cobeham & his wife Johanna *v.* Thomas, parson of Chartham church in Lyngtrefeld

19*th* *Edward I*

210 Simon de Goldburg & his wife Agnes *v.* William de Eton in Eggeham & Ingefeld

1*st* *Edward II*

3 John fil' Robert de Clere & his wife Johanna *v.* James le Bel of Fermesham in Chert

1*st* and 2*nd* *Edward II*

7 John Joce & his wife Cristiana *v.* John de Liston in Suthwerk

9 John de Ethebrigg & his wife Margery *v.* William de Esthall in Retherheth, Suwerk, Camerwell & Bermundeseye

6*th* and 7*th* *Edward II*

84 Gilbert de Clare Earl of Gloucester & Hertford & his wife Matilda by Adam de Brom *v.* Gilbert de Sancto Audoeno in Bechesworth

9*th* *Edward II*

116 William de Basyngestok *v.* Robert fil' William le Tannur of Kyngeston & his wife Margaret in Kyngeston

118 Hugh de Hereford of London *v.* John le Frenshe of London joynour, & his wife Juliana in Westgrenewych & Camerwelle

10th *Edward II*

144 Simon fil' Simon de Wodeham & his wife Katherine *v.* John de Matham in Certeseye, Wodeham & Pyryford

11th *Edward II*

150 William de Pyncebek *v.* William de Derham & his wife Alice in Hacchesham

11th & 12th *Edward II*

165 Isabella widow of Hugh Bardolf *v.* Master James de Moun in Adyngton

13th & 14th *Edward II*

189 Robert fil' John Allard of Wynchelse by Bertram de Suthwerk *v.* Hugh de Hereford of London in Westgrenewich & Camerwell

190 Robert fil' John Allard of Wynchelse by Bertram de Suthwerk *v.* Hugh de Hereford of London in Westgrenewich & Camerwell

191 Hugh de Audele junior & his wife Margaret *v.* Hugh le Despenser junior & his wife Alianora in Chelsham & Warlingham

192 John de Hastynges by Robert de Lalleford *v.* John Bernard parson of Wenreret Church & Ralph de Bockyng in Westcote

14th *Edward II*

204 John de Hastynges by Robert de Lalleford *v.* John Bernard parson of Wenreret Church & Ralph de Bockyng in Westcote

205 John le Latymer & his wife Johanna & Robert fil John *v.* Lambert de Trikyngham in Est Shenes, Mortelake & Wymbeldon

15th *Edward II*

209 Robert de Stenesgrave & his wife Johanna *v.* John Mason chaplain & Roger atte Pyrie in Blecchyngelegh, Wolkestede, Crowehurst, Lingefelde, Tanregge, Okstede & Lemenesfeld

17th *Edward II*

Robert Fitz-Payn & his wife Ela *v.* Jordan de Byntre parson of Wrocheshale church & Geoffrey de Godemanston parson of Wodelouch in Whisshele

231 John Inge parson of Lynleye church *v.* Fremmund Inge & his wife Cristiana by John de Bledelawe in Neudegate & Cherlewode

2nd *Edward III*

17 Alan le Fraunceys of Wrydelyngton & John Seman of Berton *v.* Nicholas le Fraunceys of Wrydelyngton & his wife Florence in Micham & Morden

3rd & 4th *Edward III*

72 Elizabeth widow of John de Spyneye *v.* Master John de Everdon in Wymeldon

3rd & 5th *Edward III*

78 William de Langeleye & his wife —— *v.* John de Moleyns & his wife Egidia & Bartholomew Galian & his wife Johanna in Fetcham

5th *Edward III*

87 Eustace de Eton chaplain & Geoffrey de Skardeburgh chaplain *v.* John de Haudlo & his wife Matilda in Retherhuth, Camerwell, Hacchesham, Westgrenewych, Suthwerk, Bermundeseye & Hamme

105 Roger de Northwode & his wife Elizabeth *v.* Durand de Widmerpol & John fil' John de Bikenore & his wife Elizabeth in Suthwerk

6th *Edward III*

119 John fil' Edmund de Berners & his wife Elizabeth by John de D—— guardian of Elizabeth & John de Bissopeston parson of Westhorsele in Westhorsele

3rd & 6th *Edward III*

124 James le Botiller Earl of Dormound & his wife Alianor *v.* James Laules in Shire & la Vacherie

6th *Edward III*

129 Nicholas Fraunceys & his wife Florence *v*. Geoffrey le Ros parson of Danseye church in Suthwerk

8th *Edward III*

153 William —— & his wife Cristina *v*. John de Hungerford & Thomas de Freitmantel in Adynton

9th *Edward III*

170 William Roce of Totingbek *v*. Robert de la More of Sutwerk & his wife Johanna in Sutwerk & Neuton juxta Sutwerk

11th *Edward III*

211 Thomas de Brewes & his wife Beatrice by John de Slopham *v*. Robert de Harperdesford in Bokham & Bromlegh

217 Thomas atte More & his wife Johanna *v*. Robert de Parnycote in Farnham

12th *Edward III*

225 Robert de la Haye parson of Dachette church *v*. John de Molyns in Henle

232 William Fillol & his wife Mary *v*. Robert fil' John de Latymer Kt & Hugh Fillol in Nobright

13th *Edward III*

267 John Dabernoun *v*. Thomas de Pernycote & Thomas atte Doune in Fecham, Aldebury, Stoke Dabernoun, Estwyke & Lamhuthe

14th *Edward III*

276 Geoffrey de Skardeburgh parson of Onebury church & Thomas Asselote parson of Wolstanton church *v*. John de Haudlo in Retherheth, Camerwell, Hachesham, Westgrenewych, Suthwerk, Bermundeseye & Hamme juxta Kyngeston

283 Nicholas de la Beche chivaler *v*. John fil' John de Sutton on Trent & his wife Isabella in Middleton

17th *Edward III*

322 Bartholomew de Burgherssh chivaler *v.* John Badesele & his wife Alianor in Horne & Lynggefeld
19*th* Edward III

356 John fil' John de Cobeham chivaler by John de Crukern his guardian *v.* Thomas de Alkham parson of Southflete church & John de Sheldon parson of Conlyng church in Werplesdon & Hacchesham juxta London
20*th* Edward III

434 Thomas Huscarl chivaler & his wife Lucy *v.* Master William de Carreu portioner of Bedyngton church & Nicholas Carreu senior in Bedyngton & Horlee
21*st* Edward III

406 Henry Husse chivaler *v.* Johanna widow of Thomas de Huntyngfeld in Hascumbe, Bromleye, Stoke, Fanne & Godalmyng
22*nd* & 23*rd* Edward III

435 Guy de Montfort & his wife Margaret *v.* Richard de Budiford chaplain, Thomas de Cumpton chaplain, Walter de Hereford & John Cullecuppe of Fosshawe in Asshstede
23*rd* Edward III

443 Henry de Bekwell & his wife Agnes by Henry Wykwan *v.* John Notte of London spicer, Thomas de Sudbury vicar of Camerwell church & John Shrympe chaplain in Camerwell
29*th* Edward III

519 William Pynkhurst & Alexander vicar of Ruggewyk church *v.* Adam Geffray of Horsham & his wife Letice in Shaldeford & Shire.
30*th* Edward III

525 Hawise atte Welle *v.* William de Stofold & his wife Juliana in Chidyngfold

528 Hawise de Wysham *v.* Thomas de Morton parson of Sheldeslegh Beauchamp church in Borstowe

32ⁿᵈ *Edward III*

570 Richard parson of Rocheford church, John Botiler of Waleden & Adam de Eirdale *v.* John de Nevill of Essex Kt in Ocstede & Stubbington

33ʳᵈ *Edward III*

584 John de Breouse chivaler & his wife Elizabeth *v.* Thomas de Breouse chivaler & his wife Beatrice in Imworth & Emilbrigge

35ᵗʰ *Edward III*

596 Thomas de Beauchamp Earl of Warwick *v.* John de Bukyngham, Ralph Basset of Sapcote, Richard de Pyriton, William de Salwarp, Richard de Sutton & William de Sutton in Cranelee

16ᵗʰ & 36ᵗʰ *Edward III* (*among fines of* 16ᵗʰ *Ed. III*)

303 Reginald de Cobeham & his wife Johanna by Walter de Kildesby *v.* Thomas de Frythyng in Stonhurst & Estgrenstede

37ᵗʰ *Edward III*

628 Nicholas de Lovayne chivaler & his wife Margaret *v.* John, Bishop of Worcester & William de Chirchell in Effyngham

40ᵗʰ *Edward III*

663 John Duke of Lancaster son of the Lord King, Humfrey de Bohun Earl of Hereford the King's kinsman, Henry de Beaumont, Roger Lestrange, Guy de Brien, Warin de Insula, Henry de Percy, Thomas de Lodelowe, John de Delues, Walter de Hopton, John de Lodelowe, William Banastre, Robert de Halsham, John Botiller, Roger de Delyngrugge, John de Kyngesfold & Henry de Wynnesbury *v.* Richard Earl of Arundel & Surrey in Reygate, Dorkyng and Bechesworth

664 Richard Earl of Arundel & his wife Alianor fil' Henry lately Earl of Lancaster *v.* John Duke of Lancaster most beloved son of the Lord King, Humfrey de Bohun (remainder as in 663)

665 Nicholas de Loveyne chivaler *v.* Henry atte Held & Richard de Brustowe in Brustowe
  41*st* Edward III
673 Alexander the Vicar of Rugewyke Church & John Bury of Rugewyke *v.* Robert Taillour of Rugewyke & his wife Letice in Iwehurst
676 John de Burlee & his wife Agatha *v.* Peter Beaumond chaplain & William de Islefold chaplain in Wonersh
  41*st* & 42*nd* Edward III
683 John de Garlon & his wife Margaret & Katharine widow of James de Bereford Kt *v.* John Pecche citizen of London & Robert de Gayton in Stokewell & Southwerk
  44*th* Edward III
700 Robert Lyncolne & William de Tarente clerk *v.* John Brok & his wife Johanna in Lyngefeld
  45*th* Edward III
726 Nicholas de Carreu *v.* William Dovill & his wife Juliana in Bedinton & Horlee
  46*th* Edward III
728 John Spycer & John Coresle *v.* John Isely junior & his wife Margery in Lymenesfeld & Crouhurst
  45*th* & 46*th* Edward III
730 John Mabunt *v.* Robert Eggyshawe & his wife Agnes in Shyre
  47*th* Edward III
740 Richard de Arundell junior & his wife Elizabeth *v.* Andrew Peverel senior chivaler & his wife Katharine in Reygate, Dorkyng, Bechesworth, Guldeford & Suthewerk
  51*st* Edward III
805 William de Brantyngham *v.* William Randolf & his wife Katharine in Aldershote

1ˢᵗ *Richard II*

7 Richard Prudhum of the county of Lancaster *v.* Thomas Ladde & his wife Agnes in Lyngefeld

50ᵗʰ *Edward III & 1ˢᵗ Richard II*

16 John Boyle *v.* Geoffrey Sonnynglegh & his wife Johanna in Lyngefeld

7ᵗʰ *Richard II*

91 Reginald Cobham chivaler by John Blast *v.* John Hert & his wife Agnes in Lyngefeld

95 Master Arnold Brocas clerk, John de Chitterne clerk, Peter Golde clerk, William Hermyte chaplain & Henry Holte *v.* Bernard Brocas knight in Piperharwe & Polyngfold

8ᵗʰ *Richard II*

131 Henry Vannere citizen of London, William More citizen of London & John Roce citizen of London *v.* William de Weston & his wife Johanna in Batreseye

10ᵗʰ *Richard II*

164 John Neudegate, Walter Knolle & Giles Taillour *v.* Thomas Eldrich & his wife Alice in Dorkyng

12ᵗʰ *Richard II*

184 Henry Boresworth *v.* William Badby & his wife Alice in Suthwark

14ᵗʰ *Richard II*

204 John Cobham esquire Thomas Tuttebury clerk William Burgoyne, Robert Lacy clerk *v.* John de Grey of Ruthin & his wife Elizabeth in Stoke Daburnon, Fechham & Estwyk

216 John Cobham esquire, Robert de Whitteby clerk, William Keteryng & Thomas Tuttebury clerk *v.* Elizabeth widow of John de Grey of Ruthin in Stoke Daubernon, Fecham & Estwyk

17ᵗʰ *& 19ᵗʰ Richard II*

233 Thomas, archbishop of York, John bishop of Salisbury &

Thomas Percy Kt *v.* William Heron Kt & his wife Elizabeth in Hecchesham & Bertyngherst

19th *Richard II*

289 John de Starle clerk & William Rikhill *v.* John de Cobeham chivaler in Werplesdon & Hacchesham juxta London

20th *Richard II*

301 Thomas Bokeherst & his wife Agnes *v.* John Hadresham & John Aleyn in Lyngefeld & Lemnesfeld

14th & 22nd *Richard II*

317 John Plecy *v.* Peter Plecy in Hethele

15th *Richard II* & 2nd *Henry IV*

16 Robert bishop of London, John bishop of Hereford, John de Roos of Hamelak, John Bagot Kt, Robert de Haryngton Kt, Gerard de Braybrok Kt senior, Gerard de Braybrok Kt junior, Philip Okore & John Hull *v.* Reginald de Grey of Ruthin chivaler in Westcote & Suthwerk

17 Same *v.* Same in Padyngden

2nd *Henry IV*

26 Walter Hoke & Thomas Joop *v.* Philip Seintcler chivaler & his wife Margaret in Lagham Meredene Heggecourt & Burstowe

4th *Henry IV*

54 Robert Whityngham, William Ledrede & William Godehowe *v.* Roger Belton & his wife Alice in Effyngham

65 Henry Pountfreyt, John Weston, John Hall, Thomas Sharp, Richard Lentwareyn clerk & Henry Gardiner clerk *v.* John Norton & his wife Johanna in Colesden, Watyngdon & Chepstede

5th *Henry IV*

77 William Brenchesle Kt, William Skrene, William Makenade & William Cherteseye of Essex *v.* William Rikhill Kt. in Patynden

6th *Henry IV*

87 John Dodde of Stanys & John Bere clerk *v.* Thomas Hurt of Stanys & his wife Cecilia in Egham

7th *Henry IV*

99 Richard Berners esquire & his wife Isabella *v.* John Bryan, John Denne clerk & John Ogham in Westhorselee

9th *Henry IV*

118 Robert Pobelewe clerk, Nicholas Stallyngburgh clerk, Thomas Pacchyng & John Double *v.* William Neel & his wife Alice in Southwerk Lambehythe & Rederhede

119 John Hadresham & William Newenham *v.* John Selverton & his wife Johanna in Hoorne, Burstowe, Nutfeld, Blecchynglegh, Wolkenestede, Lyngfeld & Croweherst

125 Richard Wakehurst *v.* William Crulling & his wife Elizabeth in Hoorne, Lyngfeld, Wolkestede, Tanrigge & Burstowe

126 John Prophete clerk, Hugh Luterell Kt, John Martyn, John Drax & William Cave *v.* John Oldcastell Kt & his wife Johanna in Retherhithe & Worpelesdon

8th & 9th *Henry V*

100 William Cave & John atte Trave *v.* Walter Herman & his wife Alice in Alfold, Cranle & Shyre

9th *Henry V*

107 Geoffrey Gebon, John Horlok, Thomas Conquer, Thomas Flyntesseind chaplain *v.* Henry Longspe & his wife Alice in Clopham

10th *Henry V*

110 John atte Ryde & Thomas Hylle *v.* Richard Lokke & his wife Lucy in Wyndysham

3rd *Henry VI*

40 Robert Whyte *v.* John Eddeshale & his wife Johanna in Farnham & Radshote

15

5th Henry VI

52 William Empyngham & Richard Hempton *v*. Richard Tyrell & his wife Anna in Great Bokeham & Walton on Thames

63 Thomas Dufhous *v*. Clement Yerdeley & his wife Juliana in Egham

2nd & 6th Henry VI

68 John Halle of Hellynglegh Sussex & John Aston of Somerton Oxon *v*. Thomas Seyntcler esquire in Bristowe

6th Henry VI

76 John Harpedon Kt & his wife Johanna Thomas Brook Kt & his wife Johanna, John Golafre esquire, William Warbelton esquire, John Tracy, John Bamburgh, Robert Fitz Robert, Nicholas Rykhull, Robert Colbrook, Robert Clynton, Robert Olyver esquire, Nicholas Waddon & Robert Vobe *v*. Reginald Kentwode clerk, Thomas Chaucers esquire, William Paston & John Chiche in Retherheth, Werpelysdon & West Grenewyche

8th & 9th Henry VI

111 William Catton & his wife Johanna & Agnes Basset *v*. Nicholas Banastre & his wife Isabella in Potenham, Burgham & Bromley

10th Henry VI

120 Nicholas Carreu senior & his wife Mercy *v*. John Martyn, Roger Heroun clerk, John Gaynesford & Thomas Heryng in Karsalton, Bandon & Nutfeld

123 William Purlee clerk senior *v*. William Perlee clerk junior *v*. John Cammell in Hethele

13th Henry VI

170 Hugh Willughby & his wife Margaret *v*. John Wodehouse clerk, Richard Byngham & Hugh Teveray in Asshestede & Newedegate

14th Henry VI

184 Nicholas Dixson clerk & William Halleclyff chaplain *v.* Henry Norbury Kt, & his wife Anna in Stoke Dauburn, Fecchem, Aldebury, Wyldewod & Estwyk

15th Henry VI

193 Thomas Broune, William Venour & Thomas Yonge *v.* Alianora Arundell daughter & heir of Thomas Arundell Kt in West Bechesworth

16th Henry VI

215 John Wakeryng clerk *v.* Robert Warner & John Gaynesford in Hampton Poyle, Guldeford, Stoke, Slyfeld, Chidyngfold, Neudegate & Capell

20th Henry VI

264 Richard Combe William Palmer & William Denys *v.* John Bourghchier & his wife Margery in Westhorslegh

21st Henry VI

268 Richard Waller, Thomas Uvedale, John Thornebury, William Port *v.* Thomas Batayle & John Monke in Wodyton & Okkele

271 Robert Ponynges Kt & his wife Margaret *v.* Thomas Lyseres clerk Richard Corner clerk, John Fooche clerk, William Clerk clerk & John Norton in Suthwerk

23rd Henry VI

300 Guy Porkelee & his wife Elizabeth *v.* William Bokelond esquire & his wife Alice in Egham & Thorp

26th Henry VI

330 John, archbishop of Canterbury, William, Marquis of Suffolk, Marmaduke bishop of Carlisle, Adam bishop of Chichester, Ralph Cromwell Kt, John Duddeley Kt, John Vampage senior, William Sydney senior, Thomas Baret & William Ernele *v.* William, Earl of Arundell in Bukkelond & Colley

27th Henry VI

343 John Olney, Thomas Broune esquire, William Cantlowe,

William Baron & William Benet *v.* Richard, Duke of York & his wife Cecilia in Shire

31st *Henry VI*

376 Richard Neder & William Humfrey & his wife Johanna in Croydon

377 Robert Payn of Bekenham & his wife Isolde & John Chapman *v.* Philip Roughhede & his wife Agnes in Croydon

32nd *Henry VI*

381 Simon Terry *v.* Nicholas Mason & his wife Elena in Batersey

33rd *Henry VI*

389 John Fortescu Kt, William Yelverton, John Markham & Thomas Tyrell Kt *v.* Ralph, Earl of Westmoreland & his wife Margaret & Thomas Cobham in Sterburgh, Prynkham, Oxtede, Lyngfeld and Tychesey

36th *Henry VI*

430 John Yngowe, John Matsale of London & Richard Colvil of Lenn Episcopi mercer *v.* John Colvile citizen & grocer of London & his wife Margaret in Clopham

431 William Catesby Kt, Henry Grene esquire, Thomas Littelton sergeant at law, Thomas Billyng sergeant at law, Thomas Wake esquire, Robert Tanfeld & William Cumberford *v.* Humfrey, Duke of Buckingham & wife Anna in Effyngham, Chepstede, Waldyngham, Tyllyngdowne, Caterham, Porkele, Upwode, Gaters, Halyngbury, Tanrigg & Caterham

VARIOUS COUNTIES.

49th *Henry VI*

3 John Anne esquire, Henry Spelman, William Constantyn, William Raynford esquire, Richard Adyf of London taillour *v.* John Elmebrugge senior & his wife Isabella in Suthwerk

5 Laurence, bishop of York, John bishop of Exeter, Roger
   Radclyff clerk, Richard Bothe esquire, [Seth Worsley
   esquire & Robert Bothe *v*. Thomas Stanley Kt in
   Batrichsey Wannesworth & Wassingham

   5*th* *Edward IV*
42 John Wodeward clerk & William Philip citizen and goldsmith of London *v*. William Davy & his wife Blanche in
   Sutton
43 Richard Martyn, Richard Forthe, Thomas Tycheburne &
   John Seylyard *v*. Richard Dene & his wife Margery in
   Flore

DIVERS COUNTIES.

5th Edward IV

33 Thomas Wareham & William Nele clerk *v.* John Massam
   & his wife Margery in Batersey
42 John Goryng, Thomas Covert & John Sturmyn *v.* John
   Turnour & his wife Margery in Hamme, Chertesey,
   Coveham or Coham, Waybregge & Egham
44 Thomas Batter & Robert Mauser *v*. John Upnore & his
   wife Elizabeth in Gildeford

8th Edward IV

57 Alexander Fayreford esquire & his wife Agnes *v*. William
   Bokelond & his wife Alice in Strode
64 Thomas Hoo esquire, Richard Leukenore esquire, Bartholo-
   mew Bolney, Henry Kyghley esquire, Roger Philpot,
   Henry Assheburn, William Lemyng, John Sherman &
   Thomas Boket *v*. John, Duke of Norfolk & his wife
   Elizabeth & Henry Bradfield clerk in Houghley, Gatton,
   Groveshed, Bradley, Reygate, Gatton, Mestham, Lye,
   Charlewode, Horle, Neudegate, Est Bechesworth &
   Dorkyng

12th Edward IV

85 William Edward citizen & alderman of London, John

SURREY FINES.

Edmund citizen & salter of London, Thomas Luce gentleman & Edmund Kervyle citizen & grocer of London *v.* John Colvyle citizen & grocer of London & his wife Margaret in Clopham

15th Edward IV

102 The King *v.* Richard Martyn clerk in Walton

16th Edward IV

116 Elizabeth the Queen, Thomas archbishop of Canterbury, Thomas bishop of Lincoln, William bishop of Winchester, William bishop of Durham, Edward bishop of Carlisle, Thomas, Marquis of Dorset, Henry, Earl of Essex, Anthony, Earl Ryvers, William Hastyngs Kt of Hastyngs, Thomas Burgh Kt & William Huse *v.* Elizabeth, Duchess of Norfolk in Reygate, Dorkyng, Guldeford & Suthewerk

122 John Grofham & Robert atte Legh *v.* John atte Legh of Effyngham & his wife Agnes in Lymnesfeld & Lyngfeld

VARIOUS COUNTIES.

1st Edward IV

6 John Hay, Richard Castell & Thomas Joly *v.* John Payne & his wife Margaret widow of Henry Hill in St Olave's Suthwerk

12th Edward IV

9 The King *v.* Oliver Manyngham Kt & his wife Alianor widow of Robert Hungerford Kt in Ditton

21st Edward IV

12 The King *v.* Thomas Stanley of Stanley & his wife Margaret Countess of Richemound in Bagshote

DIVERS COUNTIES.

1st Edward V

2 Reginald Sonde gentleman *v.* Ralph Josselyn gentleman & his wife Katharine in Dorkyng

3rd *Richard III*

10 Thomas Wode esquire, Edward Bartelot & Marten Ferrers v. John Gaynesford son & heir of William Gaynesford & Roland Ludworth & his wife Margaret in Lyngfeld

4th *Henry VII*

John Onley v. John Burgh & his wife Margery in Wotton & Okkle

5th *Henry VII*

Reginald Bray Kt, William Hody Kt, Henry Colet Kt, William Smyth clerk, Richard Emson, Bartholomew Rede, Thomas Riche, John Shaa & William Coope v. Edward Dudley knight Lord Dudley & his wife Cecilia in Nether Shepperton

3rd *Henry VII*

John Arundell Kt, Thomas Kebeell sergeant at law, John Brown, Robert Nevyll, John Capell & Thomas Boucher v. Edward Burgh & his wife Amy & William Capell Kt in Okestede

10th *Henry VII*

William bishop of Lichfeld & Coventry, Reginald Bray Kt, William Hody Kt, Henry Colet Kt, Richard Emson, Bartholomew Rede, Thomas Riche, John Shaa & William Coope v. Edward Dudley knight Lord Dudley & John Dudley esquire in Upper Shepperton

14th *Henry VII*

William bishop of Lincoln, Reginald Bray Kt, William Hody Kt, Hugh Oldam, Humfrey Conyngesby sergeant at law, Richard Emson, William Cope & Oliver Sandys v. Ralph Rympyngden & his wife Amy in Craneley

15th *Henry VII*

William Draycote clerk & William Hyde v. John Marton esquire & his wife Johanna in Maldon & Chessyngden

15th & 16th *Henry VII*

William Campion, Richard Emson, William Cutler,

William Holt, Robert Hill, William Byrell, Richard Herlewes & Robert Tendryng *v.* Henry Poyser & his wife Constance in Newenton

16th *Henry VII*

Reginald Bray Kt, Thomas Lovell Kt, James Hobert, Richard Emson & Thomas Lucas *v.* Thomas Darcy Kt & his wife Edith in Talworth

19th *Henry VII*

Edward Ponynges Kt, Thomas Fenys Kt, Thomas Marrowe sergeant at law, Edward Ferrers esquire & William Rote clerk *v.* Maurice Berkeley brother & heir of William late Marquis of Berkeley & his wife Isabel in Reygate, Dorkyng, Guldeford & Suthwerk

22nd *Henry VII*

Robert Bekyngham grocer *v.* Thomas Mosage & his wife Johanna in Suthwerk

I. INDEX NOMINUM.

ABBOT, EDITH, 166
    John, 115, 166
    Stephen, 69
    William, 85
de Abboteston, Roger, 68
Abbyngeworth, Richard, parson of, 104
de Abecroft, Beatrice, 67
    Thomas, 67
Abell, Elizabeth, 200
    John, 200
de Abernun, Dabernun or Dabernoun
    Constance, 70
    Gilbert, 9
    John, 27, 70, 77, 219
    Matilda, 9
Abraham, William, 183
de Abyndon, Peter, 52, 214
Ace, Adam, 60
    Hilditha, 60
Aclond, William, 191
de Acres, Edmund, 120
Acton, Gilbert, 146
Adam, Elizabeth, 152
    Johanna, 156
    John, 121, 156
    Katharine, 121
    Robert, 152
fil' Adam, Pagan, 36
    Isabel, wife of, 36
    William, 43
        Elicia, wife of, 43
de Adburton, William, 22
Adrian, or Adryan
    Cecilia, 54, 56
    John, 27, 56
    John fil' John, 54, 120
    Margaret, 120
fil' Adrian, John, 26
Adyf, Richard, 200, 228
de Adyngton, Edith, 65

de Adyngton, Maurice, 65
Agmondesham, Agmundesham, Amotesham, or Ammotson
    Isabella, 148, 162
    John, 198, 205 (2), 206
    Milicent, 190
    Philip, 177 (2), 178, 190
    Ralph, 148, 162, 190, 191
Aguilun, Agyloun, Aquillun, or Aiquillun
    Dionisia, 85
    Emma, 65
    Johanna, 11
    Roger fil' William, 85
    William, 11, 59, 65
fil' Ailbric, Alexander, 3
    William, 14
fil' Ailvard, John, 3
fil' Ailward, Gocelin, 3
fil' Ailwin, Henry, 6 (2)
Akr, William, 5
fil' Alan, John, 55
    Roger, 8
fil' Albred, John, 28
fil' Albric, Roger, 9
de Aldebyr, Isabel, 41
    Peter fil' William, 41
de Aldefeld, Adam, 118
Aldenham, Alice, 142
    John, 142
de Aldested, William, 118
fil' Aldwin, Emma, 3
de Alegate, Edmund, 81
de Alemaiyne, Margaret, 105
    Peter, 105
Alfat, Henry, 136
    Johanna, 136
Algod, John, 11
de Alkham, Thomas, 220
fil' Alexander, William, 31
Aleyn, or Alayn
    Cristina, 193

Aleyn, or Alayn
    Johanna fil' Thomas, 156
    John, 70, 108, 145, 157, 158, 183, 224
    Juliana, 167
    Katharine, 177
    Margery, 70
    Robert, 167
    Roger, 177
    Stephen, 82
    Thomas, 193
    William, 165 (2)
Alfray, John, 118, 170 (2)
    Agnes, 118
Alfrede, Agnes, 176
    William, 176, 177
Alfroun, William fil' Thomas, 100
fil' Algod, John, 10
fil' Alice, Isabel, 63
Alisaundre, or Alexaundre
    Margaret, 146 (2)
    Robert, 146 (2)
Allard, Robert fil' John, 217 (2)
Allerton, Johanna, 203
    Thomas, 202
Alot, Agnes, 161
    Robert, 161
de Alreford, William, 80
de Althorp, Walter, 151
Alvyn, John, 190
Alvyne, William, 144
Alwyne, Juliana, 171
    Thomas, 171
Alye, Edward, 207
    John, 207
Ambresbiry, Felicia, Prioress of, 21
de Ambresbiry, de Ambresbury, or de Aumbresbir
    Martin, 62, 67
    Rosamund, 62, 67
    William, 21
fil' Amfred, Jordan, 10
Ammory, John, 162
    Juliana, 162
Ammotson, or Amotesham, *see* Agmundesham
Ancroft, William, 149, 150
Ande, Edith, 75, 80, 82
    Thomas, 75, 80, 82, 88, 106
de Andham, Henry, 55
Andreu, Andrew, or Andrewe
    Alice, 172, 208
    James, 139
    John, 174

Andreu, Andrew, or Andrewe
    Mabel, 88, 93
    Matilda, 110
    Richard, 110
    Richard fil' Walter, 92
    William, 88, 93, 172, 208
de Anesti, Hubert, 7
    Matilda, 7
Anio, Dionisia, 113
    John, 113
Ankerwyk, Margery, Prioress of, 42
Anne, John, 228
Anshard, James, 29
de Aperdele, de Aperderle, or de Appilderleye
    Alice, 73
    Henry, 34
    John, 73
    John fil' John, 157
    Nicholas, 73
    Roger fil' Adam, 85
    William, 34, 41
de Appelby, Alice, 133
    Robert, 133
de Appeltrefeld, Gilbert, 60
Appelton, John, 155
Appulton, Florence, 191
    Henry, 191
Apsle, or Apsele
    Emma, 66
    John, 196
    Richard, 66, 196
Aquillun, *see* Aguilun
Aquitaine and Wales, Edward, Prince of, 133
    Johanna, wife of, 133
Arblaster, Areblaster, or le Arblester
    Thomas, 182
    Walter, 38
    William, 40 (2)
Archer, John, 204
de Archiaco, Fulk, 80
Ardern, Arderne, or de Ardern
    Agnes, 87, 101
    Alice, 142
    Isabella, 153 (2)
    John, 87, 101
    Richard, 142, 153 (2)
    Thomas, 32
    William, 153
Argentyne, John, 202
Arle, Agnes, 182
    John, 182

le Armeror, Emma, 69
   William, 69
Arnold, Agnes, 196
   Cristiana, 150
   Johanna, 205
   John, 150, 205
   Matilda, 113
   Richard, 113
   Simon, 196
   William, 144
fil' Arnulf, Agnes, 30
de Arras, William, 31
Arundell, or de Arundell,
   Alianor, 182, 227
   Elizabeth, 222
   John, 195, 231
   Katharine, 195
   Nicholas, 19
   Richard, 222
   Robert, 79
   Thomas, 182, 227
Arundell, William, Earl of, 227
Arundell and Surrey, Richard, Earl of, 119, 131, 134, 136, 143, 221 (2)
   Alianor fil' Henry, Earl of Lancaster, wife of, 221
fil' Ascelina, Margery, 24
de Ashurst, or de Asshurst
   Alice, 69
   Richard, 129
   Robert, 69
Askern, Cristiana, 143
   Thomas, 143
Asketyn, William, 147
Askewe, William, 180
de Aspeleg, Henry, 40
   Matilda, 40
Aspey, Isolde, 121
   Robert, 121
Asplion, John, 164
Asselote, Thomas, 219
Asselyn, Elias, 127
   Margery, 127
de Assesham, Johanna fil' Walter, 92
   William, 40
de Asshburnham, Johanna, 137
   John, 137
Asshwell, John, 177
atte Asshe, Isabel, 72
   John, 72
de Asshe, John fil' Ralph, 86
de Asshebrok, Alice, 124 (2)

de Asshebrok, John, 124 (2)
Asshebourne, Elizabeth, 121, 122
   John, 121, 122
Assheburn, Henry, 229
Assheburneham, William, 204
Asshebury, Hugh, 184
   Johanna, 184
de Assheby, John, 98
Assheby, Hugh, 181 (2)
Asshele, Johanna, 170
   William, 170
de Assherygg, Fremund, 68
Assheton, John, 194
Asshurst, Gilbert, 169
   Johanna, 170
   John, 164
   Richard, 170
   Thomas, 172 (2), 174
   William, 169, 174
de Asshyndon, Cecilia, 75
   Robert, 75
Aston, John, 158, 179, 226
   Thomas, 147, 156
Aswy, Assewy, Ayswy, or Eswy
   Adrian fil' Ralph, 10
   Thomas, 22, 25, 32, 35, 213
Ateruwebern, Peter, 19 (2)
Attefrith, Alice, 53
   Robert, 53
Attenovene, Walter, 59
Attewyk, Brunning, 40
de Attewyk, Walter, 43
le Attorne, Agnes, 89
   John, 89
Atwode, John, 203
Auberkin, Gilbert, 44
   Richard, 34 (2)
de Aubervyle, Richard, 81
Aubrey, Elizabeth, 201
   Johanna, 182
   John, 182
   Richard, 194, 201, 208
   Robert, 179 (2)
Aubyn, John, 145
de Audele, Hugh, 100, 217
   Margaret, 100, 217
Audeley, James, 204
   Johanna, 204
Aufray, Robert, 82
fil' Augustin, Robert, 24
de Aulburn, Agatha, 70 (2)
   Alice, 70
   Johanna, 70
de Aulton, John, 113

Aumesas, Aumbesas, or Ambesas
    Elizota, 92
    Johanna, 52, 53 (2), 55, 57, 71,
        73, 77, 87, 93
    William, 52, 53 (2), 55, 57, 71,
        73, 77, 87, 92, 93
Aumener, Peter, 180
Auncell, John, 207
Aunger, Alice, 196
    Isabel, 112
    John, 196
    Ralph, 112
Averay, or Auverey
    Cecilia, 156
    Edith, 48
    Walter, 48
    William, 156
Axsmyth, Anna, 177
    Richard, 177
de Axsted, or de Aksted
    Isabella, 24
    Roland, 9, 11, 24
Aygnel, Edith, 64
    Elias, 64
Aylesham, Thomas, 163
de Ayleston, or de Aylistone
    John, 106 (2)
    Katharine, 111
    Philip, 111
Aylmer, or Aylmere
    John, 203
    Lawrence, 203 (2), 206
    Thomas, 203 (2)
Aylove, or Eylove
    Agnes, 197 (2)
    Thomas, 197 (2)
Ayssheton, Nicholas, 188

Babbe, Agnes, 126
    Thomas, 126
de Babbegrave, Robert, 216
Bachelir, or de Bachelir
    Johanna, 100, 149
    Nicholas, 100, 149
Bachelor, Nicholas, 90
le Bachelor, Agnes, 60
    Walter, 31, 60 (2)
Bachemus, Francis, 98
    Johanna, 98
Bacon, Bacoun, or Bacun
    Henry, 5
    John, 174, 176
    Katharine, 174
de Bacsete, Geoffrey, 27

de Bacsete, William, 27
Badby, Alice, 223
    William, 223
de Baddeby, John, 122
de Badeham, John fil' Reginald, 58
    John, 58, 59
de Badelesmere, Peter, 8 (2)
Badesele, de Badeselle, de Badeshil, or de Badeshulle
    Alianor, 115, 220
    Anna, 102 (2)
    Edmund fil' John, 102 (2)
    John, 91, 115, 220
de Badrichesey, Peter fil' Walter, 2
de Baerne, Felicia, 56
    John, 56
de Baggeshete, Johanna, 109
    William, 109
de Baggeworth, Thomas, 88
Bagot, or Bagod
    Alice, 136, 160
    Andrew, 136, 160
    John, 224 (2)
de Bagschate, Robert, 11
Baillemunt, Robert, 12
Bakepuz, William, 173
Baker, or Bakere
    Agnes, 206
    Albrea, 3
    Albreda, 16
    Idonia, 158
    Johanna, 202, 203
    John, 16, 186, 206
    Margery, 152
    Robert, 16
    Thomas, 152, 158, 202, 203
    W——, 3
le Baker, or le Bakere
    Alice, 78
    Amphusia, 104
    Beatrice, 49
    Geoffrey, 49
    Ralph, 104
    William, 78
de Bakewrth, William, 15
Baldewin, or Baldewyne
    Alice, 139
    Constance, 73
    John, 73
    Mabel, 23
    William, 23, 139
fil' Baldric, Matilda, 19
fil' Baldwin, or fil' Baldewin
    Cristina fil', 2

fil' Baldwin, or fil' Baldewin
    Peter, 21
    William, 7
de Balesford, Robert, 54
    Sampson, 213
de Balesham, Gilbert, 92
    John, 64
Balford, Henry, 193
Balham, John, 155
    Juliana, 155
Balhorn, or Balhorne
    Stephen, 177, 189
le Balk, John, 44
Balknap, or Belknapp
    Henry, 194, 195
Balle, Thomas, 134
Balsham, Matilda, 147
    Thomas, 147
Balton, John, 161
de Balun, Henry, 28
Bamburgh, John, 226
Banaster, or Banastre
    Isabella, 226
    John, 200
    Nicholas, 181, 226
    William, 8, 221
de Bandon, Adam, 81
    Alice, 36
    Richard, 58
    Robert, 28
    Thomas fil' Richard, 36
de Banelingham, Mabel, 12
    Thomas, 12, 16
Banell, Cristiana, 153
    John, 153
Bank, John, 199
    Margery, 199
    Ranulph, 199
Barat, John, 161
Barbarius, John, 16
Barbon, Thomas, 203, 208
le Barbur, Barbour, or Barber
    Alice, 49
    Beatrice, 84
    Cecilia, 95
    Dyonisia, 57
    Elias, 89
    Hawyse, 76
    Helewysa, 19
    Henry, 19
    Hugh, 66
    Idonia, 66
    John, 76
    Jordan, 47, 49

le Barbur, Barbour, or Barber
    Juliana, 89
    Ralph, 61
    Symon, 36
    Thomas, 84, 161
    William, 57, 95
Bardolf, Hugh, 217
    Isabella, 217
Bardsey, or Bardesey
    Robert, 194, 195
Barentyn, Druo, 157
Baret, Agnes, 104
    Johanna, 148
    John, 31
    John fil' Peter, 104
    Matilda, 31
    Thomas, 227
    William, 148
de Bareville, Robert, 5
Barley, Richard, 201
Barnard, Alice, 199
    John, 199
Barnes, Anna, 201
    Henry, 201
    Richard, 201
de Barnett, Thomas, 145
Barnewell, Margaret, 209
    Thomas, 209
Baron, William, 228
Barowe, William, 199
Barre, John, 192
atte Barre, Johanna, 112
    John, 144
    William, 112, 128
de la Barre, Richard, 35
Bartelot, Edward, 231
fil' Bartholomew, Bartholomew, 27
    Matilda, wife of, 27
Bartlot, John, 185, 191
de Barton, Johanna, 75
    Philip, 75
    William, 75
Barton, Alice, 187
    Humfrey, 208
    John, 168, 173
    Simon, 156
    Thomas, 187
Base, Agnes, 134
    Robert, 134
    William, 134
de Basevill, Gilbert, 22
de Basing, de Basyng, or de Basinges
    Adam, 37
    Isabel, 45

de Basing, de Basyng, or de Basinges
    Johanna, 37
    Margery, 59
    Matilda, 19
    Nicholas, 45
    Robert, 19, 59
Basket, Isabel, 123
    Thomas, 123
Basset, Agnes, 226
    Alan, 37
    Amy, 195
    Anna, 209
    Ela, 214, 215
    Petronilla, 37
    Philip, 214, 215
    Ralph, 151, 221
    Richard, 209
    Thomas, 140, 195
    William, 171
Bastard, William, 5
de Basyngestok, Matilda, 81
    Petronilla, 119
    Richard, 119
    William, 81, 216
Bataille, Batayle, de la Bataille, Botayle, or Botaile
    Henry, 11
    John, 67, 97, 99
    Margeret, 97, 99
    Thomas, 227
    William, 7
Bate, John, 185
    Margaret, 186
    Simon, 186
    Thomas, 198
Batell, William, 212
Bath and Wells
    John, Bishop of, 92
    Robert, Bishop of, 53, 54, 56, 60
de Bath, Robert, 28
    William, 9
Batter, Thomas, 229
Battle, Odo, Abbot of, 2
    Ralph, Abbot of, 21, 27, 39
    Reginald, Abbot of, 46
    ——— Abbot of, 14, 25
Batyn, Johanna, 175
    Richard, 175
Batyson, William, 201
Baudewyn, Geoffrey, 108, 109
Baudri, John, 52
    Mabel, 52
    William, 52
Baven, Margaret, 192

Baven, William, 192
Bavent, or Bavet
    Roger, 213 (2)
    Sarra, 213 (2)
Baxster, Peter, 194
Baynard, Henry, 101, 104
Bays, John, 143
Beauchamp, Beuchamp, de Beauchamp, or de Bello Campo
    Cecilia, 80
    Gilbert, 123
    Hawyse, 86
    Johanna, 140
    John, 80 (2)
    Juliana, 123
    Petronilla, 68
    Simon, 68
    Thomas, 140
    Thomas, Earl of Warwick, 221
    Walter, 86
Beaufoy, Agnes, 144
    William, 144
Beaumond, Peter, 222
    Thomas, 183
de Beaumont, Henry, 221
Bec Dionisia, 18
    Henry, 18
de Bechampton, Robert, 44
atte Beche, Emma, 109, 114
    Symon, 109, 114
de la Beche, Johanna, 86
    Nicholas, 86, 219
de Bechum, Baldewin, 12
    Johanna, 12
de Beck, Agnes, 35
    Ralph, 35
Bedell, Bedel, or le Bedel
    Avice, 138
    Felicia, 96
    John, 192
    Simon, 96
    William, 138
de Bedenstede, Agnes, 140
    Laurence, 140
    Walter, 47
Bedewynd, Richard, 151
Bedford, John, 186
de Bedinton, or Bedington
    Isabel, 14
    Johanna, 212
    John, 14, 212
    Peter, 25
Beel, or le Beel
    John, 105, 175

INDEX NOMINUM.   239

Beel, or le Beel
    John, fil' James, 81
    Suzanna, 175
Beere, Elias, 169
de Bekeham, John, 35
    Robert, 11
    William, 12
de Bekensfeld, de Bekenesfeld, or
    de Bekennesfeld
    Andrew, 132
    Cristina, 94
    Johanna, 65, 132
    Thomas, 65
    William, 87, 94
le Bekere, Robert, 66
Beket, John, 151
    Matilda, 151
de Bekwell, or de Bekewell
    Agnes, 123, 124, 127, 220
    Henry, 117, 123, 124, 127, 220
    Johanna, 180
    Nicholas, 180
Bekyngham, Robert, 232
le Bel, James, 25, 36, 216
    John, 104
Belami, Geoffrey, 30
de Belce, William, 12
Belde, John, 191
le Belde, Alice, 85
    Gunnilda, 76
    Roger, 85
    Thomas, 76
Bele, John, 168
Belebarbe, Dionisia, 64
    Ralph, 64
Belemeyns, John, 21
de Beleshale, Lecia, 42
    Robert, 42
Belet, Alice, 10
    Emma, 214
    Michael, 10
de Bellevale, Petronilla, 13 (2)
Belot, John, 17
Belton, Alice, 224
    Roger, 224
de Benchesham, Philip, 14, 16
de Bendenges, Geoffrey, 4
    Peter, 14
    Stephen, 2
fil' Benedict, William, 12, 13, 18
Benefait, Constance, 143
Benefait, William, 143
Benek, or Benyk
    Agnes, 206

Benek, or Benyk
    John, 206
    Richard, 155
le Benere, Johanna, 80, 97
    Walter, 80, 97
Beneroche, John, 152, 156
Benet, Henry, 194
    Isabel, 148
    Johanna, 192
    John, 192, 199
    Thomas, 203
    William, 228
    William fil' Giles, 148
Benge, Edmund, 173
Bengeman, Richard, 198
Benstede, Agnes, 137
    Laurence, 137
Benteley, or de Bentele
    Johanna, 175
    John, 154, 175
    William, 83
de Benyngworth, Robert, 86
Berard, William, 133
de Bercherst, Alan, 11
de Berdefeld Gilbert, 114
Bere, John, 225
atte Bere, Johanna, 129
    John, 128, 129
de la Bere, Johanna, 96
    John, 96
    Lucy, 22
    Richard, 22
    William, 22
de Bereford, James, 222
    Katharine, 222
de Beregh, Matilda, 52
    Robert, 52
de Bereleye, Margery, 43
    Richard, 43
Berenger, Ingelran, 77
de Berewyk, John, 53, 60, 63, 71
Berford, Baldewyn, 157
de Berg, de Bergh, de Berge, de
    Berges, or de Berghes
    Nicholas fil' Henry, 105
    Peter, 9 (2), 10
    William, 37
Bergh, William, 168
de Berham, Gilbert, 27
    Lucy, 27
Berkeley, Isabel, 232
    Maurice, 232
    William, Marquis of, 200, 232

le Berker, Henry, 29
   Sibil, 29
de Berkes, Simon, 2
de Berking, de Berkynge, de Berkinges, de Berkinkes, or de Berekinges
   Alice, 23, 26, 29, 34 (3), 35 (2), 36
   John, 23, 26, 29, 34 (3), 35 (2), 36
   Margaret, 14
   Ralph, 14
   Richard, 92
   Roger, 54
   Stephen, 10
de Berleston, Ralph, 67
Berlyng, Matilda, 113
   Roger, 113
Bermundesey, Hugh, Prior of, 5 (2), 12, 13, 18
   Hymbert, Ymbert, or Imbert, Prior of, 26, 28, 31 (3), 32, 33, 39
   John, Prior of, 45
   Peter, Prior of, 53, 56
Bermundesey, Wyschard, Prior of St. Saviour's, 21
Bernard, John, 217 (2)
   Katharine, 123
   Roger, 122
   Roysia, 49
   Symon, 49
   William, 61
Bernardine, Alice, 74
   Pinus, 74
de la Berne, Alexander, 33
Berners, or de Berners
   Cristiana, 47, 53, 84
   Elizabeth, 106, 218
   Isabella, 225
   John fil' Edmund, 106, 218
   Ralph, 47 (2), 53, 84
   Richard, 84, 168, 225
   Thomas fil' Richard, 106
atte Bernette, Juliana, 96
   Robert, 96
de Bernewell, or de Bernewelle
   Agatha, 76
   Isabel, 43, 46, 50
   Margaret, 76
   Symon, 76, 77
   William, 43, 46, 50
de Bernham, Richard, 86
de Beroudon, Peter, 112, 116
de la Berwe, Alice, 26
   Hamo, 26

Berwell, or Birwell
   Katharine, 146 (2)
   Roger, 146 (2)
de Besevile, or de Beseville
   Hugh, 3 (2), 212 (3)
   Johanna, 212
   John, 99
   Robert, 4 (2)
   William, 13, 14, 212
Besouth, William, 169
de Besseford, Nicholas, 101
Best, John, 211
   Thomas, 168, 211
Beswill, John, 90
Betaigne, Robert, 152
de Betoigne, Johanna, 101
   Thomas, 101
de Beverlay, Cecilia, 50
   Robert, 50
Beverley, Johanna, 183
   John, 183
Bevyll, John, 199
de Bibury, Nicholas, 104
de Bidun, see de Bydun
Bierden, Elizabeth, 163
   John, 163
de Bifeld, or de Byfeld
   Hawyse, 76, 80
   John, 76, 80
   Thomas, 173
Bigge, John, 200
Bigod, Roger, Earl of Norfolk, 215
   Alina, wife of, 215
Bigot, Hugh le, 37
de Bikenore, Elizabeth, 218
   John fil' John, 218
Bilby, Robert, 206
Billesdon, Robert, 195
de Billinghurst, Richard, 35
Billyng, Thomas, 228
de Billyngford, James, 161
Billyngton, Johanna, 198
   Thomas, 198
   Ranulph, 198
Bircham, Geoffrey, 160
   Juliana, 160
Birchedenne, Cecilia, 126
   Thomas, 126
   Johanna, 119
de Birton, Ralph, 119
   Richard, 116, 119
Bishopton, John, 166
Bisshop, or Bysshop
   Alice, 200

INDEX NOMINUM.

Bisshop, or Bysshop
  John, 211
  Nicholas, 155, 167, 175
  William, 200
atte Bissh, or atte Bisshe
  Agnes, 141
  William, 113, 141
Bissopesgate, the Prior extra, 213
de Bissopeston, Johanna, 93
  John, 218
  Robert, 93
le Biterle, Richard, 95
Bitterley, John, 184
  Juliana, 184
Black, Ralph, 7
  Thomas, 18
atte Blakefenne, Henry, 66
de la Blakefanne, Henry, 109
  Robert, 109
le Blake, Alice, 119
  Nicholas, 119
Blake, Constance, 171
  Robert, 171
de Blakelond, Margery, 87
  William, 87
Blanche, Robert, 10
Blast, John, 146, 223
Blaunche, Alice, 186
  John, 186
Blawere, Matilda, 141
  Nicholas, 141
de Blechyngelegh, Adam, 50
  Agnes, 62
  Emma, 48
  Ingeram, 62
  Symon, 48
de Bledelawe, John, 218
  Thomas, 131
le Blenche, John, 22 (2)
Blenche, Frechisent, 9
  William, 9
Blewet, John, 188
de Blonham, Cristina, 124
  John, 124
Blund, or le Blund
  Agnes, 39
  Akina, 3
  Gilbert, 7
  John, 1, 39
  Matilda, 21
  Paul, 21
  Philip, 3 (2)
  Robert, 7
  William, 1, 9

Blundel, or Blundell
  Cecilia fil' Ralph, 27
  Walter, 172
  William, 208
le Blunt, Walter, 56
de Bobyngeworth, Isolde, 78
  Walter, 78
Bocher, Adam, 163
  Henry, 128
  Mary, 163
  Matilda, 96
  William, 96
le Bocher, Henry, 110
de Bockyng, Ralph, 217 (2)
de Bocland, de Boclaunde, or de Bokelaund
  Cristiana, 57
  Gilbert, 57
  Johanna, 49
  John, 49
  John fil' John, 61
de Boclinton, de Boclynton, or de Bokelynton
  Alice, 60
  Richard, 60, 97, 105 (2)
  Robert, 56, 60
Bocok, Thomas, 149
de Bodekesham, Alice, 116
  John, 90, 116
  Rose, 90
Bodely, Emma, 193
Boghay, Henry, 152 (2)
  John, 152
de Bohun, or de Boun
  Henry, Earl of Hereford and Essex, 88, 215
  Humfrey, or Umfrey, Earl of Hereford and Essex, 214 (2), 215, 221 (2)
  Johanna, 214
Bokeherst, Agnes, 224
  Thomas, 224
Bokelond, Alice, 227, 229
  William, 227, 229
Bokenham, Alice, 169
  John, 169
Boket, Thomas, 229
Bolaun, William, 24
Bolayn, or Boleyn
  Margaret, 203
  William, 203 (2)
le Bole, William, 8
  Letice, widow of William le Bole, 8

Bole, or Bolle
  Agnes, 27, 28
  Avice fil' Hugh, 4
  William, 27, 28, 39
de Bolingbrok, Richard, 94
Bolne, or Bolney
  Bartholomew, 229
  John, 177, 179
Boltford, John, 129 (2)
  Margaret, 129 (2)
Bolton, Edmund, 163
  Margaret, 163
  Roger, 178, 195
de Bolton, Agnes, 107
  Roger, 107
Bonchrestien, Stephen, 7, 8
Bonde, Johanna, 208
  William, 208
de Bonebroke, Isabel, 138
  Robert, 135, 138
Bonejoie, Godfrey, 24
  Letitia, 24
Bonet, Agnes, 151
  John, 146, 151, 157
  Matilda, 90
  William, 90
Bonvadlet, William, 29
Bonvalet, Richard, 142
de Bonynges, Henry, 54
Boresworth, Henry, 223
de Boresworth, Roger, 124
Borley, John, 184
  Matilda, 184
Borneford, John, 186
·Bornere, Johanna, 174
  Thomas, 174
de Bosco, John fil' Simon, 54
  Simon, 54
  Thurbert, 3
  William, 70
Boteler, Botiller, Botiler, Butiler,
  le Botiller, le Buteler, or le
  Butiller
  Adam, 27
  Alan, 128
  Alianor, 218
  Alice, 159, 173
  Dulcia, 33
  Isabella, 187
  John, 68, 187, 221 (2)
  John, Earl of Dormound, 218
  Juliana, 128
  Margery, 34
  Robert, 33, 34

Boteler, Botiller, Botiler, Butiler,
  le Botiller, le Buteler, or le
  Butiller
  Simon, 97
  Thomas, 159, 173
  William, 176
Bothe, Richard, 229
  Robert, 229
Botolf, Henry, 164
Botreux, Johanna, 186
  Robert, 186
de Botteleg, John, 42
de Botteleye, John, 77
Bottlegh, Johanna, 151
  William, 151
Bouch, Agnes, 77
  William, 77
Boucher, Adam, 165
  Mary, 165
  Thomas, 231
Bouchier, Edward, 202
Bouet, Alice, 111
  John, 111
Boughton, Margaret, 199
  Robert, 199
Bouk, John, 87
  Matilda, 87
Boure, or Bowre
  Thomas, 198, 200
Bourer, Johanna, 150
  John, 150
Bourghchier, John, 227
  Margery, 227
  Thomas, 197, 198, 199
de Bourstalle, John, 129
  Robert, 96
Bouth, Robert, 178
de Boveleye, John, 57
de Boveney, or de Boveneye
  Gilbert, 5
  John, 65
de Bovill, or de Bovile
  Henry, 26
  John fil' Mathew, 60
  Mathew, 35
  Petronilla, 60
de Bovyndon, Alice, 109
  Thomas, 109
Bowebrok, John, 166
Boweland, Adam, 173
  Margery, 173
Boweman, Isabella, 193
  Robert, 193
Box, Cristina, 55 (4), 56, 63

INDEX NOMINUM.

Box, John fil' Robert, 107
   Margaret, 107
   Thomas, 55 (2), 56, 58, 63
   Walter, 39, 45
   William, 110
de la Boxe, Henry, 29
de Boxhale, Richard, 128
Boydon, Alice, 134, 149
   John, 134, 149
Boyle, John, 137 (2), 223
Boys, George, 186, 187
   Johanna, 119
   John, 119
   Katharine, 120, 187
   Walter, 120
Brabasun, Masera, 128
   Robert, 128
Bracy, or Bracey
   John, 177, 180, 186
atte Bradeford, John, 141
de Bradel, or de Bradele
   Basilia, 23
   Ralph, 23, 29
Bradfield, Henry, 229
de Bradmer, or de Bradmere
   Alice, 32
   William, 8, 32, 214
Bradsha, Robert, 197
Braghynge, Elias, 125
Brampton, James, 176
   William, 163
de Brandon, Geoffrey, 79, 82
de Brantyngham, or Brantyngham
   William, 151, 222
Braunche, Andrew, 113
   Johanna, 28
   William, 28
Braunthwayt, Alice, 166
   John, 166
Bray, Johanna, 194
   John, 149, 166
   Nicholas, 194
   Reginald, 201, 202, 204, 205, 206, 231 (3), 232
   Richard, 193
   William, 194
de Bray, Adam, 65
   Erneburga fil' Ralph, 59
   Nicholas, 93
   William, 93
de Braybof, or de Braybœf
   Geoffrey, 33, 43
Brayborne, John, 212
   Thomas, 212

de Brayborne, William, 212
de Braybrok, Gerard, 224 (2)
   Margery, 101, 118
   William, 101, 118
Brayham, Nicholas, 152, 156
de Braynford, or de Breynford
   Agnes, 45, 54
   Alice, 60
   John, 54, 60
   John fil' Adam, 45
Braynt, or de Braynte
   Alice, 141, 147
   William, 141, 147
Brayton, 164
Breaux, Thomas, 151
de la Breche, Henry, 28
de Brecia, Frechusant fil' Hamo, 53
de Brecles, William, 92
de Breges, Richard, 1
atte Bregge, Margery, 84
   Rose, 99
   Walter, 84, 99
   William, 84, 99
de Bremingefeld, Richard, 48
Bremysgrove, Bremmesgrave, Brymmesgrave, or Brymmesgrove
   Alan, 186
   Alice, 186
   John, 164, 166, 170
Brenchelee, John, 152
Brenchesle, William, 224
Brent, William, 204
Brentfeld, Alice, 177
   Roger, 177
Breouse, de Brewes, de Brewosu, de Breus, or de Brywes
   Alice, 214
   Beatrice, 56, 219, 221
   Elizabeth, 221
   Eva, 56
   Isabel, 112
   John, 56, 221
   Mary, 70
   Peter, 70
   Richard, 214
   Robert, 37
   Thomas, 219, 221
   William, 49, 59, 70 (2), 112, 214
Bretinghull, Reginald, 10
de Bretinghurst, or de Brittinghurst
   Johanna, 84
   Reginald, 12, 13, 17
   Robert, 84

Brette, Henry, 157
    Johanna, 157
le Brewere, Richard, 84
Brian, Bryan, de Briane, de Brien,
    or de Bryene
    Alice, 94 (3)
    Guy, 116, 120, 221
    John, 163, 225
    Thomas, 94 (3), 97, 196
le Brid, Alice, 78
    John, 78
Bridbrok, William, 154
Brigham, Alice, 102
    William, 101
Bright, or Bryght
    Johanna, 169
    Thomas, 182
    William, 169
Brikelisworth, or de Briklesworth
    John, 111, 127
    Peter, 169
    Richard, 174
    William, 111
de Brisle, Roger, 78 (2)
Bristowe, or Brystowe
    Agnes, 156
    Geoffrey, 156
    John, 203
fil' Britgive, Walter, 14
Brittinghurst, see Brelinghurst
de Brius, John, 7
    Margery, 7
del Broc, Eva, 2, 4 (2)
Brocas, Brokas, or de Brokas
    Arnald, or Arnold, 156, 159,
        191 (2), 223
    Benedict, 189
    Bernard, 132, 137, 223
    Cecilia, 189
    Elizabeth, 159
    John, 106, 107
    Margaret, 107, 119, 191 (2)
    Oliver, 119
    Thomas, 159
    William, 191 (2)
de Brockhale, Johanna, 68
    William, 68
Brode, Johanna, 178
    Richard, 178
Broghton, John, 164
Brok, Johanna, 222
    John, 222
de la Brok, Robert, 67 (2)
Broke, Alice, 171

Broke, Henry, 171
    John, 156
    Margaret, 156
    Richard, 211
    William, 156
atte Broke, Agnes, 141
    Richard, 144
    Walter, 141
Brokere, Edith, 54
    John, 160
    William, 54
de Brokes, Cristiana, 61
    John, 61, 69
Broket, Thomas, 180
Brokham, Johanna, 168
    William, 168
Brokholes, John, 184, 189
Brokhull, Robert, 138
de Brokshote, Johanna, 94
    Ralph, 94
Brokwode, Henry, 139
    Matilda, 139
de Brom, Adam, 216
Bromehale, Alice, 164
    John, 164
Bromersshe, Emma, 157
    Robert, 157
le Bromere, Lecia, 55
    William, 55
Brombale, Agnes, prioress of, 52
de Bromleg, John, 31
    Matilda, 31
Brompton, Henry, 180
Brond, Geoffrey, 24
    John, 176
Brook, Johanna, 226
    John, 163
    Thomas, 226
    William, 181, 185
Brother, John, 29, 30
de Brounyerd, David, 77
    Margery, 77
Brounyng, Agnes, 180
    John, 163
    Ralph, 176
    Robert, 180
Brown, Browne, Browene, Broun,
    or Broune
    Agnes, 85
    Anna, 162
    Elias, 156
    Gilbert, 85
    Henry, 135, 156
    Isabella, 135, 156

Brown, Browne, Browene, Broun, or Broune
  Johanna, 131
  John, 131 (2), 199, 206, 231
  Margaret, 113, 116
  Matthew, 206, 211
  Philip, 149
  Richard, 183
  Robert, 144, 146, 162
  Sarra, 131 (2)
  Thomas, 113, 116, 133, 150, 182, 187, 227 (2)
  William, 131
le Brudeford, John, 90
de Brugeford, de Brugford, or de Brygeford
  Henry, 111
  John, 96
  Lucy, 63
  Peter, 63
de Bruge, Juliana, 106
  Robert, 106
atte Brugg, or atte Brugge
  Beatrice, 61
  Nicholas fil' Nicholas, 61
  William, 129
Bruggeman, Alice, 146
  John, 146
de Brugges, Walter, 29
Brule, John, 5
de Brumle, Alexander, 37
de Brummore, Johanna, 55
  Philip, 55
Brun, William, 13
le Brun, Hamo, 32
  Henry, 32
Brunyng, Gunnilda, 51
  Henry, 51
le Brus, Robert, 26
de Brustowe, Richard, 222
Bruton, John, 190
Brutteby, Beatrice, 153
  William, 153
le Bruys, Alice, 103
  John, 103
Bryan, or Bryene, see Brian
Brydeyngton, Thomas, 171
Brygeford, see Brugeford
Brygge, Agnes, 189
  William, 189
Bryghtlamton, Johanna, 129
  John, 129
de Brymarton, Robert, 38
Brymmesgrene, John, 153

Brymmesgrove, see Bremysgrove
de Brynkehurst, Robert, 45 (2)
Brynkes, Margaret, 183
  William, 183
Brystowe, see Bristowe
Bryt, Stephen, 178
Brywes, see Breouse
de Buchurst, Robert, 84
Buck, Clement, 68
Buckingham, Humfrey, Duke of, 228
  Anna, wife of, 228
de Budele, or de Bodel
  Edward, 5
  William fil' Edward, 11, 17
Budiford, Richard, 220
le Bufle, Dionisia, 26
  Walter, 26, 37
de Bugbrigge, William, 127
de Bughton, Robert, 66
  Sarra, 66
Buk, Adam, 166
le Bukere, Robert, 15
Bukke, William, 199
Bukyngham, or de Bukyngham
  John, 150, 221
  Roger, 185
  William, 9
Bulchild, Thomas, 192
Bule, Lewin, 15
Bundy, John, 16
  Margaret, 16, 71
  Richard, 71
Bunt, Terricus, 28
Buntyng, John, 48
Burcote, William, 147
de Burdegala, Oliver, 80
  Sibil, 40
  William, 40
de Burdens, Johanna, 182
  John, 182
  Sibil, 39
  William, 39
Burdeyn, John, 128
  Margaret, 128
Burdon, John, 141
atte Bure, Alice, 84
  Richard, 84
de Burefeld, or de Burghfeld
  Gilbert, 94 (2)
de Burewe, Matilda, 89
  Richard, 89
Burel, John, 29
de Bures, John, 14, 38, 120

de Bures, Richard, 8
Bures, Alan, 103, 107
    Johanna, 111
    John, 107 (2), 111
    Juliana, 103, 107
    Robert, 138
    Stephen, 103
    William, 170
Burford, Agnes, 203
    Cristofer, 203
atte Burgate, Johanna, 116
    William, 116
de Burg, Cecilia, 113
    Hubert, Earl of Kent, 13
    Margaret, 13
    Thomas, 113
    Vitalis, 21
de Burgate, Philip, 48
Burgeys, Gilbert, 127
    Johanna, 127 (2), 177
    John, 110, 134, 144
    Margery, 134, 144
    Richard, 127
    Robert, 110
    Thomas, 177, 201
    William, 204
de Burghersh, or de Burghersh
    Alice, 135
    Bartholomew, 115, 220
    William, 135
Burgh, Alice, 197
    Amy, 231
    Edward, 231
    John, 163, 167 (2), 176, 179, 231
    Katharine, 179
    Margery, 231
    Thomas, 197 (2), 230
atte Burgh, William, 169
de Burgh, John, 215
de Burghton, Johanna, 92
    John, 92
Burgoyne, Elias, 128
    John, 165 (2)
    Juliana, 128
    William, 223
Buristrete, William, 99
de Buritton, William, 51
Burle, Robert, 133
de Burlee, Agatha, 222
    John, 222
de Burn, Matilda, 37
atte Burnebrig, Peter, 98
Burnel, or Burnell
    Philip, 60, 61

Burnel, or Burnell
    Robert, 47
    Robert fil' William, 56, 61
    Thomas, 211
Burouhard, Ralph, 44
de Bursebrigg, Alice, 127
    Richard fil' Richard, 127
    Walter fil' Adam, 127
Bursebrygg, John, 158
le Burser, Felicia, 46
    Thomas, 46
Burstowe, Robert, 192
de Burstowe, or de Burstohe
    Alice, 61, 71
    John, 35, 61, 71
    John fil' William, 118
    Margery, 118
    Peter, 35
    Randulf, 10
Burstowe, Richard, parson of, 102
Burstowe, Robert, 193
    William, 193
de Burton, Johanna, 95, 129
    John, 95, 121, 149
    William, 130
Burton, Edmund, 207
    Edward, 211
    Henry, 204, 206
    Isabel, 211
    John, 198
    Simon, 188
    William, 188, 190
Burwell, John, 150
atte Bury, Alice, 146
    Godfrey, 146
Bury, John, 222
de Bury, Thomas, 119
le Buscher, Baldewin, 55
Bussebrigge, or Bussebrygge
    Robert, 162 (2)
le Buteler, le Butiller, Butiler, or Botiller, *see* Boteler
de Butteford, William fil' Walter, 72
Buttry, or Buttrye
    William, 209 (2)
Butvside, Thomas, 203
de Buxton, Emma, 116
    Henry, 116
de Bydun, de Bydon, or de Bidun
    Peter, 19, 27
    Roger, 19
Bykenore, Agnes, 148, 150
    Alexander, 148, 150, 161

Bykerton, John, 185
Byknell, William, 203
de Bylissersse, Juliana, 43
    William, 43
Byllyngey, Robert, 187
Bylney, Henry, 166
Byndewyn, Richard, 193
Byngham, John, 215
Byngle, John, 175
Bynham, John, 164
de Bynteworth, Hugh, 81
de Byntre, Jordan, 218
atte Byrchette, Edith, 61
    Robert, 61
Byrell, William, 232
Byrkehede, John, 185
Byrte, John, 198
Bys, Alianora, 154, 158
    John, 148
    Matilda, 148
    William, 145, 154, 158
Bysbrygge, Richard, 205
Byssh, Thomas, 180

Cabous, Juliana, 117
    Richard, 117
de Caburg, John, 20
Cace, Agnes, 168
    Richard, 168
Cade, Margery, 209
Cafhous, John, 105
Calan, Isabella, 161
    John, 161
Calcot, Thomas, 210
Calke, William, 129
Calle, Thomas, 173
le Caller, Elias, 90
    Matilda, 90
Cambrugg, William, 176
de Cameis, de Cameys, de Cammeys,
    or de Kameis
    Margaret, 70
    Matilda, 9
    Ralph, 7, 9, 20, 70, 213
de Camera, Mabel, 27
    William, 27
Cammell, John, 226
Camoys, Roger, 181
de Campania, Robert, 50
Campeden, or de Campeden
    John, 151, 152 (2), 157 (3)
Campion, William, 231
de Campo, Hamo, 57
de Candevere, Herbert, 50

de Canductu, Charles, 94
de Canefold, or de Canefeld
    John, 128
    Margery, 67
    Walter, 67
Canoun, Edmund, 115
    Johanna, 115
Canterbury, Prior of Christ
    Church, Geoffrey, 3, 6
    Prior of Holy Trinity, John, 212
    Prior of Holy Trinity, Nicholas, 32 (2), 35
    Bishop of, B., 36
    Bishop of, John, 227
    Bishop of, S., 9 (3)
    Bishop of, Thomas, 230
    Prior of, Thomas, 55
de Canterbury, Margery, 110
    Walter, 113
de Cantilupe, Emma, 32
    Eva, 34
    William, 32, 34
Cantlowe, William, 227
Canyn, or Kanyn
    Henry, 85, 86
    Lucy, 85, 86
Capell, John, 231
    William, 199 (2), 207, 231
Capenore, Isabella, 141
    John, 141
Cappe, Elizabeth, 152
    John, 152
    William, 152
Capron, or Caperon
    Margaret, 178, 181 (2), 184, 185
    Thomas, 178, 181 (2), 184, 185
Carbonel, Carbonell, or Karbonell
    Johanna, 32, 143, 144
    John, 152
    Maisent fil' William, 8
    Ralph, 8
    Ralph fil' Ralph, 12
    Richard, 143, 144
    William fil' Ralph, 32
Cardon, Peter, 28
Carkeke, William, 205
de Carleton, Alice, 83
    William, 83
Carlisle, Bishop of, Edward, 230
    Marmaduke, 227
Carpenter, or le Carpenter
    Avice, 10
    Elena, 9

Carpenter, or le Carpenter
    Emma, 59
    Henry, 187
    Johanna, 130 (2)
    John, 9, 144, 179
    Martin, 10
    Matilda, 144
    Ralph, 88
    Richard, 59, 209
    Robert, 162
    Thomas, 130 (2)
    William fil' William, 15
Carrou, Carrew, Carewe, de Carrew, or de Carreu
    Mercy, 226
    Nicholas, 118, 120, 125, 132, 133, 141, 144, 146, 147, 149, 159 (2), 220, 222, 226
    Richard, 204
    William, 118, 125, 220
Carter, Cartere, or le Cartere
    Agnes, 180
    John, 180
    Richard, 155
    Robert, 16
    Rose, 206
    Thomas, 137, 206
    William fil' William, 136
Carvile, John, 165
Cary, Hugh, 172
Caryll, John, 205
Castell, Johanna, 201
    John, 201
    Richard, 230
atte Castell, or atte Castelle
    Agatha, 154
    Isabel, 130
    John, 154
    William, 130
de Castleacre, Alice, 102, 106
    Isabel, 106
    William, 102 (2), 106
Caterall, Thomas, 210
de Caterham, Godard, 12
Cateryk, John, 168
Catesby, William, 192, 228
Catteslond, Johanna, 180
    Thomas, 180
Catton, Johanna, 226
    William, 226
Caundyssh, Robert, 182
Caunterbury, Stephen, 177
Causton, Alianor, 166
    William, 166

Cave, William, 225 (2)
de Caversham, Johanna, 132
    John, 132
Cawode, Robert, 180, 184
Caxton, Robert, 179
    Thomas, 179
Caym, Richard, 161
    Sarah, 161
Cecū, Alexander, 3
de Cesterton, Valence fil' William, 33
de Cestrehunt, *see* de Chesthunte
Chabbok, John, 152, 156
de Chabeham, Alice, 10, 57
    Gilbert, 10
    John, 74
    Margery, 74
    Matilda, 48
    Peter, 48
    Sibil, 57
    Walter, 57
    William fil' Peter, 57
de Chaddesle, Cristina, 136
    John, 136
    Robert, 131
de Chakedon, Emma, 77
    Peter, 77 (2)
    Ralph, 77
Chaloner, Margaret, 191 (2)
    Thomas, 191 (2)
le Chaloner, Grace, 9
    John, 9
Chamberlain, Chamberleyn, or Chaumberleyn
    Fulc, 18
    Thomas, 20
le Chamberleg, William, 42
de Chamberleyn, Robert, 51
Chambre, Richard, 198
    Thomas, 182, 191
de or le Champeneys, or Champeneys
    Osbert, 39
    Ralph, 37
    Thomas, 206
Champ, Johanna, 161
    John, 161
Champyan, or Champyon
    Arnold, 197
    Richard, 100
    Walter, 208
Chancy, Johanna, 189, 191, 192
    John, 189, 191, 192
de Chanente, Cecilia, 71

INDEX NOMINUM. 249

de Chanente, Stephen, 71
Chanri, Richard, 135
le Chanu, John, 19, 20
    Jordan, 32
    Katharine, 20 (2)
Chaplain, Adam, 18
    Godefrey, 10
    Ralph, 8
    Robert, 5
    Walter, 20
le Chapman, John, 76
    Letice, 76
Chapman, John, 137, 228
    Matilda, 157
    Peter, 157
    Thomas, 160
    Walter, 139
Chapre, or Chaper
    John, 4
    Roger, 54
Charleton, Thomas, 147
de Charlewode, Juliana, 110
    Thomas, 110
Charteseye, Robert, 188
Chartham, Thomas, Parson of, 216
Chatkulne, William, 82
Chattok, Johanna, 193, 194
    John, 193, 194
Chaucers, Thomas, 226
le Chaumberleyn, Edmund, 64
    Lucy, 64
atte Chaumbre, Johanna, 125 (2)
    John, 125 (2)
de la Chaunbre, Elias, 42, 57
    Johanna, 42, 57
    John, 71
    John fil' John, 71
de Champayn, Margery, 120
Chaunce, Roger, 137, 173, 174
Chaundeler, or le Chaundeler
    Adam, 67, 77, 85
    Alan, 63 (2)
    Edward, 77
    Johanna, 63 (2), 85
    Richard, 178
Chaunterel, Alesia, 96
    John, 96
    Thomas, 204
Chauntrell, William, 182
Chawry, or Chawery
    Richard, 197, 199
de Chayham, John, 25, 35
    Symon, 35

Chaynel, Alice, 117
    William, 117
de Chedingefeld, Bruna, 16
de Chedwode, John, 84
de Chelberton, Beatrice, 66
    Robert, 66
Cheldewell, Roger, 150, 160
Cheleman, Alice, 187
    Thomas, 187
de Chelese, Warin, 11
Chelesfeld, Stephen, 101
de Chelmereford, de Chelmersford, or de Chelmeresford
    John, 85 (2), 100
    Katharine de, 79
    Nicholas, 79
de Chelsfeld, Johanna, 82
    Stephen, 82
de Chelsham, or Chelesham
    Adam, 51, 69
    Alice, 50
    Dionisia, 71, 74, 76
    John, 17, 20
    Lora, 51, 69
    Reginald, 50, 71, 74, 76
Chene, John, 122
atte Cherche, *see* atte Churche
Cherde, Isabel, 130
    William, 130
de Chereburg, John, 15
Cherlton, Robert, 152
le Chernere, William, 129
atte Chert, William, 85
Chertesey, or Certesey
    Abbot of, Alan, 18, 19, 26 (2), 28 (2), 33, 36, 40
    Abbot of, Bartholomew, 50, 51, 52
    Abbot of, John, 41, 46, 47, 48
    Abbot of, Martin, 2 (2), 4 (2), 5
    Abbot of ——, 88, 94, 117
de Chertesey, de Certesey, de Certeseye, de Certeshey, or Cherteseye
    Adam, 30
    Alice, 30
    Godwin, 2
    Henry, 65
    John, 137
    Matilda, 48
    Ralph, 18, 23
    Richard, 30 (2)
    Robert, 79, 84
    William, 224

Chesere, John, 141
de Chesewyk, John, 83
de Chesham, Richard, 133
Chesilden, John, 173
Chesterford, Johanna, 169
    John, 169
    Robert, 169
de Chesthunte, or de Cestrehunt
    Dyonisia, 37
    Margery, 74
    William, 74
de Chestre, Agnes, 122
    John, 122
de Chetwode, Alice, 116
    John, 116
    Lucy, 116
    Nicholas fil' John, 116
    Ralph, 14
le Chevaler, Peter, 35
de Chevynton, Richard, 84
de Cheyham, Agnes, 109, 114
    William, 109, 114
Cheyne, John, 147
    William, 174
de Cheyny, Ralph, 61
Chiche, John, 226
Chichele, Elizabeth, 173
    Robert, 173
Chichester, Adam, Bishop of, 227
de Chikewell, or de Chygewell
    Agnes, 68, 76
    Richard, 68, 76
Child, or le Child
    Agnes, 95
    Alice, 63
    Isabel, 130
    John, 95, 136
    Matilda, 136
    Peter, 63, 66
    Richard, 63
    Stephen, 130
Childewale, or Childewall
    Alice, 170, 174
    Robert, 170, 174
de Chinthurst, Cristina, 76
    Henry, 76
Chipsted, or Chipstede
    John, 153, 154
    Thomas, 166
    William, 154
atte Chirche, *see* Churche
atte Chirchegate, Thomas, 95
de Chirchell, William, 221
de Chirefold, Thomas, 67

de Chiriton, William, 2
Chiryngworth, John, 165
Chisenhale, Robert, 151
de Chissedon, Gerard, 19
    Germanus, 7
    Matilda, 19
        Alice, sister of, 19
    William, 7
de Chitterne, John, 223
Chivaler, William, 142
de Chivening, or de Chyvenyngg
    Adam, 66
    Simon, 66
Chonneson, Robert, 156
Chontere, John, 144
Chowne, John, 211
Chuddelegh, James, 169
Chudham, Walter, 158
atte Churche, atte Cherche, or atte
    Chirche
    Alice, 42
    Alice fil' Walter, 97
    Dionisia, 68
    Emma, 139
    Godefrey, 68
    Henry, 42
    John, 87, 139
    Richard, 145
    Robert, 76
    Simon, 133
    Simon fil' Walter, 120
    William, 75
atte Churchegate, Beatrice, 122
    Richard, 122
Churn, William, 13
de Chusendale, Robert, 123
de Chussebury, Dionisia, 75
    William, 75
Chylterne, John, 171
de Chynham, Nicholas, 111, 116 (2)
Chytyngelegh, John, 155
    Margaret, 155
de Cirencester, or de Cyrencester
    Robert, 27, 31
Citronen, Anthony, 99
de Clare, Gilbert, Earl of Gloucester, 44, 216
    Matilda, wife of, 216
    Richard, Earl of Gloucester and Hertford, 28, 38
    Alice, 21, 213
    Roger, 21, 213
Clate, Margery fil' Osbert, 30, 31
    Matilda fil' Osbert, 30, 31

INDEX NOMINUM.   251

Clate, Richard, 31
Claidich, or Claydiche
   Richard, 176 (2), 179
Claydon, John, 154
de Claygate, Juliana, 83
   Reginald, 83
Clay, Johanna, 179
   Margaret, 150
   Robert, 150, 158, 188
   Thomas, 179
Clays, Lambert, 62
   Margaret, 62
Clement, Alice, 78, 93
   Johanna, 194
   John, 169
   Seman, 78, 93
   William, 194
Clerk, le Clerk, or le Clerc
   Agnes, 152
   Alice 30 (2), 136
   Alina, 100
   Amflisia, 61
   Basilia fil' William, 31
   Clement, 201
   Dionisia, 95
   Emma, 80
   Geoffrey, 61
   Homund, 4
   Isabel, 41, 143
   Johanna, 71, 81, 82, 94
   John, 6, 95, 100, 135, 136, 143, 152, 191
   John fil' William, 93
   Margaret, 31
   Martin fil' William, 137
   Matilda fil' William, 31
   Pagan, 41
   Philip, 30 (2)
   Reginald, 10
   Richard, 81, 82, 85, 94, 152, 205, 208
   Robert, 174
   Simon, 31
   Simon fil' William, 93
   Stephen, 80
   Thomas, 166
   William, 71, 109, 152, 183, 227
de Clere, Hugh, 24
   Johanna, 216
   John fil' Robert, 216
   Roger, 27, 215
de Clerholt, Alice, 28
   William, 28
de Cleye, Lora, 97

de Cleye, Thomas, 97
Clifford, or Clyfforde
   Elizabeth, 145
   John, 154 (2)
   Lodewic, 204
   Thomas, 202
   Thomas fil' Roger, 145
de Clifton, Reginald, 4 (2)
Clipsham, Alice, 168
   John, 168, 176
le Clive, Adam, 44
   Elicia, 44
Clon, William, 188, 190, 191, 192
de Clopton, Alice, 58
   Isabel, 131
   Robert, 58
   Simon, 131
Clough, Henry, 201
Clow, William, 185
Clun, William, 186
Clynton, John, 136
   Robert, 226
de Clynton, William, Earl of Huntingdon, 124
Clyston, Gervase, 196
Cobbe, Henry, 161
   Isabella, 161
de Cobham, de Cobeham, Cobham, or Cobeham
   Johanna, 216, 221
   John, 47, 60, 223 (2), 224
   John fil' John, 220
   John fil' Reginald, 175
   Ralph, 163
   Reginald, 181, 216, 221, 222
   Richard, 198
   Thomas, 190 (2), 228
de Codeham, Frechisent, 53
   Thomas, 53
de Codestone, Walter, 53, 84
de Codington, or Codyngton
   John, 197
   Peter, 213
   Ralph, 168
le Codyngwych, Johanna, 103
   Walter, 103
de Coggeshale, Johanna, 92
   Richard 92
Cok, Agnes, 170, 171
   John, 138 (2), 150, 170, 171
   Roger, 187
   Thomas, 179
Cokayn, John, 176
Coke, Thomas, 179

de Cokfeld, Cecilia, 78
    Walter, 78
de Cokefeld, Robert, 48
Cokerell, William, 157
Cokespur, Richard, 18
Cokke, Dionisia, 179
    John, 179
Cokkys, John, 211 (2)
Cokogh, Johanna, 132
    John, 132
Colard, John, 189
Colas, Henry, 131, 135
    Johanna, 131, 135
    Walter, 135
Colbrook, Robert, 226
Colcock, or Colkok
    Richard, 187, 191
Coldmawe, Matilda, 81
    Roger, 81
Cole, Agnes, 195
    John, 87, 97
    Rosamund, 87, 97
    Stephen, 195
de Colecestre, Johanna, 64 (3)
    John, 64 (3)
Coleman, Adam, 104
    Auda, 75
    Gilbert, 42
    Roesia, 42
    Thedric, 35
    Thomas, 80, 104
de Coleshull, William, 83
    Geoffrey, 168
Colet, Henry, 200, 231 (2)
de Colevill, or de Colevile
    John, 35
    Milicent, 35
    Robert fil' Philip, 79
    William, 13, 212 (3)
de Colewyk, Hugh, 110
Colgrym, Walter, 156
Collard, John, 194
de Collee, or de Collye
    Thomas fil' Walter, 97
    Walter, 9, 15, 60
Colles, Matilda, 121
    William, 121
Collowe, William, 197
Colman, Anna, 174, 179
    John, 155
    Thomas, 174, 179
Colney, Colneye, de Colney, or de Colneye
    Alice, 160

Colney, Colneye, de Colney, or de Colneye
    John, 130, 137 (2), 138
    Thomas, 160, 206
Colrede, Thomas, 158
Colston, John, 107
de Colverdene, Johanna, 112
    William, 112
Colvil or Colvyle
    John, 228, 230
    Margaret, 228, 230
    Richard, 228
Colyer, Alice, 170
    John, 170
le Colyer, Alice, 66
    Roger, 66
Colyn, Alice, 157
    Robert, 157
de Colyngham, Thomas, 66
Colyns, Alice, 159
    John, 159, 205
Combe, Johanna, 166
    John, 166 (2), 171, 172 (2)
    Juliana, 171
    Margery, 172
    Richard, 227
Comporth, John, 203
Compton, Margaret, 200
    Nicholas, 203, 205
    Thomas, 200
Con de Cive, Margaret, 11
Conde, John, 155
Conners, Elena, 137
    Thomas, 137
Conquer, Thomas, 225
Consell, or Counseyll
    Nicholas, 187, 189 (2)
Constable, Conestable, Constabull, or le Constable
    Alice, 208
    Andrew, 87, 101
    Johanna, 205
    Juliana, 102
    Mirabel, 101
    Richard, 41, 205, 208
    Thomas, 102
    Walter, 87, 101, 102
Constantyn, William, 228
Conyngesby, Humfrey, 198, 203, 204, 205, 206, 231
Cook, Adam, 6
    Alianor, 148
    Alice, 28
    Eylena, 15

Cook, Godfrey fil' William, 23
    Henry, 15
    John, 180
    Mabel, 23, 33
    Richard, 148, 192 (2), 202
    Robert, 23, 33
    Sibil, 192 (2)
    Theobald, 28
    Thomas, 6, 131, 191
Cooke, William, 203
Coope, William, 204, 205, 231 (2)
Cope, William, 206, 231
Corbet, Juliana, 89, 93
    Robert, 121, 122
    Thomas, 89, 93
le Corder, Martin, 9
le Cordwaner, Beatrice, 36
    Dyonisia, 46
    Walter, 36, 46
Coresle, John, 223
Corf, Corfe, or Corff
    Agnes, 170
    John, 170, 175, 179
de Cornburg, Osbert, 29
Corner, Richard, 227
de Cornhull, Reginald, 2
le Corniser, William, 44
le Cornmangere, or le Cornemonger
    Edith, 61, 93
    John, 61
    Nicholas fil' William, 100
    William fil' William, 93
atte Cornere, William, 141
Cornu, William, 196
Cornwaleys, Elizabeth, 203
    John, 170
    Robert, 203
Coronere, Richard, 183
Corpsty, John, 133
Corve, Alice, 177
    John, 177, 178, 181
Cosin, see Cusin
Costentyn, Nicholas, 91, 93
    Simon, 91
le Costretbyndere, Agnes, 82
    Walter, 82
Cosynton, Alice, 143
    Thomas, 143
le Cotiler, Emma, 84
    Peter, 84
de Cottesdon, Isabella, 136
    Johanna, 136

de Cottesdon, William, 136
Cotton, Thomas, 211
    Walter, 172
Coumbe, Alice, 168
    John fil' Thomas, 138
    William, 168
de Coumbe, Thomas, 156
atte Coumbe, John, 167
    Margery, 167
Couper, Coupere, or le Coupere
    Adam, 75
    Gilbert, 163
    Isabella, 75, 163
    John, 84, 197, 210
    Juliana, 143
    Thomas, 187
    William, 143, 197
de Coushete, Agnes, 108
    Jordan, 108
de Covel, Matilda, 4
de Covelyndenne, Juliana, 98
    William, 98
de Covenham, Alice, 44
    Eva, 9
    Martin, 9
    William, 44
Coventre, de Coventre, or de Covyntre
    Edmund, 106, 110, 121
    Emma, 168
    Margaret, 110
    Margery, 121
    Robert, 168
    William, 162
Coventry and Lichfield, Reginald, Bishop of, 191
de Covereworthe, Alice, 78
    Thomas, 78
Covert, or de Covert
    Alianor, 181
    John, 105
    Margaret, 185
    Roger, 50
    Thomas, 181, 194, 229
Cowefold Ralph, 177
Cowper, or Coweper
    Gilbert, 160
    Richard, 174
    Thomas, 181 (3)
Craan, Johanna, 175
    John, 175
de Craft, Roger, 25
Crakall, John, 189
de Cramplingesham, Margery, 50

de Cramplingesham, Peter, 50
Crane, John, 18
de Craneford, Richard, 24
de Cranstok, Isabel, 67 (2)
    Roger fil' William, 67 (2)
Cras, Cristina, 131
    William, 131
de Crawestok, or de Crauestok
    Albreda, 46
    Gilbert, 46
    William, 10
de Crawedon, Nicholas, 40
Credy, Agnes, 176
    John, 170, 176
de Cresauton, Hugh, 56
Cressewyk, Alice, 149
    William, 142, 149
de Crevquor, Robert, 50
le Crew, Matilda, 6
    Robert, 6
Crikebade, Alice, 155
    Richard, 155
de Criol, John, 11
    Thomas fil' Odo, 11
Crips, Ailward, 16
le Crisp, Peter, 13
fil' Cristiana, Margaret, 20
Croc, Gunnilda, 6
    William, 6
de Croft, Johanna, 105
    William, 105
Crofter, Edmund, 196
de Crokford, Adam, 57
    Johanna, 57
    Lucy fil' Adam, 57
    William, 130
Crokhere, Richard, 162
de la Croiz, Agnes, 56
    Henry, 56
Crome, Roger, 175
Cromwell, Ralph, 227
Crophill, William, 169
Cros, John, 154
le Cros, Agatha, 62
    Robert, 62
Cross, or Crosse
    Adam, 74
    Agnes, 92
    Alice, 181
    John, 181, 184
    Lora, 74
    William 92
atte Crouche, Agnes, 87
    Elena, 182

atte Crouche, John, 182
    Roger fil' Agnes, 87
Crowe, Thomas, 148
Crowherst, de Crouhurst, or de Crawhurst
    Agnes, 98
    Dronisia, 172
    John, 98, 172
    John fil' John, 58
    Odo, 28
de Croydon, John, 101, 106, 111
    Reginald, 45
le Croys, Robert, 51
de Cruce, Alice, 10
    Gilbert, 10
    John, 3
    Reginald, 2
atte Cruch, Agnes, 133
    Nicholas, 133
Crukerne, or de Crukern
    John, 125, 220
Crullyng, Agnes, 86
    Elizabeth, 225
    Eustace, 86
    William, 225
de Crumbewell, Idonia, 91
de Crumbewell, John, 91
de Cryel, Nicholas fil' Nicholas, 215
de Cudinton, or Cudyngton
    Adam, 29
    Alice, 137
    Gunnora, 11
    John, 31
    Peter, 4
    Richard, 137
de Culcham, Agnes, 142
    Peter, 142
Culham, or de Culham
    Agnes, 135, 139, 140, 142
    William, 135, 139, 140, 142
Cullecuppe, John, 220
Culpepyr, or Culpeper
    Elizabeth, 204
    Margaret, 204
    Nicholas, 204
    Richard, 193, 204
    Sibil, 193
    Walter, 204
de Cumbe, Richard, 12, 13
    Sibil, 13
Cumberford, William, 228
de Cumpton, John, 220
Cumin, John, 4

de Cumpewrthe, Adam, 6
le Cunners, or le Conners
    Andrew, 40
    Johanna, 62, 64
    John, 62, 64
de Cunton, Ralph fil' Walter, 4
Curdhope, William, 121
Currour, Mary, 166
    Thomas, 166
le Curt, Richard, 3
Curteis, Roger fil' Walter, 84
le Curteis, William, 212
Curteys, Walter, 66
    William, 201
Cusin, Cusyn, Cosin, or Cosyn
    Adam, 133
    Alice, 38
    Beatrice, 88
    Elizabeth, 183
    Johanna, 122
    John, 158
    Peter, 49 (2), 53
    William, 38, 88, 121, 122, 183
de Cuslingeburst, Stephen, 79
le Cutiller, Richard, 29
Cutler, William, 231
le Cuver, Ralph, 23

de D . . . , Philip, 13
Daber, Roger, 121, 123
Dabernoun, or Dabernun, *see* de Abernun
Dabrichcourt, or Dauberichecourt
    Elizabeth, 133
    Eustace, 133
    Thomas, 191
de Daggenhal, Agnes, 26
    John, 26
de Dagworth, or de Dageworth
    Alianor, 114
    John, 135
    Thomas, 114
    Thomasina, 135
Dale, Geoffrey, 173
    Johanna, 173
Daly, Johanna, 208
    Nicholas, 208
de Dalynton, Hugh, 119
Damlet, Hugh, 196
Dammory, Elizabeth, 86 (2)
    Roger, 86 (2)
Dane, John, 174
    Richard, 130, 137

de Danhurst, de Danehurst, or Danhurst
    Agnes, 137, 141, 148
    Johanna, 204
    John, 204
    Katharine fil' Robert, 137 (2)
    Margaret, 178
    Robert, 137 (2), 141, 148, 178
    Roger, 89
    Thomas, 89
    William, 78
de Dantesy, Matilda, 213
    Roger, 213
Dantre, Edmund, 196
Danvers, Thomas, 206
    William, 195, 206
Danyell, or Danel
    John, 121
    Richard, 175
    Thomas, 194
    William, 127
Darcy, Edith, 232
    Thomas, 232
Darnel, Richard, 74
Daubeny, Giles, 210
de Daumartin, Daunmartin, Daumartin, or Damartin
    Agnes, 17
    Alice, 28, 31
    Avelina, 17
    Margery, 213 (2)
    Mary fil' William, 41
    Mathew, 17
    Odo, 213 (2)
    William, 23
Dase, Richard, 145
Daventre, William, 179 (2)
Davesoun, John, 186
    Margaret, 186
David, Alice, 75
    Richard, 75
Davy, Blanche, 229
    William, 49, 229
Dawene, Richard, 185
Dawse, or Dause
    Agnes, 196
    Arnald, 196
    Robert, 202
Daye, Margaret, 208
    Nicholas, 208
Debenham, Amy, 209
    William, 131
Degon, John, 211
de Delves, John, 211

de Delyngrugge, Roger, 221
Dene, Edmund, 160
    Margery, 229
    Richard, 229
atte Dene, Alice, 158
    Cristina, 131
    Geoffrey, 158
    John, 126
    Richard, 131
de Dene, Alwin, 14
    Robert, 13
    William, 14
de la Dene, Edelina fil' Osbert, 10
    Vitalis, 17
Denewey, Agnes, 184
    John, 184
Deneys, Emma, 106
    John, 106
Denham, John, 194
Denne, John, 168, 225
atte Denne, Johanna, 116
    William, 116
Denny, Denney, or Deny
    Anna, 161, 168, 170
    Edmund, 196, 200 (3), 202 (2), 203, 205, 208 (3), 209, 210, 211, 212
    Robert, 161, 168, 170
    Thomas, 161
Dent, Agnes, 131
    Richard, 131
Denton, or de Denton
    Margaret, 199
    Robert, 123, 133, 136
    Thomas, 199
Denyas, William, 145
atte Denye, Matilda, 163
    Richard, 163
    Robert, 163
    Walter, 163
Denys, Thomas, 227
de Depyng, Ismania, 79
    Margaret, 101, 102, 114
    Robert, 101, 102
    Thomas, 102
    Thomas fil' Philip, 101
    William, 79
Deraunt, John, 173
de Derby, de Dereby, or Derby
    Cristiana, 43, 46, 48, 49, 57
    Henry, 57
    Richard, 43, 46, 48, 49, 57, 64, 211
de Derham, Alice, 217

de Derham, Thomas, 165
    William, 217
de Derleton, Adam, 119
Derlyng, Alice, 124
    John, 124
Derman, Richard, 182 (2), 190
    William, 182
le Despenser, Adam, 62
    Alianora, 217
    Gilbert, 141
    Hugh, 73, 74, 89, 91, 92, 217
Deumars, Johanna, 144
    Robert, 53, 55, 144
le Deveneys, or de Deveneys
    Geoffrey, 28
    Margery, 28
    William, 51
Devenyssh, John, 196
Dewy, John, 107
    Margery, 107
le Deyere, Matilda, 81
    Symon, 81
Deyes, John, 183
    Walter, 61
Deyrell, Ralph, 12
Deys, Elizabeth, 183
Deyvill, John, 88
Dierden, Elizabeth, 182
    John, 182
Digge, Roger, 102
de Dighton, Hawise, 128
    John, 128
Dignus, Richard, 2
Dikes, Isabel, 60
    Richard, 60
de Dilewis, Henry, 23
de Dinggeleg, John, 43
Diridenne, Emma, 144
    Richard, 144
de Ditton, or de Dytton
    Johanna, 57, 59, 84, 86
    John, 64
    Nicholas, 214
    Ralph, 57, 59, 84
    Ralph fil' Ralph, 86
    William, 15
Dixson, Nicholas, 227
Dockyng, Johanna, 169
    Simon, 169
Dodche, Margaret, 180
    Robert, 180
Dodde, John, 225
Dodekin, Constance, 17

INDEX NOMINUM. 257

Dodekin, Godfrey, 17
   William, 43
Dodge, Robert, 186
Dogge, Johanna, 180
   William, 180
Dokesworth, Robert, 164, 169
de Dol, Hugh, 7
   Richard, 4, 6, 7
Dolfyn, Agnes, 172
   John, 172
Dolsely, Johanna, 127
   Thomas, 127
de Domelton, John fil' Robert, 105
de Dommere, or de Domere
   John, 48
   Margaret, 48 (2)
   Reginald, 48
   William, 48 (2)
de la Done, Peter, 60
   Robert, 15
Donmowe, John, 151
Donnyngton, William, 196
Donton, John, 206
   Leonell, 206
Dony, John, 147
Dony, Katharine, 150
Donyle, Alice, 147
   John, 147
Doo, or Do
   Matilda, 159, 166, 170
   William, 159, 166, 170
de Dool, Robert, 99
Doppelane, Katharine, 104
   Richard, 104
Doreward, John, 152, 156
Dorgoyl, or Dorgoyle
   Gerard, 75, 81
de Dorking, or de Dorkinges
   Agnes, 63, 64
   Avice, 16, 35, 37
   Aylard, 37
   Gilbert, 63, 64
   Gunnilda, 25
   Reginald, 35
   William fil' John, 42
Dorset, Thomas, Marquis of, 230
de Dorsete, Luuina, 44
   Ralph, 44
Double, Alice, 139, 154
   John, 225
   Ralph, 139, 154
le Doul, Thurstan, 29
Doune, Henry, 153

Doune, John, 209
   Margery, 209
   Samithia, 209
   Thomas, 209
   Valentine, 198
atte Doune, Alice, 101, 106
   Henry fil' Geoffrey, 103
   John, 101, 106, 160
   Margery, 107, 160
   Robert, 125 (2)
   Thomas, 151, 219
   William, 107
de la Doune, Alditha, 52
   Henry, 52
de Dounton, Alice, 112
   William, 112
de Doure, Clement, 11
   Isabel, 11
de Dovere, Robert, 41
Dovill, Juliana, 222
   William, 222
Dowens, Laurence, 195
   Margery, 195
Dowenys, Geoffrey, 195
Down, Johanna, 200
   John, 200
Doxhey, or Doxeye
   Alice, 122
   Richard, 122, 132
   Sabina, 132
Doyle, Alice, 208
   Thomas, 208
Draghsper, Hugh, 89
Dragun, Walter, 42, 56
le Draper, John, 11
Drat, Alice, 56
   Robert, 56
Drax, Cecilia, 211
   John, 225
   Lambert, 211
   Richard, 183
Draycote, William, 231
de Drokeneford, Philip, 98
Dru, or Drui
   Adam, 27, 33
   Peter, 33
de Dryfeld, Isabel, 129
   Symon, 129
le Duc, William, 22, 134
Duddel, William, 18
Duddeley, John, 227
de Dudelea, Edward, 2
de Dudeswell, John, 97
   Letice, 97

17

de Dudham, John, 51
   Matilda, 51
Dudley, Cecilia, 231
   Edmund, 207, 208, 210
   Edward, 231 (2)
   John, 231
Dufhous, Thomas, 226
Duk, John, 136
Duke, William, 167
Dulle, Agnes, 161
   Richard, 161
de Dune, Henry, 47
   Isabel, 47
de Dune, or de Dunes
   Agnes, 6, 7, 11, 12
   Deodatus, 6, 7, 11, 12
de la Dune, Alice, 17
   Ascer, 20, 36
   Gregory, 17
   Robert, 19
   Roger, 17
de Dunelm, Thomas, 26
de Dunle, or de Dunlee
   Matilda, 104
   Richard, 79
de Dunmere, John, 28
Dunmowe, William, 127
Dunne, Valentine, 196
fil' Dunning, Geoffrey, 7
Dunning, or Dunnyng
   Hugh, 66
   Johanna, 66
   John, 88, 89, 90, 160, 169
   Margaret, 88, 89, 90
Dunnom, Richard, 79
de Dunstanstede, Agnes, 41
   Andrew, 41
de Dunstaple, or de Dunestaple
   Beatrice, 36
   John, 21, 99
   Symon, 36
de Dunsterre, Humphrey, 63
Durant, or Duraunt
   Margaret, 145
   Simon, 145
   Thomas, 69
Durbarn, Johanna, 174
   Richard, 174
de Durele, Thomas, 123
Durham, Bishop of, Laurence, 196
   ,,   William, 230
de Dunton, Agatha, 62
   Gilbert, 38
   Johanna, 51

de Dunton, Ralph, 51, 62
Dyer, Agnes, 178
   Reginald, 178
le Dyghere, Alice, 132
   Richard, 132
de Dygneneton, Cecilia, 69
   Hugh, 69
Dygun, Margery, 39
   Richard, 39
Dyke, Amicia, 157
   William, 157
le Dyke, Nichola, 51
   Richard, 51
le Dyn, or le Dyne
   Geoffrey, 29, 38
Dyne, Cecilia, 155
   William, 155
Dyneley, or de Dyneley
   Elena, 100
   James, 100
   Margaret, 151, 154
   Robert, 151, 154
Dynham, John, Lord Dynham, 199
Dyry, William, 91
Dytton, *see* Ditton
Dyveyn, or Dyueyn
   John, 123, 126
   Matilda, 123, 126

de Ebbegate, John, 43
   Juliana, 43, 45 (2), 46, 49
   Robert, 43, 45 (2), 46, 49
de Ebbesham, or de Ebesham
   John, 36, 118
   Matilda, 118
   William, 38
Ebesham, Richard, Vicar of, 103
de Ebor, Alice, 124
   Henry, 124
   John, 71 (3)
   William, 27
de Echyngham, William, 86
de Ecton, Alice, 66, 68 (2)
   Gilbert, 66, 68 (2)
de Eddeshale, Johanna, 225
   John, 225
Ede, Robert, 164
fil' Edelina, Matilda, 17
fil' Edgar, Beatrice, 20
Edlon, Emma, 135
   Roger, 135
Edmund, John, 230
Edolfi, Beatrice, 141
   Stephen, 141

INDEX NOMINUM. 259

Edward, Alice, 198
  Elizabeth, 196
  John, 198
  Richard, 197
  William, 209, 229
fil' Edwin, Gilbert, 15
Edyall, Henry, 201
Edyngton, Alice, 191
  John, 191
Edyth, Geoffrey, 137
de Eggeham, Robert, 18
Eggyshawe, Agnes, 222
  Robert, 222
de Egoblaunche, Peter, Bishop of Hereford, 34
de Einton, Juliana, 16
  Mathew, 16
de Eirdale, Adam, 221
Ekton, Alice, 164
  John, 164
  Matilda, 180
  William, 180
Eldrich, Alice, 223
  Thomas, 223
de Eldynge, Nicholaa, 123, 124
  Robert, 123, 124
fil' Elias, Herbert, 20
  John, 16
de Elingham, Thomas, 86
Eliot, or Elyot
  Agnes, 155
  Cristofer, 201, 205
  Henry, 155
  Nicholas, 203
  Richard, 199, 202
  Thomas, 178, 182 (2), 187 (2), 191, 192
de Elkington, Gilbert, 113
  Isabel, 113
de Ellebrugge, Richard, 115, 121
Ellefor, William, 176
le Ellerker, John, 89 (2)
Elmebrugge, or Elmebrigge
  Isabella, 193, 228
  John, 190, 193, 228
  Thomas, 204 (2)
Elmedon, William, 11
Elmet, William, 201
Elriche, Alice, 151
  Thomas, 151
Elryngton, John, 201
de Eltham, Richard, 36
de Eluminor, Johanna, 38
  Thomas, 38

de Ely, Alice, 83
  John, 59
  Katharine, 214
  Robert, 83
Elyngbrigge, Thomas, 201
Elys, or Elis
  Elena, 73
  Johanna, 117
  John, 73, 117
  Richard, 58
  Roger, 77
  William, 77
le Em, Elizabeth, 94
  John, 94
Emeryson, George, 211
Empyngham, William, 236
Emson, Richard, 203-206, 231 (4), 232
le Enfaunt, Alice, 32
  William, 32
Enganet, Roger, 4
le Engleis, Emma, 5
  Henry, 5
  Ralph, 5
Englond, Thomas, 193
den Ensinge, John, 58
le Enveyse, Henry, 214
le Eremite, Alice, 64
  Richard, 64
Ermener, Thomas, 110
le Ermeners, Cristina, 76
  Richard, 76
Ermyn, William, 151
Ermyte, Adam, 139
  Agnes, 139
Ernald, Felicia, widow of, 7
Erneld, Richard, 154
Ernele, William, 227
Eryth, Agnes, 174
  John, 174
de Esche, Robert, 48
le Escot, Adam, 43
de Escote, Peter, 114
de Esford, Philip, 14
de Essex, Ranulph, 42
  William, 194, 195
Essex, Henry, Earl of, 230
de Essinge, John fil' Robert, 15
Estfeld, William, 179
de Esthall, William, 216
atte Estmulle, Johanna, 117
  John, 117
  Juliana, 117
  Matilda, 117

17—2

INDEX NOMINUM.

Estney, Richard, 190
de Eston, Agnes, 41
    John, 41
le Estreis, John, 30
le Estrishe, Henry, 64
    Margery, 64
Eswy, *see* Aswy
de Ethebrigg, John, 216
    Margaret, 216
de Eton, Agnes, 84
    Eustace, 218
    Nicholas, 89
    Ralph, 170
    Richard, 170
    Tiphania, 170
    William, 206
    William fil' Roger, 84
de Everdon, John, 218
de Ewaken, Maurice, 15 (2)
del Ewe, Matilda, 66
    Peter, 66
    William, 66
Ewelle, or de Ewelle
    Agnes, 22, 42, 43
    Alice, 85, 95
    Gilbert, 22, 42, 43
    Siward, 6, 8
    William, 85, 95, 104
Exeter, John, Bishop of, 229
    William, Bishop of, 19
Exton, Nicholas, 139
Exwold, John, 197
    Margaret, 197
de Eylenehaghe, Johanna, 100
    Robert, 100
Eylone, Elizabeth, 175, 190
    Thomas, 175, 190
Eylove, see Aylove
Eynesham, John, 154
    William, 154
Eyton, Eytun, or Euyton
    Emma, 27, 34
    Juliana, 74
    Ralph, 170
    Tiphania, 170
    William, 27, 34, 75

fil' Faber, John, 28
Fabian, Johanna, 92
    Robert, 92
Fairfax, Guy, 196
Fairher, or Fayrher
    John, 142, 149
    Margaret, 142

de Fakeham, William fil' William, 26
Fallan, William, 189
atte Fan, *see* atte Fen
de la Fanne, *see* de la Fenne
Fareman, Goda, 17
    Robert, 17
de Farenham, Ingelran, 87
Farman, Constance, 86
    John, 139
    William, 86
de Farnbergh, Johanna, 82
    Matilda, 82
    Richard, 82
de Farndon, Matilda, 119
    Roger, 119
de Farneberwe, Richard, 104
de Farnecroft, Adam, 111
    Cecilia, 111
    Elias, 111
de Faseby, William, 153
Fastolf, John, 188
Fauconer, John, 123
Faukes, Alice, 14
    Gunnilda, 72 (2)
    Thomas, 72 (2)
    William, 14, 28
Faunt, Matilda, 129
    Salamon, 123, 129
le Faunt, Alice, 23
    William, 23
de Fay, de Faye, or de la Faye
    John, 19, 20, 21
    Matilda, 28, 30
Fayreford, or Faireford
    Agnes, 194, 229
    Alexander, 194, 229
    Juliana, 177, 181
    Robert, 177, 181
Fedecok, Alice, 153
    Elias, 153
de Fednes, William, 22
de la Feld, or de la Felde
    Agatha, 40
    Gilbert, 4
    Henry, 52
    Johanna, 52
    Matilda, 4
    Walter, 40
de Felde, Richard, 117
atte Felde, Grecia, 84
    Isabel, 82
    Philip, 84
    Thomas, 82

de Felton, John, 99
    Richard, 67
    Sibil, 67, 99
de Felyhurst, Alice, 112
    William, 112
atte Fen, atte Fan, atte Feen, atte Fenn, or atte Fenne
    Margaret, 115, 125, 144
    Margery, 130
    Nicholas, 125
    Robert, 94
    Thomas, 94
    Walter, 94, 144
    William, 105, 108, 115, 130
    William fil' Richard, 100, 102
Fencote, John, 123
de Fenles, or de Fyenles
    Ingeram, 39
    John, 68
Fenne, Hugh, 194
de Fenne, de la Fenne, or de la Fanne
    Emma, 3
    John, 44
    Thomas, 52
    William, 3, 44
    William fil' William, 3
Fenner, John, 210
Fenrother, Richard, 199
    Robert, 210, 211
Fenys, Anna, 203, 208
    James, 184
    John, 197, 203
    Roger, 184
    Thomas, 197, 232
    Thomas, Lord Dacre, 203, 208
Feriby, or Feryby
    Johanna, 181
    John, 181, 182
de Ferkcles, Richard, 28
de Ferminger, Theobald, 6
Fermory, Thomas, 192
Ferre, Alianor, 109
    Guy, 62, 68 (2), 109
Ferrers, Edward, 204, 232
    Martin, 231
le Ferun, Johanna, 46
    John, 48
    Vincent, 48
le Ferur, le Ferour, le Ferrour, or Ferrour
    Alice, 89, 93, 98, 100, 106
    Margery, 45

le Ferur, le Ferour, le Ferrour, or Ferrour
    Thomas, 89, 93, 98, 100, 106
    Walter, 45
    William, 180
Ferthyng, John, 173
    Mary, 173
Feveresham, William, 169
le Fevre, le Fevere, or le Feure
    Henry, 82
    John, 47, 48
    Margery, 47, 48
    Matilda, 42
    Odo fil' Walter, 42
    Peter fil' Richard, 69
    Petronilla, 61
    Reginald, 43
    Richard, 61
    Sarra fil' Thomas, 55
    William, 61
Feyrchild, Beatrice, 22
    Robert, 22
de Fifhid, Richard, 132
Filiol, or Fillol
    Hugh, 219
    Mary, 134, 219
    William, 134, 219
de Finchingfeld, or de Fynchyngfelde
    Margaret, 67
    Ralph fil' William, 67
    William, 120
Fisher, Fissher, Fiscer, le Fissere, le Fissher, or le Fisshere
    Alban, 14
    Alice, 57, 73, 122 (2), 125
    Johanna, 134
    John, 73 (2), 122 (2), 125
    Mazeline, 32
    Nicholas, 134
    Ralph, 57, 73
    Robert, 32, 89
    William, 200
Fissh, or Fysche
    Alice, 127, 152
    Thomas, 127, 152
Fitzherbert, Anthony, 211
    John, 199
Fitz-Johan, or Fitz-John
    Agnes, 148 (2), 153
    Edmund, 148
    Johanna, 167
    John, 187, 194
    Nicholas, 167

Fitz-Johan, or Fitz-John
    William, 141, 148 (2), 150, 151,
      153, 155
Fitzmichel, Johanna, 126
    William, 126
Fitz-Payn, Ela, 218
    Robert, 218
Fitz Piers, William, 152, 156
Fitz Robert, Robert, 165, 177, 226
Fitzwater, William, 186
Flandr', William, 4
Fleccher, Andrew, 179
le Fleming, Golda, 18, 20
    John, 28
    William, 20, 28
Flemyng, or Flemmyng
    Alice, 121
    Gilbert, 144
    Henry, 121
    John, 163
    Juliana, 163
    Margaret, 121
    Richard, 192
Flete, Alice, 164
    Thomas, 164
    William, 171
Fleynsford, or Fleynesford
    Agnes, 160
    Henry, 160, 168
de Flore, John, 49 (2)
de Florence, Alice, 62
    Pinus, 62
Flyntesseind, Thomas, 225
Foche, John, 183
Fogel, Agnes, 119
    John, 119
le Foghel, John, 105
    Matilda, 56
    Robert, 56
Foldhay, Richard, 169
Foleburn, Cristiana, 61
    Matthew, 61
de Foleham, Johanna, 82
    Richard, 82
Folevill, John, 140
    Mary, 140
Folke, John, 175
de la Folkelaunde, Thomas, 29
Folvill, John fil' Robert, 129
de Fonte, Peter, 5
Fontevraud, Abbess of, Alice, 19
      " Johanna, 39
Fooche, John, 227
Forde, Anthony, 208 (2)

Forde, Agnes, 199
    Marcia, 189
    Mercia, 194
    Richard, 184, 188, 189, 194, 199
    Walter, 196
atte Forde, Alice, 62
    Henry fil' Adam, 62
de Ford, de Forde, de la Ford, or
    de la Forde
    Agnes, 20
    Beatrice, 52
    Henry, 20, 29
    William, 52 (2)
Forder, Richard, 175
Forester, or le Forester
    Adam, 138
    Alice, 138
    John, 109
    Matilda, 109, 119, 120
    Reginald, 43, 109, 117, 119,
      120
    Richard, 20
    William, 120
de Forneys, William, 38
Forster, Humfrey, 195
    John, 133, 196
    Robert, 196
le Fort, Agnes, 71
    Nicholas, 71
Fortescu, John, 228
Forthe, Richard, 229
Foscue, Benedict, 211
    Matilda, 211
Fot, John, 98, 133
    Margery, 98
Foucher, Mathew, 184, 187
Fouler, Alice, 166
    William, 166
Foulmere, Richard, 169
Fountaynes, John, 184
de Fourneux, John, 123
de Foxton, Johanna, 140
    John, 101, 107, 140
    Juliana, 107
Frankcheyney, John, 169
Fraunceys, Frauncheis, Fraunsoys,
    le Fraunceys, or le Frauncheis
    Agnes, 90, 188
    Alan, 98, 218
    Daniel, 117
    Florence, 98, 103, 107, 108, 218,
      219
    Geoffrey, 39
    Henry, 189 (2)

Fraunceys, Fraunceis, Fraunsoys, le Frauceys, or le Fraunceis
  John, 6
  Nicholas, 98, 103, 107, 108, 218, 219
  Pagana, 215
  Richard, 215
  Robert, 90
  Thomas, 188
  William, 4, 74
de Fraunkelee, Philip, 31
Fraunkeleyn, le Frankeleyn, le Franklein, or le Fraunkelyn
  Alice, 14
  Hugh, 14
  Margery, 103
  Richard, 60, 61
  Sabina, 60, 61
  William, 103
de Fraxino, William, 28
Fray, John, 178, 180
le Freke, or Freke
  John, 157, 178
  Thomas, 153
Freland, or Frelond
  John, 167
  Richard, 122
  Walter, 142
Freman, Agnes, 177
  Richard, 177
Fremantel, John, 160
de Fremelesworth, Johanna, 112
  John, 112
de Fremeswrth, Margaret fil' Robert, 54
de Frendesbury, John, 83
Frenshe, le Frenshe, le Frensshe, or le Freynssh
  Johanna, 74
  John, 148, 164, 216
  Juliana, 216
  Nicholas, 120
  Richard, 104
  Roger, 97
  Thomas, 125
  William, 72, 74
Frere, Johanna, 91
  Robert, 91
de Freschenevil, Ralph, 213
Freshfish, Johanna, 78
  John, 78
Frestelyng, Bartholomew, 127
de Freton, Nicholas, 40
  Roger, 147

de Fridelee, Roger, 157
Frilent, Matilda, 21
  Roger, 21
  William, 21
de Froggewelle, Isabel, 86
  Walter, 86
Froil, John, 86
de Frollebiry, de Frollebury, de Frolleburgh, or Frolbury
  Alice, 72
  Johanna, 64, 72, 184
  John, 184
  Margaret, 99, 109
  Richard, 25
  Stephen, 72, 99, 109
  William, 64, 72
de Frowik, de Frouwyk, or Frowyk
  Geoffrey, 17
  Henry, 120, 205
  Margaret, 205
  Thomas, 207
  Walter, 37
le Frutyer, Alice, 72
  William, 72
Frye, Richard, 101
  Robert, 156
de Fryland, Walter, 124
Frysel, Walter, 113
de Frythyng, Thomas, 221
de Fulbrok, John, 25
Fulbourne, Anna, 210
  Katharine, 208, 210
  Thomas, 208, 210
fil' Fulk, or fil' Fulc
  Henry, 22, 23
  Alice, wife of, 22
Fuller, Bartholomew, 178, 179
  Johanna, 146
  John, 146
le Fulur, Agnes, 14
  Algar, 14
de Funtenay, Frechesant, 17
  William, 17
le Furber, or le Fourber
  Anastasia, 24
  Anselm, 85
  Margery, 85
  Robert, 24
Furneux, Amy, 150
  William, 150
Fygge, Alice, 209
  William, 209
Fynall, Johanna, 206

INDEX NOMINUM.

Fynall, William, 206
Fynch, Alice, 135
  John, 134
  Roger, 135
Fynchyngfelde, *see* Finchingfeld
Fynderne, William, 179
de Fyndon, William, 118
Fyneford, or de Fyneford
  Alice, 139
  Robert, 121, 122, 139
atte Fynersh, Alice, 131
  Thomas, 131
Fysschwyk, Agnes, 186
  Philip, 186

de Gadynton, Alice, 135
  Richard, 135
Gage, Alice, 198
  John, 210
  Philippa, 210
  William, 198
Gairstang, Henry, 189
Galian, Bartholomew, 218
  Johanna, 218
Galley, Thomas, 186
Gamelyn, Robert, 164
de Garboldesham, Adam, 82, 83
  Cristiana, 82, 83
Gardiner, or Gardener
  Henry, 224
  John, 199, 206
de Gardino, Lucy, widow of Peter, 30, 32
  Ralph, 20
Garget, or Gargat
  Alice, 44, 48
  Dionis, 22
  Hugh, 22
  John, 131
  Richard, 44, 48
Gargrave, John, 188
Garkyn, Johanna, 129, 132
  Robert, 129, 139
Garland, Garlaunde, Gerlaund, or Gerlonde
  Adam, 91
  Alice, 91
  Henry, 34
  Johanna, 34
  John, 13, 167
  Thomas, 29
  Walter, 58
de Garscherche, or de Garschirche
  Cristiana, 64

de Garscherche, or de Garschirche
  Elias, 34
  Robert, 46
atte Garston, Walter, 104
de or de la Garston, Gerston, or Greston
  Joel, 38, 44
  John, 40, 44
  Matilda, 40, 44
  Philippa, 38, 44
  Reginald, 68
  Roger, 68
  Sarra, 68
  William, 15
de Garton, John, 137, 222
  Margaret, 137, 222
Garwinton, Thomas, 142
Gary, Cristina, 195
  John, 195
Gascoigne, Nicholas, 160
  William, 160
Gate, Roger, 147
atte Gate, Henry, 136, 139
  Johanna, 109
  Richard, 66
  Robert, 105
  Walter, 66
  William, 109
de Gatesden, John, 32, 34, 38, 215
  Letitia, 32
  Richard, 215
le Gateward, Roger fil' Walter, 73
  Walter, 73
de Gatingdon, John, 36
de Gattele, Ralph, 30
de Gatton, Alice, 96
  Giles, 94 (2), 96
  Hamo, 32 (2), 47
  Johanna, 47
  Robert, 2, 28, 67
de Gatwik, or de Gatewyk
  Elizabeth, 82
  Johanna, 99
  John, 25, 65, 99
  Katharine, 82
  Margery, 82
  Richard, 82
Gatyn, Bartholomew, 97
  John, 148, 153
  Richard, 163
  Rose, 148
Gaydon, Robert, 145
Gaynesford, Anna, 210, 211
  George, 203, 204

Gaynesford, Isabel, 203
    John, 106, 107, 112, 113 (2), 127, 167, 173, 174, 175, 181, 182 (3), 183, 190, 204 (2), 210, 211, 226, 227, 231
    Margaret, 195
    Margery, 106, 107, 112, 113 (2)
    Nicholas, 194 (2), 195, 196
    Robert, 204
    Thomas, 157
    William, 186, 187, 191, 192, 231
de Gaysham, or de Geysham
    John, 72, 73, 77 (2), 82
    Matilda, 77
de Gayton, Robert, 222
Gebon, Geoffrey, 225
de Gedding, Geoffrey, 54
    Margaret, 89, 90
    Walter, 54, 89 (3), 90
    William fil' Walter, 83
Gedner, John, 186
Geffray, Adam, 126 (2), 220
    Letice, 126 (2), 220
Geffrey, Cecilia, 86
    William, 86
Genowe, Alice, 172
    Roger, 163
Geoffrey, Wulneva, widow of, 7
fil' Geoffrey, Geoffrey, 15
    Agnes mother of, 15
    John, 36, 213 (2)
    John fil' John, 41
    Mathew, 16
        Gunnora, widow of, 21
Gerard, Henry, 59, 60, 62, 63, 66, 70
    Johanna, 71
    John, 70, 71, 178
    Matilda, 178
    William, 40
fil' Gerard, Richard, 16
Geraudon, Ernald, 32
Gerberd, Margery, 101, 111
    William, 101, 111
fil' Geri, William, 9
Gerlond or Gerlaund, see Garland
Germeyn, Agnes, 81
    Richard fil' William, 81
Germin, Alice, 99
    John, 99
de Gernemuth, Walter, 37
Gerston, see Garston

Gerveys, or Gervays
    Agnes, 62
    Johanna, 77, 103, 112
    John, 135, 154, 189
    Martin, 77, 103
    Nicholas, 62
    Robert, 112
    Thomas, 103
    William fil' Robert, 56
Gery, William, 27
de Geysham, see de Gaysham
del Geyt, William, 9
Gibbes, Rica, 143
    William, 143
Giffard, or Gyffard
    Reginald, 14
    William, 46
Gilbert, Margaret, 111
    William, 111
fil' Gilbert, Hamo, 6
    Hillary, 23
    John, 43
    Walter, 5, 6, 7
de Gildeford, see de Guldeford
Gildesburgh, Robert, 164, 172
Giles, Thomas, 203
Gilles, Alice, 79
    William, 79
de Ginnei, Matilda, 6
    William, 6
Girpen, Gilbert, 200
Glade, Alice, 110
    Margery, 73
    William, 73, 110
    William fil' William, 73
de Glastingebir, William, 29
Glene, Hugh, 178
de Gloucester, Hawyse, 70
    John, 36
    Matilda, 63
    Nicholas, 63
    Walter, 70, 86
    Walter fil' Walter, 89
le Glovere, Gilbert, 95
fil' Gocelin, Robert, 3
    Estrilda, wife of, 3
fil' Goda, Juliana, 12
de Godalming, or de Goddalmynge
    Johanna, 41
    Peter, 70
    William, 41
Godard, Alice, 121 (3), 128
    Andrew, 91
    Cristiana, 91

Godard, Elias, 121 (3)
    Isabel, 91
    John, 128
    Thomas, 91, 120
Godefray, John, 73
    Thomas, 73
Godehowe, William, 224
de Godelegh, Alice, 69
    Geoffrey, 16
    Robert, 69
Godeman, William, 10
de Godemanston, Geoffrey, 218
de Goderinton, Beatrice, 55
    Richard, 55
Goderyk, John, 134
Godesfeld, Felicia, 114
    William, 114
Godesgrace, Geoffrey, 12
Godesone, John, 175
    Matilda, 175
Godeston, Johanna, 188
    Robert, 188
Godewyn, or Godewyne
    Johanna, 178, 180
    Thomas, 178, 180
fil' Goding, Cristiana, 7
de Godinton, Matilda, 39
    Thomas, 39
Godisson, William, 148
de Godland, Heming, 38
    Matilda, 38
Godman, Johanna, 207
    Richard, 210
    Robert, 207
Godric, John fil' Robert, 21
fil Godric, Theobald, 5
Godsub, Isabel, 132
    William, 132
de Godwich, or de Gotwich
    Agnes, 96
    Alice, 96
    John, 96 (2)
fil' Godwin, Alvina, 5
    Richard, 11 (4)
Godyng, William, 189
Goghemere, Alice, 141
    Roger, 141
Golafre, or Gulafre
    Agnes, 20
    John, 226
    Richard, 20
Gold, or Golde
    John, 98 (2)
    Peter, 223

de Goldburgh, or de Goldeburgh
    Agnes, 216
    Guy fil' Simon, 84
    Simon, 216
atte, del, or de la Goldhord
    Alice, 74, 76
    Richard, 63, 74, 76
Goldmore, or Goldemore
    Agnes, 174
    Isabel, 117
    William, 117, 174
Goldsmith, or Goldsmyth
    Avice, widow of James, 29
    Beatrice fil' Warin, 20
    Cecilia, 30
    Geoffrey, 11
    Odo, 18
    Peter, 40
    Roesia, 15, 16
    Thomas, 30
    William, 15, 16, 23, 202
Goldwell, James, 194
    John, 194, 202
    Thomas, 194
Gomme, Henry, 114, 116
    Johanna, 114
    William, 107 (2), 108
Gonayre, Margaret, 152
    Peter, 152
    Richard, 139
Goode, Henry, 187
Goodlok, Geoffrey, 189
Goodman, Elizabeth, 186
    Thomas, 186
Goolde, Johanna, 176
    John, 176
Goryng, John, 194
Goseden, John, 133
Gosse, Isabella, 188
    Thomas, 188
Gosselyn, William, 149
de Gotwich, see de Godwich
Gouderyche, John, 181
    Margery, 181
Govell, Margaret, 210
    Richard, 210
Gowbrith, Gilbert, 23
Gower, Edward, 196
Goylyn, Agnes, 93
Goythur, John, 122
Grace, Johanna, 195, 202
    John, 195
    Thomas, 161, 202
    William fil' Richard, 161

INDEX NOMINUM. 267

de Graphlíngeham, or de Graphlingesham
  Acelina, 14
  Elyas, 31
  John, 14
Gras, Cristina, 124
  Walter, 77
  William, 124
le Gras, Richard, 45
  Walter, 109, 111
Grasvassal, Ralph, 24
de Grauetye, Bartholomew, 74
  Matilda, 74
Graunt, le Graunt, or le Grant
  John, 197
  Richard, 46, 49
de Grava, Ralph, 4
  Richard, 29
  Thomas, 13
Grave, Anna, 199
  John, 199
de la Grave, Alice, 36
  Gilbert fil' Robert, 64
  Richard, 36, 60
  Walter, 32
de Gravelee, Hamo, 25
de Gravemere, Gilbert, 57
de Gravenel, Cecilia, 215
  John, 34
de Graveneye, Alice, 107
  Edith, 22
  Richard, 10, 22, 107
  Richard fil' Richard, 107
Gravesende, Isabella, 162
  John, 162
de Graveshende, or de Gravesende,
  Amy, 51
  Stephen, 51
  Thomas, 106
Gray, William, 188
Greder, or le Greder
  William, 14, 16
Gregor, Johanna, 43
  John, 43
de Grendon, John, 69
  Walter, 123
Grene, or Greene
  Adam, 204
  Agnes, 204
  Alesia, 179
  Alice, 182
  Edward, 207
  Henry, 228
  Johanna, 150

Grene, or Greene
  John, 189, 192
  Richard, 182
  Matilda, 190
  Thomas, 177, 199
  Walter, 150, 179
atte Grene, Johanna, 92, 167
  John, 92
  Richard, 98
  Thomas, 79
  Walter, 136, 147, 153, 167
  William, 175
Grenebolde, Isabella, 135
  John, 135
de Grenehull, William, 55
Grenestrete, Alice, 150
  John, 150
de Grenewych, Letice, 70, 71
  Peter, 70, 71
de Grenstede, Johanna, 108, 117
  William, 108, 117
Gresley, Alice, 10
  Henry, 10
le Gresmonger, Beatrice, 35
  Philip, 35
Greston, *see* Garston
de Gretton, John, 51
atte Greuette, John, 132
de Grey, Elizabeth, 223
  John, 223
  Reginald, 224
Greyvyle, William, 210
Grick, Thomas, 91
Griffits, Grace, 152
  John, 152
Grigge, John, 208
Grofham, John, 210, 230
  Thomas, 178
le Gros, Margery, 53
  Richard, 53
  Thomas, 53
le Grouere, Alice, 105
  Robert, 105
Groute, Robert, 188
atte Grove, Adam, 74
  Beatrice, 74
  Felicia, 116
  Michael, 147
  Richard, 74
  Sibil, 147
  Thomas fil' John, 116
Groveherst, Thomas, 183
Grovere, John, 170
  William, 181

Gryffyn, Matilda, 196
    William, 196
Gryfwold, Thomas, 187
Grymesby, John, 183
    Margaret, 183
Grynford, Matilda, 127
    Ralph, 127
Gulafre, *see* Golafre
de Guldeford, de Gudeford, de Gildeford, or de Gyldeford
    Cristiana, 84, 94
    Eudo, 41, 47
    Henry, 53, 73, 75, 84, 94
    John fil' Nicholas, 60
    Peter, 39
    William, 137
de Gulden, Adam, 77
    Katharine, 77
de Gulderegg, Isabel, 64
Gundewyne, Agnes, 139
    Ralph, 139
Guonshale, Edmund, 140
Gurdon, Adam, 32, 34
Gwynne, Juliana, 198, 201
    Thomas, 198, 201
Gyan, Geoffrey, 51
Gybbe, Johanna, 158
    John, 158
Gybbon, John, 193
Gybbons, William, 173
Gyfford, William, 195
de Gyldeford, *see* de Guldeford
Gylekyn, Richard, 87
Gylle, John, 179
    Margery, 179
Gylmyn, or Gylemyn
    Richard, 188
    Thomas, 121, 188
Gylot, James, 145
Gylys, John, 157
de Gyrund, William, 22
Gysburn, William, 148
de Gyseleham, or de Gysilham
    Agnes, 40, 45
    William, 40, 45

H...arl, Thomas, 12
atte Hacche, Aveline, 44
    Matilda, 83, 87
    Nicholas, 125
    Thomas, 83
    William, 87
Haccher, John, 204, 205, 206
    Katharine, 205

Hachewulf, Gilbert, 92
Hackere, Agatha, 132
    Walter, 132
de Hadestok, Idonea, 57
    John, 46, 55
Hadinham, John, 55
de Hadresham, de Heddresham, de Hadersham, Hadresham, or Hadrisham
    Adam, 131 (2)
    Alice, 110
    Bartholomew, 46
    Emma, 59, 143, 146
    Geoffrey, 110
    James, 89
    John, 110, 131, 141, 143, 146, 153, 164, 224, 225
    John fil' James, 89
    John fil William, 156
    Nicholas, 59
de Hadyngden, John, 75
de Haghe, Roger, 128
fil' Hairun, Alan, 16
le Hakkere, Walter, 128
Halden, or de Halden
    William, 142, 143
Hale, Henry, 187
    Thomas, 183
de Hale, or de la Hale
    Edith, 23
    John, 62
atte Hale, John, 62
    William, 139
Haliwell, —— prioress of, 23
    Matilda, „ „ 12, 13
Hall, or Halle
    John, 159, 179, 224, 226
    William, 179
atte Hall, or atte Halle
    Johanna, 162, 166, 167
    John, 75, 130, 162, 166, 167, 183
    Thomas, 114
Halleclyff, William, 227
de Halling, de Haling, or de Haliuk
    Ivo, 15, 33
    Mabel, 14
    Ralph, 5, 14 (2), 15, 33
de Hallyngbiry, or de Hallyngbir
    Walter, 45
    William, 80
Halpeni, or Halpeny
    John, 160

Halpeni, or Halpeny
    Petronilla, 160
    William, 14
de Halsham, Robert, 221
de Halstede, or Halstede
    Cristina, 124
    Henry, 155, 163
    Ralph, 124
le Halveloverd, Serlo, 48
Halyday, John, 124
de Hameledon, or de Hameldon
    Alice, 93
    Richard, 93
    Robert, 8
de Hamme, de la Hamme, de Hammes, or Hamme
    Agnes, 128, 132, 134
    Alma, 72, 86
    Gilbert, 168
    Gunnilda, 61
    John, 27, 72, 86
    Matilda, 27, 101
    Philip, 128
    Reginald, 47
    Richard, 101
    Robert, 40, 96
    Roger, 61
    Thomas, 96
    Walter, 132, 134
    William, 2
fil' Hamo, John, 33
    Norman, 6
        Beatrice, wife of, 6
    Richard, 4
    Walter, 4
Hamond, William, 209
Hampden, Thomas, 195
Hampton, or de Hampton
    John, 82, 126, 142, 153, 154(2), 183
    Juliana, 82
    Sibil, 153, 154(2)
de Hanamptede, William, 134
Hanewell, William, 177
de Hangelton, Ralph, 113
Hanley, Hanlegh, or Hanlee
    Johanna, 163, 175(2)
    Thomas, 163, 175(2)
Hansard, Haunsard, or Haunshard
    Agatha, 25, 36
    Alice, 47, 51
    Aveline, 4
    Gundreda, 50 (2)
    James, 25, 36, 50 (2)

Hansard, Haunsard, or Haunshard
    James fil' William, 215
    John, 42, 50
    John fil' William, 215
    Otto, 164
    Thomas, 47, 51
    William, 4
Hapton, William, 198
Harand, Mathew, 27
de Hardebrigg, Richard, 118
Hardegray, John, 15
Hardel, William, 48
Hardele, Benedict, 145
    Margery, 145
Hardelton, Robert, 33
Hardy, John, 197
Hardyng or Harding
    Agnes, 122
    Richard, 122
    Robert, 154, 210
    Roger, 11
Hardys, Alice, 207
    Philip, 206, 207 (2)
le Hare, Johanna, 50
    William, 50
de Harewedon, William, 79
de Harewell, William, 143
de Haringe, Robert, 21
Harkestede, Agnes, 134
    William, 134
Harm, Richard, 19 (2), 26
Harpedon, Johanna, 226
    John, 226
de Harperdesford, Robert, 219
Harpur, Hugh, 22
    John, 182
atte Harryes, Alice, 143
    Stephen, 143
de Haryngton, Robert, 224
de Hascumbe, Thomas fil' Philip, 95
de Haselwode, William, 39
de Haspale, Geoffrey, 55
de Hastinges, de Hastynges, de Hastyngg, or Hastyngs
    John, 90, 217 (2)
    Robert, 18, 64
    William, 230
de Hatfeld, William, 123
Hatheway, John, 187
Hatter, Peter, 158
le Hattere, Alan, 123
    Amicia, 123
Hatton, or de Hatton
    Anabel, 90

Hatton, or de Hutton
  Henry, 90
  Henry fil' Henry, 109
  Johanna, 211
  John, 210
  Stephen, 109
Hauberger, Margery, 115
  Stephen, 115
le Haud, John, 213
de Haudlo, John, 90, 218, 219
  Matilda, 90, 218
de Haueldersh, Bartholomew, 68
Hauker, William, 143
Haukyns, Agnes, 181
  Augustin, 181
  Robert, 200, 203, 204
de Haunlegh, Clemencia, 42
  Hubert, 42
de Hautot, Hawyse, 82, 83
Hawe, Cristofer, 200, 206
  John, 200
Haweles, Henry, 174
  Margaret, 174
  Richard, 174
de Haweman, Alan, 215
  Amicia, 215
Hawys, Henry fil' Henry, 93
  William, 93
Hay, John, 230
  Juliana, 185
  Laurence, 185
atte Hay, Thomas, 155
de la Hay, Johanna, 163
  Thomas, 163
Haydok, Thomas, 181 (2)
de la Haye, Robert, 219
Hayford, Humfrey, 190
Hayne, Isabella, 183
  Stephen, 183
de Haytfeld, Matilda, 100
  Nicholas, 100
  Thomas, 80
Hayton, or Haytone
  Thomas, 164, 170
de Hayton, John, 99
Hayward, Margaret, 182
  Richard, 182
  William, 181
de Haywod, Gilbert, 16
Haywode, Agnes, 141
  Reginald, 141
de Hecheham, Hervey, 41
  Isolde, 41
de Hecstede, *see* de Hexestede

de Heddresham, *see* de Hadresham
de Hedenescumbe, Robert, 30
Hedy, John, 182
de Hege, William, 26
atte Hegge, Johanna, 130
  Richard, 130
de la Hegge, Elena, 59
  William, 59
Hegger, John, 175
de Hegham, Isabel, 60
  Nicholas, 26
  Paulina, 86
  Robert, 30
  Thomas, 60
  Thomas fil' Thomas, 60
de Heghfeld, Cecilia, 106
  John, 106
  Richard, 128
de Hegstede, Ralph, 42
de Hegthon, Ralph, 53
  Roesya, 53
de Heiwude, Agnes, 7
de Hekestede, *see* de Hexestede
atte Helde, atte Held, or atte Heelde
  Agnes, 144
  Henry, 136, 222
  Johanna, 125 (2), 168
  Nicholas, 125 (2)
  Robert, 168
  William, 144
Heldere, Alice, 169
  Richard, 169
le Helere, Alice, 107
  William fil' Geoffrey, 107
fil' Hemeric, Hemeric, 20
Hemery, John, 136 (2), 143 (2)
Hempton, Richard, 226
le Hen, Juliana, 73
  Richard, 73
le Hende, Johanna, 112
  John, 112
de Hengham, Hugh, 55
  Ralph, 57, 58, 59, 68
  Robert, 55
de Henle, or de Henley
  Isabel, 69, 70, 88
  John, 48, 71, 88
  William, 69, 70, 88, 106
de Henleg, or de Henlegee
  Philip, 17, 20
Henley, Johanna, 177, 186
  Thomas, 177, 186
fil' Henry, Alexander, 1, 2

fil' Henry, Alice, 31
    Saerus, 30, 33, 213
Henry, Henry fil' William, 103
    Isabel, 103
de Henxton, Giles, 70
    Margery, 70
le Heore, Isabel, 75
    Thomas, 75
Hereford, John, Bishop of, 192, 224
Hereford, Thomas, 180
de Hereford, Felicia, 19
    Hugh, 216, 217 (2)
    Richard, 19
    Walter, 220
Heremitam, Geoffrey, 10
Hereward, Agnes, 125
    Mabel, 41
    Robert, 125
    William, 4
Herfray, Laurence, 127
    Matilda, 127
Hergreve, John, 173
    Juliana, 173
de Herlawe, Agnes, 130
    Philip, 130
Herle, or de Herle
    Alice, 178
    Henry fil' William, 178
    Margaret, 103
    William, 90, 103, 107, 108, 117
Herlewes, Richard, 232
Herman, or Hereman
    Alan, 94
    Alan fil' Walter, 62
    Alice, 174, 225
    Margaret, 53, 94
    Matilda fil' Alan, 140
    Robert, 24
    Walter, 53, 54, 174, 225
de Hermesthorp, John, 138
Hermyte, William, 223
atte Herne, Elena, 42
    Ralph, 42
Herneys, Edmund, 146
    Elizabeth, 146
Hernyng. *see* Hirnyng
Heron, Elizabeth, 224
    William, 224
Heroun, Roger, 226
Herry, William, 146
de Hersetelesheye, or de Hershetelslegh
    Edmund, 41, 81
    John fil' Edmund, 81

Hert, Agnes, 223
    Isabella, 199
    John, 199, 223
    Richard, 208
    Thomas, 186
le Hert, Matilda, 106
    Nicholas, 106
    Ralph, 130
de Hertforde, Amicia, 120
    William, 120
de Hertmere, Philip, 38
    Thomas, 38
    William, 4
fil' Hervey, Edith, 46
    John, 31
    Thomas, 2
Hervey, Hervi, Hervy, or de Hervy
    Agnes, 169
    Aylith, 38
    Henry, 38
    Margaret, 82, 119
    Ralph, 82, 119
    Stephen, 169
    William, 44, 53, 182
Herveys, Edward, 174
    Elizabeth, 174
Heryng, Edmund, 149
    Nicholas, 142
    Richard, 132
    Thomas, 178, 182, 185, 186 (3), 226
de Hesse, Gunnilda, 1, 2
Heter, John, 169
    Nicholaa, 169
atte Hethe, Laurence, 61
    Rose, 160
    Walter, 160, 163
de la Hethe, or de la Hathe
    Godfrey, 60
    Henry, 60
Hethere, Agnes, 142
    John, 142
de Heton, Elizabeth, 157
    John, 157
le Hettere, Hugh, 88
de Heure, de Heuere, or de Hewere
    Agnes, 70
    Hawyse, 70, 75
    Johanna, 47
    John, 47, 70
    John fil' Roger, 11
    Mabel, 77
    Nicholas fil' Robert, 77
    Ralph, 70, 75

de Heure, de Heuere, or de Hewere
    Robert, 77
    William, 11
de Hexestede, de Hecstede, or de Hekestede
    Alan, 96
    Eva, 96
    Matilda, 5
    Robert, 19, 30
    Simon, 19
    Walter, 3, 5, 30
Hexstall, Amy, 193
    Edward, 199, 200
    Elizabeth, 199, 200
    Thomas, 193
de Heyford, Adam fil' Geoffrey, 81
    Emma, 72, 82
    Geoffrey, 72, 81, 82
    Richard, 41
    Richard fil' Geoffrey, 95
    Stephen fil' Geoffrey, 81
    Thomas fil' Geoffrey, 81
de Heyfull, Margaret, 78
    Richard, 78
le Heymonger, Benedict, 35
    Matilda, 35
Heynes, John, 176
le Heyr, Thomas, 135
de Heysulle, Johanna, 118
    Peter, 118
Heythorn, Helewisia, 52
    John, 52
Heyward, Henry, 201, 206
    Johanna, 170
    William, 170
le Heywood, or le Heyward
    Katharine, 89, 90
    Thomas, 89, 90
de Hibernia, or de Hybern
    Ralph, 22, 30
de la Hide, *see* de la Hyde
Higham, Richard, 199
Hildersham, or Hyldersham
    Thomas, 210, 211
Hill, Edith, 173
    Henry, 230
    John, 173
    Robert, 232
    See also Hylle
Hillary, Richard, 91
atte Hille, Adam, 105
Hilton, John, 159
Hirnyng, or Hernyng
    William, 149, 150

atte Hirst, William, 162
de Ho, *see* de Hoo
Hobert, James, 232
Hochard, Alice, 133
    John, 133
    Thomas fil' John, 133
Hochepount, William, 154 (2)
de Hockele, *see* de Hokkele
Hodersale, Robert, 174
Hog, Mathew, 19
Hoge, Robert, 196
Hogeson, Edward, 210
Hogham, Henry, 168
de Hoghelere, Alice, 115
    William, 115
Hoghton, William, 141 (2)
Hoke, Walter, 159, 224
atte Hoke, Cristiana, 46
    Isabel, 112
    John, 112
    Thomas, 46
    Walter, 160
Hokele, Thomas, 124
le Hokere, Johanna, 113
    William, 113
de Hokkele, or de Hockele
    Isabel, 112
    Thomas, 112, 124
Holand, Robert, 176, 177
Holbech, William, 124
Holcombe, John, 170
Holderness, Agnes, 172
    John, 172
Hole, Margaret, 211
    Richard, 211
de Holebrok, Richard, 57
de Holeburne, John, 65
    Mabel, 65
de Holeg, or de Holeghe
    John, 65
    Mabel, 65
    Roger, 6
    Thomas, 37
de Holeherst, John fil' Walter, 66
    Walter, 6, 8, 66
Holgrave, John, 197
atte Holilande, atte Holylonde, or de la Holilonde
    John, 163
    Matilda, 80
    Robert, 65, 80 (2)
Hollewey, or Holewey
    Margaret, 135
    Robert, 135

Hollewey, or Holewey
    William, 143
Holm, or de Holm
    Richard, 149
    Eylerd, 19
Holmes, Thomas, 167
Holnherst, John, 198
Holt, Henry, 223
    William, 190, 232
Holym, John, 176
    Margaret, 176
Holyngborne, or Holyngburn
    Alice, 160
    John, 160, 166
de la Hombreth, William fil' Odo, 29
atte Hone, Agnes, 155
    Richard, 155
de Honewaldesham, Johanna, 34
    William, 34
Honsom, Henry, 192
Hoo, Thomas, 171, 198, 229
atte Hoo, Alice, 131
    Walter, 131
de Hoo, de Ho, or de Heo
    Agnes, 76
    Alianor fil' Ralph, 94
    Alice, 101
    Elena, 67
    Geoffrey, 18
    Johanna fil' Ralph, 94
    John, 67, 101, 112
    John fil' John, 40
    Juliana, 101
    Ralph, 94, 101
    Richard, 76
    William, 216
Hoppeschort, Ralph, 11
de Hopton, Walter, 221
Hore, John, 147, 165
    William, 149
Horell, John, 180
de Horkesle, Henry, 78, 87
de Horlete, Ralph, 139
Horlok, Agnes, 80
    John, 225
    Thomas, 80
de Hormed, Robert, 17
Horn, Horne, de Horn, or de Horne
    Alice, 91, 118, 150
    Andrew, 83, 93, 96
    Geoffrey, 108
    Isabel, 83
    Jeremia, 88

Horn, Horne, de Horn, or de Horne
    John, 62, 68, 88, 91, 118
    John fil' John, 94
    John fil' Richard, 150
    Matilda, 44, 51, 91
    Richard, 15, 82, 83
    Robert, 46, 185
    Roger, 22, 44, 51, 68
    Roger fil' John, 94
    Simon, 91
    William, 171, 182
Hornby, Thomas, 160
    William, 160
Horncastel, or Horncastell
    Johanna, 112
    John, 112
    Thomas, 206
de Horncumbe, Cristiana, 65
    Thomas, 65
Hornwode, James, 208
    Oliva, 208
Horpol, Richard, 146
Hors, Osbert, 6
Horscroft, William, 150, 151
de Horse, or de la Horse
    Leuina, 24
    Richard, 14, 24
Horseham, Mercy, 204
    William, 204
Horsele, Agnes, 155
    Nicholas, 155
atte Horseye, or atte Horseheye
    Alice, 76, 83
    William, 76, 83
de Horsie, Hugh, 7
de Horslee, or de Horslegh
    Edith, 3
    Gilbert, 68
    Margery, 68
Horspole, John, 177
de Horton, Agnes, 89
    Albreda fil' Aylbright, 22
    Ingelran, 89
    Johanna, 47
    John, 15, 55
    John fil' Gilbert, 22
    Richard, 47, 66
de Horwode, Cristiana, 69
    William, 69
de Horyshill, Agatha, 40
    William, 40
Hosebonde, Alice, 107
    Nicholas, 107
Hothom, Henry, 166

INDEX NOMINUM.

Hough, Katharine, 184
    Nicholas, 184
de Houghton, Johanna, 92
    John, 92
    Michael, 92
atte Houke, Hawise, 137
    Nicholas, 137
le Hounere, Alice, 103
    William, 103
de Houweton, Amicia, 124
    Herlewin, 124
atte Howe, Alice, 131
    Walter, 131
    William, 164
Howel, Agnes, 158
    John, 158
de Howell, Ela, 119, 125
    Robert, 119, 125
fil' Hubert, William, 11
de Hubray, Nigel, 13
Huchecok, Alice, 203
    Richard, 206
    Thomas, 206
Huet, Agnes, 164
    John, 167
    Margaret, 167
    Matilda, 167
    Michael, 118
    Peter, 164
fil' Hugh, John, 44
    Nicholas, 36, 38
        Margery, wife of, 36, 39
Hughe, William, 67
de Hughendene, Geoffrey, 104
Hughes, John, 151
    Margery, 151
Hugblot, or Hughelot
    John, 118
    Matilda, 118
    Robert, 195
Hughson, Nicholas, 210, 211
Hull, John, 160, 224
de Hull, John, 110
atte Hulle, Agnes, 106
    Henry, 66
    John, 75, 106, 113 (3)
    Richard, 83, 118
    Robert, 103
    Sarra, 75
    Walter, 67
Huller, Bartholomew, 179
Humfrey, or Humfray
    Johanna, 228
    Walter, 158

Humfrey, or Humfray
    William, 228
Hungerford, Alianor, 230
    Richard, 202, 208
    Robert, 208
de Hungerford, John, 219
Hunt, Hunte, le Hunt, or le Hunte
    Agnes, 80
    Alice, 185
    Dionisia, 165
    Emma, 79, 87
    Gilbert, 123
    Henry, 204
    Isabel, 87, 204
    John, 161, 165
    Margaret, 204
    Margery, 147, 154
    Richard, 79, 87, 185
    Robert, 204
    Walter, 80
    William, 147, 154
Hunteleye, John, 143
de Huntingfeld, Ismania, 65 (2)
    Johanna, 220
    Peter, 65 (2)
    Thomas, 220
de Hurcle, Annora, 19
    Mathew, 19
de Hurell, Katharine, 27
    Richard, 27
Hurelond, Richard, 91
de Hurle, John, 88, 104
atte Hurst, Alice, 130
    Thomas, 130
Hurste, Elizabeth, 206, 207
    John, 206, 207
Hurt, Cecilia, 225
    Richard, 138
    Thomas, 225
Husbond, or Husebond
    David, 195
    Roger, 86
Huscarl, Lucy, 220
    Rolland, 70
    Thomas, 102, 220
Husé, or Husee
    Isabel, 69, 72, 106
    Henry, 69, 70, 72, 106 (2), 220
    Henry fil' Mark, 142, 144
    Margaret, 142, 144
    William, 230
Huskard, William, 35
de Hybern, *see* de Hibernia
Hyde, —— abbot of, 12

Hyde, John, abbot of, 4
   William „ „ 42
Hyde, Henry, 164, 172 (2)
   William, 231
de la Hyde, or de la Hide
   Alditha, 57
   Robert, 38, 57
   Roger, 34
le Hyede, Robert, 121
Hyldere, Johanna, 184
   Richard, 184
Hyldersham, *see* Hildersham
at Hyll, John, 207
   Margaret, 207
atte Hyll, Alice, 197
   John, 197
Hylle, Edmund, 209
   Edward, 209
   Stephen, 208
   Thomas, 225
Hyrner, John, 145
Hystede, Hilda, 146
   John, 146

de Ifeld, or de Yfeld
   John, 76, 91, 92, 97, 99
   Margery, 99
   William, 31
de Iham, John, 21
Illyngworth, Anna, 207
   Richard, 194 (2), 200, 201, 207
de Immeworth, de Inworthe, or de Ymewrthe
   John, 18, 66
   Matilda, 46, 54
   Ralph, 27, 34
   Reginald, 46, 54
de Inegefeld, Agnes, 23
   Robert, 23
Inge, Cristiana, 123, 218
   Fremund, 123, 218
   John, 218
   Margaret, 75
   William, 75, 80
Ingel, John, 15
   Swonilda, 15
Ingelard, William, 94
de Ingeston, Laurence, 58
   Matilda, 58
Ingram, Inggram, or Yngeram
   Elias, 190
   Johanna, 158
   John, 160
   Richard, 164

Ingram, Inggram, or Yngeram
   Thomas, 167
   William, 158
Inkel, Henry, 23, 24
   Robert, 30
Inkpenne, Petronilla, 177
   William, 177
Innocent, John, 154
de Insula, Baldewyn, 36, 39, 40
   Warin, 221
Inthenalders, John, 152, 156
Inyngfeld, Dionisia, 137
   James, 137
Irelond, Johanna, 208
   William, 208, 209
fil' Isabel, John, 53
de Isdle, Margaret fil' John, 115
Isely, John, 222
   Margery, 222
de Islefold, William, 222
Ismongere, Ismongre, or Ismanger
   John, 128, 141
   Richard, 19
Iter, Agnes, 177
   John, 177
Ive, Henry, 208
   John, 143
   Thomas, 168
Ivory, William, 132
Iwardeby, John, 181
   Katharine, 181
Iwe, Richard, 201
   Thomas, 201
Iwun, John, 58

Jacob, Alice, 125
   Nicholas, 36
   William, 125
Jakeman, Cecilia, 177
   John, 177
James, Agnes, 185 (2)
   John, 176
   Nicholas, 185 (2)
Janecok, Geoffrey, 160
   Henry, 160
   Margaret, 160
Janyn, Dionisia, 192
   Elizabeth, 185
   James, 192
   John, 181 (2), 185
de Jarkevill, John, 86
de Jarpenvill, or de Jarpunvyll
   Gilbert, 24
   Lora, 103

INDEX NOMINUM.

de Jarpenvill, or de Jarpunvyll
  Roger, 103
  Thomas, 64, 66 (2)
  William, 103
Jay, Richard, 183, 192
Jekes, Thomas, 131
Jenyn, Stephen, 199
Jermeyn, Agnes, 79
  Richard fil' William, 79
Jerusalem, Robert, Prior of the Hospital of, 7
  Robert, Treasurer of the Hospital of, 7
the Jew, Isaac, 23, 31
Joce, Cristiana, 216
  John, 216
Jocelin, John, 14
fil' Joceus, Nicholas, 24
Johan, Thomas, 131
fil' John, Elwin, 6
  John, 36, 43
  Lecia, 29
  Peter, 16
    Lucy, wife of, 16
  Ralph, 14
  Richard, 3, 6, 16
  Robert, 5, 7
  Walter, 14, 16
Johnson, Alan, 187
  Roger, 198
Jolipace, Henry, 147
Joly, Thomas, 230
Jolyf, Agnes, 153, 154
  Beatrice, 141
  Richard, 141
  Thomas, 153, 154
Joop, or Jop
  Henry, 158
  Johanna, 158
  Thomas, 158, 163, 183, 224
fil' Jordan, Geoffrey, 28
  Henry, 15
Josselyn, Katharine, 230
  Ralph, 230
Jour, John, 156
Joye, John, 132
  Juliana, 132
  Robert, 20
fil' Juliana, John, 51
  Alice, wife of, 51
  Mathew, 20
Juvenis, or le Jevenis
  John, 58
  Philip, 41

Juvenis, or le Jevenis
  Reginald, 6 (2), 8 (2), 12

de Kameis, see de Camoys
Kanyn, see Canyn
Karbonell, see Carbonel
de Karingeham, Cristina fil' Norman, 76
  Felicia, 76
  Norman, 76
Karlill, Thomas, 164
de Katenham, Thomas, 8
de Katerham, Alice, 46
  Peter, 46
Kebeell, Thomas, 231
Kebyll, Elizabeth, 211
  William, 210, 211
de Keisney, Eva, 5
Kele, William, 193
Keleburn, Margery, Prioress of, 31
  Matilda, Prioress of, 44
de Keleseye, de Kellesey, or de Kelleseye
  Robert, 84, 85, 88
de Kelleshulle, William, 47
Kelet, Richard, 198
de Kemesing, or de Kemesinges,
  Idonea, 14, 17
  John, 14, 17
Kempe, Gilbert, 20
Kempsall, Sibil, 207
  Thomas, 207
Kempton, Margaret, 145 (3)
  Robert, 145 (3)
Kemsale, John, 188
le Ken, Isabel, 56
  Johanna fil' John, 77
  Robert, 56
  William, 47
de Kendal, Cecilia, 39
  Richard, 39
Kene, John, 152
  Robert, 167
de Kenele, Isabel, 117
  Walter, 117
de Keniton, Cristiana, 38
  Warin, 38
Kent, Alice, 150
  John, 150
  Thomas, 150
de Kent, Adriana, 43, 45
  Dionisia, 9
  Isabel, 122
  John fil' Roger, 122

de Kent, Nicholas, 43, 45
    Reginald, 9
Kentebury, Alice, 149, 160
Kentebury, Reginald, 149, 160
Kentecoumbe, John, 149
Kentwode, Reginald, 226
Kentwyn, Johanna, 23
    Thomas, 23
Kentyngg, Isabel, 147
    John, 147
de Kenyngton, John, 135
Kerle, John, 154
    Margaret, 154
Kersere, Gilbert, 3
de Kertling, Alice, 55
    Nicholas fil' Richard, 55
Kervyle, Edmund, 230
Kete, or Keete
    Emma, 101, 106, 112
    Nicholas, 101, 106, 112
de Ketene, John, 151
Keteryng, William, 223
Keynes, Thomas, 127
de Kilcham, Matilda, 17
de Kildesby, Walter, 221
the King, 59 (2), 129, 197, 214, 215, 230 (3)
de Kingeston, or de Kyngeston
    Adam, 98
    Agnes, 110
    Alianor, 132
    Henry, 110
    Richard, 32
    William, 132, 213
de Kingeswod, Luke, 12
Kirkeby, or Kyrkeby
    John, 176
    Thomas, 184
de Kirkeby, or de Kyrkeby
    Cristiana, 216
    Ralph, 62
    William, 216
Kirkeman, Johanna, 197, 199
    John, 197, 199
Kirketon, or Kyrketon
    John, 148
    William, 181, 184, 185
Knappere, William, 139
Kneesworth, Thomas, 208
Knicht, Almar, 15, 16
Knight, or Knyght
    Henry, 207
    Johanna, 175
    John, 175

Knight, or Knyght
    Oliver, 198
    Ralph, 144
    William, 171
the Knights Templars in England,
    Brother Abelard, Master of, 43
    Robert de Sanford, Master of, 24, 25 (2), 28, 32
Knolle, Walter, 223
atte Knolle, Henry, 104, 113
    Matilda, 104
de Knolle, Richard, 215
de la Knolle, Henry, 79
    Kassandra, 79
    Peter, 73
Knolles, Thomas, 170
    Walter, 153
Knotte, John, 39
    Richard, 31
    Roger, 39
    Stephen, 33
Knyll, Eustace, 208
le Knyt, Beatrice, 52
    Peter, 52
Kockel, Alan, 36
    Leuina, 36
Kolswein, Beatrix, 11
    Hugh, 11
de Kulsham, Peter, 59
Kyghle, or Kyghley
    Henry, 229
    Isabella, 185, 186
    John, 185, 186
Kymbell, John, 147
de Kymberle, Richard fil' John, 94
Kyme, John, 142 (2)
Kympton, John, 174
Kympynden, John, 190
de Kynardele, or de Kynardesle
    Alice, 28, 37
    John, 28
    Walter, 28, 35
    William, 37
Kyng, or Kynge
    Agnes, 204
    Hawise, 131
    Johanna, 175
    John, 170
    Kersandria, 191
    Richard, 131
    Thomas, 204
    William, 175, 181, 191
le Kyng, Elisea, 85
    Matilda, 141

le Kyng, Robert, 141
    Symon, 59
    Walter, 85
la Kynges, Petronilla, 95
de Kyngesfold, John, 221
Kyngesmyll, John, 208
de Kyngeston, *see* de Kingeston
Kyngeston, Hugh, 190
    Johanna, 190
Kyriell, Kyryell, or Kiriell
    Alianor, 146, 147
    Cristiana, 169 (2)
    John, 146, 147, 169, 184
    Nicholas, 215
de Kyrkeby, *see* de Kirkeby
Kyrketon, *see* Kirketon
Kyrkham, Robert, 189
atte Kythe, Juliana, 187
    Walter, 187
le Lacer, Geoffrey, 92
Lacy, John, 175
    Robert, 223
de Lacy, Henry, 40
Lad, Thomas, 188
le Ladde, or Ladde
    Agnes, 97, 222
    Thomas, 222
    Walter, 97
    William fil' Walter, 97
de Lageham, Margaret, 125
    Nicholas, 125, 126
Laken, John, 186
    Richard, 207
de Lakenham, Cristina, 141
    Richard, 141
de Lalleford, Robert, 217
Lambard, Agnes, 158
    Walter, 158
Lambert, Margaret, 192
    Richard, 192
de Lambhith, de Lambhithe, or de Lamhuthe
    Agnes, 133
    Edmond fil' Thomas, 85
    Richard, 133
    William, 123
Lambyn, John, 84
    Juliana, 48
    Robert 48
Lammesse, Alice, 44, 45
    Thomas, 44, 45
Lancaster, John, Duke of, 221 (2)
Lancock, Ismania, 166
    Robert, 166

atte Lane, Agnes, 120
    Johanna, 114
    John, 114
atte Lane, Margery, 127
    Richard fil' Roger, 127
    William fil' William, 120
Lanere, Matilda, 172
    William, 172
Lanewell, Isabella, 149
    Thomas, 149
Lange, Walter, 158
de Langeford, Johanna, 75, 94
    Richard, 72, 75, 94
de Langele, de Langeley, or de Langeleye
    Alice, 130
    William, 97, 130, 218
de Langenacre, Letice, 100 (2)
de Langenhurst, Alice, 76
    Robert fil' Gregory, 76
Langeston, Elizabeth, 159
    John, 159
de Langeton, or de Langgeton
    Florence, 128
    John, 112
    Reginald, 128
de Langeton, Walter, Bishop of Coventry and Lychfeld, 88
Langford, Robert, 187
Langham, Richard, 188
de Langhurst, Alice, 12
    Richard, 12
Langle, or Langlee
    Emma, 161
    John, 169
    Margaret, 169
    William, 161
Langriche, Margaret, 148
    Mathew, 148
Langrygge, Blanche, 177
    John, 177
Langwich, John, 185
de Lascy, John, 213
Lathell, Nicholas, 197, 199
Laton, Thomas, 180
Latymer, or le Latymer
    Edmund fil' John, 90
    Johanna, 90, 217
    John, 88, 90, 100, 217
    Robert, 217
    Robert fil' John, 219
    Thomas, 123
    William, 83
Laules, James, 218

INDEX NOMINUM. 279

Laurence, or Lawrence
   Agnes, 81
   David, 81
Laurence, or Lawrence
   Elizabeth, 188
   John, 188
de Laval, Hugh, 51
   Matilda, 51
de Lavender, Agnes, 117
   Peter, 117
Lavyngton, Thomas, 187
de Le, Robert, 17
Lecche, Alice, 170
   John, 170
Lechard, Hugh, 208
le Leche, Alice, 116
   John, 116
   William, 116 (2)
Lechford, or Leccheford
   Henry, 125, 127, 133
   William, 143
de Ledebury, see de Lodebury
Ledet, John, 144
   Margaret, 144
de Ledred, de Ledrede, or de Leddrede
   Geoffrey fil' William, 33
   Gilbert, 113, 129 (2)
   Johanna, 113, 129
   John, 62
   John fil' John, 62
   Mabel, 74, 75
   Nicholas fil' John, 62
   Robert, 116
   Thomas, 74, 75
   William fil' Baldewin, 29
Ledrede, Ledredd, Leddrede, or Lederede
   Henry, 187
   Juliana, 158
   Thomas, 186
   William, 158, 224
Lee, Richard, 211
   William, 170, 185
a Lee, Humfrey, 208
   John, 208
atte Lee, Cristiana, 175
   Henry, 203
   Isabella, 141, 144
   John, 164
   Margaret, 203
   Richard fil' Stephen, 175
   Stephen, 166
   William, 110. 141, 144
Leeper, Robert, 147

atte Leese, see atte Lese
de Lega, or de Lehe
   Philip, 3, 4
Leget, Johanna, 191, 192
   Thomas, 191, 192
Legg, John, 141, 144
Legh, Agnes, 210
   John, 200 (3), 201 (2), 202, 203, 204, 205 (2), 207, 208 (2), 209, 210 (3), 211, 212
   Ralph, 195, 202 (2), 203, 205 (2), 208 (2), 210, 211, 212
   Roger, 210
atte Legh, Agnes, 230
   Isabel, 69
   John, 230
   John fil' Richard fil' John, 69
   Richard, 76
   Richard fil' John, 69
   Robert, 230
de Legh, Alice, 185
   Anna, 149
   James, 185
   Ralph, 186
   Thomas, 149
de la Legh, de la Leie, or de la Leye
   Margaret, 54
   William, 6, 51, 54
atte Leghe, John, 173
Leigh, Ralph, 185
Lemman, John, 177
   Thomas, 169, 188
Lemyng, William, 229
de Lenn, Alice, 24
   Henry, 47
   Robert, 24
Lentewardyn, Richard, 165
Lentwareyn, Richard, 224
le Leper, Godfrey, 59
   Margery, 59
atte Lese, atte Leese, or de la Lese
   Agnes fil' Robert, 215, 216 (2)
   Matilda, 62, 68, 81
   Robert, 62, 68, 81
Lestrange, Roger, 221
Letice, Nicholas, 77
fil' Letitia, Hugh, 53
Lettres, Agnes, 197
   William, 197
de Leuesham, Agnes, 116
   Amisius, 116
Leuesone, Agnes, 142

Leuesone, Thomas, 142
Leukenore, Richard, 198, 229
    Roger, 202 (2)
de Leukenore, Lucy, 59, 60
    Thomas, 45, 59, 60
Leuote Adam, 114
fil' Leuric, Ailleva, 10
fil' Leufric, Edith, 6
de Levedale, Johanna, 134 (2)
    John, 134 (2)
Levelord, *see* Lovelord
Leviger, Simon, 186
Lewes, John, 211
    Thomas, 194
de Lewes, William, 39
Leweston, Margaret, 190
    Philip, 189
de Leycester, John fil' John, 130
    Thomas, 88
Leycestre, Alice, 184
    John, 177, 184
atte Leye, Richard, 141
de la Leye, *see* de la Legh
de Leython, John, 39
Leyton, William, Prior of, 19
Libard, Isabella, 180
    Nicholas, 180
Libbesofte, Johanna, 144
    Robert, 144
Lichepole, or Lychepol
    Johanna, 57, 82
    William, 57, 82
de Lichefeld, or de Lychefeld
    Alice, 132
    John, 132
    Simon, 136
de Lichesfeld, Walter, 26
Lichfield and Coventry, William, Bishop of, 203, 231
    See also de Langeton
de Lightebirches, Alice, 87
    Ranulph, 87
de Lilleswrth, Alice, 39
    William, 39
de Lincolle, Alice, 90
    Robert, 90
Lincoln, Thomas, Bishop of, 230
    William, Bishop of, 204, 205, 206, 231
de Lincoln, Johanna, 130
    John, 58
    Katharine, 58
    Thomas, 110, 111, 115, 130
de la Linde, Edgar, 8

de la Linde, Gunnilda, 8
de Lingeteld, Agnes, 23
    Walter, 3
de Liston, John, 216
de la Lithe, Henry, 30
de Litlebury, Robert, 216
de Litlemondene, Agnes, 59
    Richard, 59
de Litleton, Robert fil' William, 10
Littelton, Thomas, 228
Little, Litle, or Lytle
    Johanna, 139, 143, 149
    Robert, 139, 143, 149
de Livermore, John, 215
de Lobright, or de Lobricth
    Felicia, 20, 23, 24
    John, 20, 23, 24
de Lodebury, or de Ledebury
    Isabel, 56, 57, 58
    Richard, 56, 57, 58
de Lodelowe, John, 221
    Katharine, 99
    Thomas, 99, 221
Lodere, Johanna, 161
    John, 161
Lodlowe, Edmund, 168
atte Loge, Roger fil' Roger, 99
de Loges, Roger, 41
de Logos, Hugh, 4, 5
    Margaret, 4, 5
de Lokedon, Alice, 137
    Reginald, 137
le Lokiere, or le Lokyere
    Henry, 111
    Matilda, 82, 111
    Richard, 82
Lokke, Lucy, 225
    Richard, 225
London, Johanna, 157
    John, 157
de London, Alianor, 97, 102, 103
    Alice, 102, 119
    Johanna, 29
    Katharine, 102
    Matilda, 98
    Pentecost, 18
    Ralph fil' Roger, 102
    Robert, 98
    Roger, 1, 18, 20, 21, 97, 102 (2), 103, 119
    Roger fil' Roger, 102, 103
    William, 17, 93
    William fil' Benedict, 13
    William fil' William, 93

London, Bishop of, Fulc, 37, 212
    Richard, 55, 56, 67
    Robert, 224
    Stephen, 105
    William, 9
London Bridge, William fil' Richard, the keeper of, 40
Long, le Longe, or Longe
    Agnes, 171, 188
    Beatrice, 167
    Emma, 79
    Richard, 79, 188
    William, 11, 167, 179
atte Longbregge, Alice, 71
    John, 71
de Longebrigge, Avice, 92
    John, 92
Longereg, or Longeregge
    John, 155, 172
Longespey, Matilda, 36
    William, 36
Longherst, or Longhurst
    Alice, 207
    John, 207
    Simon, 170
de Longhurst, Edith, 109
    John, 109
    William, 109
de Longo Campo, John, 71
Longspe, Alice, 225
    Henry, 225
Longy, Richard fil' Alan, 113, 114
Longys, Cecilia, 103
    Richard, 103
Lorchon, or Lorchun
    John, 141
    Juliana, 140
    Ralph, 140
Lorkyn, John, 154
de Loseneressh, John, 78
atte Lote, Alice, 136
    Margaret, 164
    Robert, 136
    William, 164
de Lotegereshale, see de Lutegarshale
de Lovayne, or de Loveyne
    Margaret, 221
    Nicholas, 221, 222
Lovechild, Herding, 30
    Henry, 24, 36 (2)
Lovekyn, or Luvekyn
    Cecilia, 87

Lovekyn, or Luvekyn
    Edward, 53
    Emma, 77, 89
    John fil' Edward, 87
    Matilda, 53
    Robert, 31, 77, 89
Lovel, Lovell, or Luvel
    Johanna, 193
    Robert, 193
    Thomas, 232
Lovelord, or Levelord
    Adam, 176, 181 (2), 184 (2), 185, 187
Loveney, Margaret, 162
    William, 162
Lovestede, or Louestede
    John, 171 (2)
de Lovetot, John, 63
Loxle, or Loxsley
    Agnes, 153 (2)
    John, 166
    Robert, 153 (2)
de Loxle, de Loxlce, de Loxelegh, or de Loxeleye
    Alice, 81
    John, 81
    Henry, 115
    Margaret, 128, 136
    Robert, 128, 136
Lucas, Adam, 113, 149
    Isabel, 209
    John, 76, 82
    Margaret, 180
    Thomas, 180, 209, 232
Luce, Thomas, 230
de Lucy, John, 74
Ludford, John, 186
de Ludbam, Richard, 65
    Robert, 38, 55
    Roger, 65
    William, 35
Ludlowe, William, 182
Ludworth, Margaret, 231
    Roland, 231
Luggeford, Luggesford, or Luggersford
    Alan, 176, 179, 182, 183
    Alice, 176
    Matilda, 192
    Richard, 192
fil' Luke, William, 36
Lumbard, or le Lumbard
    John, 62 (2), 73
    Lucy, 63 (2)

Lumbard, or le Lumbard
    Matilda, 134
    Roger, 140, 145
    Thomas, 139, 148
de Lund, Warin, 55
le Lung, Agnes, 65
    John, 37
    Simon, 65
de Lungis, Isabel, widow of Ralph, 13
de Lurdune, Robert, 7
de Lutegarshale, de Lutegareshale, de Lotegereshale, or de Lutgereshale
    Henry, 78, 86
    John, 133
    Matilda, 133
    William, 69
Luterell, Hugh, 225
fil' Luth, William, 32
Lutte, Reginald, 30
de Lychefeld, *see* de Lichefeld
Lychepol, *see* Lichepole
de Lye, Thomas, 144
atte Lye, Johanna fil' William, 84
    John, 171
Lyende, Elizabeth, 194
    John, 194
de Lyftwych, Isabel, 122
    Richard, 122
Lygard, Disoria, 129
    John, 129
Lygon, Thomas, 171
Lylborn, Johanna, 181
    Stephen, 181
Lylly, Elizabeth, 203
    William, 203
de Lymbernere, Johanna, 50
    John fil' Richard, 50
Lyncolne, Robert, 222
Lynde, William, 190
atte Lynde, Beatrice, 142
    William, 142
Lynder, Isabella, 192
    Richard, 192
Lyndon, Adam, 139
Lyndwyk, Alice, 144
    Robert, 144
Lyngfeld, Master and Chaplain of St. Peter's College, 190
Lynster, Henry, 184
    Margaret, 184
de Lyntesford, Richard, 129
Lyon, Alice, 112

Lyon, John, 112, 116
    Margaret, 202
    William, 202
Lyseres, Thomas, 227
Lysurs, John, 143
Lytelgrome, William, 173
Lytewyn, or Lytewyne
    Agnes, 97
    John, 97, 151
    Stephen, 97
atte Lythe, Bartholomew, 74
    Cecilia, 74
    John, 128
Lythfot, Isabel, 55
    Richard, 55
Lytholf, John, 108
Lytle, *see* Little
Lyveryng, Johanna, 172
    Peter, 172

Mabonk, Alice, 126
    Simon, 126
Mabunt, John, 222
Macche, Agnes, 177, 184
    John, 167, 177, 184
    Thomas, 177
Machun, or le Machun
    Agnes, 74
    Cristina, 95
    Richard, 95
    Walter, 74
le Macone, Emma, 40
    Richard, 40
Maddele, de Maddelee, or de Maddeleye
    Matilda, 108 (2), 109
    William, 108 (2), 109
Madefray or Madefrey
    Hugh, 95
    John, 121, 122
    Juliana, 95
de Madham, John, 103
Madys, Thomas, 201
Magant, Alice, 6
    Hugh, 6
Maheu, John, 86
Makenade, William, 155
Makenheved, John, 114
Maldon, Alice, 151
    John, 183
    Thomas, 183
    William, 151
de Maldon, Alice, 63
    William, 63

INDEX NOMINUM.

Malemeins, Malemeyns, or Malesmeins
  Gilbert, 35
  Margery, 24
  Nicholas, 8, 32 (2), 34, 54
  Robert, 30
Malemoillier, Agnes, 3
  Thomas, 3
Malet, Agnes, 111
  Thomas, 111
de Malevill, Eustace, 66, 68 (2)
de Mallyng, Peter, 53 (2)
Maltesone, John, 125
Malton, John, 176, 188 (2)
de Malton, Isabel, 71
  John, 71, 100, 101
de Malvern, Alesia, 103
  Bartholomew, 103
Man, Letice, 105
  William, 105
le Man, Alice, 150
  John, 150
  Matilda, 96
  Thomas, 96, 151
de la Mandeleyne, John, 108
Mandut, or Manduit
  Ralph, 9
  Robert, 5 (2), 7 (2)
  William, 18
Manion, Ferand, 119, 120
  Margery, 119, 120
Manyngham, Oliver, 230
de Mara, Mathias, 40
  William, 40
Marble, Richard, 211
March, Agnes, 152
  Robert, 152
Marchall, Mareschal, Mareschall, Marescall, Marshall, le Mareschal, le Marescall, or le Marschal
  Agnes, 62, 147
  Alice, 142, 189
  Elizabeth, 201
  Gilbert, 20, 48
  Henry, 51, 53, 56, 147
  John, 7 (2), 46, 62, 64, 117, 201
  John fil' William, 87
  Nicholas, 192
  Philip, 3
  Richard, 28, 56, 189
  Robert, 54
  Walter, 142
  William, 87

Marchant, John, 162
  Katharine, 162
  Margaret, 162
  Richard, 162
  William, 162
de Mardwyr, William, 45
de la Mare, Alianor, 79, 87
  John, 58, 79, 87
  William, 21 (2)
Marewe, Isabel, 111
  William, 111
de Mares, Henry, 214
  John, 214
  Richard, 214
  William, 214
Mareys, Alice, 117, 118
  William, 117, 118
de Marisco, Cristiana, 65
  William, 60, 61 (2)
Mark, Cristina, 152
  Roger, 152
Markham, John, 228
Markle, Beatrice, 151
  Robert, 151
Markwyk, Richard, 124
de Marlebergh, John, 120
Marler, Marlere, or le Marler
  Johanna, 79
  John, 152, 156
  John fil' Robert, 93
  Robert, 79, 93, 196
  Salomon, 79
de la Marlere, Henry, 103
  Margaret, 103
Marlin, Matilda, 116
  William, 116
Marlond, see Merland
del Marreys, Nicholas, 92
Marrowe, or Marowe
  Thomas, 208, 232
Marston, William, 210
Marten, Elizabeth, 202
  Richard, 202
fil' Martin, Henry, 43
  Saerus, 43
Martin, or Martyn
  Alianor, 201
  Emma, 141
  Geoffrey, 149
  Henry, 43, 155 (2), 176, 195
  John, 141, 155 (2), 168, 174, 195, 201, 205, 226
Martin, or Martyn
  Lucy, 155 (2)

Martin, or Martyn
  Mabel, 120
  Richard, 120, 198, 209, 229, 230
Marton, Johanna, 231
  John, 231
  fil' Mary Simon, 23
  Avice, wife of, 23
Marycie, Frank, 202
  Isoda, 202
Maryner, William, 201
Maryotte, Alice, 192
  John, 192
Masham, Richard, 207
Mason, Elena, 228
  John, 217
  Nicholas, 228
  Walter, 153
Massam, John, 229
  Margery, 229
Matany, Almaric, 177
de Matham, Hamelin fil' Sampson, 128
  Isabel, 66
  John, 66, 217
  Sampson, 128
Mathewe, John, 168, 200
  fil' Mathew, Robert, 10
  fil' Matilda, William, 35
Matsale, John, 228
Maubank, or Maubanc
  Alice, 113, 119
  Beatrice, 8
  Edmund, 119
  Gunnilda, 38
  Johanna fil' Henry, 102
  Peter, 113, 119
  Reginald, 29
  Richard, 102
  Robert, 38
  William, 5, 6
Maundevile, Alice, 83
  Geoffrey, 83
Maunsel, or Mauncell
  Adam, 115
  Alice, 49
  Cecilia, 34
  Elias, 35
  Henry, 119
  Isabel, 49
  John, 37, 73
  Ralph, 49 (2)
  Richard, 107
  Richerus, 34 (2)

Maunsel, or Mauncell
  Roger fil' Ralph, 49
de Maurdyn, or de Mawardyn
  John, 67, 68
Mauser, John, 68
Mawetson, John, 196
May, Chelsa, 55
  Henry, 87
  John, 55
Maybank, Agnes, 149
  William, 149
Maynard, Agnes, 192 (2)
  John, 192 (2)
Mayster, John, 146
de Meandon, Dulcia, 36
de Mecham, see de Micham
de Medburn, Walter, 68
Mede, Edith, 205
  John, 161
  Margaret, 161
  William, 205
de Medersh, Felicia fil' John, 70
  John, 105
  Robert, 105
de Medewell, William, 119
de Mees, William, 70
Melbourn, Milbourne, or Melbourne
  Agnes, 173
  Isabella, 150
  John, 150
  Margaret, 138
  Richard, 173
  William, 138, 173, 199
de Meldon, Robert, 86
de Meleburn, or de Meleburne
  Emma, 37
  Henry, 214
  Robert, 37
  William, 37
Melersh, John, 138
de Melewys, Johanna, 18
  Thomas, 18
le Melkere, Gilbert, 45
  Matilda, 45
Melksop, de Melksope, or de Melkesope
  Cecilia, 81
  John, 125
  Margery, 125
  Robert, 81
  William, 69 (2)
atte Melle, Agnes, 163

atte Melle, William, 163
Menne, William, 122
de Menyl, William fil' Hugh, 41
Mercator, Gunnora, 30
    Henry, 30
le Mercer, Augustin, 24
    Bella, 24
Merden, Nicholas, 210
Merdene, Alice, 161
    Hugh, 161
atte Mere, John, 142
    Richard, 147
de Merehurst, Agnes, 85
    John, 85
de Merewe, Alice, 51
    Thomas, 51
Merk, Alice, 93
    Richard, 93
Merkyngfeld, or de Merkyngfeld
    John, 88
    Laurence, 125
Merland, Merlond, or Marlond
    Henry, 194 (2), 195
    Richard, 200, 201, 205, 206, 208
Merlawe, or de Merlawe
    John, 42
    Richard, 167
atte Mersh, or atte Merssh
    Alice, 142
    Margery, 149
    Peter, 142
    Stephen, 149
Mersher, Alice, 196
    Anna, 210
    John, 196
Mershton, John, 134
    Scolastica, 134
de Merstham, Thomas, 66
    Walter, 120
Merston, Amy, 205
    Anna, 196
    Henry, 175
    John, 187, 188
    Margaret, 151, 191
    Richard, 191
    Rose, 187
    William, 151, 196
de Merston, William, 96
Merton, Juliana, 206
    Ralph, 206
de Merton, Avice, 53
    David, 21

de Merton, Richard, 51
    Robert, 53
    Walter, 22, 27, 35, 213, 214 (2), 215
Merton, ——, Prior of, 1
    Eustace, Prior of, 40, 41
    Gilbert, Prior of, 44, 49, 51
    Henry, Prior of, 18 (2), 21
    Robert, Prior of, 26, 27, 31
    Thomas, Prior of, 10
    Walter, Prior of, 4, 5, 7, 8 (4), 9, 29
ap Meryk, James, 208
le Messager, Milo, 215
    Ralph, 52
Mesyngleghe, Margaret, 163
    Thomas, 163
de Metyngham, John, 64
Meyne, John, 170
fil' Michael, Michael, 25
de Micham, de Micheham, or de Mecham
    Edward fil' Ailwin, 5
    Ernald, 4, 5
    Helewysia, 46
    Peter, 46
    Symon, 58
de Michehale, Thomas, 120
Michel, or Michell
    Elizabeth, 196
    Geoffrey, 149
    Thomas, 196
    William, 34, 196
Michelgrove, Henry, 146
de Michelham, Thomas fil' Robert, 116
de Mickelham, de Mikelham, de Mikkelham, or de Mikeleham
    Alice, 56
    Gilbert, 56
    John, 29, 107
    John fil' John, 106
    Robert, 33
Middelton, Cristofer, 202
    John, 143
    Margaret, 202
de Middleton, de Middelton, or de Myddelton
    Geoffrey, 5
    Henry, 9, 67
    John, 46
    Matilda, 67
    Richard, 38, 54

de Middleton, de Middelton, or de
    Myddelton
  Robert, 65 (3), 67
  Thomas, 141, 146
de Mikkesham, Isabel, 72
  Thomas, 72
Milbourne, *see* Melbourn
Milcent, Alice, 99
  Beatrice, 99
  William, 99
Mildenhale, de Mildenhale, or de
    Mildenhall
  Katharine, 39, 45
  Robert, 179
  Roger, 39, 45
  William, 49
le Mileward, Robert, 92
Mille, Thomas, 192
atte Mille, Alice, 166
  John, 166
  Robert, 166
Miller, Avelina, 10
  Robert, 10
  Stephen, 22
Milward, Henry, 174
  Isabella, 174
Milys, Alice, 188
  John, 188
de Minthurst, William, 7
Mirfeld, William, 157
le Minur, John, 35
Mitford, Thomas, 175
de Mockyngg, de Mokkyngg, or
    Mokkyngg
  Alice, 132, 137
  Idonia, 89
  John, 89, 99, 132, 137, 141
    (2)
  Nichola, 99
  Nicholas, 141
  Robert, 179 (2)
Mogge, William, 106
le Moigne, *see* le Moyne
Mokway, Henry, 73
  Johanna, 73
Molde, William, 15
de Molendino, or de Molendinis
  John fil' Henry, 28
  Robert, 19
de Molond, Agnes, 129
  John, 129
Molton, John, 193
del Molyn, or atte Mulne
  Alice, 47, 53, 54

del Molyn, or atte Mulne
  Hugh, 53, 54
  William, 47, 52
de Molyns, or de Moleyns
  Egidia, 218
  John, 105, 218, 219
  Margery, 129
  William fil' John, 129
de Monasterio, William, 14
le Monek, Robert, 113
Mondy, John, 207
de Moneketon, or de Munketon
  John, 71
  Roger, 88
Mongar, John, 209
Monke, John, 227
  William, 15
Monkoye, Henry, 96
  Thomas, 96
Monouxe, Amy, 210
  George, 210
de Monte, or de Montibus
  Jordan, 15, 26
de Monte Acuto, Agnes, 32
  Fyna, 78
  William, 78, 96
de Monte Canis, Warin, 28
de Monte Regali, Imbert, 53
de Montfort, or de Montefort
  Guy, 220
  Henry, 36
  John fil' Peter, 216
  Margaret, 220
  Matilda, 49
  Peter, 49, 216
Montgomery, Cristina, 204
  John, 204
Moordon, John, 171
Moraunt, Agnes, 159
  Richard, 159, 171
  Thomas, 170
  William, 187, 192
Morden, Alice, 198
  Richard, 198
de Mordon, Alice, 145
  Simon, 145
More, Thomas, 169, 190
  William, 223
atte More, Gilbert, 89
  Isabel, 89
  Johanna, 219
  John, 85
  Robert, 114
  Thomas, 219

INDEX NOMINUM.   287

de More, or de la More
   Cecilia, 60
   Cristina, 88
   Elyas fil' Nicholas, 29
   Ida, 57
   Johanna, 219
   John, 57
   John fil' William, 92
   Robert, 219
   Scodland, 88
Morestede, or Morstede
   Juliana, 171, 181
   Thomas, 171, 181
Morice, John, 90
Morin, le Morin, or Moryn
   Eudo, 25
   Gilbert, 1
   John, 29
   Ralph, 11, 17
   William, 123
Morison, Peter, 194
de Morlane, Mabel, 86
   Robert, 86
Morris, or Morys
   Cristina, 88, 93
   Lucy, 165 (2)
   Nicholas, 165 (2)
   Thomas, 165 (2)
   William, 88, 93
de Mortimer, de Mortemer, de Mortymer, or de Mortuo Mari
   Elena, 190
   Hugh, 40
   Isabel, 124
   Jocosa, 51
   Johanna, 120
   Robert, 51
   Thomas, 120, 124 (2), 190
   William, 40, 46, 120
de Mortinger, Reginald, 40
Morton, Agnes, 180
   Robert, 180
   John, 201
   Thomas, 180, 201
de Morton, Richard, 102
   Thomas, 220
   Walter, 24, 28
   William, 103
Morvile, Felicia, 133
   John, 133
Moryn, *see* Morin
Morys, *see* Morris
Mosage, Johanna, 232
   Thomas, 232

Mose, or le Mose
   John, 184
   William, 135
Mot, Alice, 132 (2), 144
   Henry, 132 (2), 144
   John, 153
   Juliana, 153
Mote, Cecilia, 147
   John, 147
atte Mote, Juliana, 159 (2)
   Thomas, 159 (2)
Motte, Agnes, 195
   Margaret, 179
   Thomas, 179, 195
Moukoy, Henry, 85
   Isobel, 85
de Moun, James, 217
Mounde, Johanna, 82
   Walter, 82
de Moundele, Johanna, 112
   Thomas, 112
Mounkoy, Alice, 122
   John, 122
le Mouner, Elicia, 39
   Emma, 55, 62
   John, 44, 55, 62
   Mabel, 44
   Walter, 39
   William fil' Nicholas, 63
Mounford, Richard, 170
de Mounpelers, Margery, 168
   William, 168
Mounteney, Thomas, 133
de Mounteney, Theobald, 121
Mounyng, Richard, 107
Mousherst, Moushirst, or Moushurst
   Richard, 144, 167, 168
Moushill, John, 189
   Margaret, 189
Mowbray, Elizabeth, 135
   John, 135
Moy, John, 111
Moylle, Roger, 189
   Walter, 186
   William, 189
le Moyne, or le Moigne
   John, 39, 40
Moyse, Johanna, 81
   John, 81
Mugge, Geoffrey, 180
   Johanna, 180
   Stephen, 184
   Thomas, 189

le Mukere, Ralph, 14
de Mulesey, Samson, 5, 9
le Muleward, Alice, 132
    Henry, 132
    Richard, 85
Mulle, John, 174
atte Muln, *see* del Molyn
Multon, Agnes, 165
    Thomas, 165
de Multon, Walter, 138
de Mumbrai, or de Mumbre, 1, 2
Mundy, John, 187
de Munested, William, 14
de Munketon, *see* de Monckton
Munnyng, Richard, 106
Munpelers, Robert, 55
    Roesia, 55
Muriele, Johanna, 162
Muryweder, Alice, 132
    John, 132
de Muscote, James, 68
de Muskham, Isabella, 112
de Mussendene, Simon, 107
de Myddelton, *see* de Middleton
Mydenale, John, 209
Myles, Robert, 95
Mylle, John, 212
Myllys, John, 205
    Margaret, 205
Mylshe, Alianor, 207
    Matthew, 207
Mymmys, Emma, 139
    Nicholas, 139
Myre, Letice, 189
    William, 189

atte Nalerette, Johanna, 100
    John, 100
Nantes, John, 178
de Naples, William, 115
Nappere, le Nappere, or le Naper
    Hugh, 15
    Mabel, 21
    Robert fil' Ralph, 21
    Walter, 131
Narburgh, William, 165
atte Nasshe, Johanna fil' John, 86
    John, 86
    Margaret fil' John, 86
Naward, Margery, 171
    Walter, 171
Naylyngherst, Clement, 199
    Elizabeth, 199
Neder, Richard, 228

de la Nedre, Robert, 54
Neel, or Nele
    Alice, 225
    John, 195
    William, 225, 229
le Neir, or le Neyr
    Giles, 27
    Philip, 29
    Thomas, 18
Netelfold, Hugh, 156
    Johanna, 156
de Nethersole, Robert, 127
de Netoelfeld, John, 76
de Neubir, Reginald, 11
Neubrigg, de Neubrigg, Neubrigge,
    or Neubrugge
    William, 112, 115, 120 (2),
        123 (2), 126, 127 (2), 128
Neudegate, *see* Newdegate
Neulond, *see* Newelond
Neuport, William, 139
de Neuport, Quintin, 37
    Sabinia, 37
Neuton, John, 202
de Neuton, Richard fil' Nigel, 41
Nevill, Nevile, or Nevyll
    George, 204
    Richard, 162
    Robert, 231
de Nevill, Hugh, 11, 212
    Johanna, 11, 212
    John, 40, 149, 221
    Philippa, 213
Newark, Geoffrey, Prior of, 44,
    48 (2), 52, 53
    John, Prior of, 6, 8
    Richard, Prior of, 37, 38 (2), 40
    Roger, Prior of, 100
    Thomas, Prior of, 19, 26, 29, 30
    Walter, Prior of, 65
Newcastle under Lyme, Master Peter of, 83
de Newcastle, Geoffrey, 28
    Peter, 62
de Newdegate, de Newedegate, de
    Neudegate, Neudegate, or
    Neudigate
    Isabella, 202, 204
    John, 180, 202, 204, 210, 223
    Richard, 15, 20
    William, 38, 133, 135, 137
Neweam, Matilda, 179
    Thomas, 179

INDEX NOMINUM.   289

atte Neweland, Edmund, 23
de la Newelond, or de la Neulond
   Isabel, widow of Walter, 12
   Lucy fil' Walter, 11
le Neweman, John, 84
   Matilda, 84
Newenham, William, 225
de Newenham, John, 48
Newerk, John, 182
   Katharine, 182
Newetymbyr, Nicholas, 180
Newman, John, 15
Nichol, or Nichole
   Johanna, 90
   John, 87, 92
   John fil' John, 90
   Scolastica, 87, 92
fil' Nicholas, David, 15
Nicholas, Isabella, 17
   Stephen fil' Thomas, 17
Nicolet, Johanna, 171
   William, 171
de la Nobrith, or de Nobrihte
   Felicia, 22
   John, 22
   Nicholas, 22
Noel, Robert, 80
de Norboton, Forthwin, 16
Norbrigge, Northbrigge, or Norbrugge
   Alice, 209
   Henry, 199, 203, 205, 209 (2)
   Peter, 182, 187
Norbury, Anna, 227
   John, 194
   Henry, 227
atte Nore, Juliana, 126
   Simon, 126
Noreys, le Noreys, le Norreys, or la Noresche
   Hugh, 45
   John, 78
   John fil' John, 93
   Mary, 45
   Peter, 124
   Robert fil' Robert, 45
Norfolk, Elizabeth, Duchess of, 229, 230
   John, Duke of, 229
de Norhamton, Henry, 32 (2)
Norman, Agnes, 139
   Alice, 38
   Geoffrey, 38, 51
   Johanna, 129, 130

Norman, Walter, 129, 130, 139
   William, 55, 56, 75
fil' Norman, Geoffrey, 31
   Alice, wife of, 31
Normanton, Laurence, 202
   Mary, 202
de Normenvile, or de Normenwil
   Emma, 1 (2), 2
   Julia, 1
   Rose, 2
   Margaret, 1
North, Gilbert, 35, 83
   William, 168
de North, Henry, 28
Northbrigge, or Northbrugge, see Norbrigge
de Northbury, Johanna, 133
   William, 133
de Northland, John, 108
Northrigge, Johanna, 155
   Robert, 155
Northrug, or Northrugge
   Agnes, 65
   Alice, 144
   Beatrice, 65
   John, 65
   John fil' John, 65
   Margery, 83
   Robert, 83, 144
Northwod, John, 161
   Juliana, 161
de Northwode, Agnes, 53
   Elizabeth, 218
   John, 61, 71
   Nicholas, 102
   Roger, 56, 215, 218
   Roger fil' Peter, 48
   Thomas fil' William, 77
   William, 53, 71, 77
   William fil' William, 48
de Northwyk, William, 79, 104
de Nortoft, Matilda, 213
   William, 213
Norton, Johanna, 164, 165, 224
   John, 156, 163, 164, 165, 169, 183, 224, 227
   Margery, 169
   Robert, 168
de Norton, John, 88
   Margaret, 150
   Ralph, 150
   Richard, 61
de Norwich, Richard, 121
   William, 80

19

Norwych, Robert, 134
Notebourne, Robert, 145 (2)
Notte, John, 220
de Notton, Isabel, 124
    William, 123, 124
Notyngham, Isabella, 153
    Richard, 153
de Notyngham, Matilda, 124
    Richard, 120
    Roger, 124
atte Novene, Mabel, 104
    Richard, 104
    Thomas, 104
Nowel, or Nowell
    Alice, 128
    Matilda, 135
    Robert, 128, 135
Nutfeld, John, 195
Nutheuseband, Henry, 19
Nynes, Nicholas, 199
de Nytymbre, Margery, 113
    William, 113

de Ockeleye, or de Okkelyghe
    Agatha, 104
    Matilda, 75
    Walter, 104
    William, 75
Ode, Agnes, 190
    William, 190
Odyerne, Juliana, 78
    William, 78
le Ofham, John, 111, 124
Ogger, Johanna, 178
    William, 178
Ogham, John, 225
Oisel, or Oysel
    Gilbert, 19
    Richalda, 19
    Richard, 37, 38
    Richard fil' Richard, 37, 38
atte Oke, Alan, 54
de Okebourne, John, 128
    Margery, 128
de Okham, or de Ocham
    Nicholas, 69
    Thomas, 50, 51
de Okhurst, John, 126
Okore, Philip, 224
Okstede, Roger, Parson of, 114
de Okstede, Isabel, 108
    John, 108
    Thomas, 85
    William, 60

Okwod, Alice, 138
    John, 138
Oky, Elena, 59
    John, 59
Oldam, or Oldham
    Hugh, 203, 204, 205, 206, 231
de Oldbridge, Thomas, 17
Oldcastell, Johanna, 225
    John, 225
Oliver, or Olyver
    Emma, 37 (2)
    Johanna, 160
    John, 141, 160
    John fil' Thomas, 119
    Katharine, 119
    Robert, 95
    Thomas, 89
    Walter, 92
    William, 89, 94
fil' Oliver, Hugh, 27
    Mary, wife of, 27
Olmestede, William, 140
Olney, John, 227
de Olneye, John, 151
Onderheld, John, 181 (2)
Onley, John, 231
del Ore, Agnes, 29
    Osbert, 29
le Orfevere, or le Orfeure
    Beatrice, 58
    James, 58
    John, 54
    Peter, 36
Orgar, Alice, 124
    Thomas, 124
Ormesby, Arthur, 177, 186
    Mercy, 186
Ormond, Thomas Lord, 203
de Orreby, Florence, 79, 87 (2), 90
    Philip, 79, 87 (2), 90
Osbarn, Osbern, Osebarn, or Osebern
    Gocelyn, 98
    Margaret, 126
    Margery, 98
    Richard, 173, 176
    Thomas, 126, 184
    William, 110
Oslang, Gilbert, 25
Ospreng, William Gracien, Master of the Hospital of St. Mary of, 21
de Osyngehurst, Abraham, 45 (2)
    Letitia, 45

INDEX NOMINUM. 291

Oter, John, 19
   Lucy, 19
Otewell, John, 208
atte Otlond, Robert, 60
   Sibil, 60
Otte, Alice, 72 (2)
   John, 72
   Stephen, 72, 82
   Stephen fil' Stephen, 72, 82
de Otteford, John, 63
   Juliana, 63
Otteley, Robert, 180
Otteworth, de Otteworth, de Ottewurth, de Ottewirthe, de Ottewrth, de Ottewrthe, or de Uttewrth
   Edmund, 57
   Ida, 20
   Laurence, 57
   Thomas, 30, 34, 39, 53
   Walter, 14, 20, 23, 24 (2), 30, 34
   William, 176
Ottour, Isabella, 187
   John, 187
Otwey, John, 200
Oundel, Henry, 147, 156
Owen, David, 210
   Jasper, 210
Oxbrygge, Thomas, 197
de Oxehagh, Hugheline, 24, 25
   Richard, 24, 25
de Oxenecroft, Gilbert, 15
Oxeneye, Salamon, 156, 177
de Oyldebof, Hugh, 49, 50
Oysel, *see* Oisel

P——, Ralph, 3
Paas, Johanna, 157
   John, 157
Pacchyng, Thomas, 158, 225
de Padbroke, or de Padebrok
   Cassandra, 55
   John, 55, 78
fil' Pagan, John, 24
   Emma, wife of, 24
Page, Agnes, 139
   Alice, 127
   Henry, 139
   John, 127, 140
   Matilda fil' Adam, 96
   William, 32
de Pakenham, Lucy, 117
   William, 117

Pakkere, 174, 186, 189 (2), 191
Palmer, John, 154
   Philip, 172
   Thomas, 172, 198
   William, 227
le Palmere, James, 112 (2)
   Sarra, 112
Palmes, Brian, 207
   Guy, 207
Palsbudde, Thomas, 191
Papellioun, William, 99
de Papeworth, de Pappeworth, de Papewrth, or de Pappewrth
   Agnes, 94
   Alice, 44, 78
   Johanna, 44
   John, 42, 44 (2)
   Juliana, 44
   Ralph, 20
   Robert, 29
   Thomas fil' Robert, 55
   Walter, 78
   William, 8
Paramurs, Isabel, 16
   William, 16
de Parco, Alexander, 22
   Emma, 22
   Geoffrey, 13
   John, 25
de Paris, le Parys, or Parys
   Agatha, 94 (2)
   Alice, 65, 200
   John, 65
   Matilda, 81, 82
   Richard, 81, 82
   Robert, 200
   Simon, 94 (2)
Park, John, 169
atte Park, Juliana, 171
   Roger, 171
Parker, le Parker, or le Parkere
   Agnes, 108
   Alice, 137, 165
   Cassandra, 79
   Elicia, 57
   Emma, 134
   John, 108, 110, 137, 165, 186, 187 (2), 192, 200
   Margaret, 186, 187 (2)
   Paulina, 52
   Peter, 79
   Robert, 57
   Thomas, 134
   Walter, 52, 53, 108

atte Parkgate, Nicholas, 72
Parlebien, Richard, 156
le Parmenter, Alice, 52
    Edelina, 19
    John, 52
    William, 19
de Parnycote, de Pernycote, or Pernecote
    Robert, 105, 219
    Thomas, 74, 219
Parnyng, Isabel, 115
Pasmer, John, 204
Passelewe, Symon, 40
Paston, William, 226
Pathorn, Thomas, 141, 142
de Patmere, Clemence, 102
    Richard, 102
Patrik, Isabel, 115
    Robert, 114
Paul, John, 95
le Paumer, Alured, 11
    Edith, 16
    Edward, 16
    William, 49
Pavy, Richard, 172
Pawelyn, Richard, 177
Payn, or Payne
    Agnes, 155
    Alice fil' Robert, 73
    Andrew, 95
    Henry, 155, 168
    Isolde, 228
    Johanna, 93, 96 (2), 100
    John, 76 (2), 77, 93, 96, 100, 173, 187, 230
    Lucy, 76
    Margaret, 230
    Philip, 96
    Richard, 96
    Robert, 41, 95, 228
    Simon, 76
Paynel, or de Paynel
    Margaret, 69, 73
    William, 61, 69, 73
Payto, John, 209
Peche, or Pecche
    Adam, 152
    Elizabeth, 211
    John, 211, 222
    Mary, 152
le Pedeler, or le Pedelere
    William, 102 (2), 103
Pedewyn, William, 168
Pegge, Reginald, 200, 209 (2)

Pego, Nicholas, 146
Pelham, Johanna, 147
    William, 147
Pemberton, Hugh, 204
Pembroke, Margery, 162
    Walter, 162
atte Pende, Agnes, 146
    Johanna, 142
    Nicholas, 146
    Richard, 142
de Penhurste, Ralph, 2
Penne, Isabella, 172
    William, 172
atte Penne, Thomas, 162
de la Penne, Elicia, 56 (2)
    Robert, 56 (2)
Pentecost, John, 101
    William, 4 (2), 13
Peny, John, 173
    Nicholas, 150
Penycod, William, 209
Penycot, Johanna, 190
    John, 190
Peper Osbert, 15
Percy, Thomas, 224
de Percy, Henry, 221
Peres, John, 173
de Perham, Johanna, 56
    William, 56
Perkyns, Agnes, 197
    John, 197
Perlee, William, 226
Pernel, Thomas, 139
Pernersh, or Pernersshe
    Johanna, 126
    Matilda, 164
    Richard, 164
    Walter, 126
de Pernestede, Geoffrey, 75
    Isabel, 75
Perneys, John, 183 (2)
de Pernycote, see de Parnycote
Person, Alice, 154
    John, 142, 154
Pertrych, Margery, 172
    William, 172
Perveys, John, 176
Peryn, William, 193
de Pesemere, William, 32
Peshauwe, Agnes, 136
    Richard, 136
le Pessuner, Alice, 22
    Richard, 22
le Pestur, Cecilia, 42

INDEX NOMINUM. 293

le Pestur, Matilda, 33, 48
  Robert, 33
  Roger, 42
  William, 48
le Pesur, Jocens, 12
  Mary, 12
fil' Peter, Robert, 5
  Roger, 5
  William, 27, 48
Petirburgh, Robert, 165 (2)
Petit, Emma, 74, 95
  William, 74, 95
Petresfeld, Frebern, 146
de Petresfeld, Alice, 118
  John, 118
de Pettestede, Ada, 47
  John, 47
de Pettys, Archangelus, 187
  Margaret, 187
Pevensey, Henry, 185
  Johanna, 185
Peverel, Andrew, 222
  Katharine, 222
Peyforer, Lora, 82
  William, 82
le Peyntur, Johanna, 69
  John, 68
  Richard, 52
  Robert, 69
Peyntwyn, Hugh, 207
le Peystur, John, 65
  Margery, 65
fil' Philip, Alice, 30
  Thomas, 2
Philip, or Phylyp
  David, 202
  Mathew, 188
  William, 229
Philpot, or Philipot
  Johanna, 196
  Roger, 196, 198, 199, 229
Picot, or Pykot
  Alice, 55
  Henry, 55
  William, 39
  William fil' William, 23
Piers, James, 198
  Johanna, 198
Pikerin, Geoffrey, 21
Pilketon, John, 165
  Margaret, 165
Pilton, or Pylton
  John, 164 (2), 176, 171
  Margaret, 164 (2), 167, 171

Pinchun, or Pynchon
  Cecilia fil' John, 74
  Thomas, 15, 104
Pinget, Cristiana, 7
  Reginald, 7
Pippard, Edmund, 41
  Margaret, 41
Pirie, Pirye, or Pyrye
  Alice, 129, 172
  John, 172, 176
  Juliana, 108
  Peter, 106, 108, 129
  Richard, 172
de Pirifrith, de Pirifright, de Pyrefrith, or Pyrefryth
  Juliana, 22
  Peter, 22, 37, 212
de Pirile, de Pirlee, de Purle, or de Pyrle
  Alice, 116
  Johanna, 21
  John fil' Peter, 116 (2)
  John fil' William, 64
  Nicholas, 12, 21
  Walter, 4
de Piriton, or de Pyriton
  John fil' William, 109
  Richard, 221
Piryman, Gilbert, 156
  Matilda, 156
de Piwelesdon, or de Pyuelesdon
  Elena, 50
  Emeline, 69
  Roger fil' Thomas, 69
  Thomas, 50
Planez, John, 17
Playter, Juliana, 212
  Thomas, 212
Plecy, John, 224
  Peter, 224
Plegge, Agnes, 182
  William, 182
de Plesyngton, Robert, 149
de Pleyshamel Johanna, 46
  Richard, 46
atte Pleystowe, Alice, 130
  Richard, 130
Plofyld, Edmund, 186
Plomer, Plomere, le Plomer, or Plummer
  Johanna, 100, 103
  John, 100, 103
  Simon, 122, 125, 130
Pobelowe, Robert, 157, 225

INDEX NOMINUM.

Pode, Cristina, 207
de Podenhale, Margaret, 129
    Richard, 129
de Podeshal, Peter, 11
de Podyndenne, de Podyndenn, de Podydene, de Pudindon, de Pudindene, de Pudingden, or de Putindene
    Adam, 119, 123
    Gilbert, 2, 12
    Johanna, 119
    Lucy, 2
    Philip, 52
    Simon, 22. 55
    William, 2
le Poer, Alice, 55
    Geoffrey, 55
Poignaunt, Adam, 99
de Pokeuord, John, 95
    Juliana, 95
Polbre, Margery, 50
    Robert, 50
Pole, Elizabeth, 201
    Richard, 129, 201
atte Pole, Johanna, 131
    Walter, 131
de Polesdon, de Polesden, or de Polesdene
    Godwyn, 65
    Gunnilda, 16
    Herbert, 2
    Sarra, 23
    Thomas, 23
    Walter, 5
le Poleter, Isolde, 85
    Walter, 85
Poleyn, Alice, 110
    John, 110
    William, 20
Pollard, John, 146
    William, 23
Polle, Emma, 74
    Martin, 74
Pollebroke, Alice, 187
    Walter, 187
de Pollingfold, or de Polyngfold
    Robert, 105
    Stephen, 23
Pollowe, John, 125
de Polsted, de Polstede, or de Polested
    Cecilia, 1, 8
    Hugh, 1, 40
    John, 199

de Polsted, de Polstede, or de Polested
    Michael, 8
    Thomas, 210, 211
de Polton, Isabel, 72
    Thomas, 72
Polynge, Matilda, 154
    Richard, 154
de Ponshurst, de Poneherst, de Ponisherst, or de Ponshurst
    Alice, 69, 72 (2), 76 (2), 82, 83
    Basilia, 11
    John, 72 (2), 76 (2), 83
    John fil' John, 69
Ponte, Johanna, 136
    Richard, 136
Pontrell, John, 190
Ponynges, or Ponyngges
    Edward, 232
    Margaret, 227
    Robert, 183, 227
de Ponynges, Michael, 134
    Robert, 179
Pope, Johanna, 135
    John, 108, 135
    Thomas, 61, 63
le Pope, Ralph, 131
Popy, Robert, 155
Porkelee, Elizabeth, 227
    Guy, 227
de Porkele, William fil' William, 97
Porland, William, 160
Port, William, 227
atte Port, Richard, 157
de la Porte, Emma, 44
    Thomas, 44
Porter, Agnes, 156
    John, 156
    Richard, 164
le Porter, Alice, 122
    John, 122
de Portesmuth, Walter, 52
Portyngton, Thomas, 196
Postel, Gilbert, 85
    Margery, 85
    Ralph, 89
le Potager, Agnes, 100
    Walter, 100
de Potenhale, Richard, 11
    Rose, 118
le Poter, Peter, 13
Pothel, Ralph, 6

INDEX NOMINUM.   295

Potom, John, 111
de Pottenhethe, or de Puttenhuthe
   John, 138
   Margaret, 138
   Thomas, 98
Potter, Johanna, 202
   John, 202
   Richard, 202
Potyer, John, 181
Potyn, Margaret, 96
   Nicholas, 142
   Walter, 96
Poulche, Beatrice, 90
   Peter, 90
Pounde, Thomas, 195
Pountfreyt, Henry, 224
   Juliana, 149
   Robert, 149
Povy, William, 193
Powe, William, 160
Power, Lucy, 99
   Robert, 99
Poydras, Walter, 71
de la Poylle, de la Puylle, or de la Pyle
   Alice, 30 (2), 72
   Margaret, 123
   Robert, 123
   Thomas, 34, 72
   Walter, 42
de Poynton, William, 113
Poynt, Alice, 188
   Richard, 188
Poyser, Constance, 232
   Henry, 232
Prat, Thomas, 98, 165
Pratyn, Agnes, 161
   John, 161
Predome, Prodom, Prodomme, Prodhomme, or Prudhum
   Adam, 85, 92
   Emma, 85, 92
   Helewisia, 10
   Johanna, 74, 96, 100, 158
   John, 74, 82, 96, 100
   Richard, 222
   Simon, 158
   Swein, 10
Prentout, Simon, 178
Prentys, or Pryntys
   Margaret, 170
   Thomas, 159, 163, 164, 169
   William, 170, 174
Pressen, John, 175

Prest, Preest, or le Prest
   Geoffrey, 33
   Goldyna, 33
   Isabel, 42
   Nicholas, 181
   William, 33, 42
Preston, Johanna, 182
   John, 161, 182
de Preston, Alice, 79
   Daniel, 76
   Margaret, 56, 58
   Robert, 56, 58
   Stephen, 73
Primerole, Cecilia, 66
   Richard, 66
de Prinkeham, Odo, 16
Prior, Priour, or Priur
   Ingebran, 173
   John, 66
   Lecia, 66
   Matilda, 173
   Robert, 161
   Thomas, 165 (2)
Prodom, Prodomme, or Prodhomme, see Predome
Profale, John, 98
Profyt, Alice, 159
   William, 159
Prophet, Thomas, 160
Prophete, John, 225
Prou, Agatha, 130
   Walter, 130
Prowet, Hugh, 54
Prudhum, see Predome
Pruet, Johanna, 115
   Richard, 112, 113, 115, 117, 133
Prynce, John, 190
Puddyng, John, 155
de Pudindon, de Pudindene, or de Pudingden, see de Podyndenne
Puffe, Richard, 151
Puke, Adam, 19
Pukelyn, John, 80
   Matilda, 80
Pulpit, or Pulpyt
   William, 179, 191
Pultebem, Robert, 91
le Pulter, Nicholas, 129
Punchard, Richard, 47
Punshurst, John, 153
del Punt, Peter, 29
de Puntinton, Robert, 12
Purbyk, Dulcia, 53
   Margaret, 115

Purbyk, Roger, 115
    Walter, 53
Purchase, Henry, 181
de Purle, *see* de Pirile
Purnoche, Thomas, 206
Purse, Agnes, 95
    Richard, 95
Purte, Geoffrey, 81
Purwoche, Thomas, 208
de Puthurst, John, 53
de Putindene, *see* de Podyndenne
de Puttenhuthe, *see* de Pottenhethe
Puttock, Anabel, 185
    Emerus, 140
    Isabella, 140
    John, 140, 185
    Margaret, 140, 200
    Richard, 200
de la Puylle, *see* de la Poylle
Pyard, John, 117
Pycard, Agnes, 176
    Thomas, 176
Pycas, John, 178
Pycher, John, 190
    Margaret, 190
Pygas, John, 158
Pygot, Alianor, 206
    Lawrence, 187
    Richard, 196
    William, 206
Pykeman, Adam, 95, 183
    Andrew, 133, 145
    Emma, 183
    Johanna, 133, 145, 192
    Matilda, 95
    Richard, 192
    Robert, 49
Pykenot, John, 35
Pykeryng, John, 205
Pykeslegh, William, 151
Pykot, *see* Picot
Pykworth, John, 176
de la Pyle, *see* de la Poylle
de Pylefrith, Peter, 45
Pylgrym, Agnes, 125
    Roger, 125
Pympe, Reginald, 204
de Pyncebek, William, 217
Pynchon, *see* Pinchun
Pynde, Thomas, 198
Pynkhurst, Pynkehurst, or de Pynkhurst
    Adam, 126, 140
    Johanna, 126

Pynkhurst, Pynkehurst, or de Pynkhurst
    Letice, 110
    Thomas, 110
    Walter, 110
    William, 220
Pynnok, Nicholas, 114, 124
Pynselegh, John, 121
    Katharine, 121
Pynwell, William, 175
le Pyp, Robert, 97
Pypart, Emma, 33
    John, 33
Pyrefrith, *see* Pirifrith
atte Pyrie, or atte Pyrye
    Agnes, 141
    Alice, 159
    Gilbert, 42
    Godfrey, 159
    Henry, 141
    Roger, 217
de Pyriton, *see* de Piriton
de Pyrle, *see* de Pirile
Pyrot, Henry, 55
Pyrun or Pyron
    Alice, 67
    Emma, 41
    Henry, 29, 41
    Robert, 67
Pyrye, *see* Pirie
de Pyuelesdon, *see* de Piwelesdon

atte Quarere, Thomas, 118
de la Quarere, Agnes, 25
    Ralph, 25
Quatremars, Beatrice, 40
    Nicholas, 40
Quecche, Hugh, 164
Queen, Elizabeth the, 230
de Quenhethe, Avice, 92
    William, 92
Quynaton, Robert, 176
Quyntyn, John, 138

Rabus, John, 6
    Walkelyn, 6
Radclyff, Roger, 229
de Radelee, Adam, 111, 115
    Matilda, 111, 115
de Radesole, John, 112, 115
    Margaret, 112, 115
de Rading, Margery, 22
    William, 22
le Rakyere, Hagenilda, 102

INDEX NOMINUM.

le Rakyere, Roger, 102
de Ralegh, Mabel, 213
    Godelot, sister of, 213
    Margaret fil' John, 86
    Ralph, 213
fil' Ralph, Brian, 7, 8 (2)
    Gunnora, wife of, 8 (2)
    Elyas, 11
    Gerard, 12
    Gilbert, 2, 5
    Hamo, 10
    Henry, 15
    John, 21
    Osbert, 5
    Richard, 9, 11
        Cecilia, wife of, 9
    Robert, 44
    Vitalis, 3
    William, 20, 29, 32
de Rameseye, Agnes, 48
    Alexander, 38
    John, 48
    Matilda, 38
    Robert, 124
de Rameshulle, William, 87
Ramsey, Thomas, 195
Rand, John, 183
Randolf, or Randolph
    Elizabeth, 120
    Emma, 70
    Katharine, 145, 222
    John, 120, 197
    Nicholas, 172
    Walter fil' Robert, 70
    William, 145, 222
de Rankedich, Thomas, 41
fil' Ranulph, Amabel, 4
    Isabel, 4
    Richard, 6
    Robert, 2
    Suanilda, 4
de Rattescroft, Alice, 62
    Robert, 62
Rauf, Alice, 26
    Gilbert fil' William, 26
Raum, Philip, 130
Ravelyn, John, 211
Raven, or Ravon
    Johanna, 135
    Robert, 135
    Sarra, 14, 27
    Thomas, 14, 27
de Ravenser, John, 138
Rawelyn, William, 194

Raynford, William, 228
de Recchynge, John, 107
fil' Recluse, Wlric, 3
Rede or Reed,
    Bartholomew, 201, 202, 205, 207, 231 (2)
    Edmund, 172, 177
    Isabella, 167, 172
    John, 167, 172, 207, 210
    Petronilla, 161
    Ralph, 161
    Robert, 197, 199
de Rede, or de Reda
    Adam, 73
    Alice, 92
    Clemence, 45, 47
    Edith, 73
    John, 45, 47, 92
    Mabel, 70, 83
    Robert, 64, 70, 83
Redeforde, or Redforde
    Johanna, 177
    John, 209
    William, 177
Redeknapp, William, 193
de Redenhale, Amicia, 67, 70
    Roger, 67, 70
Redeston, William, 158, 188
Redhond, Alice, 125
    Richard, 125
de Redinghersth, *see* de Ridyngersh
Redmane, Mathew, 134
Redyng, Cecilia, 149
    John, 149
le Rees, Matilda, 93
    Thomas, 93
Reeve, Agnes, 22
    Robert, 22
Reffawe, John, 180
    Margaret, 180
Regaud, Matilda, 54
    Richard, 54
Regge, John, 168
fil' Reginald, William, 14
fil' Reiner, Reginald, 16
de Remdon, Roger, 8
de Remenham, Robert, 102
    Thomas, 102
Remys, Thomas, 158, 167, 170
Renecester, Richard, Prior of, 15
Renehawe, Annora, 158
    John, 158
de Resham, Richerus, 84, 96
    John, 84, 109

Reson, William, 134
de Retherhee, Agnes, 18
atte Revere, Richard, 176
de Reygate, or de Regate
    Cristina, 76
    John, 44 (2), 76
Reygate, Brother Henry, Master of the Hospital of, 34
de Reygni, de Reingny, or de Reney
    Robert, 19, 21 (2), 25
Reyner, Cristina, 109
    Isabel, 62
    Johanna, 62
    John, 62, 180
    Thomas, 62, 109
de Reynham, or de Reyngham
    Alesia, 141, 143
    Edmund, 104, 110
    Isolde, 104, 110
    Nicholas, 141, 143
Reynold, or Reynald
    Johanna, 135
    John, 133, 183, 194
    Mabel, 133
    Margaret, 194
    William, 135
    Richard, Johanna, 99, 185
    John, 90, 169
    Robert, 78
    Thomas, 99
    William, 185
fil' Richard, Henry, 15
    Richard, 16
    Symon, 27
    Thomas, 20
    William, 21, 24
        Tephania, wife of, 21, 24
Richardson, John, 210
Riche, Thomas, 231 (2)
Richebele, Isabel, 118
    Peter, 118
Richemund, Margaret, Countess of, 197, 230
Richer, John, 158
de Richescumbe, Drugo, 20
le Rideler, William, 126
le Ridere, Geoffrey, 13
de Ridyngersh, de Rydingehers, or de Redinghersth
    John, 110
    Margery, 110
    Matilda, 69
    Robert, 47, 69

atte Rigge, Richard, 99
Riggeley, Alice, 207
    Humfrey, 207
de Rikethorn, Elena, 85
    William, 85
Rikhill, Rikill, Rykhull, or Rykkell
    John, 198, 201 (2)
    Nicholas, 226
    Richard, 201
    William, 151, 224 (2)
de Rinssam, Robert fil' Reginald, 5
Ripon, John, 183
Riseberger, Agnes, 193
    Henry, 193
de la Rithe, Cecilia, 54
    William, 54
Robelot, William, 163
Rober, John, 204
fil' Robert, Floerin, 26
    Henry, 3, 5
    Luke, 12
    Milo, 5
        Alice, wife of, 5
    Ralph, 14
    Richard, 4
    Robert, 1
    Stephen, 15
    Thomas, 10
    Vitellus, 4
    William, 2, 11, 17
        Cristina, wife of, 17
Roberth, Walter, 204
Robkyn, Alice, 153
    William, 153
Robyn, Alice, 146
    William, 146
Roce, Hillary, 87 (2)
    John, 121, 223
    Margery, 87 (2)
    Walter, 95
    William, 102, 103, 219
Rocheford, Richard, Parson of, 221
de Rockele, Grecia, 35
    Reginald, 35
Rodelond, Elena, 188
    Robert, 188
de Rodesham, William, 118
Rodford, John, 200
atte Rodgate, Adam, 77
    Matilda, 77
de la Roede, John, 43
Roger, Johanna, 90
    John, 90

Roger, Walter, 94
fil' Roger, Gilbert, 11
    Hagenilda, 24
    Reginald, 16
    Simon, 4
    William, 16
Roghheye, Johanna, 159
    John, 159
Roke, John, 163
de Rokelond, John, 88
    Margery, 88
de Rokenham, Annora, 82
    Thomas fil' Thomas, 82
de Rokesbiry, Ranulph, 6
    William, 8
Rokesburgh, William, 176
de Rokesle, de Rokeslee, or de Roukeslee
    Lucy, 45, 47, 58
    Reginald, 47
    Sarra, 73
    Thomas fil' Thomas, 108
    Walter, 45, 47, 58
    William, 73
    William fil' Reginald, 59
de Rokwyk, John, 126
Roland, or Rouland
    John, 97, 147
    Juliana, 97
    Roland fil' Robert, 71
Rolf, Agnes, 122
    Emma, 149
    Henry, 187
    Johanna, 187
    Thomas, 149, 156, 179
    William, 122
le Romayn, Romeyn, or Romyn
    Adam, 80
    Cecilia, 80
    Juliana, 63, 64, 71 (2), 74
    Thomas, 63, 64, 71 (2), 74
Rombem, Isabella, 174
    William, 174
Rommyng, Anna, 212
    Stephen, 212
de Rontele, John fil' Walter, 81
    Walter, 81
de Ronthhale, Margery, 130
    Thomas, 130
Rook, Richard, 147
de Roos, John, 224
Ropere, Simon, 126
le Ros, Geoffrey, 219
    John, 85

Rose, Cristina, 126
    John, 126
    Robert, 49
atte Rose, Adam, 81, 87
    Cecilia, 81, 87
Rosefeld, Alianor, 161
    Henry, 161
Rote, John, 175
    Simon, 100
    William, 232
Rotheley, William, 194
Rothyng, Cristina, 146
    Eustace, 146
    Richard, 146
de Rothyng, Emma, 127
    John, 126, 127
    Richard, 111 (2)
atte Rouberne, or atte Roughebern
    John, 130, 148
    Katharine, 148
de Rouebern, de la Ruebern, de Roughberne, or de Rughebern
    Peter, 9, 101
    Ralph, 85
    Richard, 85
    William, 17
Roughhede, Agnes, 228
    Richard, 228
de Roukeslee, *see* de Rokesle
Rouland, *see* Roland
de Rouleboys, John, 46
de Rouleye, John, 128
Rous, John, 134, 139
    John fil' John fil' William, 154
le Rous, Richard, 69
Ruch, Margery, 131, 137
    Robert, 131, 137
de Ruda, Walter, 10
Ruddeston, Walter, 207
atte Rude, Anastachia, 83
    Cristiana, 169
    John, 169
    Walter, 83, 169
    Walter fil' Walter, 83
de la Rude, Beatrice, 40
    William, 18, 40
    William fil' Walter, 22
    William fil' William, 22
de la Ruebern, *see* de Rouebern
de Ruerhee, Fulk, 3
    Robert, 3
Ruffus, Adam, 2
    Gilbert, 10

Ruffus, Robert, 18
Rufin, William, 15
le Ruge, Dionisia, 64
    Isabel, 64
    Simon, 64
Rugespere, Katharine, Prioress of, 17
Rugewyke, or Ruggewyk
    Alexander, Vicar of, 220, 222
de Rugge, John, 23
    John fil' John, 19
de Rughebern, *see* de Rouebern
de Rugwik, Walter, 36
Rukbare, Henry, 193
de Rumeham, Cecilia, 12
    Thomas, 12
Rumney, Johanna, 193
    John, 193
Rundel, Juliana, 130
    Robert, 130
Rus, Katharine, 138, 148
    Robert, 138, 148
le Rus, Adam, 61
    Agnes, 58
    Letitia, 61
    Peter, 41
    William, 58
Russel, Adam, 214
    Cecilia, 31, 32
    Johanna, 180
    John, 31, 32
    Matilda, 57
    Richard, 37, 43, 57
    Robert, 182
Russham, Hawise, 131
    Thomas, 131
de Russham, Petronilla, 79
    William, 79
Rusthall, Agnes, 144
    John, 144
de Rustington, Lawrence, 84, 89
Ryall, Thomas, 205
atte Ryde, John, 225
Rydere, Alice, 150
    Cristiana, 55
    Geoffrey, 55
    William, 150
Rydlay, Owen, 200
    Roger, 200
Rykhull, or Rikkell, *see* Rikhill
Rykoun, Alice, 136
    Walter, 136
Rykyld, Haverilda, 86
    William, 86

Rympyngden, or Rympynden
    Amy, 231
    John, 205, 206
    Ralph, 231
    Thomas, 206
Rynge, John, 206
Ryngeburn, William, 152
Ryngewode, Emma, 171, 176
    Nicholas, 171, 176
Ryngston, Thomas, 196
de Ryngwode, John, 111
    Juetta, 111
Ryplyngham, John, 207
de Rypon, Aunger, 61
de Ryppeleye, John fil' John, 50
de Ryselberge, Henry, 39
    Margery, 39
de Rytlyng, Cristiana, 86
    John, 86
de Ryvall, Peter, 33 (3)
Ryvel, Walter, 87
de la Ryvere, Isabel, 143
    Thomas, 143
Ryvers, Anthony, Earl, 230
Ryxton, Nicholas, 183

de Sabaudin, Peter, 214
de Sabrichesworth, Amiel, 113
    Johanna, 113
fil' Saerus, John, 212 (2), 214 (2)
de Safray, Henry, 32
Saft, Roger, 10
le Sagiere, Johanna, 126
    John, 126
de Saham, Matilda, 69
    Stephen, 69
de St. Albans, Adam, 98
    Elias, 3
de Sancto Audoeno, Gilbert, 216
St. Augustine's, Canterbury, Robert, Abbot of, 18
de St. Cristofer, Thomas, 7
de St. Edmund, Johanna, 78
    William, 78
"de loco sancti Edwardi," Robert, the Abbot, 27
de St. Fide, Gilbert, 59
    Pavya, 59
de St. German, or de St. Jerman
    Joel, 23, 29
    Emma, 71
de St. Giles, Roger, 71. *See also* de Seyntgyle
de St. John, Edward, 90

INDEX NOMINUM. 301

de St. John, Eva, 90
    John, 13, 56, 91
    John fil' Roger, 60
    Margaret, 56
    Margery, 91
    Peter, 98, 126
    Peter fil' John, 100
    Roger, 28, 33, 42, 126
    Roger fil' John, 125, 126
    William, 21
St. John's Church, Colecestre, Robert, Abbot of, 59
St. John of Jerusalem, Priors of the Hospital of
    Joseph, 51
    Roger de Ver, 43
    Terricus, 30
de St. Laud, Beatrice, 50
    Ralph, 50
St. Leofrid, Ralph, Abbot of, 18
de St. Martin, Margery, 17
    Thomas, 17
St. Mary Magdalen of Sindon, the Master of the Hospital of, 23
St. Mary Suthwerk, Adam, Prior of, 215
    Alan, Prior of, 39, 42
    Humfrey, Prior of, 18, 21
    Stephen, Prior of, 29 (3), 30, 32
    William, Prior of, 3
de St. Michael, Laurence, 21, 54
    Thomas, 97, 104
    Walter, 5
    William, 95
de St. Omer, William, 116, 131
St. Paul's, London, Alexander, Treasurer of, 26
    Master Henry, Deacon and Chaplain of, 26
    John, Dean of, 215
de St. Swythun, Andrew, 22
St. Thomas de Acre, Adam, Master of the Hospital of, 38
    William, Master of the Hospital of, 40
St. Thomas the Martyr, in Suthwerk, Amisius, Master of the Hospital of, 9 (3)
    Robert, Master of the Hospital of, 11
    William, Master of the Hospital of, 17
    ——— Master of the Hospital of, 121

St. Wlfmar Bonon, Walter, Abbot of, 28
le Sakkere, Adam, 86
    Edith, 86
de Saklesford, or de Shakleford
    Alice, 15
    Gerard, 15
    Hugh, 62
    John, 62
    Juliana, 62
    Richard, 62
de la Sale, Alice, 57
    Isabel, 53
    John, 55
    Laurence, 53
    Lucy, 52
    Richard, 84
    Robert, 57
    William, 42
de Saleby, Gilbert, 89 (2)
    Matilda, 89 (2)
Saleman, Alice, 97, 102
    Roger, 110 (2)
    Roger fil' Ralph, 97, 99, 102 (2)
de Salford, Alice, 122
    John, 122
Salisbury, Alice, 185
    John, 185, 223
    Richard, 12
    Robert, 17
de Salisbury, John, 119
    Margaret, 119
Salman, William, 157
le Saltere, Henry, 16
de Salvo, Nicholas, 99
de Salwarp, William, 221
Salyng, John, 145
    Margaret, 145
fil' Samar, Pagan, 2
Samford, Henry, 197
Sampson, Margaret, 187
    Richard, 187
fil' Sampson, Gregory, 24
Sande, Cristina, 209
    John, 209
Sandeford, de Sandeford, or de Sandford,
    John, 173
    Thomas, 115
    William, 136
de Sandes, Lucy, 8
    Ruald, 14, 19
    William, 8
Sandewych, John, 173

INDEX NOMINUM.

de Sandon, Gilbert, 19
    Nicholas, 39
    Thomas fil' John, 80
Sandon, Richard, Master of the Hospital of the Holy Ghost of, 24
Sandon, or Saundon
    Giles, Prior of, 33
    Richard, Prior of, 19
de Sandres, Beatrice, 5
Sandys, Oliver, 206, 231
Sankhurst, Richard, 128
    William, 128
de Sarterie, Alexander, 94
    Alice, 94
de Sarum, Amicia, 94
    Cecilia, 111
    John, 111
    William, 94
de Saukevill, Geoffrey, 13
Saundelford, John, Prior of, 27
Saunder, Saundre, Saundir, or Saundyr
    Henry, 199, 203, 210
    Johanna, 189, 194
    John, 196
    Margaret, 196
    Thomas, 170, 188
    William, 184, 188, 189, 194
Saundon, *see* Sandon
de Saunford, Isabel, 46
    Ralph, 46
le Saunner, Richard, 31
Sauntere, or Saunterre
    Agnes, 49
    John, 49
    Thomas, 72
Sauser, or le Sauser
    John, 71
    Reginald, 50
    Robert, 90, 166
del Sauserye, Matilda, 151
    Robert, 151
Savage, le Savage, Sauvage, or le Sauvage
    Aveline, 59
    Geoffrey, 59
    Hawysia, 59
    Isabel, 87, 88
    Johanna, 165
    John, 59, 183
    John fil' John, 58
    Lucy, 68
    Robert, 2, 8, 157, 165

Savage, le Savage, Sauvage, or le Sauvage
    Roger, 87, 88
    William, 158
fil' Savaric, William, 10
Savereye, Juliana, 179
    Peter, 179
Savery, Agatha, 69
    Philip, 69
Saxilby, Richard, 184
de Say, Johanna, 71
    Henry, 71, 72
    William, 30
Sayer, Agnes, 189
    John, 171
    Thomas, 189
de Sayten, William, 32
de Scaldeford, *see* de Scaudeford
Scamaile, or Scamaille
    Dionis, 136
    John, 128
    Sibil, 128
    Walter, 136
Scapereng, Geoffrey, 45
Scarbrugh, William, 174
Scarlet, John, 163
de Scaudeford, or de Scaldeford
    Jocelin, 7
    John, 15
    Peter, 32
    Philip, 9
Schayl, Inga, 35
    Richard, 35
Schench, Clarice, 68
    Martin, 68
de Scheyntone, Adam, 59
de Schorne, Matilda, 51
    Richard, 51
Schort, Cristiana, 39
    William, 39
Schurley, Thomas, 202
le Scolmaystre, William, 112
Scopeham, Katharine, 198
    Richard, 198
Scory, Johanna, 169
    Richard, 169
de Scoteslye, Robert, 75
de Scothon, Margery, 38
    Robert, 38
Scott, Scotte, Scote, or Scot
    Adam, 64
    Agnes, 174, 197, 205
    Alice, 15
    Anna, 210

Scott, Scotte, Scote, or Scot
   Cecilia, 99
   John, 93, 96, 99, 174, 194, 202, 205, 209 (2), 210, 211 (2)
   William 15, 197
Scrace, John, 206
   Margery, 206
Scragge, John, 211
Scrift, William, 20
de Scrikeston, Beatrice, 21
   Henry, 21
le Scrop, Geoffrey, 82
   Henry, 121
de Scrouby, Hugh, 65 (2)
Sebarn, Margaret, 139
   Robert, 139
Sebright, Eufemia, 74
   William, 74
Sedenye, *see* Sydney
fil' Segar, Adam, 10
de Segesford, Charles, 93
Seintcler, or Seyntcler
   Margaret, 224
   Philip, 224
   Thomas, 226
Seint Just, Alan, 170
Sekyngton, William, 163
Selde, Godfrey, 178
Seleburne, John, the Prior of, 33 (2)
de Sellesdon, Amicia, 104
   John, 104
Sellyng, John, 194
   Margaret, 194
de Sellyng, Robert, 122
Selot, Walter, 134
Selverton, Johanna, 159 (2), 225
   John, 159 (2), 225
Sely, Agnes, 107, 108
   John, 132
   Laurence, 107, 108
Seman, Adam, 64
   Avice, 64
   Edith, 189
   John, 98, 189, 218
   Martin, 154
fil' Semer, Harding, 10
Semere, Isabel, 133 (2)
   Johanna, 114
   John, 133 (2), 148
   Peter, 114, 133 (2)
   Tiphania, 114
de Sende, Alice, 65
   Thomas, 65

Sergeant, John, 149
   Matilda, 128
   William, 128
Serle, Agnes, 135, 158
   Thomas, 133, 158, 159
Sessyngham, Thomas, 175
Sevenok, William, 165
Sever, Henry, 186
Sevoghel, Ralph, 19
Sewale, Cristina, 177
   John, 177
   Thomas, 149
Seward, Richard, 78
   Sibil, 136
   William, 136
de Sewell, de Suwelle, or de Sywell
   Isabella, 37, 44
   Laurence, 53
   Symon, 31 (2), 37, 44
Sexteyn, Thomas, 185
de Sey, John, 213
Seylyard, John, 229
Seymour, Johanna, 163
   John, 163
Seyntcler, *see* Seintcler
de Seyntgyle, Emma, 83
   Roger, 83
Seynt John, William, 174
Seynt Leger, Anna, 202, 203
   James, 203 (2)
Shaa, Edmund, 194
   John, 195, 201, 205 (2), 207, 231 (2)
atte Shagh, Agnes, 142
   Robert, 142
Shakespye, Emma, 111
   Walter, 111
de Shakleford, *see* de Saklesford
Shapewyk, John, 170
Shaplee, Alice, 105
   Thomas, 105
Sharp, Roger, 57
   Thomas, 224
   William, 176, 211
Shawe, John, 202
de Sheldon, John, 220
Shelford, Henry, 172
Shelley, John, 195
de Shelveleye, Thomas, 121
de Shen, Roger, 17
de Shenholton, or de Henholte
   Thomas, 102 (2)
Shep, Katharine, 148 (2)
   Peter, 148 (2)

le Shephard, Robert, 99
Shepherd, Shepherde, or Sheperde
    Isabella, 155
    Margaret, 159 (2)
    Richard, 160
    Walter, 155
    William, 159 (2)
Sherefeld, Elizabeth, 175
    Richard, 175
Sherewynd, Edward, 75
    Elena, 75
Sherman, Cristina, 142
    John, 142, 229
Shert, William, 207
de Sherton, Alice, 64
    William, 64
Shipbroke, Margaret, 142
    Roger, 142
de Shiple, John, 113
    Mabel, 113
de Shirbourn, John, 122
    Katharine, 122
de Shirbroke, Margaret, 137
    Roger, 137
de Shire, Alice, 73
    Bartholomew, 73, 79
Shirfeld, or Shirefeld
    Richard, 173, 177, 187
Shirley, Reginald, 193, 194
    William, 187
Shirwode, Margaret, 198
    Thomas, 198
Shobyngdon, Alice, 179
    William, 179
de Shokkeburgh, Agnes, 145
    Cristofer, 145
Shordiche, or Shordych
    Alice, 158
    Amicia, 132
    John, 158
    Thomas, 132
Shorman, John, 169
Short, Alice, 163
    Thomas, 163
de Shotemere, Hamo, 26
Shouve, Thomas, 196
de Shrimpelersh, Hugh, 99
    Margaret, 99
Shropshire, Thomas, 166
Shrympe, John, 220
de Shuldham, John, 165
de Shyre, Matilda, 213
    Roger, 213
de Shyrefeld, Clementina, 52

Sibile, Sibyle, or Sybyle
    Nicholas, 182, 183, 190
de Siddene, William, 95
Sideneye, *see* Sydney
Sigmond, Agnes, 147
    John, 147
Silverton, or Sylverton
    Johanna, 174, 189, 198
    John, 174
    Nicholas, 184, 189, 198
Simion, Elizabeth, 77
    Perceval, 77
fil' Simon, or fil' Symon
    Roger, 7
    Alice, wife of, 7
    Thomas, 15
    William, 215
Sippenham, Thomas, 163
le Sire, Juliana, 93
    Simon, 93
fil' Siward, Emma, 23
    William, 8, 10
Skarburgh, Anna, 189
    John, 189
de Skardeburgh, Geoffrey, 218, 219
Skarisbrig, Cecilia, 210
    Peter, 210
Skeene, William, 163
Skelton, John, 181
    Katharine, 181
Skenefeld, John, 176
Skerne, or Skirne
    William, 179, 183, 189, 190 (2)
Skernynges, Roger, fil' Vincent, 63
    Thomas, 63
Sket, Roger, 59
Skinner, John, 145
Skipwith, Gregory, 202
Skrene, William, 224
Skryeven, Agnes, 193
    William, 193
Skylle, John, 200
Skymer, Richard, 198
Skynner, or Skynnere
    Johanna, 149
    John, 191, 192, 193, 194, 197, 200, 202, 204, 209 (2), 210, 211 (2)
    Michael, 202
    Richard, 149, 196, 200, 201
Slak, Agnes, 150
    Roger, 150
Slaplegh, or de Slappeleghe
    Alice, 98, 114 (2)

Slaplegh, or de Slappeleghe
    Thomas, 98, 114 (2)
de Slapton, Alice, 55
    Stephen, 55
Sleddale, Adam, 132
de Sleford, Thomas, 114, 115
    William, 134
Slifeld, de Slifeld, Slyfeld, de Slyfeld, Slefeld, or de Slefeld
    Agnes, 41
    Alianor, 199
    Anna, 195
    Geoffrey, 41
    Johanna, 154
    Nicholas, 126, 129, 136, 154
    Thomas, 182, 195
    William, 199
de Slopham, John, 219
de Slopundon, Elizabeth, 141
    Thomas, 141
Slow, William, 10
Slowe, John, 196
de Slyfeld, *see* Slifeld
Smart, Alice, 114
    John, 114
    William, 208
Smerehele, Gunnilda, 91
    Ralph, 91
Smert, Isabella, 161
    John, 151, 161
    Matilda, 151
Smith, or Smyth
    Alice, 12
        Cecilia, sister of, 12
        Mabel, sister of, 12
    Bartholomew, 12
    Cristina, 2
    Gunnora, 14, 16
    Henry, 5
    Johanna, 180, 183
    John, 138, 180, 183, 208
    Laurence, 148
    Mabel fil' John, 48
    Norman, 2
    Reginald, 14, 16
    Richard, 14, 180
    Walter, 138
    William, 33, 148, 178, 231
atte Smyth, Matilda, 126
    William, 126
le Smyth or le Smythe
    Johanna, 119
    John fil' Richard, 101
    Richard, 101, 110

le Smyth, or le Smythe
    Walter, 92, 132
    William, 119
Snell, Emma, 162
    John, 193
    Richard, 162
    Robert, 193
    Thomas, 193
de Snodeham, Emma, 44
    Robert, 71
    Walter, 25, 44
    Walter fil' Robert, 97
Snoute, Walter, 79
Snowe, Richard, 174
de Sodynton, John, 103
de Sogehamme, John, 127
    Margery, 127
Solace, Robert, 142
Solas, Johanna, 160
    John, 160, 162
de Solderne, Isolde, 75
    Philip fil' Thomas, 75
de la Solere, William, 98
Somer, Henry, 200, 201
    Richard, 170
de Somerbury, de Somerbergh, de Somerbyry, or de Summerbury
    Henry, 54, 63, 70, 74, 83, 104
    Herbert, 46
    Johanna, 104
    Margaret, 70, 74
    Richard, 68
    Richard fil' Henry, 104, 114 (2)
Somerset, Charles, 210
Somervylle, John, 152
    Katharine, 152
Somur, Johanna, 184
    Thomas, 184
Sonde, Reginald, 230
    William, 192
atte Sonde, Alice, 85
    Matilda, 166
    Richard, 172 (2)
    Robert, 85, 166, 175
de Sonde, William, 35
de la Sonde, Henry, 52
    Walter, 29
Sondes, Reginald, 198
Sonnynglegh, Geoffrey, 223
    Johanna, 223
Sotenham, Juliana, 157
    Philip, 157
de Sotheneye, Agnes, 99

de Sotheneye, John, 99
Southwell, John, 148
Souwy, Johanna, 48
    John, 48
Spardour, Bartholomew, 209
Spark, Hugh, 182
    Margaret, 182
Sparsulle, Robert, 164
Speleman, Stephen, 167
Spelman, Henry, 228
Spencer, Henry, 175
    Johanna, 162, 175
    Richard, 203
    Thomas, 102
Spenden, John, 182
Spenser, William, 143
le Spenser, Alice, 119
    Elizabeth, 118
    Isabel, 92
    John, 92
    Philip, 118
    Robert, 119
Spereman, Thomas, 97
    Wimarca, 97
Sperlyng, Cristiana, 45
de Spersholte, William, 88
Spicer, or Spycer
    Adam, 123
    Johanna, 123
    John, 160, 166, 222
    Matilda, 166
    William, 150
le Spicer, Matilda, 89
    Thomas, 89
de la Spineye, de Spineto, or de la Spyneye
    Elizabeth, 218
    John, 218
    Margaret, 98
    Peter, 98
    Robert, 35
Sporier, Agnes, 155
    William, 155
atte Spottenes, Johanna, 61
de Spridlyngton, William, 124
Spring, Hugh, 16
Springaunt, William, 62
Sprygy, William, 155
Spycer, *see* Spicer
Spyllebord, Margery, 42
    Richard, 42
de la Spyneye, *see* de la Spineye
Spynk, William, 205
atte Spytele, Alice, 116

atte Spytele, John, 116
Squattechese, Robert, 11
Squery, Squyry, or Squyrry
    Bartholomew, 170
    John, 193
    Juliana, 209
    Richard, 165
    Philip, 193
    Thomas, 170, 209
Stacy, Agnes, 162
    Johanna, 180
    John, 180
    Matilda, 51
    Richard, 51, 162
de Stafald, or de Stafaud
    Juliana, 5
        Haenilda, sister of, 5
    Odo, 5
    Richard, 15
Stafford, Anna, Countess of, 182
    Humfrey, Earl of, 182
Stakeford, Isabella, 162
    John, 162
Stallyngburgh, Nicholas, 225
Standen, Agnes, 164
    William, 164
Standon, Robert, 165
de Stanes, Savaric, 9
    Thomas, 80
de Stanesfeld, William, 112
Stanford, Robert, 211
de Stanford, Johanna, 82
    William, 82
de Stangrave, or de Stanigrave
    Johanna, 33, 100, 107, 114, 115
    John, 47, 115
    John fil' John, 42, 46
    Robert, 100, 107, 114
    Robert fil' John, 52
de Stanhamme, Henry fil' Simon, 95
    Simon, 95
Stanley, John, 186, 189
    Margaret, 197
    Thomas, 197, 229, 230
de Stanore, Ranulf, 11
de Stanstede, Emeric, 42
    Isabel, 42
    Simon, 42
    William, 97
Stanton, John, 160
Stanyndenne, William, 152
Stapelford, Edmund, 163
    John, 162

INDEX NOMINUM.   307

de Stapelho, Thomas, 128
de Stapelston, Nicholas, 86
Stapenhull, Johanna, 167
   John, 167
de Stapleton, de Stapletone, or de Stapelton
   Isabel, 108
   Johanna, 69
   Miles, 69, 71, 108
   Nicholas, 108
de Starith, Geoffrey, 16
Starky, Humfrey, 194
de Starle, John, 224
de Staundon, Geoffrey, 56
de Staunford, Isabel, 109
   Robert, 109
Stede, William, 194
Stef, Adam, 26
de Stenesgrave, Johanna, 217
   Robert, 217
Stepere, John, 151
Stepulton, Hugh, 197
de Sterteford, Alice, 105
   John, 105
Steven, Johanna, 200
   Richard, 200
Stevenson, Margaret, 198
   Richard, 198
Stevynton, Agnes, 175
   John, 175
Stiker, Florence, 79
   Henry, 79
Stilewell, William, 93
Stirkland, Elizabeth, 181
   Walter, 181
de Stock, Robert, 32
de la Stocket, John, 91
de Stockwell, de Stocwell, de Stokwell, or de Stokewell
   Agnes, 69, 70
   Alan, 30
   Henry, 69, 70
   John, 1
   William, 23
de Stodeye, John, 124
de Stofold, Beatrice, 56
   Juliana, 220
   Ralph, 56
   William, 220
de Stoghton, Henry, 113, 120
   Johanna, 120
   John, 120 (2)
   Juliana, 120
   Margaret, 113

de Stoghton, Matilda, 120
   Thomas, 113
Stok, John, 154
de Stoke, de Stokes, or de Stok
   Agnes, 38, 49
   Aldred, 21
   Alvina, 9, 21
   Emma, 36, 46
   Hugh, 38, 49
   Richard, 27 (2)
   Robert, 29
   Thomas, 36, 46
   William, 19
Stokes, William, 176
Stoket, Alianor, 142
   John, 142
atte Stoket, or atte Stokette
   John, 76, 115
   Matilda, 76
de Stokton, Hugh, 24
de Stokwell, or de Stokewell, *see* de Stockwell
Stokwod, Agnes, 182
   John, 182
de Stominholl, Isabel, 38
   Roger, 38
Stone, Alice, 191
   Edward, 193
   Isabella, 193
   John, 190, 191, 206
   Margaret, 190
   Richard, 201
   William, 193
atte Stone, Henry, 174
   Isabella, 174
   Johanna, 164
   Richard, 103
   Thomas, 164
de la Stonball, Agnes, 42
   Jordan, 42
de Stonham, or de Stonehame
   Simon, 41
   William, 41
atte Stonhouse, Henry, 128
de Stonle, Isabel, 112
   Simon, 112
Stonor, Thomas, 195
de Stonore, John, 113
Stopyndon, John, 183, 184, 189
de Storich, Alice, 98
   John fil' Ralph, 98
Storin, Adam, 166
de Storith, Robert, 113
Storm, Ordmer, 11

Storm, Robert, 99 (2), 105
Storme, Adam, 183
de Storteford, William, 49
Stote, Thomas, 111
Stoughton, or Stogton
    Gilbert, 205, 206
    Henry, 127, 202
    Johanna, 127, 164
    Thomas, 164, 165, 173, 178 (2)
Stoure, Elizabeth, 210
    William, 210
Stout, Thomas fil' Robert, 118
Stoute, Helewise, 103
    William, 103
de Stowe, Alice, 96
    Simon, 96
Stratford, William, 207
de Stratford, Dionis, 125
    Robert, 125
de Straton, or de Stratton
    Adam, 39, 212 (2), 214 (2)
atte Stret, Alice, 118
    John, 119
    Richard, 119
    William, 118
de la Stret, Beatrice, 52
    Roger, 52
atte Strete, Johanna, 138
    Ralph, 75
    Roger, 138
de Strete, or del Strete
    Henry, 117, 118, 121
    James, 146
de Stretton, Matilda, 83
    Roger, 71, 77, 83
de la Strode, or de Strode
    Agnes, 55, 63, 65, 69
    Albred, 13
    Matilda, 38
    Thomas, 55, 63, 65, 69
    Thomas fil' Thomas, 69
    William, 38, 67
de la Strond, Editha, 15
Stucle, or Stukle
    Peter, 175, 186
atte Stulpe, Isabella, 141
    Richard, 141
Sturgeon, John, 187
Sturmy, Henry, 72
Sturmyn, John, 191, 229
le Stut, Alice, 47
    Hugh, 10
    Milisant, 10
    Walter, 47

Styward, Thomas, 165
de Sudbury, Thomas, 220
de Sudhiwerke, *see* de Suthwerk
de Sudinton, Robert, 18
Sudwerke, *see* Suthwerk
Suel, Thomas, 20
Suffolk, William, Marquis of, 22
de Suffolk, Alan, 74
    Johanna, 74
de Sulameheth, Ralph, 31
le Sumeter, Emma, 33
    Walter, 33
de Sumpton, Margaret, 121
    Thomas, 121
de Sunderesse, Lewin, 44
le Surugien, Alan, 55
Suthcote, Katharine, 188 (2)
    William, 188 (2)
de Suthcote, Roger, 112
de Sutherst, or de Suthhurst
    Henry, 35, 44
de Suthill, or Suthull
    Alice, 22
    Gilbert, 4
    Gunilda, 4
    Reyner, 22
de Suthinton, John, 43
de Suthwerk, de Suthwerc, de Sutwerke, de Suwerk, or de Sudhiwerke
    Arnald, 65
    Avice, 65
    Bertram, 217
    Emma, 32
    Ernald, 50
    Geoffrey fil' William, 36
    Johanna, 50
    Jordan, 32
    Leuina, 16
    Peter fil' John, 22, 25
    Roger fil' Roger, 2 (2)
    Stephen, 9
    Theophania, 27
    Walter, 16
    William, 27
Suthwerk, Sutwerk, Suwerk, or Sudwerke
    The Prior of, 24, 25
    The Prior and convent of, 1, 2
de Suthwyk, John, 79
    Mary, 79
Sutor, William, 10
Sutton, Roger, Parson o 139
Sutton, George, 21

Sutton, Johanna, 153, 161
    John, 153, 161, 185, 210
    Richard, 210
    Thomas, 171
de Sutton, Helewyse, 33
    John, 25 (2)
    Richard, 221
    Robert, 23, 26
    Stephen, 33, 39
    William, 45, 221
de Sutton on Trent, Isabella, 219
    John fil' John, 219
de Sutwerke, or de Suwerk, see de Suthwerk
le Suur, Amabel, 52
    John, 52
    Stephen, 90
Suwell, Emma, 121, 126
    John, 121, 126
de Suwell, see de Sewell
de Swafham, Thomas, 74
de Swanton, John, 151
    Margaret, 151
Swayneslond, Alice, 198
    William, 198
Sweting, Matilda, 10
    William, 10
Sweyn, or Sweyne
    Richard, 76
    Richard fil' Richard, 76
    Thomas, 167
Swofeham, John, 166
Swote, Agnes, 105, 111, 123
    Katharine, 123
    Robert, 105, 111, 123
    William fil' William, 123
Swyft, Henry, 164
    Johanna, 164
    John, 164
Swyfth, Amabel, 26
    Richard, 26
de Swynebroc, or de Swynbroc
    William, 34, 38
de Swyneford, Agnes, 73, 110
    John fil' Richard, 110
    Richard, 73, 110
Sybyle, see Sibile
de Sydenye, William, 105
Sydney, Sydeney, Sydeneye, Sedenye, or Sideneye
    Elizabeth, 196
    Katharine, 134
    William, 134, 161, 174, 178, 179, 227

le Sygher, Henry, 71
de Syleby, Roger, 103
Sylverton, see Silverton
Symme, Agnes, 154
    William, 154
Symmes, William, 176
fil' Symon, see fil' Simon
Symond, John, 178
    Robert, 143, 182
    William, 170
Symson, Johanna, 177
    William, 177
de Syndlesham, Agnes, 92
    Robert, 92
Syngere, John, 177
Syward, William, 193
de Sywell, see de Sewell

de T——, Robert, 105
de Taiden, or de Taidon
    Henry fil' Henry, 12, 13
Taillour, or Tayllour
    Agnes, 148
    Giles, 156, 223
    Isabel, 124
    James, 148
    Johanna, 146, 150
    John, 150
    Laurence, 157
    Letice, 222
    Maurice, 199
    Philippa, 150
    Ralph fil' James, 150
    Reginald, 146
    Richard, 146, 210
    Robert, 222
le Taillour, le Tayllour, le Tayllur, le Thaylur, le Tailliour, or le Taillur
    Adam, 67
    Agatha, 72
    Agnes, 50, 114 (2)
    Alice, 129
    Cecilia, 85
    Edmund, 77
    Elicia, 38, 46 (2), 49
    Eustachia, 79
    Henry, 85
    Johanna, 67, 78, 85, 109, 110
    John, 129
    Letitia, 18
    Margaret, 136
    Matilda, 96
    Nicholas, 38, 46 (2), 49, 114 (2)

310   INDEX NOMINUM.

le Taillour, le Tayllour, le Tayllur,
    le Thaylur, le Tailliour, or
    le Taillur
  Peter, 79
  Ralph, 109
  Richard, 136
  Robert, 81, 110, 112
  Roger, 50, 96
  Simon, 85
  Thomas, 72
  Walter, 104
  William, 18
Talbot, Alice, 135
  Richard, 135
de Talewrth, John, 26
  Robert, 26
de Tamworth, John, 122, 139
Tanfeld, Robert, 228
de Tangel, Ernald, 54
  Matilda, 22
  Walter, 22
de Tangelegh, or de Tangeleye
  Agnes, 89
  Thomas, 89
  William, 89
Tank, William, 141
le Tanner, le Tannere, or le Tan-
    nur
  Adam, 115 (2), 137
  Adam fil' John, 89
  Agnes, 69
  Brice, 135
  Emma, 63
  John, 89
  Lucy, 89
  Margaret, 86, 216
  Ralph fil' Robert, 69
  Robert, 86
  Robert fil' William, 216
  Thomas, 63
de Tanrugge, Godfrey, 91 (2)
  William, 91 (2), 98
de Tarente, William, 222
Tasburgh, Edmund, 202
Tassel, Bartholomew, 59
  Margery, 59
Tatersale, Robert, 173
de Tatlesfeld, Walter, 17
de Tauresio, Isabel, 66
  Peter, 66
Taverner, Idonia, 142
  Robert, 142
le Taverner, Agatha, 81
  Roger, 81

le Tayllur, or le Tayllour, *see* le
    Taillour
Taylord, John, 187
le Taynturer, le Teynturer, or le
    Tynterer
  Alice, 37, 39
  David, 37
  Gilbert, 39
  Thomas, 25
Tebald, Agnes, 168
  John, 168
de Teill, Aulbrey, 10
le Teler, Gilbert, 10
Telgherst, Agnes, 158
  John, 158
Tellekin, Alured, 15
de Temeford, Alice, 105
  John, 105
de Temes Ditton, Robert, 32
le Templer, Peter, 31, 32
Tendale, Alice, 181, 185
  Robert, 181, 185
Tendryng, Robert, 232
Tenrig, or Tenrugge
  Adam, Prior of, 19
  Humfrey, Prior of, 41
  Nicholas, Prior of, 51
  Thomas, Prior of, 13
de Terling, Thomas, 49
Terry, Simon, 228
Ters, John, 166, 167
Testard, Felicia, 42
  Richard, 34, 42
  Thomas, 20
  William, 6, 9, 14, 15
de Tetteburi, Richard, 67 (2)
Teveray, Hugh, 226
Tewersle, Teweresle, or Tuerslee
  Alice, 167 (2)
  John, 167 (2)
  Richard, 165
le Teynturer, *see* le Taynturer
Textor, Gilbert, 14
de la Tey, or de la Thye
  Adam, 16, 26
le Thaylur, *see* le Taillour
Thebaud, or Thebaut
  Nicholas, 43
  William, 70
le Thecchere, Johanna, 155
  Simon, 155
Thedric, Gilbert, 41
  Mabel, 41
fil' Thedruc, Simon, 20

INDEX NOMINUM.

Thetcher, John, 198
Tholy, *see* Toly
Thomas, Johanna, 178
    John, 178
fil' Thomas, Gilbert, 36
    Alice, wife of, 36
    John, 35
    William fil' William, 35
de Thorbern, William, 98
Thorberne, Juliana, 93
    Walter, 93
Thorley, John, 184
atte Thorn, John fil' Hugh, 65
    Matilda, 65
Thorne, John, 148, 158
    Margaret, 148
    Thomas, 148
de Thorne, Alice, 106
    Peter, 106
Thornebury, John, 227
Thorney, Roger, 205
Thornton, Amy, 198
    Robert, 198
de Thoron, Richard, 136
Thorp, John, 179
    William, 176
de Thorp, or de Torp
    Alexander, 16, 20, 23
    Alice, 52, 116
    Avice, 44
    Emma, 79
    Henry, 79, 99, 103
    Isabel, 99, 103
    Johanna fil' Ralph, 84
    John, 52, 84, 116, 147
    Ralph, 44
T'hoursway, Agnes, 138
    John, 138
Threle, John, 197
de Thrikyngham, or de Trikyngham
    Lambert, 90, 217
de Thunderle, Margery, 67, 69
    Reginald, 67, 69
de Thunebrigg, Roger, 26
Thurbarn, or Thurbern
    Beatrice, 134, 140
    Gilbert, 74
    Johanna, 150
    Nicholas, 134, 140
    Ralph, 135, 139
    Thomas, 150
fil' Thurstan, Seman, 15
Thurston, John, 156

de Thurstan, or de Thurston
    Edmund, 72
    Henry, 76
Thwayt, Thomas, 152
Thwaytes, Margaret, 184
    William, 184, 185, 187, 188, 190, 191
Thwaytis, Thomas, 202
de la Thye, *see* de la Tey
Thyrsk, William, 186
de Tichefeld, John, 133
    Matilda, 133
de Tichesey, de Ticheseye, de Tichseye, or de Tycheseye
    Agnes, 12
    Eustace, 214
    Godfrey, 2
    John, 12, 13, 14, 16 (3), 35, 214
    Richard, 19
    Robert, 15
    Thomas, 47, 55, 58, 62
    Viviana, 19
    William fil' Odo, 2
Tichesey Church, Geoffrey, Parson of, 23
de Tidilmynton, John, 103
de Tighele, Avice, 87
    John, 87
le Timbermonger, or le Tymbermongere
    Adam, 36 (2)
    John, 58, 59
    Julia, 58, 59 .
de Tinbreg, Walter, 10
Tirwhit, William, 131
de la Toche, John fil' Adam, 119
de Tochewyk, Thomas, 116
le Tollere, Robert, 118
    Rose, 118
Toly, or Tholy
    Agnes, 117
    Alice, 138
    Edward, 117
    John, 138
    Peter, 7, 70 (3), 73
Tolymond, William, 178
Tom, Alvina, widow of, 7
    Gilbert fil', 7
de Tom, Roger fil' William, 8
Tonebrugge, Roger, 141
Tony, William, 14
Topplere, William, 14
Topy, William, 137
Tortington, Reyner, Prior of, 35

de Totchewyk, Thomas, 104
Totehale, Agnes, 134
    Richard, 134
de Totenhale, Edmund, 53
    Margery, 53
de Totenham, Letice, 110
    Peter, 98, 110
de Tothill, or de Tothull
    Alexander, 53
    Emma, 53
    Felicia, 49
    Stephen, 70
    William, 49
de Tournenfray, Dionisia, 75
    Mathew, 75
Tournour, Johanna, 134
    John, 134
Tracy, John, 226
Trapes, Alice, 148
    Robert, 148
Trappe, Agnes, 108
    John, 108
atte Trave, John, 225
de Traz, Herlewin, 9
Trennayle, Thomas, 197
le Treur, Adam, 43, 45, 49
    Elicia, 43, 45, 49
    Robert, 39
Trewe, Agnes, 207
    Richard, 207
de Trie, *see* de Trye
Trigge, Emma, 130
    William, 130
Trofford, William, 153
Tropmell, Avelina, 3
    Walter, 3
Trug, Olivia, 50, 59
    William, 50, 56, 57, 59
de Trumpeton, Robert, 37, 212
Trumpyngton, Alice, 161
    John, 161
Trussebut, Laurence, 165
Trut, Katharine, 114
    Richard, 114
de Trye, or de Trie
    Cristiana, 22
    Geoffrey, 33
    Giles fil' Luke, 26
    Idonea, 33
    Luke, 22
de Tudenham, William, 121
Tudham, Andrew, 204
    John, 192
Tuerslee, *see* Tewersle

Tukke, Margery, 80
    William, 80
Tumby, John, 144
atte Tunbregge, John, 113
Tunebrigg, John, Prior of, 26
de Tunstalle, Johanna, 103, 117
    Nicholas, 103, 117
    William, 76
Turbervyle, or Turburvyle
    Robert, 200, 201
Turbut, Andrew, 28, 34
    Matilda, 28
fil' Turebut, Turebut, 5
Turgis, or Turgys
    Geoffrey, 49
    Katharine, 107 (2), 108, 109
    Matilda, 49
    Maurice, 107 (2), 108, 109
    Simon, 92
Turk, Idonea, 113
    Walter, 113
Turney, John, 90
    Matilda, 90
de Turnham, or de Turneham
    Edelina, 8, 212
    Stephen, 8, 212
Turnour, Alice, 167
    John, 167, 229
    Margery, 229
le Turnur, Matilda, 40
    Robert, 40
Turpyn, Cecilia, 70
    John, 70
de Turri, Robert, 12
Turton, George, 209 (2)
Tuttebury, Roger, 166
    Thomas, 223 (2)
de Twangham, Richard, 47
Twisaday, Thomas, 200
atte Twychene, Alice, 83
    John, 83
    William, 123
de Twyford, Robert, 84
de Twyneham, Walter, 131
de Twywell, Geoffrey, 117
Tycheburne, Thomas, 229
de Tychefeld, Walter, 53
de Tycheseye, *see* de Ticheseye
de Tychewell, Hugh, 67
atte Tyele, Johanna, 116
    Ralph, 116
le Tyg, Matilda, 16
    Robert, 16
Tygre, John, 78

Tykkell, Tykkyll, Tykhill or, Tykhull
   Henry, 200, 201, 202
   Ralph, 202
Tylare, Philip, 143
de Tyle, Avice, 94
   John, 94
Tylle, Alice, 209
   Thomas, 209
le Tymbermongere, see le Timbermonger
Tymmell, William, 174
Tyndale, John, 175
Tyngewyke, Agnes, 174, 178 (2)
   William, 174, 178 (2)
Tyngylden, or Tynkylden
   Richard, 196, 199
le Tynterer, see le Taynturer
Typet, John, 130
Tyrell, Anna, 226
   Richard, 226
   Thomas, 228
de Tytyngge, Henry, 120
de Tywele, Aylwyn, 48
   Margaret, 48
Tywell, Robert, 202

de Udelicote, Thomas, 118
Ufford, Isabel, 147
   John, 147
de Ulsefeld, Cristiana, 35
Umfray, or Umfrey
   John, 172, 179
Underdych, John, 155
Underheld, or Underhelde
   John, 159, 175
Underhill, or Underhyll
   Elizabeth, 210
   John, 193
   Richard, 210
Upfold, Hugh, 164
   Johanna, 164
Upnore, Elizabeth, 229
   John, 229
Uppelegh, William fil' Hugh, 101
de Upton, Geoffrey, 117
   Isabel, 117
   Johanna, 99, 106
   John, 99
   Philip, 129
   Roger, 19
   William, 106
Upton, Johanna, 160
   Nicholas, 160

Urry, Walter, 174
de Uttewrth, see de Otteworth
de Uttokeshather, Robert, 109
Uvedale, Anna, 196
   Thomas, 196
   William, 227
de Uvedale, Isabel, 86
   John, 68 (2), 86, 140
   Margaret, 121
   Thomas, 115, 121
   William, 68 (2)
atte Uvere, Emma, 75
   William fil' William, 75

de la Vache, Richard, 45
de Vadis, William, 40
Valance, or Valaunce
   Robert, 167, 174
Vale, Johanna, 122
   Margery, 158
   Peter, 122
   William, 158
de Valetort, see de Vautort
de Vallibus, William, 24
de Valoynes, or de Valeignes
   Hamo, 22
   Ladereyna, 60
   Matilda, 2
   Robert, 2
Vampage, John, 227
Van, or Vanne
   John, 81
   John fil' John, 96
   Stephen, 107, 108
   Margaret, 107, 108
Vanner, or Vannere
   Henry, 143, 223
le Vaps, Agnes, 118
   Michael, 118
Vaus, Robert, 194
de Vautort, de Valetort, or Vautort
   Alice, 214
   Johanna, 123
   John, 73, 74, 123, 214
Vavasour, Alice, 201
   Henry, 201
le Vavasour, Robert, 79
le Veil, Goldina, 19
   Richard, 19
le Veille, Richard, 90
atte Velde, Peter, 90
de la Venele, Isabella, 54
   Henry, 54
Venour, William, 162, 188, 227

le Venour, Agnes, 113
   William, 113
Ventre, Elena, 96
   John, 96
de Ver, *see* St. John of Jerusalem
de Verlay, Thomas, 68
de Verney, Margery, 88
   Walter, 88
Vernon, Johanna, 198, 199, 200
   William, 198, 199, 200
le Verrer, Margery, 85
   Nicholas, 85
Vese, John, 211
   Margaret, 211
Vicars, Thomas, 208
le Vinetor, William, 47
Vinitor, Lecia fil' Walter, 6
Virley, Alice, 159, 162, 174
   Richard, 159, 162, 174
Virse, Agnes, 163
   Richard, 163
de Visia, Beumunde, 59
Vitdeners, Vitdeniers, or Wytdeniers
   Agnes, 35
   Alice, 35
   Alice fil' Philip, 28
   Philip, 5, 12, 13 (2)
Vobe, Robert, 226
Vocatour, Thomas, 199
Vyel, Cecilia, 56
   Thomas, 56, 93
Vygerous, William, 105
Vylers, Agnes, 151
   John, 151
Vyncent, Alice, 139
   John, 139, 154
atte Vyne, Johanna, 142
   John, 70
   Richard, 142
   Sarra, 70
Vynent, Thomas, 157
Vynt, Robert, 152, 154
Vytele, Walter, 173

Wacche, John, 142
Wace, Hawyse, 38
   Walter, 38
de Wachesham, John, 74
Waddon, Nicholas, 226
de Waddon, Andrew, 25
   Avice, 25
Wadelehurst, Adam, 138
   Agnes, 138

Wadelehurst, John, 138
Waddysle, John, 159
   Stephen, 138
Wadlose, Emma, 202
   Henry, 202
de Waie, Robert, 7 (2)
   Roger, 50
Wake, Thomas, 228
Wakefeld, William, 149
de Wakeherst, William, 19
Wakeherst, or Wakehurst
   Richard, 164, 174, 181, 225
Waker, Edward, 199
   Margery, 199
Wakeryng, John, 227
de Walberton, John, 100
   William, 100, 149
Walbroun, Thomas, 148
Waldecart, Robert, 80
Walden, John, 165
   Roger, 161
Waldeshef, Johanna, 83
   Walter, 83
de Waldon, Ralph, 68
de Walecote, Alice, 18
   Richard, 18
   Roger, 18
de Waleden, Alice, 80
   Richard, 80
de Walehale, Geoffrey, 50 (2)
   Matilda, 50
Walemund, Henry, 39
Walensis, Gilbert, 14
Waleram, Henry, 206
Walerand, Gilbert, 25
Walesby, William, 189
Walet, John, 143
de Waleton, Adam, 58
   Beatrice, 37
   Gilbert, 4
   Isabel, 58
   John, 4, 82
   Juliana, 82
   Leneva, 58
   Luke, 8
   Robert, 2, 29, 37, 58, 82
   William, 85
Walewayn, or Walwayn
   John, 89 (2), 90
Waleys, Agnes, 138
   John, 168
   William, 138
le Waleys, Richard, 28
Walford, John, 157

INDEX NOMINUM. 315

de Walingford, *see* de Walyngford
Walkelyn, Isabel, 87, 88
    John, 87, 88
Walle, Emma, 125
    Thomas, 125
atte Walle, Cristina, 92
    John, 92
Waller, Johanna, 182
    Richard, 227
    Thomas, 182
de Walleworth, *see* Walworth
Wallyng, Isabella, 169
    William, 169
Walshe, or Walsshe
    Alice, 196
    John, 196
    William, 141
Walsheman, Alice, 114
    Margaret, 114
Walsyngham, Alan, 169
Walter, Alice, 155
    Henry, 203
    Johanna, 195
    John, 155
    William, 195
atte Walter, Robert fil' William, 105
fil' Walter, Reginald, 25
    Walter, 6
Waltham, Richard, 149, 152
Waltham, Symon, Abbot of, 41
de Waltham, Cristiana fil' Gilbert, 67
    Gilbert, 61, 67 (2)
    Isabel, 58, 101
    Isabel fil' Gilbert, 67
    Richard fil' Gilbert, 61
    Roesia fil' Gilbert, 67
    Thomas, 58, 101
    Thomas fil' Gilbert, 61, 67
Walton, William, 168, 192
Walwayn, *see* Walewayn
Walworth, John, 160
    Margaret, 179
    William, 179
de Walworth, or de Walleworth
    Margaret, 140 (3)
    William, 139, 140 (3), 143
de Walyngford, or de Walingford
    Alice, 64, 112
    Bartholomew, 103
    John, 64, 112 (2)
Wambergh, Peter, Vicar of, 98

de Wandeleswurth, de Wandeswurth, de Wandeswrde, de Wandleswrd, de Wendleswrth, de Wendlesworth, or de Wendleswurth
    Herbert, 3
    John, 46 (2), 47
    Juliana, 3
    Pentecost, 1, 11
    William, 21, 27, 32, 54
de Wansted, Baldewin, 101
Wantele, John, 155
de Wanting, Agatha, 95
    William, 95
de Wapfold, Nicholas, 25
Waram, Thomas, 182
Warbelton, William, 226
Warberton, or Warbulton
    Isabella, 172
    John, 172
de Warblington, or de Warblinton
    Thomas, 31, 41
    Thomas fil' William, 53
Warboys, William, 198
Warde, Cristofer, 199
    Juliana, 118
    William, 118
le Warde, Robert, 101
Wardedu, John, 142
Warden, Agnes, 187
    Thomas, 165, 187
Ware, Richard, 167
atte Ware, Giles, 115
    Margery, 115
Wareham, Thomas, 229
Warham, Thomas, 190, 192 (2)
    William, 191
fil' Warin, Geoffrey, 64, 66
    Johanna, wife of, 64, 66
    Walter, 16
de Waring, John, 40
Warley, *see* Worley
de Warlingehem, William, 9
de Warmyngton, or de Wermyngton
    Richard, 139, 143
Warner, Geoffrey, 3
    Robert, 227
    Thomas, 203
de Warnham, Walter, 126, 131-136
    William, 132
le Warnyr, Alice, 58
    Richard, 58

Warre, Agnes, 209
  William, 209
la Warre, John, 40
Warreham, Thomas, 185, 186, 188, 191, 192
Warrenne, William, Earl, 13, 213
de Warrenne, John, Earl of Surrey, 45, 51, 52, 98, 100, 101
de Warwik, de Warwyk, or de Warewyk
  Alan, 97, 113
  Emma, 97, 113
  Juliana, 25
    Johanna, sister of, 25
  Richard, 25
Waryn, John, 147
  Margaret, 147
Waryng, John, 159
Wastell, Agnes, 192
  John, 192
Wasthuse, Margaret, 137
  Stephen, 137
de Watdone, Henry, 50
atte Water, atte Watre, or atte Watere
  Adam, 140
  Alice, 63 (2)
  Edith, 125
  Johanna, 81, 142
  John, 81, 125, 142
  Matilda, 142
  Richard, 176
  Robert, 81
  Thomas, 63 (2)
de la Watere, Avice, 52
  Richard, 52
de Watervill, or de Wattervill
  Alma, 18
  Egidia, 27
  Robert, 18 (2)
  William, 27
de Watevile, de Watevill, or de Watville
  Agnes, 57
  Peter, 57
  Robert, 34
  William, 20, 36
Watford, Mariota, 123
  William, 123
de Watford, John, 131
  Margaret, 131
atte Watre, *see* atte Water
de Wattervill, *see* de Watervill
Wattys, Thomas, 193

de Wauerchyn, John, 114
Waukelin, 31
  Beatrice, wife of, 31
Waukelin, Richard, 29, 43
  Lucy, 43
de Waure, or de Wauere
  Cristiana, 72 (3), 73, 77, 82, 110
  William, 72 (3), 73, 77, 82, 110
de Wauton, Alice, 213
  Bogo, 78 (2)
  John, 68, 213
  Margery, 78
  William, 10
Wauton-on-the-Hill, Stephen, the Parson of, 174
Wavendon, Nicholas, 133
Waverle, or Waverleg
  Gyffard, Abbot of, 28 (2)
  John, Abbot of, 2, 5
Waynflete, Simon, 184
le Wayte, William fil' John, 84
de Wdebam, *see* de Wodeham
Webbe, Johanna, 153
  John, 159
  Richard, 128
  Matilda, 128
  William, 198
le Webbe, Felicia, 135
  Gilbert, 80
  Gunnilda, 80
  Henry, 135
  Matilda, 80
  Richard, 129
  Robert, 80
  Thomas, 100
Wedowysson, Isabella, 189
  John, 189
  William, 189
Wegge, Matilda, 157
  Robert, 157
Weggewode, William, 139
de Welaund, Thomas, 57
Welbek, John, 195
  Richard, 195, 196
  William, 195, 196
Welburn, Cecilia, 147, 153
  John, 147, 153
Welde, John, 147
  Margaret, 147
le Welere, Agnes, 39
  John, 39
de Welkestede, or de Wolkenestede
  Alice fil' Alice, 47

de Welkestede, or de Wolkenestede
    Amice fil' Alice, 47
    Clemence fil' Alice, 47
    Gilbert, 71
atte Welle, Hawise, 220
    Johanna, 160, 166
    John, 176 (2)
    John fil' Nicholas, 122
    Matilda, 176
    Nicholas, 122
    Richard, 118
    William, 160, 166, 173
Weller, Cristiana, 179
    John, 192
    Richard, 179
Welles, John, 176
de Welles, Odierna, 130
    Thomas, 130
Wellesworth, or Welusworth
    Clarice, 78 (2)
    Roger, 78 (2)
Welton, Johanna, 171
    Thomas, 171
de Welwes, John, 45 (2)
    Matilda, 45 (2)
de Welwyk, Henry, 45
    Margery, 45
Wely, Thomas, 155
Wenbrigge, Johanna, 128
    John, 128
Wenche, Johanna, 51
    William, 51
de Wendlesore, *see* de Windesoure
de Wendleswrth, de Wendlesworth, or de Wendleswurth, *see* de Wandeleswurth
Wenge, John, 143
de Wengham, Walter, 64
Wenright, Clemence, 211
    Richard, 211
Wentebrigg, John, 143
Wenton, John, 176
    Katharine, 176
Wermere, John fil' Thomas, 80
le Wermore, Emma, 92
    John, 92
de Wermyngton, *see* de Warmyngton
Wesenham, Thomas, 190, 192
le Wessere, Simon, 10
West, Clement, 40
    Emma, 40
    Geoffrey, 115
    Isabel, 58
    Juliana, 115

West, Robert, 148, 152
    Thomas, 172, 210
    Walter, 58
    William, 172
de Westbrok, Bona, 104
    Robert, 104
    Robert fil' Richard, 72
Westbroke, Alice, 209
    Johanna, 206
    John, 197, 199, 202
    Thomas, 209
Westbury, Alice, 145
    John, 145
de Westcote, Avice, 16
    Giles, 31
    Richard, 16
Westminster, the Abbot of, 212
    Ralph, the Abbot of, 6, 37
    Richard, the Abbot of, 19
    William, the Abbot of, 10
de Westminster, Edith, 77
    Edward, 212
    Odo, 49, 56, 57
Westmoreland, or Westmerland
    Ralph, Earl of, 190 (2), 228
    Margaret, Countess of, 190 (2), 228
de Westok, Avice, 66
    Walter, 66
Weston, Elizabeth, 165
    Idonia, 162
    Johanna, 150, 151 (2), 157, 192
    John, 157, 167, 172, 178, 192, 224
    Milicent, 157
    Robert, 165, 199
    William, 150, 151 (2), 157, 162, 168 (2), 195
de Weston, Alice, 63
    Idonia, 138, 140
    Johanna, 111, 136, 223
    John, 35, 138, 140
    Margery, 105
    Matilda, 42, 97
    Nicholas, 75
    Robert, 28
    Robert fil' David, 42
    Swan, 25
    Thomas, 35, 97, 111 (2)
    Thurstan fil' Geoffrey, 25
    William, 63, 96, 105 (2), 136, 223
de West Pirle, John, 95
    Juliana, 95

de West Pirle, William fil' John, 95
de Westwod, or de Westwode
    Cristiana, 20
    Giles, 20
    John, 60
    Letitia, 60
de Westwyk, Hugh, 140
    John, 68 (2)
    Margery, 68 (2)
de Wetham, Roger, 61
Wether, Lucy, 183
    Richard, 183
de Wetherdeleye, Robert, 138
Wethewelle, Letice, 156
    Roger, 156
le Weyte, Alice, 25
    Geoffrey, 25
Wharff, Thomas, 184
Wheler, or Whelere
    John, 155, 166, 198
    Thomas, 198
le Whelere, Ralph, 67
Whenelare, Margaret, 162
    Richard, 162
Wheoly, Thomas, 165
Wherwell, or Wherewell
    Abbess of, 23, 25 (2), 26
    Mabel, Abbess of, 53
Whissh, Whisshe, Whyssh, or Whysh
    Henry, 107, 109, 111, 112, 115, 116 (2), 153, 155, 165
    Johanna, 153, 155, 165
    Katharine, 107, 109, 111, 112, 115, 116 (2)
White, or Whyte
    Alice, 188
    John, 156
    Robert, 191, 192, 225
    Thomas, 188
de Whitewell, John, 139, 143
Whithors, or Whythors
    Elizabeth, 162
    Ralph, 162
    Walter, 138
de Whitteby, Robert, 223
Whityngham, Robert, 224
Whyssh, or Whysh, see Whissh
Whyte, see White
le Whyte, Hawyse, 98
    Margery, 123
    Richard, 98
    Thomas, 123
Whythors, see Whithors

de Wicford, de Wycford, de Wykford, de Wikeford, de Wykeford
    Alexander, 3, 9, 11
    Alice, 81
    Isabel, 9
    John, 53, 71
    Margaret, 53, 71
    Margery, 65
    Roland, 81
    Thomas, 65
    Walter fil' Arnold, 90
de Wico, William, 2
de Wicsted, Alexander, 10
de Wicton, or de Wichton
    Alan, 2, 3 (2), 4, 6
de Wicumb, Sailda, 10
    William, 10
de Widewell, William, 23
de Widmerpol, Durand, 78 (2), 218
de Wigepol, Andrew, 24
    Mabel, 24
    Walter, 24
de Wik, de Wyk, or de Wyke
    Alice, 13 (3), 14, 80
    Amisius, 31
    Ascelina, 13, 24, 26
    Clement, 64
    Johanna, 83
    John, 13 (3), 14, 62, 63 (2), 80, 83, 89, 94
    Lecia, 21
    Margery fil' Richard, 26
    Ralph, 13
    Richard, 83
    Robert, 21
de Wikeford, see de Wicford
de Wikkewane, William, 88
Wilde, or Wylde
    Humfrey, 207
    John, 201, 204, 207
Wilkynson, Thomas, 199
Willam, Agnes, 137
    Richard, 137
Willershey, or Willersey
    John, 164, 166, 168
William, Johanna, 180
    John, 180, 189
    Robert, 168, 189
fil' William, Elias, 29
    Frechisant, 14
    Gilbert, 29
        Rose, wife of, 29
    Henry, 21

INDEX NOMINUM. 319

fil' William, John, 38,'49
    Lawrence, 26, 27, 28 (2)
    Peter, 38
    Richard, 7
    William, 213
Willoughby, or Willughby
    Edward, 200
    Hugh, 226
    Margaret, 226
Winchester, Godfrey, Bishop of, 6
    William, Bishop of, 195, 230
    William Wykeham, or de
        Wykeham, Bishop of, 148,
        150, 152, 165
de Windesoure, de Wyndesore, de
    Windeshores, de Wyndlesor,
    de Windlessores, de Wynde-
    sor, de Winlesore, or de
    Wendlesore
    Hugh, 8, 11, 18, 23, 26
    Hugh fil' Hugh, 47 (2)
    John, 54 (2), 120, 122 (2)
    Philip, 5
    Richard, 47 (2)
    Walter, 1
de Wintersell, de Wintreshull, de
    Wintershull, de Wyntersell,
    de Wyntreshull, de Wyntere-
    hill, or de Wyntereshull
    Beatrice, 33, 37, 43, 62, 213
    Francis, 98
    Henry, 61
    Johanna, 60
    John, 37, 41, 60
    Juliana, 98
    Margaret, 9
    Peter, 50
    Robert, 9
    William, 33, 37, 43, 44, 46, 62, 213
de Witemersse, Henry, 35
de la Witesand, Thomas, 20
Witewell, John, 130
    Matilda, 130
Wityngham, Robert, 171
le Wlf, Gilbert, 58
    Margery, 58
fil' Wlwold, Matilda, 6
Wodbat, or Wodebat
    Peter, 116
    Richard, 91 (2)
Woddesdon, Isabella, 174
    Richard, 174
Wode, Elizabeth, 193

Wode, Johanna, 206, 211
    John, 15, 193
    Robert, 191
    Thomas, 198, 206, 211, 231
    William, 190, 199, 204
atte Wode, Adam, 132
    Henry, 153
    Isabella, 173
    John, 140, 173
    Juliana, 77, 106
    Laurence, 140
    Margery, 119
    Peter, 115, 116 (2), 119, 134,
        140, 143, 150, 155
    Petronilla, 143, 155
    Reginald, 147
    Roger, 137
    William, 77, 106, 175
de la Wode, Alice, 53
    Peter, 53
Wodecok, Elyot, 201
    Henry, 200, 201, 203, 205
de Wodecote, de la Wodecote, de
    Wudecote, or de la Wudecote
    Agnes, 45
    Alured fil' Walter, 36
    Cecilia, 36
    Hamo, 18
    Richard, 20
    William fil' Baldric, 45
de Wodeford, John, 117
atte Wodehacche, Robert, 137
de Wodeham, de Wodham, de
    Wudeham, or de Wdeham
    Adam, 4, 5, 112
    Isabel fil' James, 27
    James, 48, 97
    James fil' James, 60
    Katharine, 217
    Miles, 107
    Reginald, 125
    Reginald fil' Robert, 99
    Robert, 95
    Sarra, 34
    Sibil, 95
    Simon fil' Simon, 217
    Walter fil' Robert, 95
Wodehouse, John, 226
Wodeland, or Wodelond
    Johanna, 153
    Walter, 126, 153
Wodelef, John, 147
    William, 147
Wodeloc, Roger, 69

Wodemersthorne, Peter, parson of, 66
Woderone, John, 156, 157
Woderowe, Walter, 10
Wodesdon, Dionis, 200
    John, 200
de Wodesham, Letice fil' Robert, 100
    Margery fil' John, 100 (2)
    Matilda, 100
Wodeward, Johanna, 186, 187
    John, 229
    Richard, 186, 187
Wodford, Robert, 206
Wodham, Elizabeth, 205
    John, 205
Wody, Elizabeth, 203
    William, 203
Wodye, Dionisia, 137
    William, 137
Woghere, John, 181
    Margery, 181
    Richard, 154
Wokkyng, Richard, 170
Wolbergh, Margaret, 165
    Nicholas, 165
de Wolhampton, Johanna, 131
    John, 131
de Wolkenestede, see de Welkestede
Wolmar, Richard, 77
de Wolneston, John, 83
Wolseley, Ralph, 195
de Wolveston, Johanna, 78
    John, 78
fil' Wolward, John, 20
Woneham, Margaret, 207
    Robert, 207
de Wonham, William, 3
Woppefold, John, 166
    Matilda, 166
Worcester, John, Bishop of, 221
de Worldham, John, 123
Worley, or Warley
    Henry, 210, 211
    Nicholas, 210
Worsley, Seth, 229
Worsop, John, 204
Worsted, Agnes, 149
    John, 149
de Worstede, John, 123
Worthington, Robert, 198
Wortyngge, William, 140
Wotton, or Wotten
    Elizabeth, 178

Wotton, or Wotten
    Johanna, 173
    John, 188
    Nicholas, 178
    Robert, 173, 178
de Wouburn, or de Wuburn
    Adam, 38, 44, 95
    Matilda, 41
    Nicholas, 41
Wower, Johanna, 194
    William, 194
Wrethier, Alice, 207
    John, 207
Wreyford, William, 109
Wrig, Johanna, 166
    Walter, 166
Wronge, Pagan, 16 (2)
Wrotham, Richard, 154
de Wrotting, Edmund, 50 (2)
    Margery, 50 (2)
Wroughton, Henry, 189
    Margaret, 189
Wryght, Elizabeth, 212
    Thomas, 212
Wryther, Alice, 208
    John, 208
de Wuburn, see de Wouburn
de Wudeham, see de Wodeham
Wullowe, Roger, 192
le Wulmangere, Agnes, 66
    Thomas, 66
de Wulurenehampton, Richard, 68
de Wy, John, 88, 104
    Sibil, 88, 104
Wyatt, Henry, 209 (2), 211 (2)
    Richard, 209, 211
de Wycford, see de Wicford
de Wyckele, John fil' Reginald, 116
de Wycliff, Robert, 146
de Wydden, Agnes, 140
    Henry, 140
    Richard, 139, 140
Wyddene, or Wydene
    Nicholas, 173
    Richard, 153
Wydeslade, John, 188*
Wydevyle, Edward, 198
Wydyngton, Robert, 177
Wyfolde, Nicholas, 185
de Wyford, Alice, 77
    Richard, 77
Wygayn, Alice, 91
    Thomas, 91
de Wyggepyrie, William, 98

Wyght, Cecilia, 156
   Thomas, 156
de Wyghton, Katharine, 136
   William, 136
Wyghtryng, Johanna, 197, 199
   William, 197, 199
Wygyndeune, William, 175
de Wyk, or de Wyke, *see* de Wik
atte Wyk, or atte Wyke
   Isabel, 72
   Thomas, 72
   Walter, 42
Wyke, Agnes, 161
   Peter, 161
   Stephen, 162
de Wykeford, or de Wykford, *see* de Wicford
de Wykeham, John, 151, 152
   Nicholas, 157 (2)
   Peter, 151, 152
   William, *see* Bishop of Winchester
Wykes, Henry, 208
Wykwan, or Wykwane
   Henry, 111 (2), 112, 113, 115, 116 (2), 118, 119, 120, 121, 220
de Wykyngeston, William, 58
de Wylburham, Emma, 214
   William, 214
Wylcombe, Agnes, 167
   Peter, 167
Wylde, *see* Wilde
de Wylden, Richard, 139
atte Wyle, or atte Wylle
   Richard, 109, 132
   Thomas, 168
Wylegyng, Johanna, 91
   Richard, 91
de Wylehal, William, 213
Wyleman, Sibil, 47
   William, 47
Wylewes, Henry, 142
de Wylforde, Cristina, 140
   Thomas, 140
Wylkyn, John, 174
atte Wylle, *see* atte Wyle
Wyllot, Agnes, 207
   John, 207
de Wylughby, Elizabeth, 117, 118, 120, 133
   Richard, 117, 118, 120, 133
de Wymbeldon, Dionisia fil' William, 17

de Wymbeldon, Florius, 33
   Isabel, widow of Ralph, 26
Wymeldon, Wymelden, or Wymeldene
   Margery, 159, 172
   Ralph, 167, 173, 174, 177, 178, 181
   William, 155, 158, 159, 164 (2), 172 (3), 177
Wymond, or Wymund
   Agnes, 158
   Henry, 97
   John, 87
   Thomas, 158
le Wympler, William, 25
Wynbussh, Thomas, 194
Wynchester, or Wynchestre
   Emma, 137
   John, 209
   William, 137
de Wynchester, Johanna, 102
   John, 102
Wynclesham, Richard, the Priest of, 162
de Wyndes, William, 38
de Wyndesor, de Wyndesore, or de Wyndlesor, *see* de Windesoure
Wynepol, Alice, 126
   Robert, 126
de Wyngham, John, 41
de Wyngth, Richard, 17
de Wynnesbury, Henry, 221
Wynter, Agnes, 167, 168
   John, 154, 167
   Thomas, 154, 168
de Wyntersell, de Wyntreshull, de Wyntereshill, or de Wyntereshull, *see* de Wintersell
Wyntershill, Wyntereshull, or Wyntershull
   Johanna, 190
   John, 160, 164, 170, 177
   Robert, 182
   Thomas, 190
de Wynton, John, 23
   Matilda, 60
   Michael, 60
   Nicholas, 60
de Wyntryugham, Johanna, 128
   William, 128, 145
Wyppetratel, Henry, 40
de Wyrcestre, William, 119
de Wyrdrawere, Alice, 41
   William, 41

Wyring, Alice, 58
   William, 58
Wysbech, Wysebech, Wysebeche, or de Wysebech
   Alice, 138 (2), 145
   John, 129, 138 (2), 145
   Matilda, 158
   Peter, 143
   William, 158
Wysdom, Juliana, 127
   William, 127
Wysham, Hawyse, 220
   John, 171
   Katharine, 171
   Margaret, 171
   William, 171
de Wyth, Agnes, 127
   Roger, 127
de Wytham, or de Wythham
   Hugh, 70, 93
   Margery, 70
Wyther, Cecilia, 201
Wytheued, Beatrice, 80
   John, 80
de Whythewell, de Wythewell, or de Wytewell
   Alesia, 83, 112
   Cecilia, 98
   Constance, 113
   Gilbert, 80, 89, 98
   John, 108, 113, 124
   Matilda, 124
   William, 70 (2), 83, 112
Wythorn, John, 104
Wytlock, Adam, 61
   Hilditha, 61
Wytte, William, 172
de Wyveleshole, Robert, 46

Yago, Agnes, 108
   John, 108
de Yakeslee, or de Yakesley,
   Alice, 123, 136
   John, 123, 136
Yardburgh, John, 156

de Yatele, de Yatelegh, de Yattelegh, or de Yateleghe
   Isabel, 52, 54 (2)
   Laurence, 52, 54 (2)
   Robert, 30
de Yellyng, John, 115
de Yelverton, William, 228
de Yenefeld, Agnes fil' John, 23
   Isabel, 43, 52, 54
   John, 43, 52, 54
Yepeswych, Beatrice, 154
   Nicholas, 154
Yerd, John, 188
atte Yerd, Richard, 184
Yerdsley, Clement, 226
   Juliana, 226
Yevele, Henry, 145, 154 (2)
   Katharine, 145, 154 (2)
de Yfeld, see de Ifeld
de Yford, Thomas, 37
del Yl, Henry, 15
de Ymbeloge, John, 11
de Ymewurthe, see de Immeworth
Yngeram, see Ingram
de Ynglesham, John, 214
Yngowe, John, 228
de Ynyngefeud, Margaret, 46
Yokflote, Thomas, 158
Yon, Agnes, 64
   Thomas, 64
   Robert, 68, 81
Yong, or Yonge
   Alice, 200 (2)
   John, 176, 200 (2)
   Thomas, 227
   William, 209
York, Thomas, Archbishop of, 223
   Laurence, Bishop of, 229
   Richard, Duke of, 228
   Cecilia, Duchess of, 228
de York, John, 139

la Zouche, Alan, 43
   William, 214

II. INDEX LOCORUM.

ABINGER, Abbyngworth, Abingeworth, Abingewrth, Abingworth, Abyngeworth, or Abyngeworthe, 25, 64, 71, 103, 109, 151, 185, 200, 202, 207 (2)
Abymoure, 204
Addescombe, Adescombe, Adescompe, Addescompe, or Adyscomp, 173, 186, 190, 198, 208, 209
Addington, Adinton, Adington, Adynton, or Adyngton, 18, 24, 28, 29, 32, 116, 124, 141, 159, 170 (2), 171, 191, 201, 203, 217, 219
Adeworth, North, 215
Aillesford, 122
Aldebrok, or Alrebrok, 80, 119, 144, 166
Aldebury, 105, 126, 155, 160, 200, 219, 227
Aldeford, or Alfaude, 15, 125
Aldershote, 222
Aldfold, or Alfold, 78, 203 (3), 206, 225
Aldham, 84, 94
Alresford, New, 175
Apse, Apese, or Aspe, 27, 34, 35, 82, 83 (2), 119, 190
Ardern, 170
Arnyngton, 149
Arpitle, 43
Ash, Asshe, Assche, Assh, or Esche. 40, 48, 81, 86, 87, 92, 112, 144 (2)
Ashtead, Assested, Ashtede, Asshested, Asshestede, or Asshstede, 103, 129 (2), 203, 212, 216, 220, 226
Aston, 185
Awelle, or Awell, *see* Ewell
Awelton, Auton, Aulton, or Awylton, 1 (2), 3 (2), 4 (2), 6, 7 (2)

Axiholm, island of, 135
Axstede, or Aksted, 9, 24, 28, 55

Badshute, 155 (2)
Badynton, or Badyngton, *see* Beddington
Bagshot, Bageset, Baggesayte, Baggeshete, Baggeshote, Baggeshute, Bagschate, Bagshet, Bagshete, or Bagshote, 11, 19, 21, 25, 62, 73, 74, 79, 133, 169, 195, 197, 215, 230
Bandon, or Bendon, 14, 15, 17, 25, 28, 36, 45, 48, 59, 61, 69, 73, 76, 101, 109, 117, 119, 121, 122, 134 (2), 139, 158, 170, 226
Bansted, Banstede, Banested, Bensted, Bendestede, or Benested, 1, 2, 4, 13, 25, 39, 52, 72, 75, 82, 86, 111 (2), 118, 140 (2), 149, 189, 194, 215
Barnes, or Bernes, 120, 153, 199, 202, 209 (2), 215
Battersea, Bacherichesaye, Badricheshee, Badricheshey, Batericheseye, Baterycheseye, Batersey, Batreseye, Batrichesey, Batricheseye, Batrichsaye, Batrichsey, Batrycheseye, Batriseye, Betrechesey, or Patricheseye, 4, 6 (2), 23, 63, 74, 87 (2), 92 (3), 102, 110, 112, 127, 129, 130 (2), 132, 134, 135, 153, 156, 161, 176, 177, 183, 184 (2), 189, 191, 192, 196, 208, 212, 223, 228, 229 (2)
Bechinton, 83
Bechom, 3
Beddington, Badynton, Badyngton, Beddyngton, Bedinton, Bedigton, Bedynton, Bedyngton, Bedynton, Bedyntone, or Bodynton, 11, 12, 14, 15, 17, 31, 35, 44, 51, 58 (2),

62, 65, 70, 73, 75, 77, 81, 82, 83, 88, 91, 92, 94, 98, 99 (2), 101, 102, 109, 115, 116, 117, 119 (2), 120 (2), 122 (2), 125, 131, 132, 133, 139, 140 (2), 144, 146 (2), 154, 159, 161, 163, 164 (2), 169, 170 (2), 174, 177, 186, 188 (2), 191, 196, 201, 203, 204, 220, 222
Bedenescumbe, or Bednescumbe, 100 (2)
Bekenham, Beghenham, or Bekynham, 116, 182, 228
Bencham, or Benchamp, 183, 194, 202
Benchesham, or Benchisham, 14, 17, 37, 40, 106, 138, 154, 162, 165, 185 (2)
Bentele, co. Southampton, 165
Benyngton, 154, 165, 175
Berardesfeld, 74
Bercherst, 11
Bergh, Berges, Bergh, Bruges, Brugge, or Burgh, 4, 5, 9, 14, 21, 29, 37, 42
Berhes, 35
Berkyngge, 122
Bermondsey, Beremundesey, Bermondesey, Bermondeseye, Bermundesey, or Bermundeseye, 12, 31 (2), 33, 63, 70, 71, 73 (2), 75, 78, 79, 84, 105, 108 (2), 121, 123, 140, 142, 144, 148 (2), 152, 161, 164, 176, 185, 187, 198, 211 (2), 216, 218, 219
Bermondsey, St. Mary Magdalene, 176
la Berne, 26
Berners, 75 (2)
Berselegh, *see* Bisley
Berton, 98, 218
Berttemers, 43
Bertyngherst, Bredynghurst, or Bredyngherst, 149, 191, 224
Betchworth, Bechesworth, Bechesworthe, Becchesworth, Becheswrde, Bechisworth, or Bechewrth, 3, 63, 103, 111 (2), 126, 154, 175, 216, 221, 222
—— Est. 27, 56, 57, 59, 74, 107, 119, 151, 168, 169, 175, 229
—— West, 80 (2), 85, 143, 177, 182, 227
Betrecheseye, *see* Battersea
Bettegrave, *see* Britgrave

Beverink, or Boverink, 1 (2), 2
Biddyk, 67
Biflete, or Bifled, *see* Byfleet
Billesersse, or Bylysshersh, 2, 190
Bisley, Berselegh, Busseleye, or Busshelegh, 87, 117, 201
Blakehok, 23
Blechingley, Blachingeleg, Blachingelegh, Blacchynglegh, Blachingeleye, Blecchingleye, Blecchingligh, Blecchynggelegh, Blecchynglegh, Blecchyngleghe, Blecchynglee, Blecchyngley, Blecchyngleye, Blecchynglye, Blecchynlegh, Blechingel, Blechingeleg, Blechingeleye, Blechinglegh, Blechingleye, Blechynglye, Bletchyngeleye, or Bletchynggeleghe, 15, 33, 40, 47, 50, 57, 68, 72, 80, 86, 100, 106, 110, 112, 115, 121, 128, 131, 136 (3), 159 (2), 160, 161, 167, 168, 169 (2), 175, 180, 188, 190, 197 (2), 200, 217, 225
Bodynton, *see* Beddington
Bokelond, *see* Buckland
Bookham, Bocham, Bokham, Bokeham, or Boukham, 47, 52, 65, 90, 136, 208, 219
Bookham, Great, 41, 90 (2), 126, 137, 146, 195, 226
Bookham, Little, 42, 70, 148, 206, 215
Borden, 135
Bradley, or Bradel, 23, 229
Bramley, Brambelegh, Bromblegh, Bromle, Bromlee, Bromleg, Bromlegh, Bromleghe, Bromley, Bromleye, Bromleygh, Bromleyghe, Bromligh, Bromlygh, Bromlyghe, Brumleg, or Brumlegh, 14, 19, 21, 27, 28, 29, 30 (2), 43, 44, 54 (2), 56, 57, 63, 66, 69, 70, 73 (3), 76, 78, 80, 81, 91, 93, 96, 97 (2), 98 (2), 101 (2), 104, 106 (2), 110 (2), 112, 113, 114, 115, 117 (2), 120, 121 (2), 125, 126, 127, 128 (2), 132 (2), 133 (2), 140 (2), 142, 145 (2), 153, 154, 155 (2), 162, 164, 174, 178, 194, 195, 209, 213, 214, 219, 220, 226
Bromlegh-juxta-Guldeford, 87
Brande, 207

INDEX LOCORUM.

Bredyngherst, or Bredynghurst, *see* Bertyngherst
Brewe, 149
Bristowe, 135, 226
Britgrave, Bettegrave, Bretesgrave, or Bryttesgrave, 103, 117, 187, 196, 205
Brittegrene, 152
Brokesbourne, 137
Brokham, or Brocham, 25, 26, 60, 120 (2), 128 (2), 136
Bromham, 88
Bromle, Bromblegh, Bromlegh, Brumleg, or Brumlegh, *see* Bramley
Bruges, or Brugge, *see* Bergh
Brunningesfaud, 119
Brustowe, 179, 222
Buckland, Bokelond, Bokelonde, Bukkelond, or Bukelonde, 62, 68, 188, 192, 227
Budele, or Buddeleg, 17, 33
Burgavenny, 204
Burgh, *see* Bergh
Burgham, or Bourgham, 62, 77, 95, 130, 195, 226
Burstow, Burstowe, Borstowe, Bourstowe, Burghstowe, or Byrstowe, 35, 46, 71, 72, 97, 99 (2), 102, 113, 116, 118, 119, 153, 159 (2), 161, 171 (2), 175, 188, 205, 220, 224, 225 (2)
Busseleye, or Busshelegh, *see* Bisley
Byfleet, Bifled, Biflete, or Byflete, 4, 5, 182, 205 (2)
Bysshecourt, 204

Camberwell, Camberwelle, Cambrewelle, Camerwell, Camerwelle, Camerewell, Camereswell, Kamerwell, Kamerewell. or Kambreswele, 3, 4, 11, 12 (2), 13 (3), 15, 23 (2), 24, 26, 28, 30, 35, 42, 55 (2), 59, 60, 66, 71, 76, 80, 86, 88, 90, 92, 101, 104 (2), 113 (2), 117, 121, 122, 123, 124, 127, 131, 139, 142, 143, 145, 149, 163 (2), 168, 169 (2), 172, 174, 180, 183, 184, 191 (2), 207, 216 (2), 217 (2), 218, 219, 220
Cantebrigg, 93, 94
Capell, or la Capele, 126, 170, 189, 204, 207, 227
Carleton in Lyndrik, 123

Carshalton, Carsalton, Carselton, Carsaulton, Cassalton, Crassalton, Cresalton, Creshalton, Creshaulton, Creshauton, Cressalton, Karsalton, Kershalton, Kersalton, Kersawelton, Kersaulton, Kersauton, or Kershaulton, 14, 22, 28, 35, 36, 39 (2), 51, 52, 56, 58, 61, 65, 68, 71 (4), 83, 85, 87, 91, 93 (2), 94, 98, 99 (3), 104, 106, 110, 116, 118, 119, 120 (2), 123, 130 (2), 132, 139, 140 (2), 144, 146 (4), 154 (2), 163 (2) 164, 168 (2), 175 (6), 177 (2), 184 (2), 186 (2), 190, 191, 192, 204, 211, 212, 226
Caterham, Kateram, Katerham, Katenham, or Katrehamme, 8, 20, 40, 41, 50, 60, 79, 80, 93, 115, 120, 121 (2), 124, 135, 146, 156, 188, 204, 228 (2)
Catteshull, or Cateshulle, 94, 120, 142, 144, 151
Certesey, Certeseye, Certesie, Certheseye, or Certishey, *see* Chertsey
Chabham, Chabeham, or Chabbeham, 40, 46, 47, 57, 83, 94, 101, 108, 114, 123, 131, 132, 138, 141, 142 (2), 146, 163 (2), 188, 204, 215
Chabiedon, 64
Chakedon, 190
Chaldon, Chauvesdone, Chalvedon, Chelvedon, Chalvysdon, or Chauledone, 4, 41, 50, 96, 105, 181, 185
Chalk, 158
Changeton, 117
Charlewood, Charlewode, Cherlwod, Cherlwode, Cherlewod, Cherlewode, Cherlwude, Cherlewude, or Chorlwode, 4, 15, 24, 25, 33, 64, 80, 93, 96, 97, 98, 110, 112, 123, 127, 133, 141, 142, 164, 184 (2), 188 (2), 189, 192, 204, 205, 218, 229
Cheam, Cheham, Cheiham, Cheyham, or Chayham, 4, 35 (2), 173
Cheam, Est, 211
Cheam, West, 109, 114, 125, 152, 180, 189, 193
Chelewrth, or Chelewurth, 19, 23, 24 (2), 34, 53
Chelsham, Chelesham, or Chelles-

ham, 2 (2), 12, 17, 18, 22, 27, 41, 42, 47, 51 (2), 57, 61, 62 (2), 69, 71, 74 (2), 76, 88, 92, 97, 99, 110, 115, 122, 134, 140, 146, 147, 178 (2), 188, 191, 214, 217
Chelvedon, *see* Chaldon
Chenam, Est, 206
Chenam, West, 206
Chepyngnorton, 86
Cherlewod, Cherlewode, Cherlwude, or Cherlewude, *see* Charlewood
Chert, 216
Chertsey, Certesey, Certeseye, Certesie, Certheseye, Certishey, Chartiseye, Chertiseye, Chertesay, Chertesaye, Chertisey, Chertiseye, Chertseye, Chiertesaye, or Chirchsey, 2 (3), 3, 11 (4), 14, 16, 20, 33, 44, 46, 47, 48 (2), 49, 50, 52 (3), 57, 63, 64, 65, (3), 66, 68, 69 (2), 70 (3), 72, 75 (3), 76, 77, 79, 80, 83, 84, 88 (3), 89, 92, 93 (2), 94, 95, 97 (2), 98 (2), 99, 103, 105 (3), 109 (2), 110, 112, 113 (2), 114 (3), 115 (2), 128, 130, 131, 132, 135 (2), 136 (2), 137 (2), 138, 142, 148, 150, 151 (2), 153, 155, 157 (2), 167 (2), 170 (2), 176 (2), 178, 179, 180 (2), 186, 195, 200 (2), 204, 206, 217, 229
Chesington, Chessyngden, Chisseden, Chissenden, Chissingdon, Chissyndon, Chyssendon, Chyssyndon, or Chyssyngdon, 7, 23, 36, 39, 61, 63, 117, 168, 215, 231
Chiddingfold, Chedingefald, Chedingefold, Chedyngefold, Chetyngfaud, Chidingefald, Chidingefold, Chidyngfold, Chudyngfold, Chudyngefold, Chuddynfold, Chuddyngfold, Chuddyngefold, Chuddingfold, Chydingfald, Chydyngfold, or Chydynggefold, 8, 14, 16, 47, 53, 72, 74, 77, 104, 106 (2), 118, 123, 138 (3), 150, 152, 163, 195, 196, 209, 220, 227
Chiertesaye, *see* Chertsey
Chipsted, Chepstede, Chepestede, Chipstid, or Chypstede, 11, 21, 31, 37, 45, 51, 67, 80, 82 (2), 170, 198, 210, 213, 224, 228
Chirchsey, *see* Chertsey
Chorlwode, *see* Charlewood

Clandon, Clendon, or Cleyndon, 4, 26, 115, 129, 133, 145, 150, 195
Clandon, Abbatis, 54
Clandon, Regis, 107
Clandon, Est, 96, 130, 158
Clandon, West, 26, 35, 60, 63, 96, 105, 111, 119
Clapham, Clopham, or Cloppeham, 22, 33, 39, 71 (2), 94, 141, 144 (2), 166, 171, 186, 208, 209, 213, 225, 228, 230
Cleygate, or Cleigat, 6, 166
Clone, 117
Clopton, 141
Codeham, or Codham, 206, 207, 214
Codynton, Codyngton, or Codington, *see* Cuddington
Cokefeld, co. Essex, 191
Colbroke, co. Bucks, 188, 197
Cold Abbey, 202, 210
Colle, Collee, or Colley, 9, 102, 227
Combe, or Coumbe, *see* Cumbe
Compton, Conton, Comton, or Cumpton, 1, 32, 38, 40, 46, 54, 64, 73, 94 (2), 99, 102, 109, 136, 196, 206
Compton-juxta-Guldeford, 90, 109, 159, 169
Compton-juxta-Waverle, 120
Coresbrokes, 61
Coulsdon, Colesdon, Colesdone, Colisdon, Colisden, Colusdon, Colysdon, Coulesdon, Culisdon, or Cullesden, 37, 39, 44, 64, 77, 93, 94, 96, 116, 156, 185, 201, 204, 224
Coveham, or Covenham, 12, 19, 39, 51, 59, 100, 111, 122, 128, 142 (2), 146, 147 (2), 153, 155, 160, 165, 167, 182, 186, 194, 196, 229
Craneford, 24
Cranley, Cranleye, Cranle, Cranlee, Cranlegh, Cranelee, or Craineley, 40, 41, 47, 70, 74, 95, 111, 126, 129, 133, 134, 138, 178, 204, 205, 221, 225, 231
Crassalton, *see* Carshalton
Crauham, Crawham, or Crouham, 111, 215 (2), 216 (2)
Craustok, *see* Crawestok
Craweley, 205
Crawestok, Crawestoke, or Crauestok, 10, 66, 67, 77 (2), 90, 145
Cresalton, Creshalton, Creshaulton,

INDEX LOCORUM. 327

Creshauton, or Cressalton, *see* Carshalton

Crowhurst, Crowehurst, Crowehurste, Crauhurste, Crawhurst, Crowherst, Croweherst, Crowhyrst, Croherst, Crohurst, Crouherst, or Crouhurst, 12, 14, 16 (2), 22, 23 (2), 28, 46, 52, 55, 58, 74, 76, 81, 86, 91 (2), 107, 109, 112, 113 (2), 115, 119, 120, 121, 123, 127, 141 (2), 143 (2), 146, 153, 155, 156, 159 (2), 162 (4), 163, 167, 182 (2), 183, 192, 204, 210, 211 (2), 217, 222, 225

Croydon, Croindon, Croyndon, or Croyndone, 14, 33, 67, 74, 76, 80, 83, 88 (2), 89 (2), 92, 93 (3), 101, 104, 105, 106, 107 (2), 111, 115 (2), 116, 119, 123, 124, 126, 131 (2), 135 (3), 139 (2), 145 (2), 146 (3), 147 (3), 150, 153 (2), 154, 158, 159 (3), 163 (4), 165 (2), 166 (8), 167 (9), 168 (3), 169 (3), 170 (2), 172 (2), 173, 175, 178, 179 (5), 180 (2), 182 (3), 183, 185 (4), 186 (2), 188, 189, 190, 191, 192 (4), 193 (2), 194, 198 (2), 199 (2), 200 (2), 202 (2), 203 (2), 206, 207, 208, 209, 228 (2)

Cuddington, Cudinton, Cudynton, Cudyngton, Codynton, Codyngton, or Codington, 5, 7, 21, 29, 52 (2), 68, 95, 99, 104 (2), 114 (2), 127, 135, 136, 152, 174 (2), 189, 206, 211, 213

Cudeford, 14

Culisdon, or Cullesden, *see* Coulsdon

Cumbe, Combe, or Coumbe, 7, 73, 74, 165

Cumbe, Nevill, or Nevyle, 38, 174

Dalby de Wauz, 41
Danhurst, 20
Dilewis, Dilwysh, Dilwysse, Dylewish, or Dylewysh, 13, 39, 76, 80, 163
Dilewis, West, 113
Ditton, 15, 20, 27, 63, 213, 214, 230
Ditton-on-Thames, 209
Dodington, 78
Dorking, Dorkinge, Dorkinges, Dorkingg, Dorkyng, Dorkynge, or Dorkyngge, 10, 20, 25, 29 (2), 30, 32, 39, 52, 58, 65, 76, 78, 80 (2), 85 (7), 89, 90, 93, 95, 100 (2), 103, 108, 110, 115, 125 (2), 128, 132, 136, 139, 147 (2), 156, 157, 166 (2), 170, 174, 175, 177, 187 (3), 195, 200, 204, 213, 221, 222, 223, 229, 230 (2), 232

Doune, La Doune, Dun, or La Dune, 6, 8, 139, 160
Dounton, 104
Drayton, 151
Dritham, 5
Dun, *see* Doune
Dunsfold, Dunfold, Dounysfold, Duntesfold, Duntesfolde, Dunttesfold, Duntesfaud, Dountesfold, or Dunterfeld, 43, 48, 80, 117, 152, 163, 166 (3), 197, 207, 209
Dunstall, 174
Dylewish, or Dylewysh, *see* Dilewis
Dynesle, 71

Ebsham, Ebesham, or Ebbesham, *see* Epsom
Edenbridge (Pontis Edulfi), 33
Edinton, 3, 11
Effingham, Effingeham, Effyngham, or Effyngeham, 5, 29, 31, 38 (2), 41, 44, 47, 48 (2), 51 (2), 68, 70, 71, 77, 84, 88, 89 (3), 90, 101, 121, 122, 138, 148, 171, 173, 200, 205, 206, 209, 213, 221, 224, 228
Egham, Egeham, Eggeham, Eghtham, or Heggeham, 5 (2), 9, 23, 36, 43 (2), 64, 66, 67, 79, 84 (3), 92, 93, 99, 107, 112, 116, 129-13 137 (2), 138, 139 (2), 147, 14 182, 186, 197, 208, 216, 225-22 229
Eldefolde (*see* also Aldfold), 36
Elesdon, 57
Ellisworth, 98
Elstede, 105, 155
Emelbrugge, or Emilbrugge Hundred, 166, 221
Emworth, *see* Immeworth
Eppewell, 93
Epsom, Ebsham, Ebesham, or Ebbesham, 47, 52, 55, 56, 66, 76, 144, 150, 152, 174
Ertingdon, Ertyndon, Ertyngdon, Ertedon, Ertendon, Ertinden, Irtyndon, Hertindon, or Herting-

don, 25 (2), 26, 40, 58, 62, 66, 70, 71, 87, 94, 98, 102, 103, 106, 107, 126 (2), 134, 137, 144, 151, 153, 155, 161, 170, 178, 182, 191
Ertingdon-juxta-Guldeford, 170
Esche, *see* Assche
Esher, Esere, Eshere, Esschere, or Esshere, 18
—— Episcopi, 165
—— Watevill, Watviles, Watervyle, or Waterville, 57, 150, 165, 191
Eshyng, or Essinge, 48, 72, 168
Esshemeresworth, 91
Esse, *see* Hese
Estbury, 169
Ested, 21, 40
Estwyk, or Estwyke, 219, 223 (2), 227
Eton, 104, 157
Euebrigge, 43
Ewehurst, Uhurst, Iwehurst, or Ywehurst, 46, 67, 78, 104, 128, 202, 222
Ewekene, Eweykene, or Ewakne, 48, 55, 78
Ewell, Ewelle, Awell, or Awelle, 1, 6 (2), 7, 8 (2), 9, 12, 15, 19, 22 (4), 37, 41 (2), 42, 43, 52, 61-63, 71, 80, 97, 99, 109, 114 (2), 118, 127, 135-137, 152, 153, 168, 173, 186, 189, 194
Eylesham, 125
Eyneford, 215, 216 (2)

Fanne, *see* Fenne
Farley, Farleye, Farleygh, Farleg, or Farlegh, 18, 35, 116, 171, 191, 213, 214
Farncumbe, Farnecumbe, Farncombe, or Fernecombe, 54 (2), 94, 100, 143, 158, 209
Farnham, Farnam, Farneham, Farenham, or Fernham, 46, 60, 67, 70 (3), 72, 74, 85 (2), 87 (2), 93 (2), 99 (2), 112, 120, 125 (3), 138, 143, 147, 148 (2), 151, 162, 177, 181, 185, 192, 212, 219, 225
Farn†, 27
Fecham, *see* Fetcham
Felbrygg, 137
Felstede, 152, 156
Feltham, 37
Fenne, or Fanne, 3, 52, 220

Fermesham, 25, 36, 75 (2), 78 (2), 81, 105 (2), 175, 216
Fernham, *see* Farnham
Fernhurst, 75
Fernebergh, or Ferneborowe, 151, 200
Fernecombe, *see* Farncumbe
Ferryng, 189
Fetcham, Fecham, Feccham, Feccham, or Feceham, 5, 8, 27, 33, 89, 124 (2), 130, 141, 145, 153, 157, 161, 164 (2), 172, 205, 206, 210, 211, 218, 219, 223 (2), 227
Finchingfeld, or Fynchyngfeld, 82, 119
Flexwere, 87
Flore, 229
Fosshawe, 220
Frankyngham, 180

Gamelingedene, 2
Garston, 173
Gatecombe, 115
Gaters, 228
Gatton, 12, 13 (3), 21, 28, 102 (2), 134, 166, 208, 210, 229 (2)
Geldeford, *see* Guildford
Gene, 121
Gildeford, *see* Guildford
Gingeston, *see* Kingston
Glastonia, 56
Godalming, Godalmyng, Godalmynge, Godalmyngge, Godelmyng, or Godelmynge, 52, 62, 72, 73, 75, 78, 84, 91 (2), 94-96, 98, 104, 116 (2), 117, 120, 127 (2), 135, 137, 138, 150 (2), 156, 158, 159, 168, 187, 196, 206, 220
Godalming Hundred, 12
Godstone, Goddestone, or Godiston, 188, 205 (2), 207
Gomershall, Gomshelne, Gomeshulne, Gomshulne, or Gumshelf, 59, 61, 104, 128, 132, 160, 176
Goryng, 182
Graweshull, 9
Grenewich, Grenewiche, Grenewych, Grenewyche, or Grenewyk, Est, 187
—— West, 76, 107, 154, 216, 217 (2), 218, 219, 226
Grenstede, Grenstede, or Grenestede, Est, 98, 115 (2), 118, 170, 221

INDEX LOCORUM. 329

Groveshed, 229
Guildford, Gildeford, Gildeforde, Geldeford, Gudeford, Guldeford, Guldeforde, or Gyldeford, 5 (2), 8, 9, 13, 15, 16, 22, 24, 26, 34-36, 39 (3), 41, 42, 44, 47, 48, 50, 51 (2), 52, 53 (4), 54 (2), 55, 58, 59, 60, 62 (2), 63, 66, 70 (3), 71 (3), 72, 76, 77, 84, 87 (3), 90 (3), 94, 96 (2), 97, 98 (2), 102 (2), 103, 106, 107 (2), 108 (3), 110, 114 (4), 115 (2), 116, 125, 126 (2), 127, 128 (3), 131, 133 (3), 134, 135, 137, 140 (2), 141 (2), 144, 145 (3), 148 (3), 150, 152, 153 (3), 155 (2), 156 (2), 158 (2), 161 (2), 164 (2), 165, 166, 168, 170, 172 (2), 174, 178 (2), 180, 181 (3), 182 (3), 184, 187, 189 (2), 191 (3), 194, 198, 200 (2), 203, 208 (2), 209 (2), 222, 227, 229, 230, 232
—— St. Mary, 192, 197
—— St. Nicholas, 196
Guldesburgh, 103
Gumshelf, *see* Gomershall
Gundeslee, 23

Hacstede, 28
Haddarn, 176
Hadley, Hadlee, Hadleg, Hedlegh, or Hedleghe, 9, 30, 136, 160, 164
Hakeney, 172
Halgheford, 5
Hallyngbury, 228
Halresshet, 92
Halstede, 154, 156
Hamelak, 224
Hameledon, 8
Hamme, or Hame, 2, 72, 96, 124, 128, 141, 148, 167, 193, 218, 229
—— juxta-Kyngeston, 183, 219
Hampton, 195
Hampton Est, 86, 120
Hampton Poyle, 227
Hamsted, or Hemstede, 16 (2), 32, 35
Hanlegee, 17
Hascombe, Hascumbe, or Hassecumbe, 35, 43, 69, 70, 72, 197, 207, 220
Haslemere, Haselmere, or Hasulmere, 75, 155, 168, 187
Hastyngs, 230

Hatcham, Hachham, Hachesham, Hacchesham, Hagesham, Hechesham, or Hecchesham, 18, 28, 79 (2), 86, 88, 90, 101, 108, 109, 113, 121, 140, 213 (2), 217-219, 224
—— juxta-London, 220, 224
Haverychesham, 138
Haywode, or Heiwude, 7
—— juxta-Coveham, 69
Hedlegh, or Hedleghe, *see* Hadley
Heggecourt, or Heggecourte, 179, 224
Heggeham, *see* Egham
Hellynglegh (co. Sussex), 226
Hemstede, *see* Hamsted
Hendon, 127
Henley, Henle, or Henlee, 118, 219
—— juxta-Guldeford, 129
Herewardesle, 13
Hermondesworth, 146
Hertford, 132, 160
Hertingdon, *see* Ertingdon
Hertmere, 4, 38 (2), 72
Hese, co. Kent, 178
Hese, Hesse, or Esse, 1, 2, 10, 30 (2), 36
la Hethe, 63
Hethele, or Hethlegh, 155, 224, 226
Hexstede, 190
Heyford, 72, 95, 101, 112
Hocklegh, *see* Ockley
Hoddesdon, 176
Hoke, 33, 117
Holbroc, or Holebrouk, 8, 83
Holecroft, 15
Holeg, 6
Holeherst, 6
Honewaldesham, Honewoldesham, or Hunnewaldeham, 34 (2), 48
Horishill, or Horisull, *see* Horsell
Horley, Horleye, Horlee, Horlie, or Horle, 10, 11 (2), 26, 38, 41 (2), 42, 57, 77, 79 (3), 80, 83, 93 (3), 98, 102, 103, 119, 128, 131, 137 (2), 142, 143, 144, 160, 172 (2), 180, 190, 192 (2), 193, 196, 197, 203, 210, 220, 222, 229
Horne, Hoorne, or Hourne, 92, 106, 116 (2), 118, 135, 139, 141 (2), 144, 151, 159 (2), 171 (2), 175 (2), 203, 204, 205, 220, 225 (2)
Horndon-on-the-Hill (co. Essex), 201

330 INDEX LOCORUM.

Horsell, Horeshull, Horeshulle, Horeswell, Horishill, Horisull, Horsille, Horsull, Horseld, Horshill, or Horshull, 22, 37, 83, 110, 112 (2), 118, 123, 132, 134, 139, 140, 163, 188, 201
Horsham, 116, 126 (3), 190, 220
Horsley, Horsle, Horslee, Horsleg, Horslegh, Horsleghe, Horsley, Horsleye, Horselee, Horseleg, or Horsseleg, 3, 4, 8, 11, 17, 23, 41, 165
—— Est, 26, 40, 47, 62, 68, 69, 80, 84, 85, 101, 118, 130, 148, 167, 190, 205, 206
—— West, 26, 47 (2), 68, 100, 106, 108, 117, 118, 168, 177, 181, 194, 218, 225, 227
Horsmongerlond in Neweton, 211
Horton, 6, 15 (2), 22, 55, 152
Hoteressaham, 10
Houghley, 229
Houwyke, 110
Hunnewaldeham, *see* Honewaldesham
Hynton, 95

Ibenerth, 109
Ifelde, 205
Imbham, or Imham, 168, 206
Immeworth, Immewrth, Imworth, or Emworth, 34, 103, 166, 209, 221
Ingefeld, or Inggefeld, 64, 84 (2), 216
Ingworth, 125
Ipswich, 78
Irtyndon, *see* Ertingdon
Iweherst, *see* Ewehurst
Iwode, 78, 81
Ixnyngge, 111

Jernemue, 38

Kamerwell, *see* Camberwell
Katenham, Kateram, Katerham, or Katrehamme, *see* Caterham
Kayowe, 185
Kembryssheford, 181
Kennersley, *see* Kynworsley
Kennington, Kenynton, or Kenyngton, 51, 110, 210
Kent Co., 163
Kentisshestrete, 198
Kerdesforde, 152

Kersalton, Kersaulton, or Kersawelton, *see* Carshalton
Kingeswude, 4, 8
Kingston, Kingeston, Kingestun, Kinggeston, Kinggestun, Kyngeston, Kyngestone, or Gingeston, 3 (2), 6 (2), 7, 10 (4), 11, 14 (2), 15 (5), 16 (4), 19, 20, 21, 30 (4), 31 (3), 32 (2), 36 (2), 40, 51 (3), 53 (3), 54 (2), 55 (2), 57, 58 (4), 59, 61, 63 (3), 66 (3), 67, 69 (2), 71, 72, 73 (4), 74 (2), 75, 76, 77, 81 (4), 82, 85, 86 (2), 87 (4), 88, 89 (9), 90 (7), 92 (2), 93 (5), 95 (2), 96 (4), 98, 100 (5), 102
—— juxta-Tamisiam, 103, 106 (2), 108, 110, 111, 112, 115, 117 (2), 118, 119, 122 (2), 123, 126, 127, 128 (2)
—— super-Tamisiam, 129, 130 (6), 131, 132 (3), 134 (3), 135 (3), 138 (5), 139 (2), 141 (4), 142 (2), 143 (3), 144, 145, 147 (2), 148, 149 (2), 150 (3), 152, 153 (5), 154, 155 (2), 156, 157 (3), 158 (3), 160, 161 (2), 162 (4), 165, 168, 169 (3), 171, 176, 179, 191, 193, 206, 210, 211, 214, 216 (2)
Kynworsley, or Kennersley, 210, 211

Lagham, Lageham, or Legham, 74, 91 (2), 100, 125 (2), 179, 224
Lambeth, Lambeheth, Lambehethe, Lambehith, Lambehithe, Lambehuth, Lambehythe, Lambheth, Lambhethe, Lambheythe, Lambhith, Lambhithe, Lambhuth, Lambbythe, Lamehith, Lamehuthe, Lamehyth, Lameth, Lamethethe, Lameye, Lamhee, Lamheth, Lamhethe, Lamhith, Lamhithe, Lamhuth, Lamhuthe, Lamhythe, Lamibeth, or Lombeth, 5, 32 (2), 36 (2), 43, 46, 49 (2), 50, 53, 61, 62 (2), 63, 64, 65 (2), 67, 78, 81, 85, 99, 102 (2), 104, 107, 111, 115, 129, 131, 133, 139, 145, 151, 154, 159, 161, 170
—— North, 80, 86, 88, 95, 129, 130, 131, 149 (2), 161, 185, 189
—— South, 20, 24, 36, 56, 57, 59, 69, 70, 168, 171

INDEX LOCORUM.   331

Lambeth Water, 203
Lambythemersh, or Lambehythemarshe, 145, 178
Launcyng, 82
Leddred, Ledered, Ledrede, Ledride, Ledred, or Lederede, *see* Letherhead
Ledling, 17
Legh, Leghe, Leye, or Leygh, 89, 111 (2), 117, 119 (2), 154, 160, 175, 180, 200, 209
le Legh, 157
Lemefeld, Lemensfeld, Lemenesfeld, Lemmesfeld, Lemnefeud, Lemnesfeld, or Lemnysfeld, *see* Limpsfield
Lenehurst, 124
Lenn Episcopi, 228
Leshurst, 62, 106 (2), 160
Lesnes, 187
Letherhead, Leddred, Leddrede, Ledered, Lederede, Lederedd, Ledred, Ledrede, Ledride, Lethered, or Letherhed, 7, 8, 10, 15 (2), 29, 33, 34, 57, 59, 61, 62, 65, 69, 72 (2), 73, 74, 75, 76 (2), 78 (2), 82, 83, 85 (2), 87 (2), 89, 91, 93, 95 (2), 110, 104, 107, 110, 111, 112, 115, 116 (2), 117, 124, 127, 129 (2), 145, 152, 154, 156, 157, 158, 159, 164 (2), 167, 172, 189, 195, 199, 205, 206, 210, 211, 214 (2)
Leuesham (co. Kent), 150, 172
Lewes, 89
Leye, or Leygh, *see* Legh
Leye-juxta-Becheworth, 78 (2)
Leye-juxta-Derhurst, 163
Limpsfield, Lemefeld, Lemensfeld, Lemenesfeld, Lemmenesfeld, Lemmesfeld, Lemnefeud, Lemnesfeld, Lemnysfeld, Lempnesfeld, Lymenesfeld, Lymenesfeud, Lymefeld, Lymmefeld, Lymnesfeld, Lymynesfeld, or Lymnesfeld, 25, 39 (2), 45, 55, 58, 76, 81, 85, 95, 96, 107, 129, 146, 163, 177, 181 (2), 190, 195, 217, 222, 224, 230
Lincoln, 178
Lingfield, Lingfeld, Lingfeud, Lingefeld, Lingefelde, Lingefeud, Linggefelde, Lingesfeld, Lyngfeld, Lynggefeld, Lyngefelde, Lyngefeld, Lyngefeud, Lynghefeld, or Lynkefeld, 22, 23 (2), 30, 41, 42, 43, 46, 52, 55, 75, 81, 84, 87 (2), 91, 92 (2), 96, 107, 109, 115, 116, 119, 123, 127, 129, 130, 137 (4), 141 (2), 142, 143 (2), 144, 146, 147, 148 (2), 155, 156, 158, 159 (3), 163 (2), 166, 167, 169, 172, 173, 175 (2), 176, 179, 181 (3), 182 (2), 190 (2), 198, 210 (2), 211, 217, 220, 222, 223 (3), 224, 225 (2), 228, 230, 231
Litleton, Litlington, Littelington, Lytleton, or Lyttylton, 7, 10 (2), 51, 94, 168
—— juxta-Guldeford, 159
Lomheth, *see* Lambeth
London, 39 (2), 49, 55 (2), 57, 59, 61, 64, 67, 68, 71, 75, 76 (3), 78, 79, 81 (3), 82 (2), 83, 84 (2), 86 (3), 88 (3), 90, 91, 92, 93, 95, 96, 97, 99 (2), 100, 101, 103, 104 (2), 106, 107 (2), 108 (3), 109, 111 (6), 113 (5), 114 (4), 115, 117, 118 (2), 119 (2), 120, 121 (5), 122, 123 (4), 124 (5), 125, 126 (3), 127 (4), 129 (2), 130 (4), 131, 132 (3), 133 (3), 134 (2), 135 (3), 136 (2), 137, 138 (3), 139, 140 (5), 141 (2), 142 (2), 143 (4), 144, 145 (3), 146 (2), 147 (3), 148 (5), 149 (3), 150 (5), 151 (5), 152 (5), 153 (7), 154 (2), 156 (5), 158 (4), 159, 160, 161 (3), 162 (2), 163 (5), 164 (5), 165, 166, 167 (3), 168 (3), 169 (3), 171 (8), 172, 173 (2), 174, 175, 176 (6), 177 (3), 178 (5), 179 (3), 180 (8), 181 (2), 183 (8), 185 (2), 186 (6), 188, 189 (2), 190 (3), 191 (3), 192, 193 (3), 194 (2), 195 (3), 196 (4), 198 (2), 199, 200 (3), 201 (7), 205 (2), 208 (2), 209, 211 (2), 216 (2), 217 (2), 220, 222, 223 (2), 228 (3), 229 (2), 230 (3)
London Bridge, 30, 40
Long Ditton, Longe Ditton, or Long Dytton, 51, 62, 82, 114, 117, 123, 135, 138, 139, 152, 156, 161, 162, 168, 174, 199, 210, 211
Longehope, 43
Loseley, or Loselee, 7, 206
Luda, 80

Ludlingg, 73
Luk, 121
Lunnsfeld, 16
Luyton, 116
Lye, 229
Lymenesfeld, Lymenesfeud, Lymefeld, Lymmefeld, Lymmesfeld, Lymynesfeld, or Lymnesfeld, *see* Limpsfield
La Lynde, 70
Lyngefeld, Lynggefeld, Lyngefelde, Lyngefeud, Lynghefeld, or Lynkefeld, *see* Lingfeld
Lyngelegh, 60
Lyngtrefeld, 216
Lytleton, *see* Litleton

Mades, 1 (2)
Maldon, Maldone, or Meldon, 27, 51, 63, 69, 74, 117, 190, 208, 214, 231
Malet, 146
Mandon, Meandon, or Mendon, 8 (2), 20, 27, 37, 215
Manhefeud, 47
Marsham, or Mersham, 54, 65
Maufeld, 80
Maydestone, 175
Mayford, 67 (2), 77, 84 (2), 97, 103, 109, 186
Meandon, or Mendon, *see* Mandon
Meldon, *see* Maldon
Mereden, Meryden, or Merden, 91, 125, 179, 224
Merrow, Merwe, or Merewe, 17, 21, 25 (2), 40, 44, 48, 68, 70, 87, 102, 108, 111, 122, 126, 141, 145 (2), 161, 168, 176, 178
Mersey, *see* Molesey
Merstham, or Mestham, 7, 15, 26, 32, 34, 50, 64, 66, 67, 80, 82, 95, 96, 101, 103, 118, 143, 150, 161, 185, 186, 201, 208, 229
Merton, 136, 152, 161, 187, 214
Mickelham, Mikelham, Mikeleham, Mykelham, or Mykeleham, 2, 18, 27, 28, 29, 34 (2), 52, 56, 89 (2), 100, 107, 157 (3), 159, 164, 177, 189, 213
Midleton, Middelton, or Myddleton, 18, 31, 44, 76, 115, 219
Mitcham, Micham, Michham, Miccham, Micheham, Miccheham, Mecham, Mecheham, Mycham, or Mychham, 4, 5 (2), 7, 9, 10 (2), 12, 13, 18, 20, 24, 26, 31, 39, 40, 41, 50, 52, 56, 57, 58 (3), 60, 61, 63, 79, 82, 87 (2), 88, 90, 91, 98, 99, 101, 103, 107, 116, 117 (2), 118, 120 (2), 121, 122 (2), 132, 133, 139, 141, 146, 149, 172, 177, 190, 202, 205, 207 (2), 218
Molesey, Molseye, Molesye, Moleseie, Moleseye, Mulsey, Mulesey, Muleseye, or Merseye, 9, 34, 68 (2), 83, 119, 128, 193
Molesey, West, 4, 6, 16, 76, 81, 82, 152
Mordon, Morden, Moredon, or Moorden, 1, 19, 65, 98, 103, 107, 117, 146, 149, 184, 207, 211, 218
Mordon, West, 21
Mortlake, Mortelak, or Mortelake, 37, 39, 45, 88, 105, 108, 195, 202, 209, 217
Mulsey, Mulesey, or Muleseye, *see* Molesey
Mycham, *see* Mitcham
Myddleton, *see* Midleton
Mykelham, or Mykeleham, *see* Mickelham
Mylton, 207

Neobright, *see* Nobright
Netlested, 2
Neuton, Neueton, Neuweton, or Neuwynton, *see* Newington
Newdegate, Newedegate, Neudegate, or Nudegate, 14, 17, 20, 21, 60, 74, 76, 83, 96, 100 (3), 103, 110, 119, 123, 129, 171, 173, 184, 189, 192, 204, 218, 226, 227, 229
Newington, or Newington by Suthwerk, Neuton, Neueton, Neuweton, Neuwynton, Newton, Neweton, Newenton, Newyngton, Newyngton, or Niewyngton, 35, 37, 38, 43, 45 (3), 46, 49, 50, 64 (2), 65, 67, 88, 94, 113, 114, 124, 125, 126, 129, 146 (2), 152, 156, 160 (2), 161, 177, 184, 198, 201, 206, 207, 212, 219, 232
Newington-juxta-Lameheth, 67
Newington, St. Mary, 90, 181
Newington, St. Georges, 152
Newlond, la Newlond, Neulond, or Newelond, 20, 39, 135, 137
Niewyngton, *see* Newington

Nobright, Nobrychite, or Neobright, 56, 100, 134, 219
Norbinton, 10
Northampton, 193
Nudegate, *see* Newdegate
Nutfield, Notfeld, Notefeld, Notefelde, Notfeud, Nutfeld, Nutfelde, Nutefeld, or Nuttefeld, 28, 46, 65, 72 (4), 73, 77, 82, 84, 110, 125, 135, 159 (2), 160, 163, 164 (2), 174, 194, 197 (2), 204, 210, 211, 226

Ockham, Ocham, or Okham, 47, 54, 100, 108, 114 (2), 117, 122 (2), 131, 165, 167 (2), 205
Ockley, Occle, Ockel, Ockele, Ockelegh, Ockeley, Okle, Okele, Okley, Okeley, Okeleye, Okelege, Okelinge, Okkle, Okkele, Okkeleghe, or Hocklegh, 8, 11, 16, 30, 32, 34, 45 (2), 47, 48, 68, 75, 79, 82, 103, 109, 115, 125, 129, 135, 137, 178, 186, 189, 202, 204 (3), 208, 227, 231
Opping, 57
Orsete, 90
Otterworth, Ottewrth, Ottewirth, Ottewortb, Ottewurth, Utterwrth, or Uttewrth, 13, 19 (2), 24 (2), 30, 34, 53
Oxted, Ocstede, Okested, Okestede, Okestate, Oksted, Okstede, Oxsted, Oxstede, or Oxtede, 5, 45, 68, 76, 78 (2), 85, 86, 91, 95, 101 (2), 107, 114, 119, 123, 128, 135 (2), 142, 144 (4), 145 (2), 155 (4), 162 (2), 163, 166, 167 (3), 174, 177 (3), 182 (2), 183, 184, 192, 202, 217, 221, 228, 231

Pachenesham, 65, 130, 202, 208, 209
Padesdon, 32, 34
Padynden, Padyndene, Padyngden, Padyngdon, Patynden, or Putinden, 16, 92, 125, 151, 185, 200, 224 (2)
Papeworth, 20, 130, 157
Patricheseye, *see* Battersey
Patynden, *see* Padynden
Pekham, Pecham, or Peccham, 10, 12, 17, 24, 40, 59, 84, 86, 92, 101, 104, 113, 116, 117, 121, 122, 140, 165, 172, 180, 190, 210

Penehurst, 11
Penge, or Peyng, 10, 182 (2)
Pepperharrow, Piperharg, Piperharwe, or Pyperharg, 28, 113, 137, 223
Petteworth, 184
Pinkehurst, 24
Piperharg, or Piperharwe, *see* Pepperharrow
Pirbright, Purefright, Purefrith, Puryfryght, Pirifright, Purbryght, Piribright, or Pyrbright, 22, 77, 92, 97, 108, 110 (2), 129, 162, 170 (2), 172, 210
Pirford, Piryford, Pureford, Puryford, Puryforde, Pyreford, or Pyryford, 50, 74, 83, 94, 118, 123, 132, 180, 182 (3), 188, 201, 217
Pirlee, 4
Polesden, East, 89
Polesden, Polesdene, Pollesden, or Pollesdon, 2, 5, 6, 16, 195
Polested, Polsted, or Polstede, 3, 16, 49, 73 (2), 136
Polyngfold, 105, 223
Pontis Edulfi, *see* Edenbridge
Porkeleye, or Porkele 146 (2), 228
Potenhethe, 154
Preston, 84, 118 (2)
Preston-juxta-Benstede, 116
Prynkham, 228
Pureford, Puryford, or Puryforde, *see* Pirford
Purefright, Purefrith, Puryfryght, or Purbryght, *see* Pirbright
Putenham, Putham, Puttham, Puteham, Putteham, Puttenham, Poteham, or Potenham, 3, 4, 30, 33 (2), 37, 49, 50, 64, 86 (2), 109, 116 (3), 138, 192, 213, 226
Putinden, *see* Padynden
Pyperharg, *see* Pepperharrow
Pyrbright, *see* Pirbright
Pyreford, or Pyryford, *see* Pirford
Pytfaude, 36

Raby, 149
Radesole, 49
Radshote, 225
Rasebery, or Ravenesbury, 146, 149, 195
Redereye, Rederhede, or Reherth, *see* Rotherhithe
Reigate, *see* Reygate

Remdon, 4
Remenham, 102
Retherhee, Retherhey, Retherheth, Retherhethe, Retherhithe, Retherhuth, or Retherhythe, *see* Rotherhithe
Rewenhale, or Rowenhale, 152, 156
Reygate, Reigate, or Reygate, 3, 6, 31, 39, 44, 49, 52, 83, 95, 97 (2), 103, 119, 129, 131, 137, 138 (2), 144 (2), 146, 148 (2), 149 (2), 160, 161 (2), 166, 168, 172 (2), 178, 185 (2), 187, 192, 200, 210 (2), 229, 230
Rikermeresworth, 130
Ripley, Rippele, Ryppele, Ryppeleye, or Rypley, 62, 109, 113, 157 (2), 158 (2), 190
Rithereye, or Ritherheth, *see* Rotherhithe
Rokehampton, 120, 153, 209
Rokesbiry, 8
Ronewelle, 45
Rotherhithe, Redereye, Rederhede, Reherth, Retherhe, Retherhee, Retherhey, Retherbeth, Retherhethe, Retherhithe, Retherhuth, Retherhythe, Rithereye, Ritherheth, Rotherheye, Rotherhuthe, Rutherhee, Rutherhey, or Rutherheth, 5, 10, 12, 13, 17, 21, 22 (2), 26, 28 (2), 30, 31, 33, 39, 53 (2), 54, 56, 57, 60 (2), 61, 73, 79, 82, 83, 107, 108, 128, 160, 187, 188, 195 (2), 212 (2), 213, 214 (2), 216, 218, 219, 221, 222, 225 (2), 226, 232
Rothyng, 187
Roweley, 204
Rowenhale, *see* Rewenhale
la Ruebern, 9
Rugwik, Rugewyk, or Ruggewyk, 113, 126, 222 (2)
Rutherhee, Rutherhey, or Rutherheth, *see* Rotherhithe
Ruthin, 223 (2), 224
Rydon, 156
Rykford, 98
Ryppele, Ryppeleye, or Rypley, *see* Ripley

St. Paul's, London, 183
Saklesford, *see* Shakelford

Salesbiry, 104
Sande, Sandes, *see* Sende
Sandersted, Sandested, Sanderstede, Sandirstede, Sandrestede, Saunderstede, or Saundrestede, 4, 12, 50, 58, 84, 85, 89, 96, 116, 119, 139 (2), 146, 159, 170, 185, 201
Sandon, 150, 189, 194
Sandres, or Saundres, 2, 5, 26, 41
Sapcote, 221
Sarum, New, 141
Saunde, Saundes, or Saundis, *see* Sende
Saunderstede, or Saundrestede, *see* Sandersted
Scaudeforde, or Schaldeforde, *see* Shalford
Schene, *see* Shene
Schyre, or Scyre, *see* Shere
Seenes, *see* Shene
Sele-juxta-Farnham, 151
Sellesdon, Sellesdone, or Selysdone, 28, 58, 159, 170
Sende, Sande, Sandes, Saunde, Saundes, Saundis, Seende, or Sendes, 6, 8, 14, 19, 29 (2), 38 (2), 47, 52, 53, 55, 59 (2), 60, 63, 65, 66, 78, 84, 87, 91, 94, 97, 100, 101, 102, 105, 106, 107 (2), 108, 111, 113 (2), 127, 131, 133, 136, 142, 145, 149, 154, 165, 167 (2), 172, 199
Shakelford, or Saklesford, 15, 109, 136
Shalford, Shaldeford, Shaldeforde, Scaudeford, or Schaldeford, 7, 31, 32, 36, 61, 63, 78, 91, 98, 100 (3), 103, 110, 117, 126, 132, 133, 134, 140, 145, 152, 161, 165, 168 (2), 171, 173, 174 (2), 178, 182, 191 (2), 194 (2), 196, 198, 202, 207, 220
—— juxta-Guldeford, 66 (2)
—— Est, 104, 112
—— West, 164, 209
Sheldeslegh Beauchamp, 220
Shellegh, 149
Shene, Schene, Seenes, or Shenes, 10, 17, 37, 47, 53, 108, 185, 214
—— Est, 31, 32, 37, 88, 102, 151, 154, 160, 195, 217
—— West, 37, 74, 122, 189, 192, 214
Shepperton, Nether, 231

INDEX LOCORUM. 335

Shepperton, Upper, 231
Shere, Shire, Shyre, Scyre, Schyre, or Sire, 15, 19, 26, 31, 47, 66, 70, 73, 79 (3), 100 (3), 104, 105, 110, 111, 113, 114, 126, 128, 129, 133, 135, 160, 178, 203 (3), 204, 213, 215, 218, 220, 222, 225, 228
Sholaund, or la Sholaunde, 33 (3)
Shorne, 138
Shyre, *see* Shere
Shyrley, 193
Sidwode, Sydewode, or Sythwode, 61, 118, 201
Sire, *see* Shere
Slagebam, 161
Slyfeld, Slifeld, or Stlifeld, 4, 8, 12, 108, 132 (2), 227
Somerbury, 114, 134
Somerton, co. Oxon, 226
Southcote, 165
Southwark, Southwerk, Sudhiwerk, Sudhiwerke, Sudwerc, Sudwerk, Sudwurc, Sudwurk, Sutwerc, Sutwerk, Sutwerke, Suwerc, Suwerck, Suwerk, Suwerke, Suthewerk, Suthwark, Suthwerc, Suthwerk, or Suthwerke, 2 (3), 3 (2), 6 (2), 7 (2), 9 (5), 11 (2), 12, 14, 16-18 (3), 21, 22 (2), 23 (2), 24 (3), 25 (2), 26, 29 (5), 30 (5), 31 (3), 32 (5), 33-35 (2), 36 (3), 37, 38 (3), 39, 41, 42 (2), 43 (6), 44 (2), 45 (2), 46 (7), 47 (2), 48 (3), 49 (6), 50, 51, 54, 55 (2), 56 (4), 57 (2), 58 (3), 59 (4), 60, 61 (3), 64 (5), 67, 69 (4), 70, 71, (2), 73, 74 (2), 75 (4), 76 (2), 77 (2), 78 (3), 79, 80 (2), 81 (3), 82 (7), 83 (2), 84 (2), 85 (5), 86 (3), 87 (2), 88 (6), 89-92 (2), 93, 94 (8), 95 (4), 96 (3), 97 (4), 98, 99 (3), 100-102 (2), 103 (2), 104-106 (2), 107, 108 (4), 109 (2), 110, 111 (4), 112-114 (2), 115 (2), 116 (2), 119 (3), 121 (2), 122 (3), 124 (7), 125 (5), 126, 127 (2), 128 (2), 129, 130 (2), 131 (5), 132, 133 (6), 134 (4), 135, 136 (5), 137, 138 (3), 139, 140 (3), 141, 142 (6), 145, 147 (3), 148 (2), 149 (2), 150 (4), 151 (2), 152 (5), 154 (4), 155, 156 (2), 158 (3), 159 (2), 160 (2), 161 (2), 162 (5), 163 (3), 164 (3), 165 (2), 166 (2), 167, 168 (2), 169, 170, 172, 173 (2), 174 (2), 176 (2), 177 (3), 178, 179 (4), 180 (3), 181 (3), 184, 186 (2), 187 (2), 188-191 (2), 193, 195, 197-199 (2), 200, 201, 205 (2), 206-208, 210, 214, 216, (2), 218 (2), 219 (3), 222 (2), 223-225, 227, 228, 230, 232 (2)
—— St. George, 181, 184 (2), 187
—— St. Margaret, 184, 193, 206
—— St. Mary Magdalene, 136, 179, 189
—— St. Olave's, 145, 178, 179 (2), 196, 210, 211, 230
Speldherst, 144
Stanes, 84, 110
Stanley, 230
Stanore, 72
Stanstede, 28
Staunton Drewe (co. Somerset), 187
Stenyng (co. Sussex), 179
Sterburgh, 228
Stistede, 156 (3)
Stlifeld, *see* Slifeld
Stoghton, *see* Stoughton
Stoke, Stok, or Stokes, 5, 9, 21, 26, 42, 55, 57, 87, 107, 145, 153, 161, 182, 220, 227
—— juxta-Guldeford, 52, 70, 90, 91, 96, 98, 101, 102, 107, 112, 120, 126-128, 131, 133 (2), 134, 140, 145 (2), 155 (2), 165, 168, 170, 178 (2), 180, 181 (2), 182, 187, 191, 198, 202
Stoke Daberon, Dabernon, Dabernoun, Dabernun, Dauberon, or Danberon, 111, 119, 130, 195, 219, 223 (2), 227
Stokwell, or Stokewell, 36, 63, 86, 174, 205, 222
Stonhurst, 221
Stoughton, or Stogton, 115, 202
Stretham, or Stretenham, 101, 103, 180, 184
Stretford-atte-Bowe, 91
Strode, 93, 99, 194, 208, 228
Stubbington, 221
Sudinton, 18
Sudwurc, or Sutwerke, etc., *see* Southwark
Surbeton, Suberton, or Subertone, 5, 6, 10, 122
Suthton, 3
Sutton, 173, 184, 191, 198, 202, 211, 215, 228

Sydewode, or Sythwode, *see* Sidwode

Tadeswurthe, 4
Talworth, Talewrth, Taleworth, Tallworth, Talleworth, or Thaleworth, 23, 26, 59, 61, 63, 66, 82, 89, 114, 117, 152, 183, 191, 232
Talworth, North, 198
Talworth, South, 60, 71, 198
Tandridge, Tanerig, Tanerigge, Tanrich, Tanrigge, Tanrygge, Tanregg, Tanregge, Tanrugg, Tanrugge, Taunrigge, Tenrig, Tenrigg, Tenrigge, Tenrugge, or Tenrygge, 13, 19, 20, 23, 24, 27, 31, 41, 42, 46, 49 (2), 53, 79 (2), 91, 97, 98, 109, 116, 120, 131, 143, 144, 151, 158, 167 (2), 176, 179, 183, 188, 192, 205, 207, 217, 225, 228
Tattesfield, Tatesfeld, Tattysfeld, Tatlefeld, Tatlesfeld, Tatelysfeld, Thatlefeld, or Tetlesfeld, 11, 17, 50, 142, 175, 206, 207, 214
Tenrig, or Tenrugge, etc., *see* Tandridge
Tenterden (co. Kent), 179
Terrisworthe, 195
Thaleworth, *see* Talworth
Thames Ditton, Tames, Tamis, Tamyse, Temes, Temis, Temmys, Thamyse Ditton, or Dytton, 20, 32, 34, 64, 80, 82, 100, 117, 119, 123, 160, 162, 210
Thorncombe, 93
Thorp, 10, 20, 23, 33, 66, 84 (2), 98 (2), 107, 112, 115, 137, 147 (2), 227
Thrule, 19
Ticheseye, Titsey, Tytsay, Tytsey, or Tycheseye, 23, 47, 58, 66, 68, 69, 73, 78, 86, 99, 110, 115, 121 (2), 173, 206, 207, 228
Tooting, Titinges, Totinges, Totyng, or Tyting, 1 (2), 2, 20, 28, 143, 152, 208
—— Bek, or Beke, 102, 103 (2), 207
—— Graveney, or Graveneye, 99, 170, 173, 194, 204, 207
Toresworth, 62
Tortington, 122
Tuleswerthe, 4
Tunchamstede, 43
Twangham, or Twengham, 19, 27

Twyford, 74
Tydd, St. Giles (co. Camb.), 141
Tydyng, 161
Tylemundesdon, 60
Tyllyngdowne, 228
Tyngefeld, 158

Uhurst, *see* Ewehurst
Uners, *see* Wonersh
Upton, 19 (2), 29
Upwode, 228
Utteworth, or Utterwrth, *see* Otterworth

Vachery, or la Vacherie, 40, 203 (3), 218
Vinecumbe, 18

Waddon, or Waddone, 5, 14, 96, 101, 119, 201
Wakeringg, 74
Wakerle, 122
Walden, or Waldon, 131, 132
Waldingham, Waldingeham, or Waldyngham, 6 (2), 109, 122, 228
Walford, 176
Walknested, or Walkensted, *see* Wolkensted
Wallyngton, or Walyngton, 146 (2), 154, 175, 177, 186, 191, 192, 197 (2), 203, 207, 211
Waltham, 106
Waltham, Sancte Crucis, or Crosse, 101, 177
Walton, Waleton, or Walleton, 4, 8, 20 (2), 33, 34, 38, 46, 49, 61, 66 (2), 74, 75 (2), 82, 83, 85, 88, 94, 96, 101, 105, 109, 111, 118, 119, 122, 124, 128, 132, 137-139, 144, 146, 149, 169, 176, 196, 215, 230
—— on-Thames, 149, 157, 162, 194, 204, 206, 207, 226
Walworth, Walewrth, Wallewrth, Wallewurd, or Walewurth, 1, 2, 31, 44, 49, 55, 88, 198, 209, 211, 212
Walyngford, 80
Wamburgh, or Waneburgh, 109
Wandsworth, Wandelesworth, Wandelsworth, Wandeswrth, Wandesworth, Wandesworthe, Wandleswrde, Wandleswrthe, Wandleswurth, Wanlesworth,

INDEX LOCORUM.

Wannesworth, Wendesworth, Wendelesworth, Wendlesworth, Wendleswirth, Wendleswrth, Wendleswurth, or Wendeswrth, 3-6, 13, 14, 19, 25, 28, 29, 33, 34 (3), 44, 45, 53-55 (3), 56, 58, 61 (2), 63, 67 (4), 72, 81 (3), 85, 92 (3), 95, 96, 99, 101 (3), 105 (2), 107, 110-112 (2), 114, 115, 118, 121 (2), 122, 125 (3), 126 (2), 127 (3), 128 (2), 129 (2), 132, 135, 138, 139, 147, 150 (2), 151, 152, 156, 157, 160, 165 (2), 175 (2), 180, 183, 184, 186, 189, 190-193 (2), 198, 201 (2), 202, 208, 211, 229

Ware, 105, 176

Warlingham, Warlyngham, or Werlingham, 2, 23 (2), 26, 62, 88, 91, 120, 124, 146, 156, 171 (2), 217

Wassyngham, 126, 226

Watyngdon, Whatyndon, or Whatyngdon, 96, 184, 201, 204, 224

Wauton, or Waweton, 16, 63, 98, 100, 101, 154, 160, 164, 175 (2)

Wauton-on-the-Hull, 160

Waybregge, etc., see Weybridge

Wayflete, 118

Welkenested, or Welkested, see Wolkensted

Wendelesworth, Wendesworth, or Wendlesworth, etc., see Wandsworth

Wendesham, see Windlesham

Wendovere, 75

Werlingham, see Warlingham

Werplesdon, Werplusdon, or Werpelysdon, see Worplesdon

Westbergh, Westburgh, or Wysbergh, 126, 189, 194

Westcote, 31, 60, 149, 172 (2), 217 (2), 224

Westhall, 160, 195

Westlond, 202

Westminster, 64

Weston, or Westone, 15, 33, 34, 35, 59 (2), 63, 82, 111 (2), 144

Westram, 206, 207

Westwode, 80, 98

Weybridge, Waibreg, Waibrige, Waybruge, Waybrigge, Weybrigge, or Weybrigge-juxta-Byflet, 2, 4, 60, 95, 97, 124, 126, 162, 199, 205

Weyminster, 61

Whatedon, or Whatedone, 64, 156

Whatyndon, see Watyngdon

Wicham, or Wycham, 2, 214

Wike, Wikes, or Wickes, see Wyke

Wikford, or Wikeford, 10, 14

Wimbledon, Wimbeldon, Wymbaldon, Wymbeldon, Wymbildon, Wimbelton, Wymedon, Wymeldon, or Wynbelton, 17, 26, 27 (2), 28, 29, 34, 35, 63, 64, 68, 76, 77, 88, 98, 105, 108, 109, 115, 118, 132, 183, 190, 195, 196, 199, 209, 217, 218

Windlesham, Wendesham, Wyndysham, Wyndesham, Wyndlesham, Wyndelesham, or Wynelesham, 21, 35, 44 (2), 52, 69 (2), 79, 131 (2), 163 (2), 195, 215, 225

Wisley, Whysell, Wyssle, Wyssly, Wissele, Wisshele, Wyssele, Wysshele, Wyschele, Wysselegh, Wysshelaye, or Whisshele, 7, 26, 37, 47, 56, 74, 84, 111, 146, 196, 218

Witetrewe, 8

Witley, Wytle, Wytleg, Wytlye, Wyttle, Wyttele, or Wyttleye, 38, 69, 75 (2), 106, 155, 214

le Wode, 190

Wodemancote, 192

Woking, Wokyng, Wockyng, Wokkyng, Wokkyngg, Wokkynge, or Wokynghe, 18, 37, 54, 81, 101, 109, 115, 117, 126, 133 (3), 165, 167, 181, 190, 201, 206, 212, 215

Wolkensted, Walkested, Walkenstede, Walknested, Welknested, Welkested, Welkenested, Wokenysted, Wolkested, Wolksted, Wolkstede, Wolkestede, Wolkenested, Wolknested, Wolknestede, or Wolstede, 13, 14, 18, 19 (2), 20 (2), 22, 27, 28, 30, 33, 40, 42 (2), 45, 47, 49 (3), 52 (2), 68, 89, 90, 91, 97, 98, 100, 106, 109, 116, 118, 120, 125, 131, 143, 144, 151, 159 (3), 166, 168, 171, (3), 175, 176, 179, 187, 188, 192, 193, 200, 205 (2), 207, 210, 217, 225 (2)

Wolwyg, 54

Wonersh, Wonersshe, Wonerse, or Uners, 37, 105, 155, 196, 213, 222

Woodcote, Wodecote, la Wodecote, Wudecote, or la Wudcote, 6, 11, 58, 87, 101, 132, 169

Woodham, Wodham, or Wodeham, 118, 130, 216

Woodmanstern, Wodmersthorn, Wodemersthorn, Wodemeresthorn, Wodemeresthorne, or Wudemarethorn, 12, 66 (2), 80, 116, 119, 134, 140, 146, 147, 164, 174, 186, 210

Wordi Mortimer, 99

Wormele, 79

Worplesdon, Werplesden, Werplesdon, Werplusdon, Werplesdone, Werpelysdon, Worplesden, Worpulston, or Wurplesdon, 22, 43, 60, 64, 65, 70 (2), 71, 72 (2), 80, 81 (2), 83, 85, 86, 89, 99 (2), 108, 109, 113, 130, 133 (2), 135, 143, 145 (2), 155, 157, 159, 161, 164, 185, 190, 195, 197, 199, 203, 220, 224, 226

Wotton, Wodeton, Wudeton, or Wudyton, 20, 48, 54, 113, 114 (2), 123, 129, 132, 177, 181, 202, 213, 227, 231

Wrydelyngton, 98, 107, 218

Wudecote, *see* Woodcote

Wudemarethorn, *see* Woodmanstern

Wudeton, or Wudyton, *see* Wooton

Wyham, 99

Wyke, Wyk, Wickes, Wike, or Wikes, 2 (2), 4, 36, 83

Wyke-juxta-North Lambeth, 74

Wyldewod, 227

Wymbeldon, etc., *see* Wimbledon

Wynchelse, 217 (2)

Wyndesore (co. Bucks), 89, 178

Wyndysham, Wyndesham, or Wyndlesham, etc., *see* Windlesham

Wyntershull, 41

Wynthorp, 105

Wysbergh, *see* Westbergh

Wyssle, Wyssly, or Wyssele, etc., *see* Wisley

Wytheresfaud, 19

Wytle, Wytley, or Wyttle, etc., *see* Witley

Yarmouth, Great, 176

Ywehurst, *see* Ewehurst

THE END.

www.ingramcontent.com/pod-product-compliance
Lightning Source LLC
Chambersburg PA
CBHW031849220426
43663CB00006B/559